James Legge

Life and Teachings or Confucius

James Legge

Life and Teachings or Confucius

ISBN/EAN: 9783337385477

Printed in Europe, USA, Canada, Australia, Japan

Cover: Foto ©Thomas Meinert / pixelio.de

More available books at **www.hansebooks.com**

THE

LIFE AND TEACHINGS

OF

CONFUCIUS.

WITH EXPLANATORY NOTES.

BY

JAMES LEGGE, D.D.

Fourth Edition.

LONDON:
TRÜBNER & CO., 57 & 59, LUDGATE HILL.
1875.
[*All Rights reserved.*]

JOHN CHILDS AND SON, PRINTERS.

PREFACE.

WHEN the author, in 1861, commenced the publication of the Chinese Classics, with an English translation and such a critical apparatus as was necessary to the proper appreciation of the original Works, he did not contemplate an edition without the Chinese text and simply adapted for popular reading. It was soon pressed upon him, however, from various quarters; and he had formed the purpose to revise the separate volumes, when he should have completed the whole of his undertaking, and to publish the English text, with historical introductions and brief explanatory notes, which might render it acceptable for general perusal.

He is sorry that circumstances have arisen to call for such an issue of his volumes, without waiting for the completion of the last of the Classics;—principally because it adds another to the many unavoidable hindrances which have impeded the onward prosecution of his important task. A Mr Baker, of Massachusetts, in the United States, having sent forth the prospectus of a republication of the author's translation, his publisher in London strongly represented to him the desirableness of his issuing at once a popular edition in his own name, as a counter-movement to Mr Baker's, and to prevent other similar acts of piracy:—and the result is the appearance of the present volume. It will be followed by a second, containing the Works of Mencius, as soon as the publisher shall feel himself authorized by public encouragement to go forward with the undertaking.

The author has seen the first part of Mr Baker's republication, containing the English text of his first volume, and the indexes of Subjects and Proper Names, without alteration. The only other matter in it is an introduction of between seven and eight pages. Four of these are occupied with an account of Confucius, taken from Chambers' Encyclopædia, which Mr Baker says *he chooses to copy* :—so naturally does it come to him to avail himself of the labours of other men. "Convey the wise it call. Steal? Foh! A fico for the phrase!"

In the remainder of his Introduction, Mr Baker assumes a controversial tone, and calls in question some of the judgments which the author has passed on the Chinese sage and his doctrines. He would make it out that Confucius was a most religious man, and abundantly recognised the truth of a future life; that the worship of God was more nearly universal in China than in the Theocracy of Israel; that the Chinese in general are not more regardless of truth than Dr Legge's own countrymen; and that Confucius' making no mention of heaven and hell is the reason why missionaries object to his system of practising virtue for virtue's sake! Mr Baker has made some proficiency in the art of "adding insult to injury." It is easy to see to what school of religion he belongs; but the author would be sorry to regard his publication as a specimen of the manner in which the members of it "practise virtue for virtue's sake."

In preparing the present volume for the press, the author has retained a considerable part of the prolegomena in the larger work, to prepare the minds of his readers for proceeding with advantage to the translation, and forming an intelligent judgment on the authority which is to be allowed to the original Works. He has made a few additions and corrections which his increased acquaintance with the field of Chinese literature enabled him to do.

He was pleased to find, in revising the translation, that the alterations which it was worth while to make were very few and unimportant.

He has retained the headings to the notes on the several chapters, as they give, for the most part, an adequate summary of the subjects treated in them. All critical matter, interesting and useful only to students of the Chinese language, he has thrown out. In a few instances he has remodelled the notes, or made such additions to them as were appropriate to the popular design of the edition.

Hong-Kong, 26th October, 1866.

CONTENTS.

I. PRELIMINARY ESSAYS.

CHAPTER I.

OF THE CHINESE CLASSICS GENERALLY.

SECTION — PAGE

I. BOOKS INCLUDED UNDER THE NAME OF THE CHINESE CLASSICS 1

II. THE AUTHORITY OF THE CHINESE CLASSICS 3

CHAPTER II.

OF THE CONFUCIAN ANALECTS.

I. FORMATION OF THE TEXT OF THE ANALECTS BY THE SCHOLARS OF THE HAN DYNASTY 12

II. AT WHAT TIME, AND BY WHOM, THE ANALECTS WERE WRITTEN; THEIR PLAN; AND AUTHENTICITY .. 15

III. OF COMMENTARIES UPON THE ANALECTS 19

CHAPTER III.

OF THE GREAT LEARNING.

I. HISTORY OF THE TEXT; AND THE DIFFERENT ARRANGEMENTS OF IT WHICH HAVE BEEN PROPOSED 22

II. OF THE AUTHORSHIP, AND DISTINCTION OF THE TEXT INTO CLASSICAL TEXT AND COMMENTARY 26

III. ITS SCOPE AND VALUE 27

CONTENTS.

CHAPTER IV.
OF THE DOCTRINE OF THE MEAN.

SECTION		PAGE
I.	ITS PLACE IN THE LE KE, AND ITS PUBLICATION SEPARATELY	35
II.	ITS AUTHOR; AND SOME ACCOUNT OF HIM	36
III.	ITS SCOPE AND VALUE	43

CHAPTER V.
CONFUCIUS; HIS INFLUENCE AND DOCTRINES.

I.	LIFE OF CONFUCIUS	55
II.	HIS INFLUENCE AND OPINIONS	91

II. THE CLASSICS.

I.	CONFUCIAN ANALECTS	116
II.	THE GREAT LEARNING	264
III.	THE DOCTRINE OF THE MEAN	282

III. INDEXES.

I.	SUBJECTS IN THE CONFUCIAN ANALECTS	321
II.	PROPER NAMES IN THE CONFUCIAN ANALECTS	330
III.	SUBJECTS IN THE GREAT LEARNING	334
IV.	PROPER NAMES IN THE GREAT LEARNING	335
V.	SUBJECTS IN THE DOCTRINE OF THE MEAN	336
VI.	PROPER NAMES IN THE DOCTRINE OF THE MEAN	338

PRELIMINARY ESSAYS.

CHAPTER I.

OF THE CHINESE CLASSICS GENERALLY.

SECTION I.

BOOKS INCLUDED UNDER THE NAME OF THE CHINESE CLASSICS.

1. THE Books now recognized as of highest authority in China are comprehended under the denominations of "The five King," and "The four Shoo." The term *king* is of textile origin, and signifies the warp threads of a web, and their adjustment. An easy application of it is to denote what is regular and insures regularity. As used with reference to books, it indicates their authority on the subjects of which they treat. "The five King" are the five *canonical* Works, containing the truth upon the highest subjects from the sages of China, and which should be received as law by all generations. The term *shoo* simply means *writings* or *books*.

2. The five King are:—the *Yih*, or, as it has been styled, "The Book of Changes;" the *Shoo*, or "The Book of Historical Documents;" the *She*, or "The Book of Poetry;" the *Le Ke*, or "Record of Rites;" and the Ch'un Ts'ew, or "Spring and Autumn," a chronicle of events, extending from B.C. 721 to 480. The authorship, or compilation rather, of all these works is loosely attributed to Confucius. But much of the Le Ke is from later hands. Of the Yih, the Shoo, and the She, it is only in the first that we find additions said to be from the philosopher himself, in the shape of appendixes. The Ch'un Ts'ew is the only one of the

five King which can, with an approximation to correctness, be described as of his own "making."

"The four Books" is an abbreviation for "The Books of the four Philosophers." The first is the Lun Yu, or "Digested Conversations," being occupied chiefly with the sayings of Confucius. He is the philosopher to whom it belongs. It appears in this Work under the title of "Confucian Analects." The second is the Ta Hëŏ, or "Great Learning," now commonly attributed to Tsăng Sin, a disciple of the sage. He is the philosopher of it. The third is the Chung Yung, or "Doctrine of the Mean," ascribed to K'ung Keih, the grandson of Confucius. He is the philosopher of it. The fourth contains the works of Mencius.

3. This arrangement of the Classical Books, which is commonly supposed to have originated with the scholars of the Sung dynasty, is defective. The *Great Learning* and the *Doctrine of the Mean* are both found in the Record of Rites, being the forty-second and thirty-first Books respectively of that compilation, according to the usual arrangement of it.

4. The oldest enumerations of the Classical Books specify only *the five King*. The Yŏ Ke, or "Record of Music," the remains of which now form one of the Books in the Le Ke, was sometimes added to those, making with them the *six King*. A division was also made into *nine King*, consisting of the Yih, the She, the Shoo, the Chow Le, or "Ritual of Chow," the E Le, or "Ceremonial Usages," the Le Ke, and the three annotated editions of the Ch'un Ts'ew, by Tso-k'ew Ming, Kung-yang Kaou, and Kuh-lëang Ch'ih. In the famous compilation of the classical Books, undertaken by order of T'ae-tsung, the second emperor of the T'ang dynasty (B.C. 627—619), and which appeared in the reign of his successor, there are *thirteen King*; viz., the Yih, the She, the Shoo, the three editions of the Ch'un Ts'ew, the Le Ke, the Chow Le, the E Le, the Confucian Analects, the Urh Ya, a sort of ancient dictionary, the Heaou King, or "Classic of Filial Piety," and the works of Mencius.

5. A distinction, however, was made, as early as the dynasty of the Western Han, in our first century, among the Works thus comprehended under the same common name; and Mencius, the Lun Yu, the Ta Hëŏ, the Chung Yung, and the Heaou King were spoken of as the seaou King, or

"smaller Classics." It thus appears, contrary to the ordinary opinion on the subject, that the Ta Heŏ and Chung Yung had been published as separate treatises long before the Sung dynasty, and that the Four Books, as distinguished from the greater King, had also previously found a place in the literature of China.[1]

SECTION II.

THE AUTHORITY OF THE CHINESE CLASSICS.

1. This subject will be discussed in connection with each separate Work, and it is only designed here to exhibit generally the evidence on which the Chinese Classics claim to be received as genuine productions of the time to which they are referred.

2. In the memoirs of the Former Han dynasty (B.C. 201—A.D. 24), we have one chapter which we may call the History of Literature. It commences thus:—"After the death of Confucius, there was an end of his exquisite words; and when his seventy disciples had passed away, violence began to be done to their meaning. It came about that there were five different editions of the Ch'un Ts'ew, four of the Shoo, and several of the Yih. Amid the disorder and collision of the warring States (B.C. 480—221), truth and falsehood were still more in a state of warfare, and a sad confusion marked the words of the various scholars. Then came the calamity inflicted under the Ts'in dynasty (B.C. 220—205), when the literary monuments were destroyed by fire, in order to keep the people in ignorance. But, by and by, there arose the Han dynasty, which set itself to remedy the evil wrought by the Ts'in. Great efforts were made to collect slips and tablets,[2] and the way was thrown wide open for the bringing in of Books. In the time of the emperor Hsaou-woo (B.C. 139—86), portions of Books being wanting and tablets lost, so that ceremonies and music were suffering great damage, he

---

[1] For the statements in the two last paragraphs, see the works of Se-ho on "The Text of the Great Learning," Bk. I.
[2] Slips and tablets of bamboo, which supplied in those days the place of paper.

was moved to sorrow, and said, 'I am very sad for this.'
He therefore formed the plan of Repositories, in which the
Books might be stored, and appointed officers to transcribe
Books on an extensive scale, embracing the works of the
various scholars, that they might all be placed in the Repositories. The Emperor Ch'ing (B.C. 31—6), finding that a
portion of the Books still continued dispersed or missing,
commissioned Ch'in Nung, the superintendent of guests, to
search for undiscovered Books throughout the empire, and
by special edict ordered the chief of the Banqueting House,
Lew Heang, to examine the classical Works, along with the
commentaries on them, the writings of the scholars, and all
poetical productions; the master-controller of infantry, Jin
Hwang, to examine the Books on the art of war; the grand
historiographer, Yin Hëen, to examine the Books treating
of the art of numbers (i. e. divination); and the imperial
physician, Le Ch'oo-kŏ, to examine the Books on medicine.
Whenever any Book was done with, Heang forthwith arranged it, indexed it, and made a digest of it, which was
presented to the emperor. While the undertaking was in
progress, Heang died, and the emperor Gae (B.C. 5—A.D.)
appointed his son, Hin, a master of the imperial carriages,
to complete his father's work. On this, Hin collected all
the Books, and presented a report of them, under seven
divisions."

The first of these divisions seems to have been a general
catalogue, containing perhaps only the titles of the works
included in the other six. The second embraced the classical Works. From the abstract of it, which is preserved in
the chapter referred to, we find that there were 294 collections of the Yih-king, from 13 different individuals or editors;[1] 412 collections of the Shoo-king, from nine different
individuals; 416 volumes of the She-king, from six different
individuals;[2] of the Book of Rites, 555 collections, from 18
different individuals; of the Books on Music, 165 collections,
from six different editors; 948 collections of History, under

[1] How much of the whole Work was contained in each "collection" or
p'ëen, it is impossible for us to ascertain. P. Regis says:—"P'ien, quemadmo-
dum Gallicè dicimus 'des pièces d'éloquence, de poésie.'"
[2] The collections of the She-king are mentioned under the name of kwen,
"sections," "portions." Had p'ëen been used, it might have been understood
of individual odes. This change of terms shows that by p'ëen in the other
summaries, we are not to understand single blocks or chapters.

the heading of the Ch'un Ts'ew, from 23 different individuals; 229 collections of the Lun Yu, including the Analects and kindred fragments, from 12 different individuals; of the Heaou-king, embracing also the Urh Ya, and some other portions of the ancient literature, 59 collections, from 11 different individuals; and finally of the Lesser Learning, being works on the form of the characters, 45 collections, from 11 different individuals. The Works of Mencius were included in the second division, among the Writings of what were deemed orthodox scholars, of which there were 836 collections, from 53 different individuals.

3. The above important document is sufficient to show how the emperors of the Han dynasty, as soon as they had made good their possession of the empire, turned their attention to recover the ancient literature of the nation, the Classical Books engaging their first care, and how earnestly and effectively the scholars of the time responded to the wishes of their rulers. In addition to the facts specified in the preface to it, I may relate that the ordinance of the Ts'in dynasty against possessing the Classical Books (with the exception, as will appear in its proper place, of the Yih-king) was repealed by the second sovereign of the Han, the emperor Heaou Hwuy, in the 4th year of his reign, B.C. 190, and that a large portion of the Shoo-king was recovered in the time of the third emperor, B.C. 178—156, while in the year B.C. 135, a special Board was constituted, consisting of literati who were put in charge of the five *King*.

4. The collections reported on by Lew Hin suffered damage in the troubles which began A.D. 8, and continued till the rise of the second or eastern Han dynasty in the year 25. The founder of it (A.D. 25—57) zealously promoted the undertaking of his predecessors, and additional repositories were required for the books which were collected. His successors, the emperors, Heaou-ming (58—75), Heaou-chang (75—88), and Heaou-hwo (89—105), took a part themselves in the studies and discussions of the literary tribunal, and the emperor Heaou-ling, between the years 172—178, had the text of the five *King*, as it had been fixed, cut in slabs of stone, in characters of three different forms.

5. Since the Han, the successive dynasties have considered the literary monuments of the country to be an object of their special care. Many of them have issued editions of the

classics, embodying the commentaries of preceding generations. No dynasty has distinguished itself more in this line than the present Manchow possessors of the Empire. In fine, the evidence is complete that the Classical Books of China have come down from at least a century before our Christian era, substantially the same as we have them at present.

6. But it still remains to inquire in what condition we may suppose the Books were when the scholars of the Han dynasty commenced their labours upon them. They acknowledge that the tablets—we cannot here speak of *manuscripts*—were mutilated and in disorder. Was the injury which they had received of such an extent that all the care and study put forth on the small remains would be of little use? This question can be answered satisfactorily only by an examination of the evidence which is adduced for the text of each particular Classic; but it can be made apparent that there is nothing, in the nature of the case, to interfere with our believing that the materials were sufficient to enable the scholars to execute the work intrusted to them.

7. The burning of the ancient Books by order of the founder of the Ts'in dynasty is always referred to as the greatest disaster which they sustained, and with this is coupled the slaughter of many of the literati by the same monarch.

The account which we have of these transactions in the Historical Records is the following:[1]—

"In his 34th year" (the 34th year, that is, after he had ascended the throne of Ts'in. It was only the 8th after he had been acknowledged Sovereign of the empire, coinciding with B.C. 212) "the emperor, returning from a visit to the south, which had extended as far as Yuĕ, gave a feast in the palace of Hëen-yang, when the Great Scholars, amounting to seventy men, appeared and wished him long life.[2] The superintendent of archery, Chow Ts'ing-ch'in, came for-

---

[1] I have thought it well to endeavour to translate the whole of the passages. Father de Mailla merely constructs from them a narrative of his own; see *L'Histoire Générale de La Chine*, tome II., pp. 399—409. The common histories current in China avoid the difficulties of the original by giving an abridgment of it.

[2] These were not only "great scholars," but had an official rank. There was what we may call a college of them, consisting of seventy members.

ward and praised him, saying, 'Formerly, the State of Ts'in was only 1000 lê in extent, but Your Majesty, by your spirit-like efficacy and intelligent wisdom, has tranquillized and settled the whole empire, and driven away all barbarous tribes, so that wherever the sun and moon shine, all appear before you as guests acknowledging subjection. You have formed the States of the various princes into provinces and districts, where the people enjoy a happy tranquillity, suffering no more from the calamities of war and contention. This condition of things will be transmitted for 10,000 generations. From the highest antiquity there has been no one in awful virtue like Your Majesty.'

"The Emperor was pleased with this flattery, when Shun-yu Yuĕ, one of the great scholars, a native of Ts'e, advanced and said, 'The sovereigns of Yin and Chow, for more than a thousand years, invested their sons and younger brothers, and meritorious ministers, with domains and rule, and could thus depend upon them for support and aid;—that I have heard. But now Your Majesty is in possession of all within the seas, and your sons and younger brothers are nothing but private individuals. The issue will be that some one will arise to play the part of T'een Ch'ang,[1] or of the six nobles of Ts'in. Without the support of your own family, where will you find the aid which you may require? That a state of things not modelled from the lessons of antiquity can long continue;—that is what I have not heard. Ts'ing is now showing himself to be a flatterer, who increases the errors of Your Majesty, and is not a loyal minister.'

"The Emperor requested the opinions of others on this representation, when the premier, Le Sze, said, 'The five emperors were not one the double of the other, nor did the three dynasties accept one another's ways. Each had a peculiar system of government, not for the sake of the contrariety, but as being required by the changed times. Now, Your Majesty has laid the foundations of imperial sway, so that it will last for 10,000 generations. This is indeed beyond what a stupid scholar can understand. And, moreover, Yuĕ only talks of things belonging to the Three Dynasties, which are not fit to be models to you. At other times, when

[1] The T'een family grew up in the State of Ts'e, and in the early part of the 4th century B.C. supplanted the ruling House. The dismemberment of Ts'in was still earlier.

the princes were all striving together, they endeavoured to gather the wandering scholars about them; but now, the empire is in a stable condition, and laws and ordinances issue from one *supreme authority*. Let those of the people who abide in their homes give their strength to the toils of husbandry, and those who become scholars should study the various laws and prohibitions. Instead of doing this, however, the scholars do not learn what belongs to the present day, but study antiquity. They go on to condemn the present time, leading the masses of the people astray, and to disorder.

"'At the risk of my life, I, the prime minister, say,— Formerly, when the empire was disunited and disturbed, there was no one who could give unity to it. The princes therefore stood up together; constant references were made to antiquity to the injury of the present state; baseless statements were dressed up to confound what was real, and men made a boast of their own peculiar learning to condemn what their rulers appointed. And now, when Your Majesty has consolidated the empire, and, distinguishing black from white, has constituted it a stable unity, they still honour their peculiar learning, and combine together; they teach men what is contrary to your laws. When they hear that an ordinance has been issued, every one sets to discussing it with his learning. In the court, they are dissatisfied in heart; out of it, they keep talking in the streets. While they make a pretence of vaunting their Master, they consider it fine to have extraordinary views of their own. And so they lead on the people to be guilty of murmuring and evil speaking. If these things are not prohibited, Your Majesty's authority will decline, and parties will be formed. As to the best way to prohibit them, I pray that all the Records in charge of the Historiographers be burned, excepting those of Ts'in; that, with the exception of those officers belonging to the Board of Great Scholars, all throughout the empire who presume to keep copies of the She-king, or of the Shoo-king, or of the books of the Hundred Schools, be required to go with them to the officers in charge of the several districts, and burn them; that all who may dare to speak together about the She and the Shoo be put to death, and their bodies exposed in the market-place; that those who make mention of the past, so as to blame the present, be put to death along with their relatives; that officers who shall know of the violation of these rules and not inform against the offenders, be held equally guilty with them; and that whoever shall not have burned their books within thirty days after the issuing of the ordinance, be branded and sent to labour on the wall for four years. The only books which should be spared are those on medicine, divination, and husbandry. Whoever wants to learn the laws may go to the magistrates and learn of them.'

"The imperial decision was—'Approved.'"

The destruction of the scholars is related more briefly. In the year after the burning of the Books, the resentment of the Emperor was excited by the remarks and flight of two scholars who had been favourites with him, and he determined to institute a strict inquiry about all of their class in Hëen-yang, to find out whether they had been making ominous speeches about him, and disturbing the minds of the people. The investigation was committed to the Censors; and it being discovered that upwards of 460 scholars had violated the prohibitions, they were all buried alive in pits, for a warning to the empire, while degradation and banishment were employed more strictly than before against all who fell under suspicion. The Emperor's eldest son, Foo-soo, remonstrated with him, saying that such measures against those who repeated the words of Confucius, and sought to imitate him, would alienate all the people from their infant dynasty, but his interference offended his father so much that he was sent off from court, to be with the general who was superintending the building of the great wall.

8. No attempts have been made by Chinese critics and historians to discredit the record of these events, though some have questioned the extent of the injury inflicted by them on the monuments of their ancient literature. It is important to observe that the edict against the Books did not extend to the Yih-king, which was exempted as being a work on divination, nor did it extend to the other classics which were in charge of the Board of Great Scholars. There ought to have been no difficulty in finding copies when the Han dynasty superseded that of Ts'in; and probably there would have been none but for the sack of the capital, in B.C. 203, by Heang Yu, the most formidable opponent of the founder

of the House of Han. Then, we are told, the fires blazed for three months among the palaces and public buildings, and proved as destructive to the copies of the 'Great Scholars,' as those ordered by the tyrant had done to the copies of the people.

It is to be noted, moreover, that his life lasted only three years after the promulgation of his edict. He died B.C. 209; and the reign of his second son, who succeeded him, lasted only other three years. Then the reign of the founder of the Han dynasty dates from B.C. 201:—eleven years were all which intervened between the order for the burning of the Books and the establishment of that Family which signalized itself by the care which it bestowed for their recovery; and from the issue of the edict against private individuals having copies in their keeping to its express abrogation by the Emperor Hwuy, there were only 22 years. We may believe, indeed, that vigorous efforts to carry the edict into effect would not be continued longer than the life of its author,—that is, not for more than about three years. The calamity inflicted on the ancient Books of China by the House of Ts'in could not have approached to anything like a complete destruction of them.

9. The idea of forgery by the scholars of the Han dynasty on a large scale is out of the question. The catalogues of Low Hin enumerated more than 13,000 volumes of a larger or smaller size, the productions of nearly 600 different writers, and arranged in 38 subdivisions of subjects. In the third catalogue, the first subdivision contained the orthodox writers, to the number of 53, with 836 Works or portions of their Works. Between Mencius and K'ung Keih, the grandson of Confucius, eight different authors have place. The second subdivision contained the Works of the Taouist school, amounting to 993 collections, from 37 different authors. The sixth subdivision contained the Mihist writers, to the number of six, with their productions in 86 collections. I specify these two subdivisions, because they embraced the Works of schools or sects antagonist to that of Confucius, and some of them still hold a place in Chinese literature, and contain many references to the five Classics, and to Confucius and his disciples.

10. The inquiry pursued in the above paragraphs conducts us to the conclusion that the materials from which the

Classics, as they have come down to us, were compiled and edited in the two centuries preceding our Christian era, were genuine remains, going back to a still more remote period. The injury which they sustained from the dynasty of Ts'in was, I believe, the same in character as that to which they were exposed during all the time of "the Warring States." It may have been more intense in degree, but the constant warfare which prevailed for some centuries among the different States which composed the empire was eminently unfavourable to the cultivation of literature. Mencius tells us how the princes had made away with many of the records of antiquity, from which their own usurpations and innovations might have been condemned.¹ Still the times were not unfruitful, either in scholars or statesmen, to whom the ways and monuments of antiquity were dear, and the space from the rise of the Ts'in dynasty to Confucius was not very great. It only amounted to 258 years. Between these two periods Mencius stands as a connecting link. Born probably in the year B.C. 371, he reached, by the intervention of K'ung Keih, back to the sage himself, and as his death happened B.C. 288, we are brought down to within nearly half a century of the Ts'in dynasty. From all these considerations, we may proceed with confidence to consider each separate Work, believing that we have in these Classics and Books what the great sage of China and his disciples found, or gave to their country, more than 2000 years ago.

See Mencius, V. Pt. II. ii. 2.

CHAPTER II.

OF THE CONFUCIAN ANALECTS.

SECTION I.

FORMATION OF THE TEXT OF THE ANALECTS BY THE SCHOLARS OF THE HAN DYNASTY.

1. When the work of collecting and editing the remains of the Classical Books was undertaken by the scholars of Han, there appeared two different copies of the Analects; one from Loo, the native State of Confucius, and the other from Ts'e, the State adjoining. Between these there were considerable differences. The former consisted of twenty Books or Chapters, the same as those into which the Classic is now divided. The latter contained two Books in addition, and in the twenty Books, which they had in common, the chapters and sentences were somewhat more numerous than in the Loo exemplar.

2. The names of several individuals are given, who devoted themselves to the study of those two copies of the Classic. Among the patrons of the Loo copy are mentioned the names of Hea-how Shing, grand-tutor of the heir-apparent, who died at the age of 90, and in the reign of the Emperor Seuen (B.C. 72—48); Seaou Wangche, a general officer, who died in the reign of the Emperor Yuen (B.C. 47—32); Wei Heen, who was premier of the empire from B.C. 70—60; and his son Heuen-shing. As patrons of the Ts'e copy, we have Wang K'ing, who was a censor in the year B.C. 99; Yung Tan, and Wang Keih, a statesman who died in the beginning of the reign of the Emperor Yuen.

3. But a third copy of the Analects was discovered about B.C. 150. One of the sons of the Emperor King was appointed king of Loo, in the year B.C. 153, and some time after, wishing to enlarge his palace, he proceeded to pull

down the house of the K'ung family, known as that where Confucius himself had lived. While doing so, there were found in the wall copies of the Shoo-king, the Ch'un Ts'ew, the Heaou-king, and the Lun Yu or Analects, which had been deposited there, when the edict for the burning of the Books was issued. They were all written, however, in the most ancient form of the Chinese character,[1] which had fallen into disuse; and the king returned them to the K'ung family, the head of which, K'ung Gan-kwŏ, gave himself to the study of them, and finally, in obedience to an imperial order, published a Work called "The Lun Yu, with explanations of the Characters, and Exhibition of the Meaning."[2]

4. The recovery of this copy will be seen to be a most important circumstance in the history of the text of the Analects. It is referred to by Chinese writers, as "The old Lun Yu." In the historical narrative which we have of the affair, a circumstance is added which may appear to some minds to throw suspicion on the whole account. The king was finally arrested, we are told, in his purpose to destroy the house, by hearing the sound of bells, musical stones, lutes, and harpsichords, as he was ascending the steps that led to the ancestral hall or temple. This incident was contrived, we may suppose, by the K'ung family, to preserve the house, or it may have been devised by the historian to glorify the sage, but we may not, on account of it, discredit the finding of the ancient copies of the Books. We have K'ung Gan-kwŏ's own account of their being committed to him, and of the ways which he took to decipher them. The work upon the Analects, mentioned above, has not indeed come down to us, but his labours on the Shoo-king still remain.

5. It has been already stated, that the Lun Yu of Ts'e contained two Books more than that of Loo. In this respect, the old Lun Yu agreed with the Loo exemplar. Those two books were wanting in it as well. The last book of the Loo Lun was divided in it, however, into two, the chapter

---

[1] Called "tadpole characters." They were, it is said, the original forms devised by Ts'ang Kĕĕ, with large heads and fine tails, like the creature from which they were named. See the notes to the preface to the Shoo-king in "The thirteen Classics."

[2] See the preface to the Lun Yu in "The thirteen King." It has been my principal authority in this Section.

beginning, "Yaou said," forming a whole Book by itself, and the remaining two chapters formed another Book beginning "Tsze-chang." With this trifling difference, the old and the Loo copies appear to have agreed together.

6. Chang Yu, prince of Gan-ch'ang, who died B.C. 4, after having sustained several of the highest offices of the empire, instituted a comparison between the exemplars of Loo and Ts'e, with a view to determine the true text. The result of his labours appeared in twenty-one Books, which are mentioned in Lew Hin's catalogue. They were known as the Lun of the Prince Chang, and commanded general approbation. To Chang Yu is commonly ascribed the ejecting from the Classic of the two additional books which the Ts'e exemplar contained, but Ma Twan-lin prefers to rest that circumstance on the authority of the old Lun, which we have seen was without them. If we had the two Books, we might find sufficient reason from their contents to discredit them. That may have been sufficient for Chang Yu to condemn them as he did, but we can hardly suppose that he did not have before him the old Lun, which had come to light about a century before he published his Work.

7. In the course of the second century, a new edition of the Analects, with a commentary, was published by one of the greatest scholars which China has ever produced,—Ch'ing Heuen, known also as Ch'ing K'ang-shing. He died in the reign of the Emperor Heen (A.D.109—220) at the age of 74, and the amount of his labours on the ancient classical literature is almost incredible. While he adopted the Loo Lun as the received text of his time, he compared it minutely with those of Ts'e and the old exemplar. He produced three different works on the Analects, which unfortunately do not subsist. They were current, however, for several centuries; and the name of one of them—"The Meaning of the Lun Yu explained,"—appears in the Catalogues of Books in the T'ang dynasty (A.D. 624—907).

8. On the whole, the above statements will satisfy the reader of the care with which the text of the Lun Yu was fixed during the dynasty of Han.

SECTION II.

AT WHAT TIME, AND BY WHOM, THE ANALECTS WERE WRITTEN; THEIR PLAN; AND AUTHENTICITY.

1. At the commencement of the notes upon the first Book, under the heading—"The Title of the Work," I have given the received account of its authorship, taken from the "History of Literature" of the western Han dynasty. According to that, the Analects were compiled by the disciples of Confucius, coming together after his death, and digesting the memorials of his discourses and conversations which they had severally preserved. But this cannot be true. We may believe, indeed, that many of the disciples put on record conversations which they had had with their master, and notes about his manners and incidents of his life, and that these have been incorporated with the Work which we have, but that Work must have taken its present form at a period somewhat later.

In Book VIII., chapters iii. and iv., we have some notices of the last days of Tsăng Sin, and are told that he was visited on his death-bed by the officer Măng King. Now King was the posthumous title of Chung-sun Tsëi, and we find him alive (Le Ke, II. Pt. II. ii. 2) after the death of Duke To of Loo, which took place B.C. 430, about fifty years after the death of Confucius.

Again, Book XIX. is all occupied with the sayings of the disciples. Confucius personally does not appear in it. Parts of it, as chapters iii., xii., xviii., and xix., carry us down to a time when the disciples had schools and followers of their own, and were accustomed to sustain their teachings by referring to the lessons which they had heard from the sage.

Thirdly, there is the second chapter of Book XI., the second paragraph of which is evidently a note by the compilers of the work, enumerating ten of the principal disciples, and classifying them according to their distinguishing characteristics. We can hardly suppose it to have been written while any of the ten were alive. But there is among them the name of Tsze-hea, who lived to the age of about a hundrod. We find him, B.C. 406, three quarters of a century after the death of Confucius, at the court of Wei, to the prince of which he is reported to have presented some of the Classical Books.

2. We cannot therefore accept the above account of the origin of the Analects,—that they were compiled by the disciples of Confucius. Much more likely is the view that we owe the work to *their* disciples. In the note on Book I. ii. 1, a peculiarity is pointed out in the use of the surnames of Yew Jŏ and Tsăng Sin, which has made some Chinese critics attribute the compilation to their followers. But this conclusion does not stand investigation. Others have assigned different portions to different schools. Thus Book V. is given to the disciples of Tsze-kung; Book XI. to those of Min Tsze-k'een; Book XIV. to Yuen Heen; and Book XVI. has been supposed to be interpolated from the Analects of Ts'e. Even if we were to acquiesce in these decisions, we should have accounted only for a small part of the work. It is better to rest in the general conclusion, that it was compiled by the disciples of the disciples of the sage, making free use of the written memorials concerning him which they had received, and the oral statements which they had heard, from their several masters. And we shall not be far wrong, if we determine its date as about the beginning of the third, or the end of the fourth century before Christ.

3. In the critical work on the Classical Books, called "Record of Remarks in the village of Yung," published in 1743, it is observed, "The Analects, in my opinion, were made by the disciples, just like this Record of Remarks. There they were recorded, and afterwards came a first-rate hand, who gave them the beautiful literary finish which we now witness, so that there is not a character which does not have its own indispensable place." We have seen that the first of these statements contains only a small amount of truth with regard to the materials of the Analects, nor can we receive the second. If one hand or one mind had digested the materials provided by many, the arrangement and style of the work would have been different. We should not have had the same remark appearing in several Books, with little variation, and sometimes with none at all. Nor can we account on this supposition for such fragments as

the last chapters of the 9th, 10th, and 16th Books, and many others. No definite plan has been kept in view throughout. A degree of unity appears to belong to some Books more than to others, and in general to the first ten more than to those which follow, but there is no progress of thought or illustration of subject from Book to Book. And even in those where the chapters have a common subject, they are thrown together at random more than on any plan.

4. When the Work was first called the Lun Yu, we cannot tell.[1] The evidence in the preceding section is sufficient to prove that when the Han scholars were engaged in collecting the ancient Books, it came before them, not in broken tablets, but complete, and arranged in Books or Sections, as we now have it. The old Lun was found deposited in the wall of the house which Confucius had occupied, and must have been placed there not later than B.C. 211, distant from the date which I have assigned to the compilation, not much more than a century and a half. That copy, written in the most ancient characters, was, possibly, the autograph, so to speak, of the compilers.

We have the Writings, or portions of the Writings, of several authors of the third and fourth centuries before Christ. Of these, in addition to "The Great Learning," "The Doctrine of the Mean," and "The Works of Mencius," I have looked over the Works of Seun K'ing of the orthodox school, of the philosophers Chwang and Lëĕ of the Taouist school, and of the heresiarch Mih.

In The Great Learning, Commentary, chapter iv., we have the words of Ana. XII. xiii. In The Doctrine of the Mean, ch. iii., we have Ana. VI. xxvii.; and in ch. xxviii. 5, we have Ana. III. ix. and xiv. In Mencius, II. Pt. I. ii. 19, we have Ana. VII. xxxiii., and in vii. 2, Ana. IV. i.; in III. Pt. I. iv. 11, Ana. VIII. xviii., xix.; in IV. Pt. I. xiv. 1, Ana. XI. xvi. 2; V. Pt. II. vii. 9, Ana. X. xiii. 4; and in VII. Pt. II. xxxvii. 1, 2, 8, Ana. V. xxi., XIII. xxi., and XVII.

---

[1] In the continuation of the "General Examination of Records and Scholars," Bk cxcviii. p. 17, it is said, indeed, on the authority of Wang Ch'ung, a scholar of the 1st century, that when the Work came out of the wall it was named a Ch'uen or Record, and that it was when K'ung Gan-kwŏ instructed a native of Tsin, named Foo-k'ing, in it, that it first got the name of Lun Yu. If it were so, it is strange the circumstance is not mentioned in Ho An's preface.

xiii. These quotations, however, are introduced by "The Master said," or "Confucius said," no mention being made of any book called "The Lun Yu," or Analects. In The Great Learning, Commentary, x. 15, we have the words of Ana. IV. iii., and in Mencius, III. Pt. II. vii. 3, those of Ana. XVII. i., but without any notice of quotation.

In the Writings of Seun K'ing, Book I. page 2, we find some words of Ana. XV. xxx.; p. 6, those of XIV. xxv. In Book VIII. p. 13, we have some words of Ana. II. xvii. But in these three instances there is no mark of quotation.

In the Writings of Chwang, I have noted only one passage where the words of the Analects are reproduced. Ana. XVIII. v. is found, but with large additions, and no reference of quotation, in his treatise on "The state of Men in the world, Intermediate," placed, that is, between Heaven and Earth. In all these Works, as well as in those of Lëë and Mih, the references to Confucius and his disciples, and to many circumstances of his life, are numerous.[1] The quotations of sayings of his not found in the Analects are likewise many, especially in the Doctrine of the Mean, in Mencius, and in the works of Chwang. Those in the latter are mostly burlesques, but those by the orthodox writers have more or less of classical authority. Some of them may be found in the Kea Yu, or "Family Sayings," and in parts of the Lo Ke, while others are only known to us by their occurrence in these Writings. Altogether, they do not supply the evidence, for which I am in quest, of the existence of the Analects as a distinct Work, bearing the name of the Lun Yu, prior to the Ts'in dynasty. They leave the presumption, however, in favour of those conclusions, which arises from the facts stated in the first section, undisturbed. They confirm it rather. They show that there was abundance of materials at hand to the scholars of Han, to compile a much larger Work with the same title, if they had felt it their duty to do the business of compilation, and not that of editing.

[1] In Mih's chapter against the Literati, he mentions some of the characteristics of Confucius, in the very words of the 10th Book of the Analects.

SECTION III.

OF COMMENTARIES UPON THE ANALECTS.

1. It would be a vast and unprofitable labour to attempt to give a list of the Commentaries which have been published on this Work. My object is merely to point out how zealously the business of interpretation was undertaken, as soon as the text had been recovered by the scholars of the Han dynasty, and with what industry it has been persevered in down to the present time.

2. Mention has been made, in Section I. 6, of the Lun of Prince Chang, published in the half century before our era. Paou Heen, a distinguished scholar and officer, of the reign of Kwang-woo, the first emperor of the Eastern Han dynasty, A.D. 25—57, and another scholar of the surname Chow, less known but of the same time, published Works, containing arrangements of this into chapters and sentences, with explanatory notes. The critical work of K'ung Gan-kwǒ on the old Lun Yu has been referred to. That was lost in consequence of troubles which arose towards the close of the reign of the Emperor Woo, but in the time of the Emperor Shun, A.D. 126—144, another scholar, Ma Yung, undertook the exposition of the characters in the old Lun, giving at the same time his views of the general meaning. The labours of Ch'ing Heuen in the second century have been mentioned. Not long after his death, there ensued a period of anarchy, when the empire was divided into three governments, well known from the celebrated historical romance, called "The Three States." The strongest of them, the House of Wei, patronized literature, and three of its high officers and scholars, Ch'in K'eun, Wang Suh, and Chow Shung-lëě, in the first half, and probably the second quarter of the third century, all gave to the world their notes on the Analects.

Very shortly after, five of the chief ministers of the Government of Wei, Sun Yung, Ch'ing Ch'ung, Tsaou He, Seun K'ae, and Ho An, united in the production of one great work, entitled, "A Collection of Explanations of the Lun Yu." It embodied the labours of all the writers which have been mentioned, and having been frequently reprinted by succeeding dynasties, it still remains. The preface of the five compilers, in the form of a memorial to the emperor, so called, of the House of Wei, is published with it, and has been of much assistance to me in writing these sections. Ho An was the leader among them, and the work is commonly quoted as if it were the production of him alone.

3. From Ho An downwards, there has not been a dynasty which has not contributed its labourers to the illustration of the Analects. In the Leang, which occupied the throne a good part of the sixth century, there appeared the "Comments of Wang K'an," who to the seven authorities cited by Ho An added other thirteen, being scholars who had deserved well of the Classic during the intermediate time. Passing over other dynasties, we come to the Sung, A.D. 960—1279. An edition of the Classics was published by imperial authority, about the beginning of the 11th century, with the title of "The Correct Meaning." The principal scholar engaged in the undertaking was Hing Ping. The portion of it on the Analects is commonly reprinted in "The Thirteen Classics," after Ho An's explanations. But the names of the Sung dynasty are all thrown into the shade by that of Choo He, than whom China has not produced a greater scholar. He composed, in the 12th century, three Works on the Analects, which still remain:—the first called "Collected Meanings;" the second, "Collected Comments;" and the third, "Queries." Nothing could exceed the grace and clearness of his style, and the influence which he has exerted on the literature of China has been almost despotic.

The scholars of the present dynasty, however, seem inclined to question the correctness of his views and interpretations of the Classics, and the chief place among them is due to Maou K'eling, known more commonly as Maou Se-ho. His writings, under the name of "The Collected Works of Se-ho," have been published in 80 volumes, containing between three and four hundred books or sections. He has nine treatises on The Four Books, or parts of them, and deserves to take rank with Ch'ing Heuen and Choo He at the head of Chinese scholars, though he is a vehement opponent of the latter. Many of his writings are to be found also in the great Work called "A Collection of Works on the Classics, under the Imperial dynasty of Ts'ing," which contains 1400 sections, and is a noble contribution by scholars of the present dynasty to the illustration of its ancient literature.

CHAPTER III.

OF THE GREAT LEARNING.

SECTION I.

HISTORY OF THE TEXT; AND THE DIFFERENT ARRANGEMENTS OF IT WHICH HAVE BEEN PROPOSED.

1. It has already been mentioned that "The Great Learning" forms one of the chapters of the Le Ke, or "Record of Rites," the formation of the text of which will be treated of in its proper place. I will only say here that the Book, or Books, of Rites had suffered much more, after the death of Confucius, than the other ancient Classics. They were in a more dilapidated condition at the time of the revival of the ancient literature under the Han dynasty, and were then published in three collections, only one of which—the Record of Rites—retains its place among the *King*.

The Record of Rites consists, according to the current arrangement, of 49 chapters or Books. Lew Heang (see ch. I. sect. II. 2) took the lead in its formation, and was followed by the two famous scholars, Tae Tih, and his relative, Tae Shing. The first of these reduced upwards of 200 chapters, collected by Heang, to 89, and Shing reduced those again to 46. The three other Books were added in the second century of our era, The Great Learning being one of them, by Ma Yung, mentioned in the last chaper, section III. 2. Since his time, the Work has not received any further additions.

2. In his note appended to what he calls the chapter of "Classical Text," Choo He says that the tablets of the "old copies" of the rest of The Great Learning were considerably out of order. By those old copies, he intends the Work of Ch'ing Henen, who published his commentary on the Classic, soon after it was completed by the additions of Ma Yung;

and it is possible that the tablets were in confusion, and had not been arranged with sufficient care; but such a thing does not appear to have been suspected until the 12th century; nor can any authority from ancient monuments be adduced in its support.

I have related how the ancient Classics were cut on slabs of stone by imperial order, A.D. 175, the text being that which the various literati had determined, and which had been adopted by Ch'ing Heuen. The same work was performed about seventy years later, under the so-called dynasty of Wei, between the years 240 and 248, and the two sets of slabs were set up together. The only difference between them was, that whereas the Classics had been cut in the first instance in three different forms, called the Seal character, the Pattern style, and the Imperfect form, there was substituted for the latter in the slabs of Wei the oldest form of the characters, similar to that which has been described in connection with the discovery of the old Lun Yu in the wall of Confucius' house. Amid the changes of dynasties, the slabs both of Han and Wei had perished before the rise of the T'ang dynasty, A.D. 624; but under one of its emperors, in the year 836, a copy of the Classics was again cut on stone, though only in one form of the character. These slabs we can trace down through the Sung dynasty when they were known as the tablets of Shen. They were in exact conformity with the text of the Classics adopted by Ch'ing Heuen in his commentaries.

The Sung dynasty did not accomplish a similar work itself, nor has any one of the three which have followed it thought it necessary to engrave in stone in this way the ancient classics. About the middle of the 16th century, however, the literary world in China was startled by a report that the slabs of Wei which contained The Great Learning had been discovered. But this was nothing more than the result of an impudent attempt at an imposition, for which it is difficult to a foreigner to assign any adequate cause. The treatise, as printed from these slabs, has some trifling additions, and many alterations in the order of the text, but differing from the arrangements proposed by Choo Ho, and by other scholars. There seems to be now no difference of opinion among Chinese critics that the whole affair was a forgery. The text of The Great Learning, as it appears in the Book of Rites with the commentary of Ch'ing Heuen, and was thrice engraved on stone, in three different dynasties, is, no doubt, that which was edited in the Han dynasty by Ma Yung.

3. I have said that it is possible that the tablets containing the text were not arranged with sufficient care by him, and, indeed, any one who studies the treatise attentively will probably come to the conclusion that the part of it forming the first six chapters of Commentary in the present Work is but a fragment. It would not be a difficult task to propose an arrangement of the text different from any which I have yet seen; but such an undertaking would not be interesting out of China. My object here is simply to mention the Chinese scholars who have rendered themselves famous or notorious in their own country, by what they have done in this way. The first was Ch'ing Haou, a native of Loh-yang in Ho-nan province, in the 11th century. His designation was Pih-shun, but since his death he has been known chiefly by the style of Ming-taou, which we may render the Wise-in-doctrine. The eulogies heaped on him by Choo He and others are extravagant, and he is placed immediately after Mencius in the list of great scholars. Doubtless he was a man of vast literary acquirements. The greatest change which he introduced into The Great Learning, was to read *sin* for *ts'in*, at the commencement, making the second object proposed in the treatise to be the *renovation* of the people, instead of *loving* them. This alteration and his various transpositions of the text are found in Maou Se-ho's treatise on "The attested text of The Great Learning."

Hardly less illustrious than Ch'ing Haou was his younger brother Ch'ing E, known by the style of Ching-shuh, and since his death by that of E-ch'uen. He followed Haou in the adoption of the reading " *to renovate*," instead of " *to love*." But he transposed the text differently, more akin to the arrangement afterwards made by Choo He, suggesting also that there were some superfluous sentences in the old text which might conveniently be erased. The Work, as proposed to be read by him, will be found in the volume of Maou just referred to.

We come to the name of Choo He who entered into the labours of the brothers Ch'ing, the younger of whom he

styles his Master, in his introductory note to The Great
Learning. His arrangement of the text is that now current
in all the editions of the Four Books, and it had nearly displaced the ancient text altogether. The sanction of Imperial
approval was given to it during the Yuen and Ming dynasties.
In the editions of the five *King* published by them, only the
names of the Doctrine of the Mean and The Great Learning
were preserved. No text of these Books was given, and
So-ho tells us, that in the reign of Kea-tsing, the most
flourishing period of the Ming dynasty (A.D. 1522—1566),
when a Wang Wān-shing published a copy of The Great
Learning, taken from the T'ang edition of the Thirteen *King*,
all the officers and scholars looked at one another in astonish-
ment, and were inclined to suppose that the Work was a
forgery. Besides adopting the reading of *sin* for *ts'in* from
the Ch'ing, and modifying their arrangements of the text,
Choo He made other innovations. He first divided the whole
into one chapter of Classical text, which he assigned to Confucius, and ten chapters of Commentary, which he assigned
to the disciple Tsăng. Previous to him, the whole had been
published, indeed, without any specification of chapters and
paragraphs. He undertook, moreover, to supply one whole
chapter, which he supposed, after his master Ch'ing, to be
missing.

Since the time of Choo He, many scholars have exercised
their wit on The Great Learning. The Work of Maou So-ho
contains four arrangements of the text, proposed respectively
by the scholars Wang Loo-chae, Ko P'ang-san, Kaou King-
yih, and Kŏ Hoo-chen. The curious student may examine
them there.

Under the present dynasty, the tendency has been to depreciate the labours of Choo He. The integrity of the text
of Ch'ing Heuen is zealously maintained, and the simpler
method of interpretation employed by him is advocated in
preference to the more refined and ingenious schemes of the
Sung scholars. I have referred several times in the notes to
a Work published a few years ago, under the title of "The
Old Text of the sacred *King*, with Commentary and Discussions, by Lo Chung-fan of Nan-hae." I know the man
seventeen years ago. He was a fine scholar, and had taken
the second degree, or that of *Keu-jin*. He applied to me in
1843 for Christian baptism, and offended by my hesitancy

went and enrolled himself among the disciples of another Missionary. He soon, however, withdrew into seclusion, and spent the last years of his life in literary studies. His family have published the work on The Great Learning, and one or two others. He most vehemently impugns nearly every judgment of Choo Ho; but in his own exhibitions of the meaning he blends many ideas of the Supreme Being and of the condition of human nature, which he had learned from the Christian Scriptures.

SECTION II.

OF THE AUTHORSHIP, AND DISTINCTION OF THE TEXT INTO CLASSICAL TEXT AND COMMENTARY.

1. THE authorship of The Great Learning is a very doubtful point, and one on which it does not appear possible to come to a decided conclusion. Choo Ho, as I have stated in the last section, determined that so much of it was *king*, or Classic, being the very words of Confucius, and that all the rest was *chuen*, or Commentary, being the views of Tsäng Sin upon the sage's words, recorded by *his* disciples. Thus, he does not expressly attribute the composition of the Treatise to Tsäng, as he is generally supposed to do. What he says, however, as it is destitute of external support, is contrary also to the internal evidence. The 4th chapter of Commentary commences with " The Master said." Surely, if there were anything more, directly from Confucius, there would be an intimation of it in the same way. Or, if we may allow that short sayings of Confucius might be interwoven with the Work, as in the 15th paragraph of the 10th chapter, without mention of "The Master," it is too much to ask us to receive the long chapter at the beginning as being from him. With regard to the Work having come from the disciples of Tsäng Sin, recording their master's views, the paragraph in chapter 6th, commencing with " The disciple Tsäng said," seems to be conclusive against that hypothesis. So much we may be sure is Tsäng's, and no more. Both of Choo Ho's judgments must be set aside. We cannot admit

either the distinction of the contents into Classical text and Commentary, or that the Work was the production of Tsäng's disciples.

2. Who then was the author? An ancient tradition attributes it to K'ung Keih, the grandson of Confucius. In a notice published at the time of their preparation, about the stone slabs of Wei, the following statement by Kea Kwei, a noted scholar of the 1st century, is quoted:—"When K'ung Keih was living, and in straits, in Sung, being afraid lest the lessons of the former sages should become obscure, and the principles of the ancient emperors and kings fall to the ground, he therefore made The Great Learning as the warp of them, and The Doctrine of the Mean as the woof." This would seem, therefore, to have been the opinion of that early time, and I may say the only difficulty in admitting it is that no mention is made of it by Ch'ing Heuen. There certainly is that agreement between the two treatises, which makes their common authorship not at all unlikely.

3. Though we cannot positively assign the authorship of The Great Learning, there can be no hesitation in receiving it as a genuine monument of the Confucian school. There are not many words in it from the sage himself, but it is a faithful reflection of his teachings, written by some of his followers, not far removed from him by lapse of time. It must synchronize pretty nearly with the Analects, and may be safely referred to the fourth century before our era.

SECTION III.

ITS SCOPE AND VALUE.

1. THE worth of The Great Learning has been celebrated in most extravagant terms by many Chinese writers, and there have been foreigners who have not yielded to them in their estimation of it. Pauthier, in the "Argument Philosophique," prefixed to his translation of the Work, says:—"It is evident that the aim of the Chinese philosopher is to exhibit the duties of political government as those of the perfecting of self, and of the practice of virtue by all men.

He felt that he had a higher mission than that with which the greater part of ancient and modern philosophers have contented themselves; and his immense love for the happiness of humanity, which dominated over all his other sentiments, has made of his philosophy a system of social perfectionating, which, we venture to say, has never been equalled."[1]

Very different is the judgment passed upon the treatise by a writer in the Chinese Repository:—"The *Tá Hëö* is a short politico-moral discourse. *Tá Hëö*, or 'Superior Learning,' is at the same time both the name and the subject of the discourse; it is the *summum bonum* of the Chinese. In opening this Book, compiled by a disciple of Confucius, and containing his doctrines, we might expect to find a Work like Cicero's *De Officiis*; but we find a very different production, consisting of a few commonplace rules for the maintenance of a good government."[2]

My readers will perhaps think, after reading the present section, that the truth lies between these two representations.

2. I believe that the Book should be styled *T'ae Hëö*, and not *Tá Hëö*, and that it was so named as setting forth the higher and more extensive principles of moral science, which come into use and manifestation in the conduct of government. When Choo He endeavours to make the title mean—"The principles of Learning, which were taught in the higher schools of antiquity," and tells us how at the age of 15 all the sons of the emperor, with the legitimate sons of the nobles and high officers, down to the more promising scions of the common people, all entered those seminaries, and were taught the difficult lessons here inculcated, we pity the ancient youth of China. Such "strong meat" is not adapted for the nourishment of youthful minds. But the evidence adduced for the existence of such educational institutions in ancient times is unsatisfactory, and from the older interpretation of the title we advance more easily to contemplate the object and method of the Work.

3. The *object* is stated definitely enough in the opening paragraph:—"What The Great Learning teaches, is—to illustrate illustrious virtue; to love the people; and to rest

[1] Le Ta Hio, ou La Grande Etude. Paris, 1837.
[2] Chinese Repository, vol. iii. p. 98.

in the highest excellence." The political aim of the writer is here at once evident. He has before him on one side *the people*, the masses of the empire, and over against them are those whose work and duty, delegated by Heaven, is to govern them, culminating, as a class, in "the son of Heaven," "the one man," the emperor. From the 4th and 5th paragraphs, we see that if the lessons of the treatise be learned and carried into practice, the result will be that "illustrious virtue will be illustrated throughout the empire," which will be brought, through all its length and breadth, to a condition of happy tranquillity. This object is certainly both grand and good; and if a reasonable and likely method to secure it were proposed in the Work, language would hardly supply terms adequate to express its value.

4. But the above account of the object of The Great Learning leads us to the conclusion that the student of it should be an emperor. What interest can an ordinary man have in it? It is high up in the clouds, far beyond his reach. This is a serious objection to it, and quite unfits it for a place in schools, such as Choo He contends it once had. Intelligent Chinese, whose minds were somewhat quickened by Christianity, have spoken to me of this defect, and complained of the difficulty they felt in making the book a practical directory for their conduct. " It is so vague and vast," was the observation of one man. The writer, however, has made some provision for the general application of his instructions. He tells us, that from the emperor down to the mass of the people, all must consider the cultivation of the person to be the root, that is, the first thing to be attended to. As in his method, moreover, he reaches from the cultivation of the person to the tranquillization of the Empire, through the intermediate steps of the regulation of the family, and the government of the State, there is room for setting forth principles that parents and rulers generally may find adapted for their guidance.

5. The method which is laid down for the attainment of the great object proposed consists of seven steps:—the investigation of things; the completion of knowledge; the sincerity of the thoughts; the rectifying of the heart; the cultivation of the person; the regulation of the family; and the government of the State. These form the steps of a

climax, the end of which is the empire tranquillized. Pauthier calls the paragraphs where they occur instances of the sorites, or abridged syllogism. But they belong to *rhetoric*, and not to *logic*.

6. In offering some observations on these steps, and the writer's treatment of them, it will be well to separate them into those preceding the cultivation of the person, and those following it; and to deal with the latter first.—Let us suppose that the cultivation of the person is all attained, every discordant mental element having been subdued and removed. It is assumed that the regulation of the family will necessarily flow from this. Two short paragraphs are all that are given to the illustration of the point, and they are vague generalities on the subject of men being led astray by their feelings and affections.

The family being regulated, there will result from it the government of the State. First, the virtues taught in the family have their correspondences in the wider sphere. Filial piety will appear as loyalty. Fraternal submission will be seen in respect and obedience to elders and superiors. Kindness is capable of universal application. Second, "From the loving example of one family, a whole State becomes loving, and from its courtesies the whole State becomes courteous." Seven paragraphs suffice to illustrate these statements, and short as they are, the writer goes back to the topic of self-cultivation, returning from the family to the individual.

The State being governed, the whole empire will become peaceful and happy. There is even less of connection, however, in the treatment of this theme, between the premise and the conclusion, than in the two previous chapters. Nothing is said about the relation between the whole empire, and its component States, or any one of them. It is said at once, "What is meant by 'The making the whole empire peaceful and happy depends on the government of the State,' is this:—when the sovereign behaves to his aged, as the aged should be behaved to, the people become filial; when the sovereign behaves to his elders, as elders should be behaved to, the people learn brotherly submission; when the sovereign treats compassionately the young and helpless, the people do the same." This is nothing but a repetition of the preceding chapter, instead of that chapter's being made a step from which to go on to the splendid consummation of the good government of the whole empire.

The words which I have quoted are followed by a very striking enunciation of the golden rule in its negative form, and under the name of *the measuring square*, and all the lessons of the chapter are connected more or less closely with that. The application of this principle by a ruler, whose heart is in the first place in loving sympathy with the people, will guide him in all the exactions which he lays upon them, and in the selection of ministers, in such a way that he will secure the affections of his subjects, and his throne will be established, for "by gaining the people, the kingdom is gained; and, by losing the people, the kingdom is lost." There are in this part of the treatise many valuable sentiments, and counsels for all in authority over others. The objection to it is, that, as the last step of the climax, it does not rise upon all the others with the accumulated force of their conclusions, but introduces us to new principles of action and a new line of argument. Cut off the commencement of the first paragraph which connects it with the preceding chapters, and it would form a brief but admirable treatise by itself on the art of government.

This brief review of the writer's treatment of the concluding steps of his method will satisfy the reader that the execution is not equal to the design; and, moreover, underneath all the reasoning, and more especially apparent in the 8th and 9th chapters of Commentary (according to the ordinary arrangement of the work), there lies the assumption that example is all but omnipotent. We find this principle pervading all the Confucian philosophy. And doubtless it is a truth, most important in education and government, that the influence of example is very great. I believe, and will insist upon it hereafter in these prolegomena, that we have come to overlook this element in our conduct of administration. It will be well if the study of the Chinese Classics should call attention to it. Yet in them the subject is pushed to an extreme, and represented in an extravagant manner. Proceeding from the view of human nature that it is entirely good, and led astray only by influences from without, the sage of China and his followers attribute to personal example and to instruction a power which we do not find that they actually possess.

7. The steps which precede the cultivation of the person are more briefly dealt with than those which we have just considered. "The cultivation of the person results from the rectifying the heart or mind." True, but in The Great Learning very inadequately set forth.

"The rectifying of the mind is realized when the thoughts are made sincere." And the thoughts are sincere when no self-deception is allowed, and we move without effort to what is right and wrong, "as we love what is beautiful, and as we hate a bad smell." How are we to attain to this state? Here the Chinese moralist fails us. According to Choo He's arrangement of the Treatise, there is only one sentence from which we can frame a reply to the above question. "Therefore," it is said, "the superior man must be watchful over himself when he is alone." Following Choo's 6th chapter of Commentary, and forming, we may say, part of it, we have in the old arrangement of The Great Learning all the passages which he has distributed so as to form the previous five chapters. But even from the examination of them, we do not obtain the information which we desire on this momentous inquiry.

8. Indeed, the more I study the Work, the more satisfied I become, that from the conclusion of what is now called the chapter of Classical text to the sixth chapter of Commentary, we have only a few fragments, which it is of no use trying to arrange, so as fairly to exhibit the plan of the author. According to his method, the chapter on the connection between making the thoughts sincere and so rectifying the mental nature, should be preceded by one on the completion of knowledge as the means of making the thoughts sincere, and that again by one on the completion of knowledge by the investigation of things, or whatever else the phrase *kih wuh* may mean. I am less concerned for the loss and injury which this part of the Work has suffered, because the subject of the connection between intelligence and virtue is very fully exhibited in The Doctrine of the Mean, and will come under my notice in the review of that Treatise. The manner in which Choo He has endeavoured to supply the blank about the perfecting of knowledge by the investigation of things is too extravagant. "The Learning for Adults," he says, "at the outset of its lessons, instructs the learner, in regard to all things in the world, to proceed from what know-

ledge he has of their principles, and pursue his investigation of them, till he reaches the extreme point. After exerting himself for a long time, he will suddenly find himself possessed of a wide and far-reaching penetration. Then, the qualities of all things, whether external or internal, the subtle or the coarse, will be apprehended, and the mind, in its entire substance and its relation to things, will be perfectly intelligent. This is called the investigation of things. This is called the perfection of knowledge." And knowledge must be thus perfected before we can achieve the sincerity of our thoughts and the rectifying of our hearts! Verily this would be learning not for adults only, but even Methuselah would not be able to compass it. Yet for centuries this has been accepted as the orthodox exposition of the Classic. Lo Chung-fan does not express himself too strongly when he says that such language is altogether incoherent. The author would only be "imposing on himself and others."

9. The orthodox doctrine of China concerning the connection between intelligence and virtue is most seriously erroneous, but I will not lay to the charge of the author of The Great Learning the wild representations of the commentator of the twelfth century, nor need I make here any remarks on what the doctrine really is. After the exhibition which I have given, my readers will probably conclude that the Work before us is far from developing, as l'authier asserts, "a system of social perfectionating which has never been equalled."

10. The Treatise has undoubtedly great merits, but they are not to be sought in the severity of its logical processes, or the large-minded prosecution of any course of thought. We shall find them in the announcement of certain seminal principles, which, if recognized in government and the regulation of conduct, would conduce greatly to the happiness and virtue of mankind. I will conclude these observations by specifying four such principles.

First, The writer conceives nobly of the object of government, that it is to make its subjects happy and good. This may not be a sufficient account of that object, but it is much to have it so clearly laid down to "all kings and governors," that they are to love the people, ruling not for their own gratification, but for the good of those over whom they are exalted by Heaven. Very important also is the statement that rulers have no divine right but what springs from the discharge of their duty. "The decree does not always rest on them. Goodness obtains it, and the want of goodness loses it."

Second, The insisting on personal excellence in all who have authority in the family, the State, and the empire, is a great moral and social principle. The influence of such personal excellence may be overstated, but by the requirement of its cultivation the writer deserved well of his country.

Third, Still more important than the requirement of such excellence is the principle that it must be rooted in the state of the heart, and be the natural outgrowth of internal sincerity. "As a man thinketh in his heart, so is he." This is the teaching alike of Solomon and the author of The Great Learning.

Fourth, I mention last the striking exhibition which we have of the golden rule, though only in its negative form. "What a man dislikes in his superiors, let him not display in the treatment of his inferiors; what he dislikes in inferiors, let him not display in his service of his superiors; what he dislikes in those who are before him, let him not therewith precede those who are behind him; what he dislikes in those who are behind him, let him not therewith follow those who are before him; what he dislikes to receive on the right, let him not bestow on the left; what he dislikes to receive on the left, let him not bestow on the right:—this is what is called the principle with which, as with a measuring square, to regulate one's conduct."

The Work which contains these principles cannot be thought meanly of. They are "commonplace," as the writer in the Chinese repository calls them, but they are at the same time eternal verities.

CHAPTER IV.

THE DOCTRINE OF THE MEAN.

SECTION I.

ITS PLACE IN THE LE KE, AND ITS PUBLICATION SEPARATELY.

1. THE Doctrine of the Mean was one of the treatises which came to light in connection with the labours of Lew Heang, and its place as the 31st Book in the Le Ke was finally determined by Ma Yung and Ch'ing Heuen.

2. But while it was thus made to form a part of the great collection of Works on Ceremonies, it maintained a separate footing of its own. In Lew Hin's catalogue of the Classical Works, we find "Two p'een of Observations on the Chung Yung." In the Records of the dynasty of Suy (A.D. 589—617), in the chapter on the History of Literature, there are mentioned three Works on the Chung Yung;"—the first called "The Record of the Chung Yung," in two *kwen*, attributed to Tae Yung, a scholar who flourished about the middle of the 5th century; the second, "A Paraphrase and Commentary on the Chung Yung," attributed to the Emperor Woo (A.D. 502—549) of the Leang dynasty, in one *kwen*; and the third, "A Private Record, determining the Meaning of the Chung Yung," in five *kwen*, the author, or supposed author, of which is not mentioned.

It thus appears, that the Chung Yung had been published and commented on separately long before the time of the Sung dynasty. The scholars of that, however, devoted special attention to it, the way being led by the famous Chow Leen-k'e. He was followed by the two brothers Ch'ing, but neither of them published upon it. At last came Choo He, who produced his Work called "The Chung Yung, in Chapters and Sentences," which was made the text book of the Classic at the literary examinations, by the fourth emperor of the Yuen dynasty (A.D. 1312—1320), and from that time the name merely of the Treatise was retained in editions of the Le Ke. Neither text nor ancient commentary was given.

Under the present dynasty it is not so. In the superb edition of "The Five King," edited by a numerous committee of scholars towards the end of the reign K'ang-ho, the Chung Yung is published in two parts, the ancient commentaries from "The Thirteen King" being given side by side with those of Choo He.

SECTION II.

ITS AUTHOR; AND SOME ACCOUNT OF HIM.

1. THE composition of the Chung Yung is attributed to K'ung Keih, the grandson of Confucius. Chinese inquirers and critics are agreed on this point, and apparently on sufficient grounds. There is indeed no internal evidence in the Work to lead us to such a conclusion. Among the many quotations of Confucius' words and references to him, we might have expected to find some indication that the sage was the grandfather of the author, but nothing of the kind is given. The external evidence, however, or that from the testimony of authorities, is very strong. In Sze-ma Ts'een's Historical Records, published about the beginning of the first century B.C., it is expressly said that "Tsze-sze made the Chung Yung." And we have a still stronger proof, a century earlier, from Tsze-sze's own descendant, K'ung Foo, whose words are, "Tsze-sze compiled the Chung Yung in 40 p'ëen."[1] We may, therefore, accept the received account without hesitation.

2. As Keih, spoken of chiefly by his designation of Tsze-sze, thus occupies a distinguished place in the classical literature of China, it may not be out of place to bring to-

---

[1] This K'ung Foo was that descendant of Confucius, who hid several books in the wall of his house, on the issuing of the Imperial edict for their burning. He was a writer himself, and his Works are referred to under the title of K'ung Ts'ung-tsze.

gather here a few notices of him gathered from reliable sources.

He was the son of Lĭ, whose death took place B.C. 482, four years before that of the sage, his father. I have not found it recorded in what year he was born. Sze-ma Ts'een says he died at the age of 62. But this is evidently wrong, for we learn from Mencius that he was high in favour with the Duke Muh of Loo,[1] whose accession to that principality dates in B.C. 408, seventy years after the death of Confucius. In the "Plates and Notices of the Worthies, sacrificed to in the Sage's Temples," it is supposed that the 62 in the Historical Records should be 82.[2] It is maintained by others that Tsze-sze's life was protracted beyond 100 years. This variety of opinions simply shows that the point cannot be positively determined. To me it seems that the conjecture in the Sacrificial Canon must be pretty near the truth.[3]

During the years of his boyhood, then, Tsze-sze must have been with his grandfather, and received his instructions. It is related, that one day, when he was alone with the sage, and heard him sighing, he went up to him, and, bowing twice, inquired the reason of his grief. "Is it," said he, "because you think that your descendants, through not cultivating themselves, will be unworthy of you? Or is it that, in your admiration of the ways of Yaou and Shun, you are vexed that you fall short of them?" "Child," replied Confucius, "how is it that you know my thoughts?" "I have often," said Tsze-sze, "heard from you the lesson, that when the father has gathered and prepared the firewood, if the son cannot carry the bundle, he is to be pronounced degenerate and unworthy. The remark comes frequently into my thoughts, and fills me with great apprehension." The sage was de-

---

[1] Mencius, V. Pt. II. vi. 4.

[2] 82 and 62 may more easily be confounded as written in Chinese than with the Roman figures.

[3] Lĭ himself was born in Confucius' 21st year, and if Tsze-sze had been born in Lĭ's 21st year, he must have been 103 at the time of Duke Muh's accession. But the tradition is that Tsze-sze was a pupil of Tsăng Sin, who was born B.C. 604. We must place his birth therefore considerably later, and suppose him to have been quite young when his father died. I was talking once about the question with a Chinese friend, who observed:—"Lĭ was 50 when he died, and his wife married again into a family of Wei. We can hardly think, therefore, that she was anything like that age. Lĭ could not have married so soon as his father did. Perhaps he was about 40 when Keih was born."

lighted. He smiled and said, "Now, indeed, shall I be without anxiety! My undertakings will not come to nought. They will be carried on and flourish."[1]

After the death of Confucius, Keih became a pupil, it is said, of the philosopher Tsăng. But he received his instructions with discrimination, and in one instance which is recorded in the Le Ke, the pupil suddenly took the place of the master. We there read:—"Tsăng said to 'Tsze-sze, 'Keih, when I was engaged in mourning for my parents, neither congee nor water entered my mouth for seven days.' Tsze-sze answered, 'In ordering their rules of propriety, it was the design of the ancient kings that those who would go beyond them should stoop and keep by them, and that those who could hardly reach them should stand on tiptoe to do so. Thus it is that the superior man, in mourning for his parents, when he has been three days without water or congee, takes a staff to enable himself to rise.'"[2]

While he thus condemned the severe discipline of Tsăng, Tsze-sze appears in various incidents which are related of him, to have been himself more than sufficiently ascetic. As he was living in great poverty, a friend supplied him with grain, which he readily received. Another friend was emboldened by this to send him a bottle of wine, but he declined to receive it. "You receive your corn from other people," urged the donor, "and why should you decline my gift, which is of less value? You can assign no ground in reason for it; and if you wish to show your independence, you should do so completely." "I am so poor," was the reply, "as to be in want; and being afraid lest I should die, and the sacrifices not be offered to my ancestors, I accept the grain as an alms. But the wine and the dried flesh which you offer to me are the appliances of a feast. For a poor man to be feasting is certainly unreasonable. This is the ground of my refusing your gift. I have no thought of asserting my independence."

To the same effect is the account of Tsze-sze, which we have from Lew Heang. That scholar relates:—"When Keih was living in Wei, he wore a tattered coat, without any lining, and in 30 days had only nine meals. T'ëen Tsze-fang

[1] For this incident we are indebted to K'ung Foo; see note 1, p. 36.
[2] Le Ke, II. Pt. I. II. 7.

having heard of his distress, sent a messenger to him with a coat of fox-fur, and being afraid that he might not receive it, he added the message,—'When I borrow from a man, I forget it; when I give a thing, I part with it freely as if I threw it away.' Tsze-sze declined the gift thus offered, and when Tsze-fang said, 'I have, and you have not; why will you not take it?' he replied, 'You give away so rashly, as if you were casting your things into a ditch. Poor as I am, I cannot think of my body as a ditch, and do not presume to accept your gift.'"

Tsze-sze's mother married again, after Le's death, into a family of Wei. But this circumstance, which is not at all creditable in Chinese estimation, did not alienate his affections from her. He was in Loo when he heard of her death, and proceeded to weep in the temple of his family. A disciple came to him and said, "Your mother married again into the family of the Shoo, and do you weep for her in the temple of the K'ung?" "I am wrong," said Tsze-sze, "I am wrong;" and with these words he went to weep elsewhere.[1]

In his own married relation he does not seem to have been happy; and for some cause, which has not been transmitted to us, he divorced his wife, following in this, it would appear, the example of Confucius. On her death her son, Tsze-shang,[2] did not undertake any mourning for her. Tsze-sze's disciples were surprised and questioned him. "Did not your father," they asked, "mourn for his mother who had been divorced?" "Yes," was the reply. "Then why do you not cause Pih[3] to mourn for his mother?" Tsze-sze answered, "My father failed in nothing to pursue the proper path. His observances increased or decreased as the case required. But I cannot attain to this. While she was my wife, she was Pih's mother; when she ceased to be my wife, she ceased to be Pih's mother." The custom of the K'ung family not to mourn for a mother who had left it herself, or been divorced, took its rise from Tsze-sze.[4]

These few notices of K'ung Keih in his more private relations bring him before us as a man of strong feeling and strong will, independent, and with a tendency to asceticism in his habits.

[1] See the Le Ke, II. Pt. II. iii. 15. [2] This was the designation of Tsze-sze's son.
[3] This was Tsze-shang's name. [4] See the Le Ke, II. Pt. I. i. 4.

As a public character, we find him at the ducal courts of Wei, Sung, Loo, and Po, and at each of them held in high esteem by the rulers. To Wei he was carried probably by the fact of his mother having married into that State. We are told that the prince of Wei received him with great distinction and lodged him honourably. On one occasion he said to him, "An officer of the State of Loo, you have not despised this small and narrow Wei, but have bent your steps hither to comfort and preserve it;—vouchsafe to confer your benefits upon me." Tsze-sze replied, "If I should wish to requite your princely favour with money and silks, your treasuries are already full of them, and I am poor. If I should wish to requite it with good words, I am afraid that what I should say would not suit your ideas, so that I should speak in vain, and not be listened to. The only way in which I can requite it, is by recommending to your notice men of worth." The duke said, "Men of worth is exactly what I desire." "Nay," said Keih, "you are not able to appreciate them." "Nevertheless," was the reply, "I should like to hear whom you consider deserving that name." Tsze-sze replied, "Do you wish to select your officers for the name they may have, or for their reality?" "For their reality, certainly," said the duke. His guest then said, "In the eastern borders of your State, there is one Le Yin, who is a man of real worth." "What were his grandfather and father?" asked the duke. "They were husbandmen," was the reply, on which the duke broke into a loud laugh, saying, "I do not like husbandry. The son of a husbandman cannot be fit for me to employ. I do not put into office all the cadets of those families even in which office is hereditary." Tsze-sze observed, "I mention Le Yin because of his abilities; what has the fact of his forefathers being husbandmen to do with the case? And, moreover, the duke of Chow was a great sage, and K'ang-shuh was a great worthy. Yet if you examine their beginnings, you will find that from the business of husbandry they came forth to found their States. I did certainly have my doubts that in the selection of your officers you did not have regard to their real character and capacity." With this the conversation ended. The duke was silent.[1]

---

[1] See the Biographical Dictionary; Art. K'ung Keih.

Tsze-sze was naturally led to Sung, as the K'ung family originally sprang from that principality. One account, quoted in "The Four Books, Text and Commentary, with Proofs and Illustrations," says that he went thither in his 16th year, and having foiled an officer of the State, named Yŏ Sŏ, in a conversation on the Shoo-king, his opponent was so irritated at the disgrace put on him by a youth, that he listened to the advice of evil counsellors, and made an attack on him to put him to death. The duke of Sung, hearing the tumult, hurried to the rescue, and when Keih found himself in safety, he said, "When King Wǎn was imprisoned in Yew-le, he made the Yih of Chow. My grandfather made the Ch'un Ts'ew after he had been in danger in Ch'in and Ts'ae. Shall I not make something when rescued from such a risk in Sung?" Upon this he made the Chung Yung in 49 p'een.

According to this account, the Chung Yung was the work of Tsze-sze's early manhood, and the tradition has obtained a wonderful prevalence. The notice in "The Sacrificial Canon" says, on the contrary, that it was the work of his old age, when he had finally settled in Loo; which is much more likely.

Of Tsze-sze in Pe, which could hardly be said to be out of Loo, we have only one short notice,—in Mencius, V. Pt. II. iii. 3, where the Duke Hwuy of Pe is introduced as saying, "I treat Tsze-sze as my master."

We have fuller accounts of him in Loo, where he spent all the latter years of his life, instructing his disciples to the number of several hundred,[1] and held in great reverence by the Duke Muh. The duke indeed wanted to raise him to the highest office, but he declined this, and would only occupy the position of a "guide, philosopher, and friend." Of the attention which he demanded, however, instances will be found in Mencius, II. Pt. II. xi. 3; V. Pt. II. vi. 5, and vii. 3. In his intercourse with the duke he spoke the truth to him fearlessly. In the "Cyclopædia of Surnames," I find the following conversations, but I cannot tell from what source they are extracted into that work—"One day the duke said to Tsze-sze, 'The officer Heen told me that you do good without wishing for any praise from men;—is it so?' Tsze-

---

[1] See the "Sacrificial Canon," on Tsze-sze.

sze replied, 'No, that is not my feeling. When I cultivate what is good, I wish men to know it, for when they know it and praise me, I feel encouraged to be more zealous in the cultivation. This is what I desire, and am not able to obtain. If I cultivate what is good, and men do not know it, it is likely that in their ignorance they will speak evil of me. So by my good-doing I only come to be evil spoken of. This is what I do not desire, but am not able to avoid. In the case of a man, who gets up at cockcrowing to practise what is good, and continues sedulous in the endeavour till midnight, and says at the same time that he does not wish men to know it, lest they should praise him, I must say of such a man, that if he be not deceitful he is stupid.'"

Another day, the duke asked Tsze-sze saying, "Can my State be made to flourish?" "It may," was the reply. "And how?" Tsze-sze said, "O prince, if you and your ministers will only strive to realize the government of the dukes of Chow and of Pih-k'in; practising their transforming principles, sending forth wide the favours of your ducal house, and not letting advantages flow in private channels;—if you will thus conciliate the affections of the people, and at the same time cultivate friendly relations with neighbouring States, your kingdom will soon begin to flourish."

On one occasion, the duke asked whether it had been the custom of old for ministers to go into mourning for a prince whose service and State they had left. Tsze-sze replied to him, "Of old, princes advanced their ministers to office according to propriety, and dismissed them in the same way, and hence there was that rule. But now-a-days princes bring their ministers forward as if they were going to take them on their knees, and send them away as if they would cast them into an abyss. If they do not treat them as their greatest enemies, it is well.—How can you expect the ancient practice to be observed in such circumstances?"¹

These instances may suffice to illustrate the character of Tsze-sze, as it was displayed in his intercourse with the princes of his time. We see the same independence which he affected in private life, and a dignity not unbecoming the grandson of Confucius. But we miss the reach of thought and capacity for administration which belonged to the Sage.

¹ This conversation is given in the Le Ke, II. Pt. II. ii. 1.

It is with him, however, as a thinker and writer that we have to do, and his rank in that capacity will appear from the examination of the Chung Yung in the section that follows. His place in the temples of the Sage has been that of one of his four assessors, since the year 1267. He ranks with Yen Hwuy, Tsăng Sin, and Mencius, and bears the title of "The Philosopher Tsze-sze, Transmitter of the Sage."

SECTION III.

ITS SCOPE AND VALUE.

1. THE Doctrine of the Mean is a work not easy to understand. "It first," says the philosopher Ch'ing, "speaks of one principle; it next spreads this out and embraces all things; finally, it returns and gathers them up under the one principle. Unroll it, and it fills the universe; roll it up, and it retires and lies hid in secrecy." There is this advantage, however, to the student of it, that, more than most other Chinese Treatises, it has a beginning, a middle, and an end. The first chapter stands to all that follows in the character of a text, containing several propositions of which we have the expansion or development. If that development were satisfactory, we should be able to bring our own minds *en rapport* with that of the author. Unfortunately it is not so. As a writer he belongs to the intuitional school more than to the logical. This is well put in the "Continuation of the General Examination of Literary Monuments and Learned Men:"—"The philosopher Tsăng reached his conclusions by following in the train of things, watching and examining; whereas Tsze-sze proceeds directly and reaches to heavenly virtue. His was a mysterious power of discernment, approaching to that of Yen Hwuy." We must take the Book and the author, however, as we have them, and get to their meaning, if we can, by assiduous examination and reflection.

2. "Man has received his *nature* from *Heaven*. Conduct in accordance with that nature constitutes what is right and true,—is a pursuing of the proper *path*. The cultivation or

regulation of that path is what is called *instruction.*" It is with these axioms that the Treatise commences, and from such an introduction we might expect that the writer would go on to unfold the various principles of duty, derived from an analysis of man's moral constitution.

Confining himself, however, to the second axiom, he proceeds to say that "the path may not for an instant be left, and that the superior man is cautious and careful in reference to what he does not see, and fearful and apprehensive in reference to what he does not hear. There is nothing more visible than what is secret, and nothing more manifest than what is minute, and therefore the superior man is watchful over his *aloneness.*" This is not all very plain. Comparing it with the 6th chapter of Commentary in The Great Learning, it seems to inculcate what is there called "making the thoughts sincere." The passage contains an admonition about equivalent to that of Solomon,—"Keep thy heart with all diligence, for out of it are the issues of life."

The next paragraph seems to speak of *the nature* and *the path* under other names. "While there are no movements of pleasure, anger, sorrow, or joy, we have what may be called the state of *equilibrium.* When these feelings have been moved, and they all act in the due degree, we have what may be called the state of *harmony.* This equilibrium is the great root of the world, and this harmony is its universal path." What is here called "the state of equilibrium" is the same as the nature given by Heaven, considered absolutely in itself, without deflection or inclination. This nature acted on from without, and responding with the various emotions, so as always "to hit" the mark with entire correctness, produces the state of harmony, and such harmonious response is the path along which all human activities should proceed.

Finally, "Let the states of equilibrium and harmony exist in perfection, and a happy order will prevail throughout heaven and earth, and all things will be nourished and flourish." Here we pass into the sphere of mystery and mysticism. The language, according to Choo He, "describes the meritorious achievements and transforming influence of sage and spiritual men in their highest extent." From the path of duty, where we tread on solid ground, the writer suddenly raises us aloft on wings of air, and will carry us we know not where, and to we know not what.

3. The paragraphs thus presented, and which constitute Choo He's first chapter, contain the sum of the whole Work. This is acknowledged by all;—by the critics who disown Choo He's interpretations of it, as freely as by him. Revolving them in my own mind often and long, I collect from them the following as the ideas of the author:—1st, Man has received from Heaven a moral nature by which he is constituted a law to himself; 2nd, Over this nature man requires to exercise a jealous watchfulness; and 3rd, As he possesses it, absolutely and relatively, in perfection, or attains to such possession of it, he becomes invested with the highest dignity and power, and may say to himself—" I am a God; yea, I sit in the seat of God." I will not say here that there is blasphemy in the last of those ideas; but do we not have in them the same combination which we found in The Great Learning,—a combination of the ordinary and the extraordinary, the plain and the vague, which is very perplexing to the mind, and renders the Book unfit for the purposes of mental and moral discipline?

And here I may inquire whether we do right in calling the Treatise by any of the names which foreigners have hitherto used for it? In the note on the title, I have entered a little into this question. The Work is not at all what a reader must expect to find in what he supposes to be a treatise on "The Golden Medium," "The Invariable Mean," or "The Doctrine of the Mean." Those names are descriptive only of a portion of it. Where the phrase *Chung Yung* occurs in the quotations from Confucius, in nearly every chapter, from the 2nd to the 11th, we do well to translate it by "the course of the Mean," or some similar terms; but the conception of it in Tsze-sze's mind was of a different kind, as the preceding analysis of the first chapter sufficiently shows.

4. I may return to this point of the proper title for the Work again, but in the mean time we must proceed with the analysis of it.—The ten chapters from the 2nd to the 11th constitute the second part, and in them Tsze-sze quotes the words of Confucius, "for the purpose," according to Choo He, "of illustrating the meaning of the first chapter." Yet, as I have just intimated, they do not to my mind do

this. Confucius bewails the rarity of the practice of the Mean, and graphically sets forth the difficulty of it. "The empire, with its component States and families, may be ruled; dignities and emoluments may be declined, naked weapons may be trampled under foot; but the course of the Mean cannot be attained to."[1] "The knowing go beyond it, and the stupid do not come up to it."[2] Yet some have attained to it. Shun did so, humble and ever learning from people far inferior to himself;[3] and Yen Hwuy did so, holding fast whatever good he got hold of, and never letting it go.[4] Tszeloo thought the Mean could be taken by storm, but Confucius taught him better.[5] And in fine, it is only the sage who can fully exemplify the Mean.[6]

All these citations do not throw any light on the ideas presented in the first chapter. On the contrary, they interrupt the train of thought. Instead of showing us how virtue, or the path of duty, is in accordance with our Heaven-given nature, they lead us to think of it as a mean between two extremes. Each extreme may be a violation of the law of our nature, but that is not made to appear. Confucius' sayings would be in place in illustrating the doctrine of the Peripatetics, "which placed all virtue in a medium between opposite vices." Here in the Chung Yung of Tszesze, I have always felt them to be out of place.

5. In the 12th chapter Tsze-sze speaks again himself, and we seem at once to know the voice. He begins by saying that "the way of the superior man reaches far and wide, and yet is secret," by which he means to tell us that the path of duty is to be pursued everywhere and at all times, while yet the secret spring and rule of it is near at hand, in the Heaven-conferred nature, the individual consciousness, with which no stranger can intermeddle. Choo Ho, as will be seen in the notes, gives a different interpretation of the utterance. But the view which I have adopted is maintained convincingly by Maou Se-ho in the second part of his "Observations on the Chung Yung." With this chapter commences the third part of the Work, which embraces also the eight chapters which follow. "It is designed," says Choo He, "to illustrate what is said in the first chapter that the path may not be left." But more than that one sen-

[1] Ch. ix. [2] Ch. iv. [3] Ch. iv. [4] Ch. viii. [5] Ch. x. [6] Ch. xi.

tance finds its illustration here. Tsze-sze had reference in it also to what he had said—" The superior man does not wait till he sees things to be cautious, nor till he hears things to be apprehensive. There is nothing more visible than what is secret, and nothing more manifest than what is minute. Therefore, the superior man is watchful over himself when he is alone."

It is in this portion of the Chung Yung that we find a good deal of moral instruction which is really valuable. Most of it consists of sayings of Confucius, but the sentiments of Tsze-sze himself in his own language are interspersed with them. The sage of China has no higher utterances than those which are given in the 13th chapter:— " The path is not far from man. When men try to pursue a course which is far from the common indications of consciousness, this course cannot be considered *the path*. In the Book of Poetry it is said—

'In hewing an axe-handle, in hewing an axe-handle,
The pattern is not far off.'

We grasp one axe-handle to hew the other, and yet if we look askance from the one to the other, we may consider them as apart. Therefore, the superior man governs men according to their nature, with what is proper to them; and as soon as they change what is wrong, he stops. When one cultivates to the utmost the moral principles of his nature, and exercises them on the principle of reciprocity, he is not far from the path. What you do not like when done to yourself, do not do to others.

" In the way of the superior man there are four things, to none of which have I as yet attained:—To serve my father as I would require my son to serve me: to this I have not attained; to serve my older brother as I would require my younger brother to serve me: to this I have not attained; to serve my prince as I would require my minister to serve me: to this I have not attained; to set the example in behaving to a friend as I would require him to behave to me: to this I have not attained. Earnest in practising the ordinary virtues, and careful in speaking about them; if in his practice he has anything defective, the superior man dares not but exert himself, and if in his words he has any excess, he dares not allow himself such license. Thus his words have respect to his actions, and his actions have respect to his words;—is it not just an entire sincerity which marks the superior man?"

We have here the golden rule in its negative form expressly propounded:—"What you do not like when done to yourself, do not do to others." But in the paragraph which follows we have the rule virtually in its positive form. Confucius recognizes the duty of taking the initiative,—of behaving himself to others in the first instance as he would that they should behave to him. There is a certain narrowness, indeed, in that the sphere of its operations seems to be confined to the relations of society, which are spoken of more at large in the 20th chapter; but let us not grudge the tribute of our warm approbation to the sentiments.

This chapter is followed by two from Tsze-sze, to the effect that the superior man does what is proper in every change of his situation, always finding his rule in himself; and that in his practice there is an orderly advance from step to step,—from what is near to what is remote. Then follow five chapters from Confucius:—the first, on the operation and influence of spiritual beings, to show "the manifestness of what is minute, and the irrepressibleness of sincerity;" the second, on the filial piety of Shun, and how it was rewarded by Heaven with the empire, with enduring fame, and with long life; the third and fourth, on the kings Wăn and Woo, and the duke of Chow, celebrating them for their filial piety and other associate virtues; and the fifth, on the subject of government. These chapters are interesting enough in themselves, but when I go back from them, and examine whether I have from them any better understanding of the paragraphs in the first chapter which they are said to illustrate, I do not find that I have. Three of them, the 17th, 18th, and 19th, would be more in place in the Classic of Filial Piety than here in the Chung Yung. The meaning of the 16th is shadowy and undefined. After all the study which I have directed to it, there are some points in reference to which I have still doubts and difficulties.

The 20th chapter, which concludes the third portion of the Work, contains a full exposition of Confucius' views on government, though professedly descriptive only of that of the kings Wăn and Woo. Along with lessons proper for a ruler there are many also of universal application, but the mingling of them perplexes the mind. It tells us of "the five duties of universal application,"—those between sovereign and minister, husband and wife, father and son, elder and younger brother, and friends; of "the three virtues by which those duties are carried into effect," namely, knowledge, benevolence, and energy; and of "the one thing, by which those virtues are practised," which is singleness or sincerity. It sets forth in detail the "nine standard rules for the administration of government," which are "the cultivation by the ruler of his own character; the honouring men of virtue and talents; affection to his relatives; respect towards the great ministers; kind and considerate treatment of the whole body of officers; cherishing the mass of the people as children; encouraging all classes of artizans; indulgent treatment of men from a distance; and the kindly cherishing of the princes of the States." There are these and other equally interesting topics in this chapter; but, as they are in the Work, they distract the mind, instead of making the author's great object more clear to it, and I will not say more upon them here.

6. Doubtless it was the mention of "singleness," or "sincerity," in the 20th chapter, which made Tsze-szu introduce it into this Treatise, for from those terms he is able to go on to develope what he intended in saying, that "if the states of Equilibrium and Harmony exist in perfection, a happy order will prevail throughout heaven and earth, and all things will be nourished and flourish." It is here, that now we are astonished at the audacity of the writer's assertions, and now lost in vain endeavours to ascertain his meaning. I have quoted the words of Confucius that it is "singleness," by which the three virtues of knowledge, benevolence, and energy are able to carry into practice the duties of universal obligation. He says also that it is this same "singleness" by which "the nine standard rules of government" can be effectively carried out. This "singleness" is just a name for "the states of Equilibrium and Harmony existing in perfection." It denotes a character absolutely and relatively good, wanting nothing in itself, and correct in all its outgoings. "Sincerity" is another term for the same thing, and in speaking about it, Confucius makes a distinction between sincerity absolute and sincerity

acquired. The former is born with some, and practised by them without any effort; the latter is attained by study and practised by strong endeavour. The former is "the way of Heaven;" the latter is "the way of men." "He who possesses sincerity,"—absolutely, that is,—"is he who without effort hits what is right, and apprehends without the exercise of thought;—he is the sage who naturally and easily embodies the right way. He who attains to sincerity is he who chooses what is good, and firmly holds it fast. And to this attainment there are requisite the extensive study of what is good, accurate inquiry about it, careful reflection on it, the clear discrimination of it, and the earnest practice of it." In these passages Confucius unhesitatingly enunciates his belief that there are some men who are absolutely perfect, who come into the world as we may conceive the first man was, when he was created by God "in His own image," full of knowledge and righteousness, and who grow up as we know that Christ did, "increasing in wisdom and in stature." He disclaimed being considered to be such an one himself,[1] but the sages of China were such. And, moreover, others who are not so naturally may make themselves to become so. Some will have to put forth more effort and to contend with greater struggles, but the end will be the possession of the knowledge and the achievement of the practice.

I need not say that these sentiments are contrary to the views of human nature which are presented in the Bible. The testimony of Revelation is that "there is not a just man upon earth that doeth good and sinneth not." "If we say that we have no sin," and in writing this term, I am thinking here not of sin against God, but, if we can conceive of it apart from that, of failures in regard to what ought to be in our regulation of ourselves, and in our behaviour to others;—"if we say that we have no sin we deceive ourselves, and the truth is not in us." This language is appropriate in the lips of the learned as well as in those of the ignorant, to the highest sage as to the lowest child of the soil. Neither the Scriptures of God nor the experience of man know of individuals absolutely perfect. The other sentiment that men can make themselves perfect is equally wide of the truth. Intelligence and goodness by no means

[1] Ana. VII. xix.

stand to each other in the relation of cause and effect. The sayings of Ovid, "*Video meliora proboque, deteriora sequor,*" "*Nitimur in vetitum semper, cupimusque negata,*" are a more correct expression of the facts of human consciousness and conduct than the high-flown phrases of Confucius.

7. But Tsze-sze adopts the dicta of his grandfather without questioning them, and gives them forth in his own style at the commencement of the fourth part of his Treatise. "When we have intelligence resulting from sincerity, this condition is to be ascribed to nature; when we have sincerity resulting from intelligence, this condition is to be ascribed to instruction. But given the sincerity, and there shall be the intelligence; given the intelligence, and there shall be the sincerity."

Tsze-sze does more than adopt the dicta of Confucius. He applies them in a way which the sage never did, and which he would probably have shrunk from doing. The sincere, or perfect man of Confucius is he who satisfies completely all the requirements of duty in the various relations of society, and in the exercise of government; but the sincere man of Tsze-sze is a potency in the universe. "Able to give its full development to his own nature, he can do the same to the nature of other men. Able to give its full development to the nature of other men, he can give their full development to the natures of animals and things. Able to give their full development to the natures of creatures and things, he can assist the transforming and nourishing powers of Heaven and Earth. Able to assist the transforming and nourishing powers of Heaven and Earth, he may with Heaven and Earth form a ternion." Such are the results of sincerity natural. The case below this—of sincerity acquired, is as follows,—"The individual cultivates its shoots. From these he can attain to the possession of sincerity. This sincerity becomes apparent. From being apparent, it becomes manifest. From being manifest, it becomes brilliant. Brilliant, it affects others. Affecting others, they are changed by it. Changed by it, they are transformed. It is only he who is possessed of the most complete sincerity that can exist under heaven, who can transform." It may safely be affirmed, that when he thus expressed himself, Tsze-sze understood neither what he said nor whereof he affirmed. Maou Se-ho and some other modern writers explain away many of his predicates of sincerity, so that in their hands they become nothing but extravagant hyperboles, but the author himself would, I believe, have protested against such a mode of dealing with his words. True, his structures are castles in the air, but he had no idea himself that they were so.

In the 24th chapter there is a ridiculous descent from the sublimity of the two preceding. We are told that the possessor of entire sincerity is like a spirit, and can foreknow, but the foreknowledge is only a judging by the milfoil and tortoise and other auguries! But the author recovers himself, and resumes his theme about sincerity as conducting to self-completion, and the completion of other men and things, describing it also as possessing all the qualities which can be predicated of Heaven and Earth. Gradually the subject is made to converge to the person of Confucius, who is the ideal of the sage, as the sage is the ideal of humanity at large. An old account of the object of Tsze-sze in the Chung Yung is that "he wrote it to celebrate the virtue of his grandfather." He certainly contrives to do this in the course of it. The 30th, 31st, and 32nd chapters contain his eulogium, and never has any other mortal been exalted in such terms. "He may be compared to Heaven and Earth in their supporting and containing, their overshadowing and curtaining all things; he may be compared to the four seasons in their alternating progress, and to the sun and moon in their successive shining." "Quick in apprehension, clear in discernment, of far-reaching intelligence, and all-embracing knowledge,' he was fitted to exercise rule; magnanimous, generous, benign, and mild, he was fitted to exercise forbearance; impulsive, energetic, firm, and enduring, he was fitted to maintain a firm hold; self-adjusted, grave, never swerving from the Mean, and correct, he was fitted to command reverence; accomplished, distinctive, concentrative, and searching, he was fitted to exercise discrimination." "All-embracing and vast, he was like heaven; deep and active as a fountain, he was like the abyss." "Therefore his fame overspreads the Middle Kingdom, and extends to all barbarous tribes. Wherever ships and carriages reach; wherever the strength of man penetrates; wherever the heavens overshadow and the earth sustains; wherever the sun and moon shine; wherever frosts and dews fall; all who have blood and breath unfeignedly honour and love him. Hence it is said,—He is the equal of Heaven!" "Who can know him but he who is indeed quick in apprehension, clear in discernment, of far-reaching intelligence, and all-embracing knowledge, possessing all heavenly virtue?"

8. We have arrived at the concluding chapter of the Work, in which the author, according to Choo He, "having carried his descriptions to the highest point in the preceding chapters, turns back and examines the source of his subject; and then again from the work of the learner, free from all selfishness and watchful over himself when he is alone, he carries out his description, till by easy steps he brings it to the consummation of the whole empire tranquillized by simple and sincere reverentialness. He moreover eulogizes its mysteriousness, till he speaks of it at last as without sound or smell." Between the first and last chapters there is a correspondency, and each of them may be considered as a summary of the whole treatise. The difference between them is, that in the first a commencement is made with the mention of Heaven as the conferrer of man's nature, while in this the progress of man in virtue is traced, step by step, till at last it is equal to that of High Heaven.

9. I have thus in the preceding paragraphs given a general and somewhat copious review of this Work. My object has been to seize, if I could, the train of thought, and to hold it up to the reader. Minor objections to it, arising from the confused use of terms and singular applications of passages from the older Classics, are noticed in the notes subjoined to the translation. I wished here that its scope should be seen, and the means be afforded of judging how far it is worthy of the high character attributed to it. "The relish of it," says the younger Ch'ing, "is inexhaustible. The whole of it is solid learning. When the skilful reader has explored it with delight till he has apprehended it, he may carry it into practice all his life, and will find that it cannot be exhausted."

My own opinion of it is much less favourable. The names by which it has been called in translations of it have led to misconceptions of its character. Were it styled "The states of Equilibrium and Harmony," we should be prepared to expect something strange and probably extravagant. Assuredly we should expect nothing more strange or extravagant than what we have. It begins sufficiently well, but the author has hardly enunciated his preliminary apophthegms, when he conducts into an obscurity where we can hardly grope our way, and when we emerge from that, it is to be bewildered by his gorgeous but unsubstantial pictures of sagely perfection. He has eminently contributed to nourish the pride of his countrymen. He has exalted their sages above all that is called God or is worshipped, and taught the masses of the people that with them they have need of nothing from without. In the mean time it is antagonistic to Christianity. By and by, when Christianity has prevailed in China, men will refer to it as a striking proof how their fathers by their wisdom knew neither God nor themselves.

CHAPTER V.

CONFUCIUS; HIS INFLUENCE AND DOCTRINES.

SECTION I.

LIFE OF CONFUCIUS.

1. "And have you foreigners surnames as well?" This question has often been put to me by Chinese. It marks the ignorance which belongs to the people of all that is external to themselves, and the pride of antiquity which enters largely as an element into their character. If such a pride could in any case be justified, we might allow it to the family of the K'ung, the descendants of Confucius. In the reign K'ang-ho, twenty-one centuries and a half after the death of the sage, they amounted to eleven thousand males. But their ancestry is carried back through a period of equal extent, and genealogical tables are common, in which the descent of Confucius is traced down from Hwang-te, the inventor of the cycle, B.C. 2637.[1]

His ancestry.

The more moderate writers, however, content themselves with exhibiting his ancestry back to the commencement of the Chow dynasty, B.C. 1121. Among the relatives of the tyrant Chow, the last emperor of the Yin dynasty, was an elder brother, by a concubine, named K'e, who is celebrated by Confucius, Ana. XVIII. i., under the title of the viscount of Wei. Foreseeing the impending ruin of their family, K'e withdrew from the court; and subsequently, he was invested by the Emperor Ch'ing, the second of the house of

---

[1] See Mémoires concernant les Chinois, Tome XII. p. 447, et seq. Father Amiot states, p. 501, that he had seen the representative of the family, who succeeded to the dignity of the "Duke Continuator of the Sage's line," in the 9th year of K'ëen-lung, A.D. 1744. It is hardly necessary that I should say here, that the name Confucius is merely the Chinese characters, K'ung Foo-tsze, "The master, K'ung," latinised.

Chow, with the principality of Sung, which embraced the eastern portion of the present province of Ho-nan, that he might there continue the sacrifices to the emperors of Yin. K'e was followed as duke of Sung by a younger brother, in whose line the succession continued. His great-grandson, the Duke Min, was followed, B.C. 908, by a younger brother, leaving, however, two sons, Fuh-foo Ho, and Fang-sze. Fuh Ho resigned his right to the dukedom in favour of Fang-sze, who put his uncle to death in B.C. 893, and became master of the State. He is known as the Duke Le, and to his elder brother belongs the honour of having the sage among his descendants.

Three descents from Fuh Ho, we find Ching K'au-foo, who was a distinguished officer under the dukes Tae, Woo, and Senen (B.C. 799—728). He is still celebrated for his humility, and for his literary tastes. We have accounts of him as being in communication with the Grand-historiographer of the empire, and engaged in researches about its ancient poetry, thus setting an example of one of the works to which Confucius gave himself. K'aou gave birth to K'ung-foo Kea, from whom the surname of K'ung took its rise. Five generations had now elapsed since the dukedom was held in the direct line of his ancestry, and it was according to the rule in such cases that the branch should cease its connection with the ducal stem, and merge among the people under a new surname. K'ung Kea was Master of the Horse in Sung, and an officer of well-known loyalty and probity. Unfortunately for himself, he had a wife of surpassing beauty, of whom the chief minister of the State, by name Hwa Tuh, happened on one occasion to get a glimpse. Determined to possess her, he commenced a series of intrigues, which ended, B.C. 709, in the murder of Kea and the reigning Duke Shang. At the same time, Tuh secured the person of the lady, and hastened to his palace with the prize, but on the way she had strangled herself with her girdle.

An enmity was thus commenced between the two families of K'ung and Hwa which the lapse of time did not obliterate, and the latter being the more powerful of the two, Kea's great-grandson withdrew into the State of Loo to avoid their persecution. There he was appointed commandant of the city of Fang, and is known in history by the name of Fang-shuh. Fang-shuh gave birth to Pih-hea, and from him came Shuh-leang Heih, the father of Confucius. Heih appears in the history of the times as a soldier of great prowess and daring bravery. In the year B.C. 562, when serving at the siege of a place called Peih-yang, a party of the assailants made their way in at a gate which had purposely been left open, and no sooner were they inside than the portcullis was dropped. Heih was just entering, and catching the massive structure with both his hands, he gradually by dint of main strength raised it and held it up, till his friends had made their escape.

Thus much on the ancestry of the sage. Doubtless he could trace his descent in the way which has been indicated up to the imperial house of Yin, nor was there one among his ancestors during the rule of Chow to whom he could not refer with satisfaction. They had been ministers and soldiers of Sung and Loo, all men of worth; and in Ching K'aou, both for his humility and literary researches, Confucius might have special complacency.

2. Confucius was the child of Shuh-leang Heih's old age. The soldier had married in early life, but his wife brought him only daughters,—to the number of nine, and no son. By a concubine he had a son, named Măng-p'e, and also Pih-ne, who proved a cripple, so that, when he was over seventy years, Heih sought a second wife in the Yen family, from which came subsequently Yen Hwuy, the favourite disciple of his son. There were three daughters in the family, the youngest being named Ching-tsae. Their father said to them, "Here is the commandant of Tsow. His father and grandfather were only scholars, but his ancestors before them were descendants of the sage emperors. He is a man ten feet high,[1] and of extraordinary prowess, and I am very desirous of his alliance. Though he is old and austere, you need have no misgivings about him. Which of you three will be his wife?" The two elder daughters were silent, but Ching-tsae said, "Why do you ask us, father? It is for you to determine." "Very well," said her father in reply, "you will do." Ching-tsae, accordingly, became Heih's wife, and in due time gave birth to Confucius,

From his birth to his first public employment. B.C. 551—531.

---

[1] See, on the length of the ancient foot, Ana. VIII. vi., but the point needs a more sifting investigation than it has yet received.

who received the name of K'ew, and was subsequently styled Chung-ne.[1] The event happened on the 21st day of the 10th month of the 21st year of the Duke Seang, of Loo, being the 20th year of the Emperor Ling, B.C. 551.[2] The birth-place was in the district of Tsow, of which Heih was

[1] The legends say that Ching-tsae, fearing lest she should not have a son, in consequence of her husband's age, privately ascended the Ne-k'ew hill to pray for the boon, and that when she had obtained it, she commemorated the fact in the names—K'ew and Chung-ne. But the cripple, Mang-p'e, had previously been styled Pih-ne. There was some reason, previous to Confucius' birth, for using the term *ne* in the family. As might be expected, the birth of the sage is surrounded with many prodigious occurrences. One account is, that the husband and wife prayed together for a son in a dell of mount Ne. As Ching-tsae went up the hill, the leaves of the trees and plants all erected themselves, and bent downwards on her return. That night she dreamt the Black *To* appeared, and said to her, "You shall have a son, a sage, and you must bring him forth in a hollow mulberry tree." One day during her pregnancy, she fell into a dreamy state, and saw five old men in the hall, who called themselves the essences of the five planets, and led an animal which looked like a small cow with one horn, and was covered with scales like a dragon. This creature knelt before Ching-tsae, and cast forth from its mouth a slip of gem, on which was the inscription,—" The son of the essence of water shall succeed to the withering Chow, and be a throneless king." Ching-tsao tied a piece of embroidered ribbon about its horn, and the vision disappeared. When Heih was told of it, he said, " The creature must be the K'e-lin." As her time drew near, Ching-tsae asked her husband if there was any place in the neighbourhood called " The hollow mulberry tree." He told her there was a dry cave in the south hill, which went by that name. Then she said, " I will go and be confined there." Her husband was surprised, but when made acquainted with her former dream, he made the necessary arrangements. On the night when the child was born, two dragons came and kept watch on the left and right of the hill, and two spirit-ladies appeared in the air, pouring out fragrant odours, as if to bathe Ching-tsae; and as soon as the birth took place, a spring of clear warm water bubbled up from the floor of the cave, which dried up again when the child had been washed in it. The child was of an extraordinary appearance; with a mouth like the sea, ox lips, a dragon's back, &c., &c. On the top of his head was a remarkable formation, in consequence of which he was named K'ew, &c. Sze-ma Ts'een seems to make Confucius to have been illegitimate, saying that Heih and Miss Yen cohabited in the wilderness. Keang Yung says that the phrase has reference simply to the disparity of their ages.

[2] Sze-ma Ts'een says that Confucius was born in the 22nd year of Duke Seang, B.C. 550. He is followed by Choo He in the short sketch of Confucius' life prefixed to the Lun Yu, and by " The Annals of the Empire," published with imperial sanction in the reign Kea-k'ing. (To this work I have generally referred for my dates.) The year assigned in the text above rests on the authority of Kuh-lëang and Kung-yang, the two commentators on the Ch'un Ts'ew. With regard to the month, however, the 10th is that assigned by Kuh-lëang, while Kung-yang names the 11th.

the governor. It was somewhere within the limits of the present department of Yen-chow in Shan-tung, but the honour of being the exact spot is claimed for two places in two different districts of the department.

The notices which we have of Confucius' early years are very scanty. When he was in his third year his father died. It is related of him, that as a boy he used to play at the arrangement of sacrificial vessels, and at postures of ceremony. Of his schooling we have no reliable account. There is a legend, indeed, that at seven he went to school to Gan P'ing-chung, but it must be rejected, as P'ing-chung belonged to the State of Ts'e. He tells us himself that at fifteen he bent his mind to learning;[1] but the condition of the family was one of poverty. At a subsequent period, when people were astonished at the variety of his knowledge, he explained it by saying, "When I was young my condition was low, and therefore I acquired my ability in many things; but they were mean matters."[2]

When he was nineteen, he married a lady from the State of Sung, of the K̈een-kwan family; and in the following year his son Le was born. On the occasion of this event, the Duke Ch'aou sent him a present of a couple of carp. It was to signify his sense of his prince's favour, that he called his son Le (*The Carp*), and afterwards gave him the designation of Pih-yu (*Fish Primus*). No mention is made of the birth of any other children, though we know, from Ana. V. i., that he had at least one daughter. The fact of the duke of Loo's sending him a gift on the occasion of Le's birth shows that he was not unknown, but was already commanding public attention and the respect of the great.

It was about this time, probably in the year after his marriage, that Confucius took his first public employment, as keeper of the stores of grain, and in the following year he was put in charge of the public fields and lands. Mencius adduces these employments in illustration of his doctrine that the superior man may at times take office on account of his poverty, but must confine himself in such a case to places of small emolument, and aim at nothing but the discharge of their humble duties. According to him, Confucius

[1] Ana. II. iv. [2] Ana. IX. vi.

as keeper of stores, said, "My calculations must all be right:—that is all I have to care about;" and when in charge of the public fields, he said, "The oxen and sheep must be fat and strong and superior:—that is all I have to care about."[1] It does not appear whether these offices were held by Confucius in the direct employment of the State, or as a dependent of the Ke family in whose jurisdiction he lived. The present of the carp from the duke may incline us to suppose the former.

3. In his twenty-second year, Confucius commenced his labours as a public teacher, and his house became a resort for young and inquiring spirits, who wished to learn the doctrines of antiquity. However small the fee his pupils were able to afford, he never refused his instructions.[2] All that he required, was an ardent desire for improvement, and some degree of capacity. "I do not open up the truth," he said, "to one who is not eager to get knowledge, nor help out any one who is not anxious to explain himself. When I have presented one corner of a subject to any one, and he cannot from it learn the other three, I do not repeat my lesson."[3]

Commencement of his labours as a teacher. The death of his mother. B.C. 530—528.

His mother died in the year B.C. 528, and he resolved that her body should lie in the same grave with that of his father, and that their common resting-place should be in Fang, the first home of the K'ung in Loo. But here a difficulty presented itself. His father's coffin had been for twenty years, where it had first been deposited, off the road of *The Five Fathers*, in the vicinity of Tsow:—would it be right in him to move it? He was relieved from this perplexity by an old woman of the neighbourhood, who told him that the coffin had only just been put into the ground, as a temporary arrangement, and not regularly buried. On learning this, he carried his purpose into execution. Both coffins were conveyed to Fang, and put in the ground together, with no intervening space between them, as was the custom in some States. And now came a new perplexity. He said to himself, "In old times, they had graves, but raised no tumulus over them. But I am a man, who belongs equally to the north and the south, the east and the west. I must have

---

[1] Mencius, V. Pt. II. v. 4.   [2] Ana. VII. vii.   [3] Ana. VII. viii.

something by which I can remember the place." Accordingly he raised a mound, four feet high, over the grave, and returned home, leaving a party of his disciples to see everything properly completed. In the mean time there came on a heavy storm of rain, and it was a considerable time before the disciples joined him. "What makes you so late?" he asked. "The grave in Fang fell down," they said. He made no reply, and they repeated their answer three times, when he burst into tears, and said, "Ah! they did not make their graves so in antiquity."[1]

Confucius mourned for his mother the regular period of three years,—three years nominally, but in fact only twenty-seven months. Five days after the mourning was expired, he played on his lute but could not sing. It required other five days before he could accompany an instrument with his voice.[2]

Some writers have represented Confucius as teaching nis disciples important lessons from the manner in which he buried his mother, and having a design to correct irregularities in the ordinary funeral ceremonies of the time. These things are altogether "without book." We simply have a dutiful son paying the last tribute of affection to a good parent. In one point he departs from the ancient practice, raising a mound over the grave, and when the fresh earth gives way from a sudden rain, he is moved to tears, and seems to regret his innovation. This sets Confucius vividly before us,—a man of the past as much as of the present, whose own natural feelings were liable to be hampered in their development, by the traditions of antiquity which he considered sacred. It is important, however, to observe the reason which he gave for rearing the mound. He had in it a presentiment of much of his future course. He was "a man of the north, the south, the east, and the west." He might not confine himself to any one State. He would travel, and his way might be directed to some "wise ruler," whom his counsels would conduct to a benevolent sway that would break forth on every side till it transformed the empire.

4. When the mourning for his mother was over, Confucius

[1] Le Ke, II. Pt. I. i. 10; Pt. II. iii. 30; 6. See also the discussion of those passages in Keang Yung's "
[2] Le Ke, II. Pt. I. i. 22.

remained in Loo, but in what special capacity we do not
know. Probably he continued to en-
He learns music; visits the
court of Chow; and returns courage the resort of inquirers to
to Loo.
B.C. 526—517. whom he communicated instruction,
and pursued his own researches into
the history, literature, and institutions of the empire. In
the year B.C. 524, the chief of the small state of T'an[1] made
his appearance at the court of Loo, and discoursed in a
wonderful manner, at a feast given to him by the duke,
about the names which the most ancient sovereigns, from
Hwang-te downwards, gave to their ministers. The sacrifices to the Emperor Shaou-haou, the next in descent from
Hwang-te, were maintained in T'an, so that the chief fancied
that he knew all about the abstruse subject on which he
discoursed. Confucius, hearing about the matter, waited on
the visitor, and learned from him all that he had to communicate.[2]

To the year B.C. 523, when Confucius was twenty-nine
years old, is referred his studying music under a famous
master of the name of Sëang. He was approaching his 30th
year when, as he tells us, "he stood firm,"[3] that is, in his
convictions on the subjects of learning to which he had
bent his mind fifteen years before. Five years more, however, were still to pass by before the anticipation mentioned
in the conclusion of the last paragraph began to receive its
fulfilment,[4] though we may conclude from the way in which
it was brought about that he was growing all the time in the
estimation of the thinking minds in his native State.

In the 24th year of Duke Ch'aou, B.C. 517, one of the
principal ministers of Loo, known by the name of Mäng He,
died. Seventeen years before he had painfully felt his ig-

---

[1] See the Ch'un Ts'ew, under the 7th year of Duke Ch'aou.

[2] This rests on the respectable authority of Tso-k'ew Ming's annotations
on the Ch'un Ts'ew, but I must consider it apocryphal. The legend-writers
have fashioned a journey to T'an. The slightest historical intimation becomes a text with them, on which they enlarge to the glory of the sage.
Amiot has reproduced and expanded their romancings, and others, such as
Pauthier (Chine, pp. 121—183) and Thornton (History of China, vol. i. pp.
151—215) have followed in his wake. [3] Ana. II. iv.

[4] The journey to Chow is placed by Sze-ma Ts'een before Confucius' holding of his first official employments, and Choo He and most other writers
follow him. It is a great error, and has arisen from a misunderstanding of
the passages from Tso-K'ew Ming upon the subject.

norance of ceremonial observances, and had made it his subsequent business to make himself acquainted with them. On his deathbed, he addressed his chief officer, saying, "A knowledge of propriety is the stem of a man. Without it he has no means of standing firm. I have heard that there is one K'ung K'ew, who is thoroughly versed in it. He is a descendant of Sages, and though the line of his family was extinguished in Sung, among his ancestors there were Fuh-foo Ho, who resigned the dukedom to his brother, and Ching K'aou-foo, who was distinguished for his humility. Tsang Heih has observed that if sage men of intelligent virtue do not attain to eminence, distinguished men are sure to appear among their posterity. His words are now to be verified, I think, in K'ung K'ew. After my death, you must tell Ho-ke to go and study proprieties under him." In consequence of this charge, Ho-ke, Mang He's son, who appears in the Analects under the name of Mang E,[1] and a brother, or perhaps only a near relative, named Nan-kung King-shuh, became disciples of Confucius. Their wealth and standing in the State gave him a position which he had not had before, and he told King-shuh of a wish which he had to visit the court of Chow, and especially to confer on the subject of ceremonies and music with Laou Tan. King-shuh represented the matter to the Duke Ch'aou, who put a carriage and a pair of horses at Confucius' disposal for the expedition.

At this time the court of Chow was in the city of Lö, in the present department of Ho-nan of the province of the same name. The reigning emperor is known by the title of King, but the sovereignty was little more than nominal. The state of China was then analogous to that of one of the European kingdoms, during the prevalence of the feudal system. At the commencement of the dynasty, the various States of the empire had been assigned to the relatives and adherents of the reigning family. There were thirteen principalities of greater note, and a large number of smaller dependencies. During the vigorous youth of the dynasty, the emperor or lord paramount exercised an effective control over the various chiefs, but with the lapse of time there came weakness and decay. The chiefs—corresponding

[1] Ana. II. v.

somewhat to the European dukes, earls, marquises, barons, &c.,—quarrelled and warred among themselves, and the stronger among them barely acknowledged their subjection to the emperor. A similar condition of things prevailed in each particular State. There were hereditary ministerial families, who were continually encroaching on the authority of their rulers, and the heads of those families again were frequently hard pressed by their inferior officers. Such was the state of China in Confucius' time. The reader must have it clearly before him, if he would understand the position of the sage, and the reforms which, we shall find, it was subsequently his object to introduce.

Arrived at Chow, he had no intercourse with the court or any of the principal ministers. He was there not as a politician, but an inquirer about the ceremonies and maxims of the founders of the dynasty. Laou Tan, whom he had wished to see the acknowledged founder of the Taouists, or Rationalistic sect, which has maintained its ground in opposition to the followers of Confucius, was then a treasury-keeper. They met and freely interchanged their views, but no reliable account of their conversation has been preserved. In the 5th Book of the Le Ke, which is headed, "The philosopher Tsäng asked," Confucius refers four times to the views of Laou-tsze on certain points of funeral ceremonies, and in the "Family Sayings," Book xxiv., he tells Ko K'ang what he had heard from him about "The Five Te," but we may hope their conversation turned also on more important subjects. Sze-ma Ts'een, favourable to Laou-tsze, makes him lecture his visitor in the following style:—"Those whom you talk about are dead, and their bones are mouldered to dust; only their words remain. When the superior man gets his time, he mounts aloft; but when the time is against him, he moves as if his feet were entangled. I have heard that a good merchant, though he has rich treasures deeply stored, appears as if he were poor, and that the superior man whose virtue is complete, is yet to outward seeming stupid. Put away your proud air and many desires, your insinuating habit and wild will. These are of no advantage to you. This is all which I have to tell you." On the other hand, Confucius is made to say to his disciples, "I know how birds can fly, how fishes can swim, and how animals can run. But the runner may be snared, the swimmer may be hooked, and the flyer may be shot by the arrow. But there is the dragon. I cannot tell how he mounts on the wind through the clouds, and rises to heaven. To-day I have seen Laou-tsze, and can only compare him to the dragon."

While at Lô, Confucius walked over the grounds set apart for the great sacrifices to Heaven and Earth; inspected the pattern of the Hall of Light, built to give audience in to the princes of the empire; and examined all the arrangements of the ancestral temple and the court. From the whole he received a profound impression. "Now," said he with a sigh, "I know the sage wisdom of the duke of Chow, and how the house of Chow attained to the imperial sway." On the walls of the Hall of Light were paintings of the ancient sovereigns from Yaou and Shun downwards, their characters appearing in the representations of them, and words of praise or warning being appended. There was also a picture of the duke of Chow sitting with his infant nephew, the king Ch'ing, upon his knees, to give audience to all the princes. Confucius surveyed the scene with silent delight, and then said to his followers, "Here you see how Chow became so great. As we use a glass to examine the forms of things, so must we study antiquity in order to understand the present." In the hall of the ancestral temple there was a metal statue of a man with three clasps upon his mouth, and his back covered over with an enjoyable homily on the duty of keeping a watch upon the lips. Confucius turned to his disciples, and said, "Observe it, my children. These words are true, and commend themselves to our feelings."

About music he made inquiries of Ch'ang Hwang, to whom the following remarks are attributed :—"I have observed about Chung-ne many marks of a sage. He has river eyes and a dragon forehead,—the very characteristics of Hwang-te. His arms are long, his back is like a tortoise, and he is nine feet six inches in height,—the very semblance of T'ang the Successful. When he speaks, he praises the ancient kings. He moves along the path of humility and courtesy. He has heard of every subject, and retains with a strong memory. His knowledge of things seems inexhaustible.—Have we not in him the rising of a sage?"

I have given these notices of Confucius at the court of
Chow, more as being the only ones I could find, than because I put much faith in them. He did not remain there
long, but returned the same year to Loo, and continued
his work of teaching. His fame was greatly increased;
disciples came to him from different parts, till their
number amounted to three thousand. Several of those
who have come down to us as the most distinguished
among his followers, however, were yet unborn, and the
statement just given may be considered as an exaggera-
tion. We are not to conceive of the disciples as forming
a community, and living together. Parties of them may
have done so. We shall find Confucius hereafter always
moving amid a company of admiring pupils; but the
greater number must have had their proper avocations and
ways of living, and would only resort to the master, when
they wished specially to ask his counsel or to learn of him.

5. In the year succeeding the return to Loo, that State
fell into great confusion. There were three Families in it,
all connected irregularly with the ducal house, which had
long kept the rulers in a condition

He withdraws to Ts'e, and returns to Loo the following year. B.C. 516, 515.

of dependency. They appear frequently in the Analects as the Ke
clan, the Shuh, and the Mäng; and while Confucius freely
spoke of their usurpations,[1] he was a sort of dependent of
the Ke family, and appears in frequent communication
with members of all the three. In the year B.C. 516, the
duke Chaou came to open hostilities with them, and
being worsted, fled into Ts'e, the State adjoining Loo on
the north. Thither Confucius also repaired, that he might
avoid the prevailing disorder of his native State. Ts'e
was then under the government of a duke, afterwards
styled King, who "had a thousand teams, each of four
horses, but on the day of his death the people did not
praise him for a single virtue."[2] His chief minister, however, was Gan Ying, a man of considerable ability and
worth. At his court the music of the ancient sage-em-
peror, Shun, originally brought to T'se from the State of
Ch'in, was still preserved.

According to the "Family Sayings," an incident oc-

See Analects, III. i. ii. et al.   [2] Ana. XVI. xii.

curred on the way to Ts'e, which I may transfer to these pages as a good specimen of the way in which Confucius turned occurring matters to account in his intercourse with his disciples. As he was passing by the side of the T'ae mountain, there was a woman weeping and wailing by a grave. Confucius bent forward in his carriage, and after listening to her for some time, sent Tsze-loo to ask the cause of her grief. " You weep, as if you had experienced sorrow upon sorrow," said Tsze-loo. The woman replied, " It is so. My husband's father was killed here by a tiger, and my husband also; and now my son has met the same fate." Confucius asked her why she did not remove from the place, and on her answering, " There is here no oppressive government," he turned to his disciples, and said, " My children, remember this. Oppressive government is fiercer than a tiger."[1]

As soon as he crossed the border from Loo, we are told he discovered from the gait and manners of a boy, whom he saw carrying a pitcher, the influence of the sage's music, and told the driver of his carriage to hurry on to the capital. Arrived there, he heard the strain, and was so ravished with it, that for three months he did not know the taste of flesh. " I did not think," he said, " that music could have been made so excellent as this."[2] The Duke King was pleased with the conferences which he had with him,[3] and proposed to assign to him the town of Lin-k'ew, from the revenues of which he might derive a sufficient support; but Confucius refused the gift, and said to his disciples, " A superior man will only receive reward for services which he has done. I have given advice to the Duke King, but he has not yet obeyed it, and now he would endow me with this place! Very far is he from understanding me."

On one occasion the duke asked about government, and received the characteristic reply, " There is government

---

[1] I have translated, however, from the Le Ke, II. Pt. II. iii. 10, where the same incident is given, with some variations, and without saying when or where it occurred.   [2] Ana. VII. xiii.
[3] Some of these are related in the Family Sayings;—about the burning of the ancestral shrine of the Emperor Le, and a one-footed bird which appeared hopping and flapping its wings in Ts'e. They are plainly fabulous, though quoted in proof of Confucius' sage wisdom. This reference to them is more than enough.

when the prince is prince, and the minister is minister;
when the father is father, and the son is son."¹ I say
that the reply is characteristic. Once, when Tsze-loo asked
him what he would consider the first thing to be done if
intrusted with the government of a State, Confucius answered, "What is necessary is to rectify names."² The
disciple thought the reply wide of the mark, but it was
substantially the same with what he said to the Duke
King. There is a sufficient foundation in nature for
government in the several relations of society, and if those
be maintained and developed according to their relative
significancy, it is sure to obtain. This was a first principle
in the political ethics of Confucius.

Another day the duke got to a similar inquiry the reply
that the art of government lay in an economical use of the
revenues; and being pleased, he resumed his purpose of
retaining the philosopher in his State, and proposed to
assign to him the fields of No-k'e. His chief minister,
Gan Ying, dissuaded him from the purpose, saying, "Those
scholars are impracticable, and cannot be imitated. They
are haughty and conceited of their own views, so that they
will not be content in inferior positions. They set a high
value on all funeral ceremonies, give way to their grief,
and will waste their property on great burials, so that
they would only be injurious to the common manners.
This Mr K'ung has a thousand peculiarities. It would
take generations to exhaust all that he knows about the
ceremonies of going up and going down. This is not the
time to examine into his rules of propriety. If you,
prince, wish to employ him to change the customs of Ts'e,
you will not be making the people your primary consideration."³

I had rather believe that these were not the words of
Gan Ying; but they must represent pretty correctly the
sentiments of many of the statesmen of the time about
Confucius. The duke of Ts'e got tired ere long of having
such a monitor about him, and observed, "I cannot treat
him as I would the chief of the Ke family. I will treat
him in a way between that accorded to the chief of the Ke,

¹ Ana. XII. xi. ² Ana. XIII. iii.
³ See in Sse-ma's History of Confucius.

and that given to the chief of the Măng family." Finally he said, "I am old; I cannot use his doctrines."[1] These observations were made directly to Confucius, or came to his hearing.[2] It was not consistent with his self-respect to remain longer in Ts'e, and he returned to Loo.[3]

6. Returned to Loo, he remained for the long period of about fifteen years without being engaged in any official employment. It was a time, indeed, of great disorder. The Duke Chaou continued a refugee in Ts'e, the government being in the hands of the great Families, up to his death in B.C. 509, on which event the rightful heir was set aside, and another member of the ducal house, known to us by the title of Ting, substituted in his place. The ruling authority of the principality became thus still more enfeebled than it had been before, and, on the other hand, the chiefs of the Ke, the Shuh, and the Măng, could hardly keep their ground against their own officers. Of those latter the two most conspicuous were Yang Hoo, called also Yang Ho, and Kung-shan Fuh-jaou. At one time Ke Hwan, the most powerful of the chiefs, was kept a prisoner by Yang Hoo, and was obliged to make terms with him in order to secure his liberation. Confucius would give his countenance to none, as he disapproved of all, and he studiously kept aloof from them. Of how he comported himself among them we have a specimen in the incident related in the Analects, XVII. i.—"Yang Ho wished to see Confucius, but Confucius would not go to see him. On this, he sent a present of a pig to Confucius, who, having chosen a time when Ho was not at home, went to pay his respects for the gift. He met him, however, on the way. 'Come, let me speak with you,' said the officer. 'Can he be called benevolent, who keeps his jewel in his bosom, and leaves his country to confusion?' Confucius replied, 'No.' 'Can he be called wise, who is anxious to be engaged in public employment, and yet is

He remains without office in Loo, B.C. 515—501.

---

[1] Ana. XVIII. iii.

[2] Sze-ma Ts'een makes the first observation to have been addressed directly to Confucius.

[3] According to the above account Confucius was only once, and for a portion of two years, in Ts'e. For the refutation of contrary accounts, see Keang Yung's Life of the sage.

constantly losing the opportunity of being so?' Confucius again said, 'No.' The other added, 'The days and months are passing away; the years do not wait for us.' Confucius said, 'Right; I will go into office.'" Chinese writers are eloquent in their praise of the sage for the combination of propriety, complaisance, and firmness, which they see in his behaviour in this matter. To myself there seems nothing remarkable in it but a somewhat questionable dexterity. But it was well for the fame of Confucius that his time was not occupied during those years with official services. He turned them to better account, prosecuting his researches into the poetry, history, ceremonies, and music of the empire. Many disciples continued to resort to him, and the legendary writers tell us how he employed their services in digesting the results of his studies. I must repeat, however, that several of them, whose names are most famous, such as Tsang Sin, were as yet children, and Min Sun was not born till B.C. 500.

To this period we must refer the almost single instance which we have of the manner of Confucius' intercourse with his son Le. "Have you heard any lessons from your father different from what we have all heard?" asked one of the disciples once of Le. "No," said Le. "He was standing alone once, when I was passing through the court below with hasty steps, and said to me, 'Have you read the Odes?' On my replying, 'Not yet,' he added, 'If you do not learn the Odes, you will not be fit to converse with.' Another day, in the same place and the same way, he said to me, 'Have you read the rules of Propriety?' On my replying, 'Not yet,' he added, 'If you do not learn the rules of Propriety, your character cannot be established.' I have heard only these two things from him." The disciple was delighted, and observed, "I asked one thing, and I have got three things. I have heard about the Odes; I have heard about the rules of Propriety. I have also heard that the superior man maintains a distant reserve towards his son."[1]

I can easily believe that this distant reserve was the rule which Confucius followed generally in his treatment of his son. A stern dignity is the quality which a father

[1] Ana. XVI. xiii.

has to maintain upon his system. It is not to be without the element of kindness, but that must never go beyond the line of propriety. There is too little room left for the play and development of natural affection.

The divorce of his wife must also have taken place during those years, if it ever took place at all, which is a disputed point. The curious reader will find the question discussed in the notes on the second Book of the Le Ke. The evidence inclines, I think, against the supposition that Confucius did put his wife away. When she died, at a period subsequent to the present, Le kept on weeping aloud for her after the period for such a demonstration of grief had expired, when Confucius sent a message to him that his sorrow must be subdued, and the obedient son dried his tears.[1] We are glad to know that on one occasion—the death of his favourite disciple, Yen Hwuy—the tears of Confucius himself would flow over and above the measure of propriety.[2]

7. We come to the short period of Confucius' official life. In the year B.C. 501, things had come to a head between the chiefs of the three Families and their ministers, and had resulted in the defeat of the latter. In B.C. 500, the resources of Yang Hoo were exhausted, and he fled into Ts'e, so that the State was delivered from its greatest troubler, and the way was made more clear for Confucius to go into office, should an opportunity occur. It soon presented itself. Towards the end of that year he was made chief magistrate of the town of Chung-too.[3]

He holds office. B.C. 500—

Just before he received this appointment, a circumstance occurred of which we do not well know what to make. When Yang-hoo fled into Ts'e, Kung-shan Fuh-jaou, who had been confederate with him, continued to maintain an attitude of rebellion, and held the city of Pe against the Ke family. Thence he sent a message to Confucius inviting him to join him, and the sage seemed

[1] See the Le Ke, II. Pt. I. i. 27. [2] Ana. XI. ix.
[3] Amiot says this was "la ville meme ou le Souverain tenoit sa Cour" (Vie de Confucius, p. 147). He is followed of course by Thornton and Pauthier. My reading has not shown me that such was the case. In the notes to K'ang-he's edition of the "Yih King," Le Ke, II. Pt. I. iii. 4, it is simply said—"Chung-too,—the name of a town of Loo. It afterwards belonged to Ts'e, when it was called P'ing-luh."

so inclined to go that his disciple Tsze-loo remonstrated with him, saying, "Indeed you cannot go! why must you think of going to see Kung-shan?" Confucius replied, "Can it be without some reason that he has invited me? If any one employ me, may I not make an eastern Chow?"[1] The upshot, however, was that he did not go, and I cannot suppose that he had ever any serious intention of doing so. Amid the general gravity of his intercourse with his followers, there gleam out a few instances of quiet pleasantry, when he amused himself by playing with their notions about him. This was probably one of them.

As magistrate of Chung-too he produced a marvellous reformation of the manners of the people in a short time. According to the "Family Sayings," he enacted rules for the nourishing of the living, and all observances to the dead. Different food was assigned to the old and the young, and different burdens to the strong and the weak. Males and females were kept apart from each other in the streets. A thing dropt on the road was not picked up. There was no fraudulent carving of vessels. Inner coffins were made four inches thick, and the outer ones five. Graves were made on the high grounds, no mounds being raised over them, and no trees planted about them. Within twelve months, the princes of the States all about wished to imitate his style of administration.

The Duke Ting, surprised at what he saw, asked whether his rules could be employed to govern a whole State, and Confucius told him that they might be applied to the whole empire. On this the duke appointed him assistant-superintendent of Works,[2] in which capacity he surveyed the lands of the State, and made many improvements in agriculture. From this he was quickly made minister of Crime, and the appointment was enough to put an end to crime. There was no necessity to put the penal laws in execution. No offenders showed themselves.

These indiscriminating eulogies are of little value. One incident, related in the annotations of Tso-k'ew on the Ts'un Ts'ow, commends itself at once to our belief, as in

[1] Ana. XVII. v.
[2] This office, however, was held by the chief of the Mäng family. We must understand that Confucius was only an assistant to him, or perhaps acted for him.

harmony with Confucius' character. The chief of the Ke, pursuing with his enmity the Duke Chaou, even after his death, had placed his grave apart from the graves of his predecessors; and Confucius surrounded the ducal cemetery with a ditch so as to include the solitary resting-place, boldly telling the chief that he did it to hide his disloyalty. But he signalized himself most of all, in B.C. 499, by his behaviour at an interview between the dukes of Loo and Ts'e, at a place called Shih-k'e, and Këä-kuh, in the present district of Lae-woo, in the department of T'ae-gan. Confucius was present as master of ceremonies on the part of Loo, and the meeting was professedly pacific. The two princes were to form a covenant of alliance. The principal officer on the part of Ts'e, however, despising Confucius as "a man of ceremonies, without courage," had advised his sovereign to make the duke of Loo a prisoner, and for this purpose a band of the half-savage original inhabitants of the place advanced with weapons to the stage where the two dukes were met. Confucius understood the scheme, and said to the opposite party, "Our two princes are met for a pacific object. For you to bring a band of savage vassals to disturb the meeting with their weapons, is not the way in which Ts'e can expect to give law to the princes of the empire. These barbarians have nothing to do with our Great Flowery land. Such vassals may not interfere with our covenant. Weapons are out of place at such a meeting. As before the spirits, such conduct is unpropitious. In point of virtue, it is contrary to right. As between man and man, it is not polite." The duke of Ts'e ordered the disturbers off, but Confucius withdrew, carrying the duke of Loo with him. The business proceeded, notwithstanding, and when the words of the alliance were being read on the part of Ts'e,—" So be it to Loo, if it contribute not 300 chariots of war to the help of Ts'e, when its army goes across its borders," a messenger from Confucius added,— "And so it be to us, if we obey your orders, unless you return to us the fields on the south of the Wän." At the conclusion of the ceremonies, the prince of Ts'e wanted to give a grand entertainment, but Confucius demonstrated that such a thing would be contrary to the established rules of propriety, his real object being to keep his sovereign out of danger. In this way the two parties separated, they of Ts'e filled with shame at being foiled and disgraced by "the man of ceremonies," and the result was that the lands of Loo which had been appropriated by Ts'e were restored.[1]

For two years more Confucius held the office of minister of Crime. Some have supposed that he was further raised to the dignity of chief minister of State, but that was not the case. One instance of the manner in which he executed his functions is worth recording. When any matter came before him, he took the opinion of different individuals upon it, and in giving judgment would say, "I decide according to the view of so and so." There was an approach to our jury system in the plan, Confucius' object being to enlist general sympathy, and carry the public judgment with him in his administration of justice. A father having brought some charge against his son, Confucius kept them both in prison for three months, without making any difference in favour of the father, and then wished to dismiss them both. The head of the Ke was dissatisfied, and said, "You are playing with me, Sir minister of Crime. Formerly you told me that in a State or a family filial duty was the first thing to be insisted on. What hinders you now from putting to death this unfilial son as an example to all the people?" Confucius with a sigh replied, "When superiors fail in their duty, and yet go to put their inferiors to death, it is not right. This father has not taught his son to be filial;—to listen to his charge would be to slay the guiltless. The manners of the age have been long in a sad condition; we cannot expect the people not to be transgressing the laws."

At this time two of his disciples, Tsze-loo and Tsze-yew, entered the employment of the Ko family, and lent their influence, the former especially, to forward the plans of their master. One great cause of disorder in the State was the fortified cities held by the three chiefs, in which they could defy the supreme authority, and were in turn defied themselves by their officers. Those cities were like the castles of the barons of England in the time of the

---

[1] This meeting at Keä-kuh is related in Sze-ma Ts'een, the Family Sayings, and Kuh-leang, with many exaggerations.

Norman kings. Confucius had their destruction very much at heart, and partly by the influence of persuasion, and partly by the assisting counsels of Tsze-loo, he accomplished his object in regard to Pe, the chief city of the Ke, and How, the chief city of the Shuh.

It does not appear that he succeeded in the same way in dismantling Ch'ing, the chief city of the Mäng;[1] but his authority in the State greatly increased. "He strengthened the ducal House and weakened the private Families. He exalted the sovereign, and depressed the ministers. A transforming government went abroad. Dishonesty and dissoluteness were ashamed, and hid their heads. Loyalty and good faith became the characteristics of the men, and chastity and docility those of the women. Strangers came in crowds from other States. Confucius became the idol of the people, and flew in songs through their mouths.

But this sky of bright promise was soon overcast. As the fame of the reformations in Loo went abroad, the neighbouring princes began to be afraid. The duke of Ts'e said, "With Confucius at the head of its government, Loo will become supreme among the States, and Ts'e which is nearest to it will be the first swallowed up. Let us propitiate it by a surrender of territory." One of his ministers proposed they should first try to separate between the sage and his sovereign, and to effect this, they hit upon the following scheme. Eighty beautiful girls, with musical and dancing accomplishments, were selected, and a hundred and twenty of the finest horses that could be found, and sent as a present to Duke Ting. They were put up at first outside the city, and Ke Hwan having gone in disguise to see them, forgot the lessons of Confucius, and took the duke to look at the bait. They were both captivated. The women were received, and the sage was neglected. For three days the duke gave no audience to his ministers. "Master," said Tsze-loo to Confucius, "it

[1] In connection with these events, the Family Sayings and Sze-ma Ts'een mention the summary punishment inflicted by Confucius on an able but unscrupulous and insidious officer, the Shaou-ching, Maou. His judgment and death occupy a conspicuous place in the legendary accounts. But the Analects, Tsze-sze, Mencius, and Tso-k'ew Ming are all silent about it, and Keang Yung rightly rejects it, as one of the many narratives invented to exalt the sage.

is time for you to be going." But Confucius was very unwilling to leave. The time was drawing near when the great sacrifice to Heaven would be offered, and he determined to wait and see whether the solemnity of that would bring the duke back to his right mind. No such result followed. The ceremony was hurried through, and portions of the offerings were not sent round to the various ministers, according to the established custom. Confucius regretfully took his departure, going away slowly and by easy stages. He would have welcomed a messenger of recall. The duke continued in his abandonment, and the sage went forth to thirteen weary years of homeless wandering.

8. On leaving Loo, Confucius first bent his steps westward to the State of Wei, situate about where the present provinces of Chih-le and Ho-nan adjoin. He was now in his 56th year, and felt depressed and melancholy. As he went along, he gave expression to his feeling in verse :—

He wanders from State to State.
B.C. 496—483.

<blockquote>
"Fain would I still look towards Loo,
But this Kwei hill cuts off my view.
With an axe, I'd hew the thickets through :—
Vain thought! 'gainst the hill I nought can do ;"
</blockquote>

and again,—

<blockquote>
"Through the valley howls the blast,
Drizzling rain falls thick and fast.
Homeward goes the youthful bride,
O'er the wild, crowds by her side,
How is it, O azure Heaven,
From my home I thus am driven,
Through the land my way to trace,
With no certain dwelling-place ?
Dark, dark, the minds of men !
Worth in vain comes to their ken.
Hastens on my term of years ;
Old age, desolate, appears."[1]
</blockquote>

A number of his disciples accompanied him, and his sadness infected them. When they arrived at the borders of Wei, at a place called E, the warden sought an interview, and on coming out from the sage, he tried to comfort the disciples, saying, "My friends, why are you distressed at your Master's loss of office ? The empire has

[1] See Keang Yung's Life of Confucius.

been long without the principles of truth and right; Heaven is going to use your master as a bell with its wooden tongue."[1] Such was the thought of this friendly stranger. The bell did indeed sound, but few had ears to hear.

Confucius' fame, however, had gone before him, and he was in little danger of having to suffer from want. On arriving at the capital of Wei, he lodged at first with a worthy officer, named Yen Ch'ow-yew.[2] The reigning duke, known to us by the epithet of Ling, was a worthless, dissipated man, but he could not neglect a visitor of such eminence, and soon assigned to Confucius a revenue of 60,000 measures of grain. Here he remained for ten months, and then for some reason left it to go to Ch'in. On the way he had to pass by K'wang, a place probably in the present department of K'ae-fung in Ho-nan, which had formerly suffered from Yang-hoo. It so happened that Confucius resembled Hoo, and the attention of the people being called to him by the movements of his carriage-driver, they thought it was their old enemy, and made an attack upon him. His followers were alarmed, but he was calm, and tried to assure them by declaring his belief that he had a divine mission. He said to them, "After the death of King Wăn, was not the cause of truth lodged here in me? If Heaven had wished to let this cause of truth perish, then I, a future mortal, should not have got such a relation to that cause. While Heaven does not let the cause of truth perish, what can the people of K'wang do to me?"[3] Having escaped from the hands of his assailants, he does not seem to have carried out his purpose of going to Ch'in, but returned to Wei.

On the way, he passed a house where he had formerly been lodged, and finding that the master was dead, and the funeral ceremonies going on, he went in to condole and weep. When he came out, he told Tsze-kung to take one of the horses from his carriage, and give it as a contribution to the expenses of the occasion. "You never did such a thing," Tsze-kung remonstrated, "at the funeral of any of your disciples; is it not too great a gift on this

[1] Ana. III. xxiv.   [2] See Mencius, V. Pt. I. viii. 2.
[3] Ana. IX. v. In Ana. XI. xxii. there is another reference to this time, in which Yen Hwuy is made to appear.

occasion of the death of an old host?" "When I went
in," replied Confucius, "my presence brought a burst of
grief from the chief mourner, and I joined him with my
tears. I dislike the thought of my tears not being followed
by anything. Do it, my child."[1]

On reaching Wei, he lodged with Keu Pih-yuh, an
officer of whom honourable mention is made in the Analects.[2] But this time he did not remain long in the State.
The duke was married to a lady of the house of
Sung, known by the name of Nan-tsze, notorious
for her intrigues and wickedness. She sought an interview with the sage, which he was obliged unwillingly to
accord. No doubt he was innocent of thought or act of
evil; but it gave great dissatisfaction to Tsze-loo that his
master should have been in company with such a woman,
and Confucius, to assure him, swore an oath, saying,
"Wherein I have done improperly, may Heaven reject
me! May Heaven reject me!"[3] He could not well
abide, however, about such a court. One day the duke
rode out through the streets of his capital in the same carriage with Nan-tsze, and made Confucius follow them in
another. Perhaps he intended to honour the philosopher,
but the people saw the incongruity, and cried out, "Lust
in the front; virtue behind!" Confucius was ashamed,
and made the observation, "I have not seen one who
loves virtue as he loves beauty."[4] Wei was no place for
him. He left it, and took his way towards Ch'in.

B.C. 495.

Ch'in, which formed part of the present province of Honan, lay south from Wei. After passing the small State
of Ts'aou, he approached the borders of Sung, occupying
the present prefecture of Kwei-tih, and had some intentions of entering it, when an incident occurred, which it
is not easy to understand from the meagre style in which
it is related, but which gave occasion to a remarkable saying. Confucius was practising ceremonies with his disciples, we are told, under the shade of a large tree. Hwan
T'uy, an ill-minded officer of Sung, heard of it, and sent a
band of men to pull down the tree, and kill the philosopher,
if they could get hold of him. The disciples were much
alarmed, but Confucius observed, "Heaven has produced

---

[1] See the Le Ke. II. Pt. I. ii. 16.   [3] Ana. XIV. xxvi.; XV. vi.
[2] Ana. VI. xxvi.   [4] Ana. IX. xvii.

the virtue that is in me;—what can Hwan T'uy do to me?"[1] They all made their escape, but seem to have been driven westwards to the State of Ch'ing, on arriving at the gate conducting into which from the east, Confucius found himself separated from his followers. Tsze-kung had arrived before him, and was told by a native of Ch'ing that "there was a man standing by the east gate, with a forehead like Yaou, a neck like Kaou-yaou, his shoulders on a level with those of Tsze-ch'an, but wanting, below the waist, three inches of the height of Yu, and altogether having the disconsolate appearance of a stray dog." Tsze-kung knew it was the master, hastened to him, and repeated to his great amusement the description which the man had given. "The bodily appearance," said Confucius, "is but a small matter, but to say I was like a stray dog—capital! capital!" The stay they made at Ch'ing was short, and by the end of B.C. 495, Confucius was in Ch'in.

All the next year he remained there lodging with the warder of the city wall, an officer of worth, of the name of Ching,[2] and we have no accounts of him which deserve to be related here.[3]

In B.C. 493, Ch'in was much disturbed by attacks from Woo, a large State, the capital of which was in the present department of Soo-chow, and Confucius determined to retrace his steps to Wei. On the way he was laid hold of at a place called P'oo, which was held by a rebellious officer against Wei, and before he could get away, he was obliged to engage that he would not proceed thither. Thither, notwithstanding, he continued his route, and when Tsze-kung asked him whether it was right to violate the oath he had taken, he replied, "It was a forced oath. The spirits do not hear such."[4] The duke Ling received him with distinction, but paid no more attention to his lessons than before, and Confucius is said then to have uttered his complaint, "If there were any of

[1] Ana. IX. xxii.   [2] See Mencius, V. Pt. I. viii. 3.
[3] Keang Yung digests in this place two foolish stories,—about a large bone found in the State of Yuĕ, and a bird which appeared in Ch'in and died, shot through with a remarkable arrow. Confucius knew all about them.
[4] This is related by Sse-ma Ts'een, and also in the Family Sayings. I would fain believe it is not true. The wonder is, that no Chinese critic should have set about disproving it.

the princes who would employ me, in the course of twelve
months I should have done something considerable. In
three years the government would be perfected."[1]

A circumstance occurred to direct his attention to the
State of Tsin, which occupied the southern part of the
present Shan-se, and extended over the Yellow river into
Ho-nan. An invitation came to Confucius, like that which
he had formerly received from Kung-shan Fuh-jaou. Peih
Heih, an officer of Tsin, who was holding the town of
Chung-mow against his chief, invited him to visit him, and
Confucius was inclined to go. Tsze-loo was always the
mentor on such occasions. He said to him, "Master, I
have heard you say, that when a man in his own person is
guilty of doing evil, a superior man will not associate with
him. Peih Heih is in rebellion; if you go to him, what
shall be said?" Confucius replied, "Yes, I did use those
words. But is it not said that if a thing be really hard, it
may be ground without being made thin; and if it be
really white, it may be steeped in a dark fluid without
being made black? Am I a bitter gourd? Am I to be
hung up out of the way of being eaten?"[2]

These sentiments sound strangely from his lips. After
all, he did not go to Peih Heih; and having travelled as
far as the Yellow river that he might see one of the principal ministers of Tsin, he heard of the violent death of two
men of worth, and returned to Wei, lamenting the fate
which prevented him from crossing the stream, and trying
to solace himself with poetry as he had done on leaving
Loo. Again did he communicate with the duke, but as
ineffectually, and disgusted at being questioned by him
about military tactics, he left and went back to Ch'in.

He resided in Ch'in all the next year, B.C. 491, without
anything occurring there which is worthy of note. Events
had transpired in Loo, however, which were to issue in
his return to his native State. The duke Ting had de-
ceased B.C. 494, and Ke Hwan, the chief of the Ke family,
died in this year. On his deathbed, he felt remorse for
his conduct to Confucius, and charged his successor,
known to us in the Analects as Ke K'ang, to recall the
sage; but the charge was not immediately fulfilled. Ke

[1] Ana. XII. x.   [2] Ana. XVII. vii.

K'ang, by the advice of one of his officers, sent to Ch'in for the disciple Yen K'ew instead. Confucius willingly sent him off, and would gladly have accompanied him. "Let me return!" he said, "Let me return!"[1] But that was not to be for several years yet.

In B.C. 490, accompanied, as usual, by several of his disciples, he went from Ch'in to Ts'ae, a small dependency of the great fief of Ts'oo, which occupied a large part of the present provinces of Hoo-nan and Hoo-pih. On the way, between Ch'in and Ts'ae, their provisions became exhausted, and they were cut off somehow from obtaining a fresh supply. The disciples were quite overcome with want, and Tsze-loo said to the master, "Has the superior man indeed to endure in this way?" Confucius answered him, "The superior man may indeed have to endure want; but the mean man, when he is in want, gives way to unbridled license."[2] According to the "Family Sayings," the distress continued seven days, during which time Confucius retained his equanimity, and was even cheerful, playing on his lute and singing. He retained, however, a strong impression of the perils of the season, and we find him afterwards recurring to it, and lamenting that of the friends that were with him in Ch'in and Ts'ae, there were none remaining to enter his door.[3]

Escaped from this strait, he remained in Ts'ae over B.C. 489, and in the following year we find him in Shĕ, another district of Ts'oo, the chief of which had usurped the title of duke. Puzzled about his visitor, he asked Tsze-loo what he should think of him, but the disciple did not venture a reply. When Confucius heard of it, he said to Tsze-loo, "Why did you not say to him,—He is simply a man who in his eager pursuit of knowledge forgets his food, who in the joy of its attainment forgets his sorrows, and who does not perceive that old age is coming on?"[4] Subsequently, the duke, in conversation with Confucius, asked him about government, and got the reply, dictated by some circumstances of which we are ignorant, "Good government obtains, when those who are near are made happy, and those who are far off are attracted."[5]

[1] Ana. V. xxi.   [2] Ana. XV. i. 2, 3.   [3] Ana. XI. ii.
[4] Ana. VII. xviii.   [5] Ana. XIII. xvi.

After a short stay in Shĕ, according to Sze-ma Ts'een, he returned to Ts'ae, and having to cross a river, he sent Tsze-loo to inquire for the ford of two men who were at work in a neighbouring field. They were recluses,—men who had withdrawn from public life in disgust at the waywardness of the times. One of them was called Ch'ang-tseu, and instead of giving Tsze-loo the information he wanted, he asked him, "Who is it that holds the reins in the carriage there?" "It is K'ung Kew." "K'ung Kew of Loo?" "Yes," was the reply, and then the man rejoined, "*He* knows the ford."

Tsze-loo applied to the other, who was called Këĕ-neih, but got for answer the question, "Who are you, Sir?" He replied, "I am Chung Yew." "Chung Yew, who is the disciple of K'ung Kew of Loo?". "Yes," again replied Tsze-loo, and Këĕ-heih addressed him, "Disorder, like a swelling flood, spreads over the whole empire, and who is he that will change it for you? Than follow one who merely withdraws from this one and that one, had you not better follow those who withdraw from the world altogether?" With this he fell to covering up the seed, and gave no more heed to the stranger. Tsze-loo went back and reported what they had said, when Confucius vindicated his own course, saying, "It is impossible to associate with birds and beasts as if they were the same with us. If I associate not with these people,—with mankind,—with whom shall I associate? If right principles prevailed through the empire, there would be no use for me to change its state." [1]

About the same time he had an encounter with another recluse, who was known as "The madman of Ts'oo." He passed by the carriage of Confucius, singing out, "O Fung, O Fung, how is your virtue degenerated! As to the past, reproof is useless, but the future may be provided against. Give up, give up your vain pursuit." Confucius alighted and wished to enter into conversation with him, but the man hastened away. [2]

But now the attention of the ruler of Ts'oo—king, as he styled himself—was directed to the illustrious stranger who was in his dominions, and he met Confucius and con-

---

[1] Ana. XVIII. vi.   [2] Ana. XVII. v.

ducted him to his capital, which was in the present district of E-shing, in the department of Sëang-yang, in Hoo-pih. After a time, he proposed endowing the philosopher with a considerable territory, but was dissuaded by his prime minister, who said to him, "Has your Majesty any officer who could discharge the duties of an ambassador like Tsze-kung? or any one so qualified for a premier as Yen Hwuy? or any one to compare as a general with Tsze-loo? The kings Wăn and Woo, from their hereditary dominions of a hundred *le*, rose to the sovereignty of the empire. If K'ung K'ew, with such disciples to be his ministers, get the possession of any territory, it will not be to the prosperity of Ts'oo? On this remonstrance, the king gave up his purpose, and when he died in the same year, Confucius left the State, and went back again to Wei.

The Duke Ling had died four years before, soon after Confucius had last parted from him, and the reigning duke, known to us by the title of Ch'uh, was B.C. 489. his grandson, and was holding the principality against his own father. The relations between them were rather complicated. The father had been driven out in consequence of an attempt which he had instigated on the life of his mother, the notorious Nan-tsze, and the succession was given to his son. Subsequently, the father wanted to reclaim what he deemed his right, and an unseemly struggle ensued. The Duke Ch'uh was conscious how much his cause would be strengthened by the support of Confucius, and hence when he got to Wei, Tsze-loo could say to him, "The prince of Wei has been waiting for you, in order with you to administer the government;—what will you consider the first thing to be done?"[1] The opinion of the philosopher, however, was against the propriety of the duke's course, and he declined taking office with him, though he remained in Wei for between five and six years. During all that time there is a blank in his history. In the very year of his return, according to the "Annals of the Empire," his most beloved disciple,

[1] Ana. XIII. iii. In the notes on this passage, I have given Choo He's opinion as to the time when Tsze-loo made this remark. It seems more correct, however, to refer it to Confucius' return to Wei from Ts'oo, as is done by Këang Yung.

Yen Hwuy, died, on which occasion he exclaimed, "Alas! Heaven is destroying me! Heaven is destroying me!"[1] The death of his wife is assigned to B.C. 484, but nothing else is related which we can connect with this long period.

9. His return to Loo was brought about by the disciple Yen Yow, who, we have seen, went into the service of Ke K'ang, in B.C. 491. In the year B.C. 483, Yow had the conduct of some military operations against Ts'e, and being successful, Ke K'ang asked him how he had obtained his military skill;—was it from nature, or by learning? He replied that he had learned it from Confucius, and entered into a glowing eulogy of the philosopher. The chief declared that he would bring Confucius home again to Loo. "If you do so," said the disciple, "see that you do not let mean men come between you and him." On this K'ang sent three officers with appropriate presents to Wei, to invite the wanderer home, and he returned with them accordingly.

This event took place in the eleventh year of the Duke Gae, who succeeded to Ting, and according to K'ung Foo, Confucius' descendant, the invitation proceeded from him. We may suppose that while Ke K'ang was the mover and director of the proceeding, it was with the authority and approval of the duke. It is represented in the chronicle of Tso-k'ew Ming as having occurred at a very opportune time. The philosopher had been consulted a little before by K'ung Wăn, an officer of Wei, about how he should conduct a feud with another officer, and disgusted at being referred to on such a subject, had ordered his carriage and prepared to leave the State, exclaiming, "The bird chooses its tree. The tree does not chase the bird." K'ung Wăn endeavoured to excuse himself, and to prevail on Confucius to remain in Wei, and just at this juncture the messengers from Loo arrived.

Confucius was now in his 69th year. The world had not dealt kindly with him. In every State which he had visited he had met with disappointment and sorrow. Only

[1] Ana. XI. viii. In the notes on Ana. XI. vii, I have adverted to the chronological difficulty connected with the dates assigned respectively to the deaths of Yen Hwuy and Confucius' own son, Le. Keang Yung assigns Hwuy's death to B.C. 481.

five more years remained to him, nor were they of a brighter character than the past. He had, indeed, attained to that state, he tells us, in which "he could follow what his heart desired without transgressing what was right,"[1] but other people were not more inclined than they had been to abide by his counsels. The Duke Gae and Ke K'ang often conversed with him, but he no longer had weight in the guidance of State affairs, and wisely addressed himself to the completion of his literary labours. He wrote, it is said, a preface to the Shoo-king; carefully digested the rites and ceremonies determined by the wisdom of the more ancient sages and kings; collected and arranged the ancient poetry; and undertook the reform of music. He has told us himself, "I returned from Wei to Loo, and then the music was reformed, and the pieces in the Imperial Songs and Praise Songs found all their proper place."[2] To the Yih-king he devoted much study, and Sze-ma Ts'een says that the leather thongs by which the tablets of his copy were bound together were thrice worn out. "If some years were added to my life," he said, "I would give fifty to the study of the Yih, and then I might come to be without great faults."[3] During this time also, we may suppose that he supplied Tsing Sin with the materials of the classic of Filial Piety. The same year that he returned, Ke K'ang sent Yen Yaw to ask his opinion about an additional impost which he wished to lay upon the people, but Confucius refused to give any reply, telling the disciple privately his disapproval of the proposed measure. It was carried out, however, in the following year, by the agency of You, on which occasion, I suppose, it was that Confucius said to the other disciples, "He is no disciple of mine; my little children, beat the drum and assail him."[4] The year B.C. 482 was marked by the death of his son Le, which he seems to have borne with more equanimity than he did that of his disciple Yen Hwuy, which some writers assign to the following year, though I have already mentioned it under the year B.C. 488.

In the spring of B.C. 480, a servant of Ke K'ang caught a k'e-lin on a hunting excursion of the duke in the pre-

[1] Ana. II. iv. 8.   [2] Ana. IX. xiv.
[3] Ana. VII. xvi.   [4] Ana. XI. xvi.

sent district of Këa-ts'eang. No person could tell what strange animal it was, and Confucius was called to look at it. He at once knew it to be a *lin*, and the legend-writers say that it bore on one of its horns the piece of ribbon, which his mother had attached to the one that appeared to her before his birth. According to the chronicle of Kung-yang, he was profoundly affected. He cried out, "For whom have you come? For whom have you come?" His tears flowed freely, and he added, "The course of my doctrines is run."

Notwithstanding the appearance of the *lin*, the life of Confucius was still protracted for two years longer, though he took occasion to terminate with that event his history of the Ch'un Ts'ew. This Work, according to Sze-ma Ts'een, was altogether the production of this year, but we need not suppose that it was so. In it, from the stand-point of Loo, he briefly indicates the principal events occurring throughout the empire, every term being expressive, it is said, of the true character of the actors and events described. Confucius said himself, "It is the Spring and Autumn which will make men know me, and it is the Spring and Autumn which will make men condemn me."[1] Mencius makes the composition of it to have been an achievement as great as Yu's regulation of the waters of the deluge.—"Confucius completed the Spring and Autumn, and rebellious ministers and villainous sons were struck with terror."[2]

Towards the end of this year, word came to Loo that the duke of Ts'e had been murdered by one of his officers. Confucius was moved with indignation. Such an outrage, he felt, called for his solemn interference. He bathed, went to court, and represented the matter to the duke, saying, "Ch'in Hăng has slain his sovereign, I beg that you will undertake to punish him." The duke pleaded his incapacity, urging that Loo was weak compared with Ts'e, but Confucius replied, "One half of the people of Ts'e are not consenting to the deed. If you add to the people of Loo one half of the people of Ts'e, you are sure to overcome." But he could not infuse his spirit into the duke, who told him to go and lay the matter before the

---

[1] Mencius, III. Pt. II. ix. 8.   [2] Mencius, III. Pt. II. ix. 11.

chief of the three Families. Sorely against his sense of propriety, he did so, but they would not act, and he withdrew with the remark, "Following in the rear of the great officers, I did not dare not to represent such a matter."[1]

In the year B.C. 479, Confucius had to mourn the death of another of his disciples, one of those who had been longest with him,—the well-known Tsze-loo. He stands out a sort of Peter in the Confucian school, a man of impulse, prompt to speak and prompt to act. He gets many a check from the master, but there is evidently a strong sympathy between them. Tsze-loo uses a freedom with him on which none of the other disciples dares to venture, and there is not one among them all, for whom, if I may speak from my own feeling, the foreign student comes to form such a liking. A pleasant picture is presented to us in one passage of the Analects. It is said, "The disciple Min was standing by his side, looking bland and precise; Tsze-loo (named Yew), looking bold and soldierly; Yen Yew and Tsze-kung, with a free and straightforward manner. The master was pleased, but he observed, 'Yew there!—he will not die a natural death.'"[2]

This prediction was verified. When Confucius returned to Loo from Wei, he left Tsze-loo and Tsze-kaou engaged there in official service. Troubles arose. News came to Loo, B.C. 479, that a revolution was in progress in Wei, and when Confucius heard it, he said, "Ch'ae will come here, but Yew will die." So it turned out. When Tsze-kaou saw that matters were desperate he made his escape, but Tsze-loo would not forsake the chief who had treated him well. He threw himself into the mêlée, and was slain. Confucius wept sore for him, but his own death was not far off. It took place on the 11th day of the 4th month in the following year, B.C. 478.

Early one morning, we are told, he got up, and with his hands behind his back, dragging his staff, he moved about by his door, crooning over,—

"The great mountain must crumble;
The strong beam must break;
And the wise man wither away like a plant."

After a little, he entered the house and sat down opposite the door. Tsze-kung had heard his words, and said

[1] Analects, XIV. xxii. [2] Ana. XI. xii.

to himself, "If the great mountain crumble, to what shall I look up? If the strong beam break, and the wise man wither away, on whom shall I lean? The master, I fear, is going to be ill." With this he hastened into the house. Confucius said to him, "Ts'ze, what makes you so late? According to the statutes of Hea, the corpse was dressed and coffined at the top of the eastern steps, treating the dead as if he were still the host. Under the Yin, the ceremony was performed between the two pillars, as if the dead were both host and guest. The rule of Chow is to perform it at the top of the western steps, treating the dead as if he were a guest. I am a man of Yin, and last night I dreamt that I was sitting with offerings before me between the two pillars. No intelligent monarch arises; there is not one in the empire that will make me his master. My time is come to die." So it was. He went to his couch, and after seven days expired.[1]

Such is the account which we have of the last hours of the great philosopher of China. His end was not unimpressive, but it was melancholy. He sank behind a cloud. Disappointed hopes made his soul bitter. The great ones of the empire had not received his teachings. No wife nor child was by to do the kindly offices of affection for him. Nor were the expectations of another life present with him as he passed though the dark valley. He uttered no prayer, and he betrayed no apprehensions. Deep-treasured in his own heart may have been the thought that he had endeavoured to serve his generation by the will of God, but he gave no sign. "The mountain falling came to nought, and the rock was removed out of his place. So death prevailed against him and he passed; his countenance was changed, and he was sent away."

10. I flatter myself that the preceding paragraphs contain a more correct narrative of the principal incidents in the life of Confucius than has yet been given in any European language. They might easily have been expanded into a volume, but I did not wish to exhaust the subject, but only to furnish a sketch, which, while it might satisfy the general reader, would be of special assistance to the careful student of the classical Books. I had taken many

---

See the Le Ke, II. Pt. I. ii. 20.

notes of the manifest errors in regard to chronology and other matters in the "Family Sayings," and the chapter of Sze-ma Ts'een on the K'ung family, when the digest of Keang Yung, to which I have made frequent reference, attracted my attention. Conclusions to which I had come were confirmed, and a clue was furnished to difficulties which I was seeking to disentangle. I take the opportunity to acknowledge here my obligations to it. With a few notices of Confucius' habits and manners, I shall conclude this section.

Very little can be gathered from reliable sources on the personal appearance of the sage. The height of his father is stated, as I have noted, to have been ten feet, and though Confucius came short of this by four inches, he was often called "the tall man." It is allowed that the ancient foot or cubit was shorter than the modern, but it must be reduced more than any scholar I have consulted has yet done, to bring this statement within the range of credibility. The legends assign to his figure "nine-and-forty remarkable peculiarities," a tenth part of which would have made him more a monster than a man. Dr Morrison says that the images of him, which he had seen in the northern parts of China, represent him as of a dark swarthy colour.[1] It is not so with those common in the south. He was, no doubt, in size and complexion much the same as many of his descendants in the present day.

But if his disciples had nothing to chronicle of his personal appearance, they have gone very minutely into an account of many of his habits. The tenth book of the Analects is all occupied with his deportment, his eating, and his dress. In public, whether in the village, the temple, or the court, he was the man of rule and ceremony, but "at home he was not formal." Yet if not formal, he was particular. In bed even he did not forget himself;—"he did not lie like a corpse," and "he did not speak." "He required his sleeping dress to be half as long again as his body." "If he happened to be sick, and the prince came to visit him, he had his face to the east, made his

[1] Chinese and English Dictionary, char. K'ung. Sir John Davis also mentions seeing a figure of Confucius, in a temple near the Po-yang Lake, of which the complexion was "quite black." ("The Chinese," vol. II. p. 66.)

court robes he put over him, and drew his girdle across them."

He was nice in his diet,—"not disliking to have his rice dressed fine, nor to have his minced meat cut small." "Anything at all gone he would not touch." "He must have his meat cut properly, and to every kind its proper sauce; but he was not a great eater." "It was only in wine that he laid down no limit to himself, but he did not allow himself to be confused by it." "When the villagers were drinking together, on those who carried staves going out, he went out immediately after." "There must always be ginger at the table, and "when eating, he did not converse." "Although his food might be coarse rice and poor soup, he would offer a little of it in sacrifice, with a grave respectful air."

"On occasion of a sudden clap of thunder, or a violent wind, he would change countenance. He would do the same, and rise up moreover, when he found himself a guest at a loaded board." "At the sight of a person in mourning he would also change countenance, and if he happened to be in his carriage, he would bend forward with a respectful salutation." "His general way in his carriage was not to turn his head round, nor talk hastily, nor point with his hands." He was charitable. "When any of his friends died, if there were no relations who could be depended on for the necessary offices, he would say, 'I will bury him.'"

The disciples were so careful to record these and other characteristics of their master, it is said, because every act, of movement or of rest, was closely associated with the great principles which it was his object to inculcate. The detail of so many small matters, however, does not impress a foreigner so favourably. There is a want of freedom about the philosopher. Somehow he is less a sage to me, after I have seen him at his table, in his undress, in his bed, and in his carriage.

SECTION II.

HIS INFLUENCE AND OPINIONS.

1. Confucius died, we have seen, complaining that of all the princes of the empire there was not one who would adopt his principles and obey his lessons. *Homages rendered to Confucius by the emperors of China.* He had hardly passed from the stage of life when his merit began to be acknowledged. When the Duke Gae heard of his death, he pronounced his eulogy in the words, "Heaven has not left to me the aged man. There is none now to assist me on the throne. Woe is me! Alas! O venerable Ne!"[1] Tsze-Kung complained of the inconsistency of this lamentation from one who could not use the master when he was alive, but the duke was probably sincere in his grief. He caused a temple to be erected, and ordered that sacrifice should be offered to the sage, at the four seasons of the year.

The emperors of the tottering dynasty of Chow had not the intelligence, nor were they in a position, to do honour to the departed philosopher, but the facts detailed in the first chapter of these prolegomena, in connection with the attempt of the founder of the Ts'in dynasty to destroy the monuments of antiquity, show how the authority of Confucius had come by that time to prevail through the empire. The founder of the Han dynasty, in passing through Loo, B.C. 194, visited his tomb and offered an ox in sacrifice to him. Other emperors since then have often made pilgrimages to the spot. The most famous temple in the empire now rises over the place of the grave. K'ang-he, the second and greatest of the rulers of the present dynasty, in the twenty-third year of his reign, there set the example of kneeling thrice, and each time laying his forehead thrice in the dust, before the image of the sage.

In the year of our Lord 1, began the practice of conferring honorary designations on Confucius by imperial authority. The Emperor P'ing then styled him—"The Duke Ne, all-

---

[1] Le Ke, II. Pt. I. iii. 43. This eulogy is found at greater length in Tso-K'ew Ming, immediately after the notice of the sage's death.

complete and illustrious." This was changed, in A.D. 492, to—"The venerable Ne, the accomplished Sage." Other titles have supplanted this. Shun-che, the first of the Manchow dynasty, adopted, in his second year, A.D. 1645, the style,—"K'ung, the ancient Teacher, accomplished and illustrious, all-complete, the perfect Sage;" but twelve years later, a shorter title was introduced,—"K'ung, the ancient Teacher, the perfect Sage." Since that year no further alteration has been made.

At first the worship of Confucius was confined to the country of Loo, but in A.D. 57 it was enacted that sacrifices should be offered to him in the imperial college, and in all the colleges of the principal territorial divisions throughout the empire. In those sacrifices he was for some centuries associated with the duke of Chow, the legislator to whom Confucius made frequent reference; but in A.D. 609 separate temples were assigned to them, and in 628 our sage displaced the older worthy altogether. About the same time began the custom, which continues to the present day, of erecting temples to him,—separate structures, in connection with all the colleges, or examination-halls, of the country.

The sage is not alone in those temples. In a hall behind the principal one occupied by himself are the tablets—in some cases, the images—of several of his ancestors, and other worthies; while associated with himself are his principal disciples, and many who in subsequent times have signalized themselves as expounders and exemplifiers of his doctrines. On the first day of every month, offerings of fruits and vegetables are set forth, and on the fifteenth there is a solemn burning of incense. But twice a year, in the middle months of spring and autumn, when the first "ting" day of the month comes round, the worship of Confucius is performed with peculiar solemnity. At the imperial college the emperor himself is required to attend in state, and is in fact the principal performer. After all the preliminary arrangements have been made, and the emperor has twice knelt and six times bowed his head to the earth, the presence of Confucius' spirit is invoked in the words, "Great art thou, O perfect sage! Thy virtue is full; thy doctrine is complete. Among mortal men there has not been thine equal. All kings

honour thee. Thy statutes and laws have come gloriously
down. Thou art the pattern in this imperial school. Reverently have the sacrificial vessels been set out. Full of
awe, we sound our drums and bells."

The spirit is supposed now to be present, and the service
proceeds through various offerings, when the first of which
has been set forth, an officer reads the following, which is
the prayer on the occasion :—" On this....month of this....
year, I, *A.B.*, the emperor, offer a sacrifice to the philosopher K'ung, the ancient Teacher, the perfect Sage, and
say,—O Teacher, in virtue equal to Heaven and Earth,
whose doctrines embrace the past time and the present, thou
didst digest and transmit the six classics, and didst hand
down lessons for all generations! Now in this second
month of spring (or autumn), in reverent observance of the
old statutes, with victims, silks, spirits, and fruits, I carefully offer sacrifice to thee. With thee are associated the
philosopher Yen, continuator of thee; the philosopher
Tsăng, exhibiter of thy fundamental principles; the philosopher Tsze-sze, transmitter of thee; and the philosopher
Măng, second to thee. May'st thou enjoy the offerings!"

I need not go on to enlarge on the homage which the
emperors of China render to Confucius. It could not be
more complete. It is worship and not mere homage. He
was unreasonably neglected when alive. He is now unreasonably venerated when dead. The estimation with
which the rulers of China regard their sage leads them to
sin against God, and this is a misfortune to the empire.

2. The rulers of China are not singular in this matter,
but in entire sympathy with the mass of their people. It
is the distinction of this empire that education General appreciation of Confucius.
has been highly prized in it from the earliest
times. It was so before the era of Confucius, and
we may be sure that the system met with his approbation.
One of his remarkable sayings was,—"To lead an uninstructed people to war, is to throw them away."[1] When
he pronounced this judgment, he was not thinking of
military training, but of education in the duties of life and
citizenship. A people so taught, he thought, would be
morally fitted to fight for their government. Mencius,

[1] Ana. XIII. 30.

when lecturing to the duke of T'ăng on the proper way of governing a kingdom, told him that he must provide the means of education for all, the poor as well as the rich. "Establish," said he, "hsëang, seu, hsio, and hsiao,—all those educational institutions,—for the instruction of the people."[1]

At the present day education is widely diffused throughout China. In no other country is the schoolmaster more abroad, and in all schools it is Confucius who is taught. The plan of competitive examinations, and the selection for civil offices only from those who have been successful candidates,—good so far as the competition is concerned, but injurious from the restricted range of subjects with which an acquaintance is required,—have obtained for more than twelve centuries. The classical works are the text books. It is from them almost exclusively that the themes proposed to determine the knowledge and ability of the students are chosen. The whole of the magistracy of China is thus versed in all that is recorded of the sage, and in the ancient literature which he preserved. His thoughts are familiar to every man in authority, and his character is more or less reproduced in him.

The official civilians of China, numerous as they are, are but a fraction of its students, and the students, or those who make literature a profession, are again but a fraction of those who attend school for a shorter or longer period. Yet so far as the studies have gone, they have been occupied with the Confucian writings. In many school-rooms there is a tablet or inscription on the wall, sacred to the sage, and every pupil is required, on coming to school on the morning of the first and fifteenth of every month, to bow before it, the first thing, as an act of worship.[2] Thus, all in China who receive the slightest tincture of learning do so at the fountain of Confucius. They learn of him and do homage to him at once. I have repeatedly quoted the statement that during his life-time he had three thousand disciples. Hundreds of millions are his disciples now. It

---

[1] Mencius, III. Pt. I. iii. 10.

[2] During the present dynasty, the tablet of the god of literature has to a considerable extent displaced that of Confucius in schools. Yet the worship of him does not clash with that of the other. He is "the father" of composition only.

is hardly necessary to make any allowance in this statement for the followers of Taouism and Buddhism, for, as Sir John Davis has observed, "whatever the other opinions or faith of a Chinese may be, he takes good care to treat Confucius with respect.[1] For two thousand years he has reigned supreme, the undisputed teacher of this most populous land.

3. This position and influence of Confucius are to be ascribed, I conceive, chiefly to two causes:—his being the preserver, namely, of the monuments of antiquity, and the exemplifier and expounder of the maxims of the golden age of China; and the devotion to him of his immediate disciples and their early followers. The national and the personal are thus blended in him, each in its highest degree of excellence. He was a Chinese of the Chinese; he is also represented, and all now believe him to have been, the *beau ideal* of humanity in its best and noblest estate.

The causes of his influence.

4. It may be well to bring forward here Confucius' own estimate of himself and of his doctrines. It will serve to illustrate the statements just made. The following are some of his sayings.—"The sage and the man of perfect virtue;—how dare I rank myself with them? It may simply be said of me, that I strive to become such without satiety, and teach others without weariness." "In letters I am perhaps equal to other men; but the character of the superior man, carrying out in his conduct what he professes, is what I have not yet attained to." "The leaving virtue without proper cultivation; the not thoroughly discussing what is learned; not being able to move towards righteousness of which a knowledge is gained; and not being able to change what is not good;—these are the things which occasion me solicitude." "I am not one who was born in the possession of knowledge; I am one who is fond of antiquity and earnest in seeking it there." "A transmitter and not a maker, believing in and loving the ancients, I venture to compare myself with our old P'ang."[2]

His own estimate of himself and of his doctrines.

Confucius cannot be thought to speak of himself in these

[1] "The Chinese," vol. II. p. 45.
[2] All these passages are taken from the VIIth Book of the Analects. See ch. xxxiii.; xxxii.; iii.; xix.; and i.

declarations more highly than he ought to do. Rather we may recognise in them the expressions of a genuine humility. He was conscious that personally he came short in many things, but he toiled after the character, which he saw, or fancied that he saw, in the ancient sages whom he acknowledged; and the lessons of government and morals which he laboured to diffuse were those which had already been inculcated and exhibited by them. Emphatically he was "a transmitter and not a maker." It is not to be understood that he was not fully satisfied of the truth of the principles which he had learned. He held them with the full approval and consent of his own understanding. He believed that if they were acted on, they would remedy the evils of his time. There was nothing to prevent rulers like Yaou and Shun and the great Yu from again arising, and a condition of happy tranquillity being realized throughout the empire under their sway.

If in anything he thought himself "superior and alone," having attributes which others could not claim, it was in his possessing a Divine commission as the conservator of ancient truth and rules. He does not speak very definitely on this point. It is noted that "the appointments of Heaven was one of the subjects on which he rarely touched."[1] His most remarkable utterance was that which I have already given in the sketch of his Life:— "When he was put in fear in K'wang, he said, 'After the death of King Wăn, was not the cause of truth lodged here in me? If Heaven had wished to let this cause of truth perish, then I, a future mortal, should not have got such a relation to that cause. While Heaven does not let the cause of truth perish, what can the people of K'wang do to me?'"[2] Confucius, then, did feel that he was in the world for a special purpose. But it was not to announce any new truths, or to initiate any new economy. It was to prevent what had previously been known from being lost. He followed in the wake of Yaou and Shun, of T'ang, and King Wăn. Distant from the last by a long interval of time, he would have said that he was distant from him also by a great inferiority of character, but still he had learned the principles on which they all happily governed the em-

[1] Ana. IX. i.   [2] Ana. IX. iii.

pire, and in their name he would lift up a standard against the prevailing lawlessness of his age.

5. The language employed with reference to Confucius by his disciples and their early followers presents a striking contrast with his own. I have already, in writing of the scope and value of "The Doctrine of the Mean," called attention to the extravagant eulogies of his grandson Tsze-sze. He only followed the example which had been set by those among whom the philosopher went in and out. We have the language of Yen Yuen, his favourite, which is comparatively moderate, and simply expresses the genuine admiration of a devoted pupil.[1] Tsze-kung on several occasions spoke in a different style. Having heard that one of the chiefs of Loo had said that he himself—Tsze-kung—was superior to Confucius, he observed, " Let me use the comparison of a house and its encompassing wall. My wall only reaches to the shoulders. One may peep over it, and see whatever is valuable in the apartments. The wall of my master is several fathoms high. If one do not find the door and enter by it, he cannot see the rich ancestral temple with its beauties, nor all the officers in their rich array. But I may assume that they are few who find the door. The remark of the chief was only what might have been expected."[2]

Another time, the same individual having spoken revilingly of Confucius, Tsze-kung said, " It is of no use doing so. Chung-ne cannot be reviled. The talents and virtue of other men are hillocks and mounds which may be stept over. Chung-ne is the sun or moon, which it is not possible to step over. Although a man may wish to cut himself off from the sage, what harm can he do to the sun and moon? He only shows that he does not know his own capacity."[3]

In conversation with a fellow-disciple, Tsze-kung took a still higher flight. Being charged by Tsze-k'iu with being too modest, for that Confucius was not really superior to him, he replied, " For one word a man is often deemed to be wise, and for one word he is often deemed to be foolish. We ought to be careful indeed in what we

Estimate of him by his disciples and their early followers.

---

[1] Ana. IX. x.   [2] Ana. XIX. xxiii.   [3] Ana. XIX. xxiv.

say. Our master cannot be attained to, just in the same
way as the heavens cannot be gone up to by the steps of
a stair. Were our master in the position of the prince of
a State, or the chief of a Family, we should find verified
the description which has been given of a sage's rule:—
He would plant the people, and forthwith they would be
established; he would lead them on, and forthwith they
would follow him; he would make them happy, and forthwith multitudes would resort to his dominions; he would
stimulate them, and forthwith they would be harmonious.
While he lived, he would be glorious. When he died, he
would be bitterly lamented. How is it possible for him to
be attained to?"[1]

From these representations of Tsze-kung, it was not a
difficult step for Tsze-sze to make in exalting Confucius
not only to the level of the ancient sages, but as "the
equal of Heaven." And Mencius took up the theme.
Being questioned by Kung-sun Ch'ow, one of his disciples,
about two acknowledged sages, Pih-e and E Yin, whether
they were to be placed in the same rank with Confucius,
he replied, "No. Since there were living men until now,
there never was another Confucius;" and then he proceeded to fortify his opinion by the concurring testimony
of Tsae Go, Tsze-kung, and Yew Jŏ, who all had wisdom,
he thought, sufficient to know their master. Tsae Go's
opinion was, "According to my view of our master, he is
far superior to Yaou and Shun." Tsze-kung said, "By
viewing the ceremonial ordinances of a prince, we know
the character of his government. By hearing his music,
we know the character of his virtue. From the distance
of a hundred ages after, I can arrange, according to their
merits, the kings of a hundred ages;—not one of them can
escape me. From the birth of mankind till now, there
has never been another like our master." Yew Jŏ said,
"Is it only among men that it is so? There is the k'e-
lin among quadrupeds; the fung-hwang among birds;
the T'ae mountain among mounds and ant-hills; and
rivers and seas among rain-pools. Though different in
degree, they are the same in kind. So the sages among
mankind are also the same in kind. But they stand out

[1] Ana. XIX. xxv.

from their fellows, and rise above the level; and from the birth of mankind till now, there has never been one so complete as Confucius."[1] I will not indulge in farther illustration. The judgment of the sage's disciples, of Tsze-sze, and of Mencius, has been unchallenged by the mass of the scholars of China. Doubtless it pleases them to bow down at the shrine of the sage, for their profession of literature is thereby glorified. A reflection of the honour done to him falls upon themselves. And the powers that be, and the multitudes of the people, fall in with the judgment. Confucius is thus, in the empire of China, the one man by whom all possible personal excellence was exemplified, and by whom all possible lessons of social virtue and political wisdom are taught.

6. The reader will be prepared by the preceding account not to expect to find any light thrown by Confucius on the great problems of the human condition and destiny. He did not speculate on the creation of things or the end of them. He was not troubled to account for the origin of man, nor did he seek to know about his hereafter. He meddled neither with physics nor metaphysics.[2] *Subjects on which Confucius did not treat.—That he was unreligious, unspiritual, and open to the charge of insincerity.* The testimony of the Analects about the subjects of his teaching is the following:—"His frequent themes of discourse were the Book of Poetry, the Book of History, and the maintenance of the rules of Propriety." "He taught letters, ethics, devotion of soul, and truthfulness." "Extraordinary things; feats of strength; states of disorder; and spiritual beings he did not like to talk about."[3]

Confucius is not to be blamed for his silence on the subjects here indicated. His ignorance of them was to a

[1] Mencius, II. Pt I. ii. 23—28.
[2] The contents of the Yih-king, and Confucius' labours upon it, may be objected in opposition to this statement, and I must be understood to make it with some reservation. Six years ago, I spent all my leisure time for twelve months in the study of that Work, and wrote out a translation of it, but at the close I was only groping my way in darkness to lay hold of its scope and meaning, and up to this time I have not been able to master it so as to speak positively about it. It will come in due time, in its place, in the present publication, and I do not think that what I here say of Confucius will require much, if any, modification.
[3] Ana. VII. xvii.; xxiv.; xx.

great extent his misfortune. He had not learned them. No report of them had come to him by the ear; no vision of them by the eye. And to his practical mind the toiling of thought amid uncertainties seemed worse than useless.

The question has, indeed, been raised, whether he did not make changes in the ancient creed of China,[1] but I cannot believe that he did so consciously and designedly. Had his idiosyncrasy been different, we might have had expositions of the ancient views on some points, the effect of which would have been more beneficial than the indefiniteness in which they are now left, and it may be doubted so far, whether Confucius was not unfaithful to his guides. But that he suppressed or added, in order to bring in articles of belief originating with himself, is a thing not to be charged against him.

I will mention two important subjects in regard to which there is a growing conviction in my mind that he came short of the faith of the older sages. The first is the doctrine of God. This name is common in the She-king, and Shoo-king. *Te* or *Shang Te* appears there as a personal being, ruling in heaven and on earth, the author of man's moral nature, the governor among the nations, by whom kings reign and princes decree justice, the rewarder of the good and the punisher of the bad. Confucius preferred to speak of Heaven. Instances have already been given of this. Two others may be cited:—"He who offends against Heaven has none to whom he can pray."[2] "Alas!" said he, "there is no one that knows me." Tsze-kung said, "What do you mean by thus saying that no one knows you?" He replied, "I do not murmur against Heaven. I do not grumble against men. My studies lie low, and my penetration rises high. But there is Heaven;—that knows me!"[3] Not once throughout the Analects does he use the personal name. I would say that he was unreligious rather than irreligious; yet by the coldness of his temperament and intellect in this matter, his influence is unfavourable to the development of true religious feeling among the Chinese people generally, and he prepared the way for the speculations of the literati of

---

[1] See Hardwick's "Christ and other Masters." Part III. pp. 18, 19, with his reference in a note to a passage from Meadows' "The Chinese and their Rebellions."   [2] Ana. III. xiii.   [3] Ana. XIV. xxxvii.

mediæval and modern times, which have exposed them to the charge of atheism.

Secondly, Along with the worship of God there existed in China, from the earliest historical times, the worship of other spiritual beings,—especially, and to every individual, the worship of departed ancestors. Confucius recognized this as an institution to be devoutly observed. "He sacrificed to the dead as if they were present; he sacrificed to the spirits as if the spirits were present. He said, 'I consider my not being present at the sacrifice as if I did not sacrifice.'"[1] The custom must have originated from a belief of the continued existence of the dead. We cannot suppose that they who instituted it thought that with the cessation of this life on earth there was a cessation also of all conscious being. But Confucius never spoke explicitly on this subject. He tried to evade it. "Ke Loo asked about serving the spirits of the dead, and the master said, 'While you are not able to serve men, how can you serve their spirits?' The disciple added, 'I venture to ask about death,' and he was answered, 'While you do not know life, how can you know about death.'"[2] Still more striking is a conversation with another disciple, recorded in the "Family Sayings." Tsze-kung asked him, "Do the dead have knowledge (of our services, that is), or are they without knowledge?" The master replied, "If I were to say that the dead have such knowledge, I am afraid that filial sons and dutiful grandsons would injure their substance in paying the last offices to the departed; and if I were to say that the dead have not such knowledge, I am afraid lest unfilial sons should leave their parents unburied. You need not wish, Ts'ze, to know whether the dead have knowledge or not. There is no present urgency about the point. Hereafter you will know it for yourself." Surely this was not the teaching proper to a sage. He said on one occasion that he had no concealments from his disciples.[3] Why did he not candidly tell his real thoughts on so interesting a subject? I incline to think that he doubted more than he believed. If the case were not so, it would be difficult to account for the answer which he returned to a question

---

[1] Ana. III. xii.   [2] Ana. XI. xi.   [3] Ana. VII. xxiii.

as to what constituted wisdom. "To give one's-self earnestly," said he, "to the duties due to men, and, while respecting spiritual beings, to keep aloof from them, may be called wisdom."[1] At any rate, as by his frequent references to Heaven, instead of following the phraseology of the older sages, he gave occasion to many of his professed followers to identify God with a principle of reason and the course of nature; so, in the point now in hand, he has led them to deny, like the Sadducees of old, the existence of any spirit at all, and to tell us that their sacrifices to the dead are but an outward form, the mode of expression which the principle of filial piety requires them to adopt, when its objects have departed this life.

It will not be supposed that I wish to advocate or defend the practice of sacrificing to the dead. My object has been to point out how Confucius recognized it, without acknowledging the faith from which it must have originated, and how he enforced it as a matter of form or ceremony. It thus connects itself with the most serious charge that can be brought against him,—the charge of insincerity. Among the four things which it is said he taught, "truthfulness" is specified,[2] and many sayings might be quoted from him, in which "sincerity" is celebrated as highly and demanded as stringently as ever it has been by any Christian moralist; yet he was not altogether the truthful and true man to whom we accord our highest approbation. There was the case of Măng Che-fan, who boldly brought up the rear of the defeated troops of Loo, and attributed his occupying the place of honour to the backwardness of his horse. The action was gallant, but the apology for it was weak and wrong. And yet Confucius saw nothing in the whole but matter for praise.[3] He could excuse himself from seeing an unwelcome visitor on the ground that he was sick, when there was nothing the matter with him.[4] Those perhaps were small matters, but what shall we say to the incident which I have given in the sketch of his Life,—his deliberately breaking the oath which he had sworn, simply on the ground that it had been forced from him? I should be glad if I could

[1] Ana. VI. xx.
[2] See above, near the beginning of this paragraph.
[3] Ana. VI. xiii.   [4] Ana. XVII. xx.

find evidence on which to deny the truth of that occurrence. But it rests on the same authority as most other statements about him, and it is accepted as a fact by the people and scholars of China. It must have had, and it must still have, a very injurious influence upon them. Foreigners charge, and with reason, a habit of deceitfulness upon the nation and its government. For every word of falsehood and every act of insincerity the guilty party must bear his own burden, but we cannot but regret the example of Confucius in this particular. It is with the Chinese and their sage, as it was with the Jews of old and their teachers. He that leads them has caused them to err, and destroyed the way of their paths.[1]

But was not insincerity a natural result of the unreligion of Confucius? There are certain virtues which demand a true piety in order to their flourishing in the corrupt heart of man. Natural affection, the feeling of loyalty, and enlightened policy, may do much to build up and preserve a family and a State, but it requires more to maintain the love of truth, and make a lie, spoken or acted, to be shrunk from with shame. It requires in fact the living recognition of a God of truth, and all the sanctions of revealed religion. Unfortunately the Chinese have not had these, and the example of him to whom they bow down as the best and wisest of men, encourages them to act, to dissemble, to sin.

7. I go on to a brief discussion of Confucius' views on government, or what we may call his principles of political science. It could not be in his long intercourse with his disciples but that he should enunciate many maxims bearing on character and morals generally, but he never rested in the improvement of the individual. "The empire brought to a state of happy tranquillity" was the grand object which he delighted to think of; that it might be brought about as easily as "one can look upon the palm of his hand," was the dream which it pleased him to indulge in.[2] He held that there was in men an adaptation and readiness to be governed, which only needed to be taken advantage of in the proper way. There must be the right administrators, but

His views on government.

[1] Isaiah iii. 12. [2] Ana. III. xi., *et al.*

given those, and "the growth of government would be rapid, just as vegetation is rapid in the earth; yea, their government would display itself like an easily-growing rush."[1] The same sentiment was common from the lips of Mencius. Enforcing it one day, when conversing with one of the petty princes of his time, he said in his peculiar style, "Does your Majesty understand the way of the growing grain? During the seventh and eighth months, when drought prevails, the plants become dry. Then the clouds collect densely in the heavens, they send down torrents of rain, and the grain erects itself as if by a shoot. When it does so, who can keep it back?"[2] Such, he contended, would be the response of the mass of the people to any true "shepherd of men." It may be deemed unnecessary that I should specify this point, for it is a truth applicable to the people of all nations. Speaking generally, government is by no device or cunning craftiness; human nature demands it. But in no other family of mankind is the characteristic so largely developed, as in the Chinese. The love of order and quiet, and a willingness to submit to "the powers that be," eminently distinguish them. Foreign writers have often taken notice of this, and have attributed it to the influence of Confucius' doctrines as inculcating subordination; but it existed previous to his time. The character of the people moulded his system, more than it was moulded by it.

This readiness to be governed arose, according to Confucius, from the duties of universal obligation, or those between sovereign and minister, between father and son, between husband and wife, between elder brother and younger, and those belonging to the intercourse of friends."[3] Men as they are born into the world, and grow up in it, find themselves existing in those relations. They are the appointment of Heaven. And each relation has its reciprocal obligations, the recognition of which is proper to the Heaven-conferred nature. It only needs that the sacredness of the relations be maintained, and the duties belonging to them faithfully discharged, and the "happy tranquillity" will prevail all under heaven. As to the institu-

[1] Doctrine of the Mean, xx. 3. [2] Mencius, I. Pt. I. vi. 6.
[3] Doctrine of the Mean, xx. 8.

tions of government, the laws and arrangements by which, as through a thousand channels, it should go forth to carry plenty and prosperity through the length and breadth of the country, it did not belong to Confucius, "the throneless king," to set them forth minutely. And indeed they were existing in the records of "the ancient sovereigns." Nothing new was needed. It was only requisite to pursue the old paths, and raise up the old standards. "The government of Wăn and Woo," he said, "is displayed in the records,—the tablets of wood and bamboo. Let there be the men, and the government will flourish, but without the men, the government decays and ceases."[1] To the same effect was the reply which he gave to Yen Hwuy when asked by him how the government of a State should be administered. It seems very wide of the mark, until we read it in the light of the sage's veneration for ancient ordinances, and his opinion of their sufficiency. "Follow," he said, "the seasons of Hea. Ride in the state-carriages of Yin. Wear the ceremonial cap of Chow. Let the music be the Shaou with its pantomimes. Banish the songs of Ch'ing, and keep far from specious talkers."[2]

Confucius' idea then of a happy, well-governed State did not go beyond the flourishing of the five relations of society which have been mentioned; and we have not any condensed exhibition from him of their nature, or of the duties belonging to the several parties in them. Of the two first he spoke frequently, but all that he has said on the others would go into small compass. Mencius has said that "between father and son, there should be affection; between sovereign and minister, righteousness; between husband and wife, attention to their separate functions; between old and young, a proper order; and between friends, fidelity."[3] Confucius, I apprehend, would hardly have accepted this account. It does not bring out sufficiently the authority which he claimed for the father and the sovereign, and the obedience which he exacted from the child and the minister. With regard to the relation of husband and wife, he was in no respect superior to the preceding sages who had enunciated their views of "pro-

[1] Doctrine of the Mean, xx. 2.   [2] Ana. XV. s.
[3] Mencius, III. Pt I. iv. 8.

priety" on the subject. We have a somewhat detailed exposition of his opinions in the "Family Sayings."— "Man," said he, "is the representative of Heaven, and is supreme over all things. Woman yields obedience to the instructions of man, and helps to carry out his principles. On this account she can determine nothing of herself, and is subject to the rule of the three obediences. When young, she must obey her father and elder brother; when married, she must obey her husband; when her husband is dead, she must obey her son. She may not think of marrying a second time. No instructions or orders must issue from the harem. Woman's business is simply the preparation and supplying of wine and food. Beyond the threshold of her apartments she should not be known for evil or for good. She may not cross the boundaries of the State to accompany a funeral. She may take no step on her own motion, and may come to no conclusion on her own deliberation. There are five women who are not to be taken in marriage:—the daughter of a rebellious house; the daughter of a disorderly house; the daughter of a house which has produced criminals for more than one generation; the daughter of a leprous house; and the daughter who has lost her father and elder brother. A wife may be divorced for seven reasons, which may be overruled by three considerations. The grounds for divorce are disobedience to her husband's parents; not giving birth to a son; dissolute conduct; jealousy (of her husband's attentions, that is, to the other inmates of his harem); talkativeness; and thieving. The three considerations which may overrule these grounds are—first, if, while she was taken from a home, she has now no home to return to; second, if she have passed with her husband through the three years' mourning for his parents; third, if the husband have become rich from being poor. All these regulations were adopted by the sages in harmony with the natures of man and woman, and to give importance to the ordinance of marriage."

With these ideas—not very enlarged—of the relations of society, Confucius dwelt much on the necessity of personal correctness of character on the part of those in authority, in order to secure the right fulfilment of the duties implied in them. This is one grand peculiarity of his teaching. I have adverted to it in the review of "The Great Learning," but it deserves some further exhibition, and there are three conversations with the chief Kĕ K'ang, in which it is very expressly set forth. "Kĕ K'ang asked about government, and Confucius replied, 'To govern means to rectify. If you lead on the people with correctness, who will dare not to be correct?'" "Kĕ K'ang, distressed about the number of thieves in the State, inquired of Confucius about how to do away with them. Confucius said, 'If you, sir, were not covetous, though you should reward them to do it, they would not steal.'" "Kĕ K'ang asked about government, saying, 'What do you say to killing the unprincipled for the good of the principled?' Confucius replied, 'Sir, in carrying on your government, why should you use killing at all? Let your evinced desires be for what is good, and the people will be good. The relation between superiors and inferiors is like that between the wind and the grass. The grass must bend, when the wind blows across it.'"[1]

Example is not so powerful as Confucius in these and many other passages represented it, but its influence is very great. Its virtue is recognized in the family, and it is demanded in the Church of Christ. "A bishop"—and I quote the term with the simple meaning of overseer—"must be blameless." It seems to me, however, that in the progress of society in the West we have come to think less of the power of example in many departments of State than we ought to do. It is thought of too little in the army and the navy. We laugh at the "self-denying ordinances" and the "new model" of 1644, but there lay beneath them the principle which Confucius so broadly propounded,—the importance of personal virtue in all who are in authority. Now that Great Britain is the governing power over the masses of India, and that we are coming more and more into contact with tens of thousands of the Chinese, this maxim of our sage is deserving of serious consideration from all who bear rule, and especially from those on whom devolves the conduct of

[1] Analects, XII. xvii.; xviii.; xix.

affairs. His words on the susceptibility of the people to be acted on by those above them, ought not to prove as water spilt on the ground.

But to return to Confucius.—As he thus lays it down that the mainspring of the well-being of society is the personal character of the ruler, we look anxiously for what directions he has given for the cultivation of that. But here he is very defective. "Self-adjustment and purification," he said, "with careful regulation of his dress, and the not making a movement contrary to the rules of propriety;—this is the way for the ruler to cultivate his person."[1] This is laying too much stress on what is external; but even to attain to this is beyond unassisted human strength. Confucius, however, never recognized a disturbance of the moral elements in the constitution of man. The people would move, according to him, to the virtue of their ruler as the grass bends to the wind, and that virtue would come to the ruler at his call. Many were the lamentations which he uttered over the degeneracy of his times; frequent were the confessions which he made of his own shortcomings. It seems strange that it never came distinctly before him, that there is a power of evil in the prince and the peasant, which no efforts of their own and no instructions of sages are effectual to subdue.

The government which Confucius taught was a despotism, but of a modified character. He allowed no "*jus divinum*," independent of personal virtue and a benevolent rule. He has not explicitly stated, indeed, wherein lies the ground of the great relation of the governor and the governed, but his views on the subject were, we may assume, in accordance with the language of the Shoo-king:— "Heaven and Earth are the parents of all things, and of all things men are the most intelligent. The man among them most distinguished for intelligence becomes chief ruler, and ought to prove himself the parent of the people."[2] And again, "Heaven, protecting the inferior people, has constituted for them rulers and teachers, who should be able to be assisting to God, extending favour and producing tranquillity throughout all parts of the empire."[2] The

---

[1] Doctrine of the Mean, xx. 14.
[2] See the Shoo-king, V. i. Sect. I. 2, 7.

moment the ruler ceases to be a minister of God for good, and does not administer a government that is beneficial to the people, he forfeits the title by which he holds the throne, and perseverance in oppression will surely lead to his overthrow. Mencius inculcated this principle with a frequency and boldness which are remarkable. It was one of the things about which Confucius did not like to talk. Still he held it. It is conspicuous in the last chapter of "The Great Learning." Its tendency has been to check the violence of oppression, and to maintain the self-respect of the people, all along the course of Chinese history.

I must bring these observations on Confucius' views of government to a close, and I do so with two remarks. First, they are adapted to a primitive, unsophisticated state of society. He is a good counsellor for the father of a family, the chief of a clan, and even the head of a small principality. But his views want the comprehension which would make them of much service in a great empire. Within three centuries after his death, the government of China passed into a new phase. The founder of the Ts'in dynasty conceived the grand idea of abolishing all its feudal Kingdoms, and centralizing their administration in himself. He effected the revolution, and succeeding dynasties adopted his system, and gradually moulded it into the forms and proportions which are now existing. There has been a tendency to advance, and Confucius has all along been trying to carry the nation back. Principles have been needed, and not "proprieties." The consequence is that China has increased beyond its ancient dimensions, while there has been no corresponding development of thought. Its body politic has the size of a giant, while it still retains the mind of a child. Its hoary age is but senility.

Second, Confucius makes no provision for the intercourse of his country with other and independent nations. He knew indeed of none such. China was to him "The middle Kingdom," "The multitude of Great States," "All under heaven." Beyond it were only rude and barbarous tribes. He does not speak of them bitterly, as many Chinese have done since his time. In one place he contrasts them favourably with the prevailing anarchy of the empire, saying, "The rude tribes of the east and north have their princes, and are not like the States of our great land which are without them."[1] Another time, disgusted with the want of appreciation which he experienced, he was expressing his intention to go and live among the nine wild tribes of the east. Some one said, "They are rude. How can you do such a thing?" His reply was, "If a superior man dwelt among them, what rudeness would there be?"[2] But had he been an emperor-sage, he would not only have influenced them by his instructions, but brought them to acknowledge and submit to his sway, as the great Yu did. The only passage of Confucius' teachings from which any rule can be gathered for dealing with foreigners, is that in the "Doctrine of the Mean," where "indulgent treatment of men from a distance" is laid down as one of the nine standard rules for the government of the empire. But "the men from a distance" are understood to be *pin* and *leu* simply,—"guests," that is, or officers of one State seeking employment in another, or at the imperial court; and "visitors," or travelling merchants. Of independent nations the ancient classics have not any knowledge, nor has Confucius. So long as merchants from Europe and other parts of the world could have been content to appear in China as suppliants, seeking the privilege of trade, so long the government would have ranked them with the barbarous hordes of antiquity, and given them the benefit of the maxim about "indulgent treatment," according to its own understanding of it. But when their governments interfered, and claimed to treat with that of China on terms of equality, and that their subjects should be spoken to and of as being of the same clay with the Chinese themselves, an outrage was committed on tradition and prejudice, which it was necessary to resent with vehemence.

I do not charge the contemptuous arrogance of the Chinese government and people upon Confucius; what I deplore is, that he left no principles on record to check the development of such a spirit. His simple views of society and government were in a measure sufficient for the people, while they dwelt apart from the rest of mankind. His practical lessons were better than if they had been left, which but for him they probably would have

---

[1] Ana. III. v. [2] Ana. IX. xiii.

been, to fall a prey to the influences of Taouism and Buddhism; but they could only subsist while they were left alone. Of the earth earthy, China was sure to go to pieces when it came into collision with a Christianly-civilized power. Its sage had left it no preservative or restorative elements against such a case.

It is a rude awakening from its complacency of centuries which China has now received. Its ancient landmarks are swept away. Opinions will differ as to the justice or injustice of the grounds on which it has been assailed, and I do not feel called to judge or to pronounce here concerning them. In the progress of events, it could not be but that the collision should come; and when it did come, it could not be but that China should be broken and scattered. Disorganization will go on to destroy it more and more, and yet there is hope for the people, with their veneration of the relations of society, with their devotion to learning, and with their habits of industry and sobriety;—there is hope for them, if they will look away from all their ancient sages, and turn to Him, who sends them, along with the dissolution of their ancient state, the knowledge of Himself, the only living and true God, and of Jesus Christ whom He hath sent.

8. I have little more to add on the opinions of Confucius. Many of his sayings are pithy, and display much knowledge of character; but as they are contained in the body of the Work, I will not occupy the space here with a selection of those which have struck myself as most worthy of notice. The fourth Book of the Analects, which is on the subject of *jin*, or perfect virtue, has several utterances which are remarkable.

Thornton observes:—"It may excite surprise, and probably incredulity, to state that the golden rule of our Saviour, 'Do unto others as you would that they should do unto you,' which Mr Locke designates as 'the most unshaken rule of morality, and foundation of all social virtue,' had been inculcated by Confucius, almost in the same words, four centuries before."[1] I have taken notice of this fact in reviewing both "The Great Learning," and "The Doctrine of the Mean," and would be far from

History of China, vol. i. p. 209.

grudging a tribute of admiration to Confucius for it. The maxim occurs also twice in the Analects. In Book XV. xxiii., Tsze-kung asks if there be one word which may serve as a rule of practice for all one's life, and is answered, "Is not reciprocity such a word? What you do not want done to yourself do not do to others." The same disciple appears in Book V. xi., telling Confucius that he was practising the lesson. He says, "What I do not wish men to do to me, I also wish not to do to men;" but the master tells him, "Ts'ze, you have not attained to that." It would appear from this reply, that he was aware of the difficulty of obeying the precept; and it is not found, in its condensed expression at least, in the older classics. The merit of it is Confucius' own.

When a comparison, however, is drawn between it and the rule laid down by Christ, it is proper to call attention to the positive form of the latter,—"All things whatsoever ye would that men should do unto you, do ye even so to them." The lesson of the gospel commands men to do what they feel to be right and good. It requires them to commence a course of such conduct, without regard to the conduct of others to themselves. The lesson of Confucius only forbids men to do what they feel to be wrong and hurtful. So far as the point of priority is concerned, moreover, Christ adds, "This is the law and the prophets." The maxim was to be found substantially in the earlier revelations of God.

But the worth of the two maxims depends on the intention of the enunciators in regard to their application. Confucius, it seems to me, did not think of the reciprocity coming into action beyond the circle of his five relations of society. Possibly, he might have required its observance in dealings even with the rude tribes, which were the only specimens of mankind besides his own countrymen of which he knew anything, for on one occasion, when asked about perfect virtue, he replied, "It is, in retirement, to be sedately grave; in the management of business, to be reverently attentive; in intercourse with others, to be strictly sincere. Though a man go among the rude uncultivated tribes, these qualities may not be neglected."[1]

[1] Analects, XIII. xix.

Still, Confucius delivered his rule to his countrymen only, and only for their guidance in their relations of which I have had so much occasion to speak. The rule of Christ is for man as man, having to do with other men, all with himself on the same platform, as the children and subjects of the one God and Father in heaven.

How far short Confucius came of the standard of Christian benevolence, may be seen from his remarks when asked what was to be thought of the principle that injury should be recompensed with kindness. He replied, "With what then will you recompense kindness? Recompense injury with justice, and recompense kindness with kindness."[1] The same deliverance is given in one of the Books of the Lo Ke, where he adds that "He who recompenses injury with kindness is a man who is careful of his person." Ch'ing Heuen, the commentator of the second century, says that such a course would be "incorrect in point of propriety." This "propriety" was a great stumbling-block in the way of Confucius. His morality was the result of the balancings of his intellect, fettered by the decisions of men of old, and not the gushings of a loving heart, responsive to the promptings of Heaven, and in sympathy with erring and feeble humanity.

This subject leads me on to the last of the opinions of Confucius which I shall make the subject of remark in this place. A commentator observes, with reference to the inquiry about recompensing injury with kindness, that the questioner was asking only about trivial matters, which might be dealt with in the way he mentioned, while great offences, such as those against a sovereign or a father, could not be dealt with by such an inversion of the principles of justice. In the second Book of the Le Ke there is the following passage:—"With the slayer of his father, a man may not live under the same heaven; against the slayer of his brother, a man must never have to go home to fetch a weapon; with the slayer of his friend, a man may not live in the same State." The *lex talionis* is here laid down in its fullest extent. The Chow Le tells us of a provision made against the evil consequences of the prin-

[1] Ana. XXV. xxxvi.

ciple, by the appointment of a minister called "The Reconciler." The provision is very inferior to the cities of refuge which were set apart by Moses for the manslayer to flee to from the fury of the avenger. Such as it was, however, it existed, and it is remarkable that Confucius, when consulted on the subject, took no notice of it, but affirmed the duty of blood-revenge in the strongest and most unrestricted terms. His disciple Tsze-hea asked him, "What course is to be pursued in the case of the murder of a father or mother?" He replied, "The son must sleep upon a matting of grass, with his shield for his pillow; he must decline to take office; he must not live under the same heaven with the slayer. When he meets him in the market-place or the court, he must have his weapon ready to strike him." "And what is the course on the murder of a brother?" "The surviving brother must not take office in the same State with the slayer; yet if he go on his prince's service to the State where the slayer is, though he meet him, he must not fight with him." "And what is the course on the murder of an uncle or a cousin?" "In this case the nephew or cousin is not the principal. If the principal on whom the revenge devolves can take it, he has only to stand behind with his weapon in his hand, and support him."

Sir John Davis has rightly called attention to this as one of the objectionable principles of Confucius.[1] The bad effects of it are evident even in the present day. Revenge is sweet to the Chinese. I have spoken of their readiness to submit to government, and wish to live in peace, yet they do not like to resign even to government the "inquisition for blood." Where the ruling authority is feeble, as it is at present, individuals and clans take the law into their own hands, and whole districts are kept in a state of constant feud and warfare.

But I must now leave the sage. I hope I have not done him injustice; but after long study of his character and opinions, I am unable to regard him as a great man. He was not before his age, though he was above the mass of the officers and scholars of his time. He threw no new light on any of the questions which have a world-wide

[1] The Chinese, vol. II. p. 41.

interest. He gave no impulse to religion. He had no sympathy with progress. His influence has been wonderful, but it will henceforth wane. My opinion is, that the faith of the nation in him will speedily and extensively pass away.

CONFUCIAN ANALECTS.

BOOK I.

CHAPTER I. 1. The Master said, "Is it not pleasant to learn with a constant perseverance and application?

2. "Is it not delightful to have friends coming from distant quarters?

3. "Is he not a man of complete virtue, who feels no discomposure though men may take no note of him?"

TITLE OF THE WORK.—Literally, "Discourses and Dialogues;" that is, the discourses or discussions of Confucius with his disciples and others on various topics, and his replies to their inquiries. Many chapters, however, and one whole book, are the sayings, not of the sage himself, but of some of his disciples. The characters may also be rendered "Digested Conversations," and this appears to be the more ancient signification attached to them, the account being, that, after the death of Confucius, his disciples collected together and compared the memoranda of his conversations which they had severally preserved, digesting them into the twenty books which compose the work. I have styled the work "Confucian Analects," as being more descriptive of its character than any other name I could think of.

HEADING AND SUBJECTS OF THIS BOOK. The two first characters, literally, "To learn and —" after the introductory—"The Master said," are adopted as its heading. This is similar to the custom of the Jews, who name many books in the Bible from the first word in them. In some of the books we find a unity or analogy of subjects, which evidently guided the compilers in grouping the chapters together. Others seem devoid of any such principle of combination. The sixteen chapters of this book are occupied, it is said, with the fundamental subjects which ought to engage the attention of the learner, and the great matters of human practice. The word "*learn*" rightly occupies the forefront in the studies of a nation, of which its educational system has so long been the distinction and glory.

1. THE WHOLE WORK AND ACHIEVEMENT OF THE LEARNER, FIRST PERFECTING HIS KNOWLEDGE, THEN ATTRACTING BY HIS FAME LIKEMINDED INDIVIDUALS, AND FINALLY COMPLETE IN HIMSELF. 1. "The Master" here is Confucius; but if we render the original term by "Confucius," as all preceding translators have done, we miss the indication which it gives of the

II. 1. Yew the philosopher said, "They are few who, being filial and fraternal, are fond of offending against their superiors. There have been none, who, not liking to offend against their superiors, have been fond of stirring up confusion.

2. "The superior man bends his attention to what is radical. That being established, all right practical courses naturally grow up. Filial piety and fraternal submission!—are they not the root of all benevolent actions?"

III. The Master said, "Fine words and an insinuating appearance are seldom associated with true virtue."

IV. Tsăng the philosopher said, "I daily examine myself on three points:—whether, in transacting business for others, I may have been not faithful;—whether, in intercourse with friends, I may have been not sincere;—whether I may have not mastered and practised the instructions of my teacher."

handiwork of his disciples, and the reverence which it bespeaks for him. Some years ago, an able Chinese scholar published a collection of moral sayings by David, Solomon, Paul, Augustine, Jesus, Confucius, &c. To the sayings of the others he prefixed their names, and to those of Confucius the phrase of the text,—"The Master said," thus telling his readers that he was himself a disciple of the sage, and exalting him above Solomon, and every other name which he introduced, even above Jesus himself!

2. The "Friends" here are not relatives, nor even old and intimate acquaintances; but individuals of the same style of mind as the subject of the paragraph,—students of truth and friends of virtue.

3. The "man of complete virtue" is, literally, "a princely man." The phrase is a technical one with Chinese moral writers, for which there is no exact correspondency in English. We cannot always translate it in the same way.

2. FILIAL PIETY AND FRATERNAL SUBMISSION ARE THE FOUNDATION OF ALL VIRTUOUS PRACTICE. 1. Yew was a native of Loo, and famed among the other disciples of Confucius for his strong memory, and love for the doctrines of antiquity. In personal appearance he resembled the sage. See Mencius, III. Pt. II. iv. 13. There is a peculiarity in the style—"Yew, the philosopher," the title following the surname, which has made some Chinese critics assign an important part in the compilation of the Analects to his disciples; but the matter is too slight to build such a conclusion on. The tablet to Yew's spirit is in the same apartment of the sage's temples as that of the sage himself, among the "wise ones" of his followers.

3. FAIR APPEARANCES ARE SUSPICIOUS.

4. HOW THE PHILOSOPHER TSĂNG DAILY EXAMINED HIMSELF, TO GUARD AGAINST HIS BEING GUILTY OF ANY SELF-DECEPTION. Tsăng was one of the principal disciples of Confucius. A follower of the sage

V. The Master said, "To rule a country of a thousand chariots, there must be reverent attention to business, and sincerity; economy in expenditure, and love for the people; and the employment of them at the proper seasons."

VI. The Master said, "A youth, when at home, should be filial, and, abroad, respectful to his elders. He should be earnest and truthful. He should overflow in love to all, and cultivate the friendship of the good. When he has time and opportunity, after the performance of these things, he should employ them in polite studies."

VII. Tsze-hea said, "If a man withdraws his mind from the love of beauty, and applies it as sincerely to the love of the virtuous; if, in serving his parents, he can exert his utmost strength; if, in serving his prince, he can devote his life; if, in his intercourse with his friends, his words are sincere:—although men say that he has not learned, I will certainly say that he has."

from his 16th year, though inferior in natural ability to some others, by his filial piety and other moral qualities he entirely won the Master's esteem, and by persevering attention mastered his doctrines. Confucius employed him in the composition of the Classic of Filial Piety. The authorship of the "Great Learning" is also ascribed to him, though incorrectly, as we shall see. Ten books, moreover, of his composition are preserved in the Le Ke. His spirit tablet, among the sage's four assessors, has precedence of that of Mencius. There is the same peculiarity in the designation of him here, which I have pointed out under the last chapter in connection with the style—" Yew, the philosopher;" and a similar conclusion has been argued from it.

5. FUNDAMENTAL PRINCIPLES FOR THE GOVERNMENT OF A LARGE STATE. "A country of a thousand chariots" was one of the largest fiefs of the empire,—a state which could bring such a force into the field.— The last principle means that the people should not be called away from their husbandry at improper seasons to do service on military expeditions and public works.

6. DUTY FIRST AND THEN ACCOMPLISHMENTS. "Polite duties" are not *literary studies* merely, but all the accomplishments of a gentleman also: ceremonies, music, archery, horsemanship, writing, and numbers.

7. TSZE-HEA'S VIEWS OF THE SUBSTANCE OF LEARNING. Tsze-hea was another of the sage's distinguished disciples, and now placed among the " wise ones." He was greatly famed for his learning, and his views on the *She-king* and the *Ch'un Ts'ew* are said to be preserved in the commentary of Maou, and of Kung-yang Kaou, and Kuh-leang Ch'ih. He wept himself blind on the death of his son, but lived to a great age, and was much esteemed by the people and princes of the time. With regard to the scope of this chapter, there is some truth in what the commentator Woo

VIII. 1. The Master said, "If the scholar be not grave, he will not call forth any veneration, and his learning will not be solid.
2. "Hold faithfulness and sincerity as first principles.
3. "Have no friends not equal to yourself.
4. "When you have faults, do not fear to abandon them."

IX. Tsäng the philosopher said, "Let there be a careful attention to perform the funeral rites to parents when dead, and let them be followed when long gone *with the ceremonies of sacrifice;*—then the virtue of the people will resume its proper excellence."

X. 1. Tsze-k'in asked Tsze-kung, saying, "When our Master comes to any country, he does not fail to learn all about its government. Does he ask his information? or is it given to him?"
2. Tsze-kung said, "Our Master is benign, upright, courteous, temperate, and complaisant, and thus he gets his information. The Master's mode of asking information!—is it not different from that of other men?"

XI. The Master said, "While a man's father is alive, look at the bent of his will; when his father is dead, look at his conduct. If for three years he does not alter from the way of his father, he may be called filial."

says,—that Tsze-hea's words may be wrested to depreciate learning, while those of the Master in the preceding chapter hit exactly the due medium.
8. PRINCIPLES OF SELF-CULTIVATION.
9. THE GOOD EFFECT OF ATTENTION ON THE PART OF PRINCES TO THE OFFICES TO THE DEAD:—AN ADMONITION OF TSÄNG SIN. This is a counsel to princes and all in authority. The effect which it is supposed would follow from their following it is an instance of the influence of example, of which so much is made by Chinese moralists.
10. CHARACTERISTICS OF CONFUCIUS, AND THEIR INFLUENCE ON THE PRINCES OF THE TIME.
1. Tsze-k'in and Tsze-k'ang are designations of Ch'in K'ang, one of the minor disciples of Confucius. His tablet is in the outer hall of the temples. A good story is related of him. On the death of his brother, his wife and major-domo wished to bury some living persons with him, to serve him in the regions below. The thing being referred to Tsze-k'in, he proposed that the wife and steward should themselves submit to the immolation, which made them stop the matter. Tsze-kung, with the double surname Twan-muh, and named-Ts'ze, occupies a higher place in the Confucian ranks, and is now among the "wise ones." He is conspicuous in this work for his readiness and smartness in reply, and displayed on several occasions practical and political ability.
11. ON FILIAL DUTY. It is to be understood that the way of the

XII. 1. Yew the philosopher said, "In practising the rules of propriety, a natural ease is to be prized. In the ways prescribed by the ancient kings, this is the excellent quality; and in things small and great we should *thus* follow those *rules*.

2. "Yet it is not to be observed in all cases. If one, knowing *how* such ease *should be prized*, manifests it, without regulating it by the rules of propriety, this likewise is not to be done."

XIII. Yew the philosopher said, "When agreements are made according to what is right, what is spoken can be made good. When respect is shown according to what is proper, one keeps far from shame and disgrace. When the parties upon whom a man leans are proper persons to be intimate with, he can make them his guides and masters."

XIV. The Master said, "He who aims to be a man of complete virtue, in his food does not seek to gratify his appetite, nor in his dwelling-place does he seek the appliances of ease: he is earnest in what he is doing, and careful in his speech; he frequents the company of men of principle that he may be rectified:—such a person may be said indeed to love to learn."

XV. 1. Tsze-kung said, "What do you pronounce concerning the poor man who yet does not flatter, and the rich man who is not proud?" The Master replied, "They will do; but they are not equal to him, who, though poor, is yet cheerful, and to him, who, though rich, loves the rules of propriety."

father had not been very bad. An old interpretation, that the three years are to be understood of the three years of mourning for the father, is now rightly rejected.

12. IN CEREMONIES A NATURAL EASE IS TO BE PRIZED, AND YET TO BE SUBORDINATE TO THE END OF CEREMONIES,—THE REVERENTIAL OBSERVANCE OF PROPRIETY. The term here rendered " rules of propriety," is not easily rendered in another language. There underlies it the idea of *what is proper*. It is "the fitness of things," what reason calls for in the performance of duties towards superior beings, and between man and man. Our term " ceremonies" would come near its meaning here.

13. TO SAVE FROM FUTURE REPENTANCE, WE MUST BE CAREFUL IN OUR FIRST STEPS.

14. WITH WHAT MIND ONE AIMING TO BE A KEUN-TSZE PURSUES HIS LEARNING.

15. AN ILLUSTRATION OF THE SUCCESSIVE STEPS IN SELF-CULTI-

2. Tsze-kung replied, "It is said in the Book of Poetry, 'As you cut and then file, as you carve and then polish.' —The meaning is the same, I apprehend, as that which you have just expressed."

3. The Master said, "With one like Tsze, I can begin to talk about the Odes. I told him one point, and he knew its proper sequence."

XVI. The Master said, "I will not be afflicted at men's not knowing me; I will be afflicted that I do not know men."

BOOK II.

CHAPTER I. The Master said, "He who exercises government by means of his virtue, may be compared to the north polar star, which keeps its place and all the stars turn towards it."

II. The Master said, "In the Book of Poetry are three hundred pieces, but the design of them all may be embraced in *that* one sentence—'Have no depraved thoughts.'"

VATION. 1. Tsze-kung had been poor, and then did not cringe. He became rich, and was not proud. He asked Confucius about the style of character to which he had attained. Confucius allowed its worth, but sent him to higher attainments. 2. The ode quoted is the first of the songs of Wei, praising the prince Woo, who had dealt with himself as an ivory-worker who first cuts the bone, and then files it smooth; or a lapidary whose hammer and chisel are followed by all the appliances for smoothing and polishing. See the She-king, Pt I. Bk v. i. 1.

16. PERSONAL ATTAINMENT SHOULD BE OUR CHIEF AIM.

HEADING AND SUBJECTS OF THIS BOOK. This second book contains twenty-four chapters, and is named "The practice of government." That is the object to which learning, treated of in the last book, should lead; and here we have the qualities which constitute, and the character of the men who administer. good government.

1. THE INFLUENCE OF VIRTUE IN A RULER. Choo He's view of the comparison is that it sets forth the illimitable influence which virtue in a ruler exercises without his using any effort. This is extravagant. His opponents say that virtue is the polar star, and the various departments of government the other stars. This is far-fetched. We must be content to accept the vague utterance without minutely determining its meaning.

2. THE PURE DESIGN OF THE BOOK OF POETRY. The number of compositions in the She-king is rather more than the round number here given. "Have no depraved thoughts,"—see the She-king, IV. ii. 1. st. 4.

III. 1. The Master said, "If the people be led by laws, and uniformity sought to be given them by punishments, they will try to avoid the punishment, but have no sense of shame.

2. "If they be led by virtue, and uniformity sought to be given them by the rules of propriety, they will have the sense of shame, and moreover will become good."

IV. 1. The Master said, "At fifteen, I had my mind bent on learning.

2. "At thirty, I stood firm.

3. "At forty, I had no doubts.

4. "At fifty, I knew the decrees of heaven.

5. "At sixty, my ear was an obedient organ *for the reception of truth.*

6. "At seventy, I could follow what my heart desired, without transgressing what was right."

V. 1. Măng I asked what filial piety was. The Master said, "It is not being disobedient."

2. *Soon after,* as Fan Ch'e was driving him, the Master told him, saying, "Măng-sun asked me what filial piety was, and I answered him—'Not being disobedient.'"

The sentence there is indicative, and in praise of one of the dukes of Loo, who had no depraved thoughts. The sage would seem to have been intending his own design in compiling the *She.* Individual pieces are calculated to have a different effect.

3. HOW RULERS SHOULD PREFER MORAL APPLIANCES.

4. CONFUCIUS' OWN ACCOUNT OF HIS GRADUAL PROGRESS AND ATTAINMENTS. Chinese commentators are perplexed with this chapter. Holding of Confucius, that "He was born with knowledge, and did what was right with entire ease," they say that he here conceals his sagehood, and puts himself on the level of common men, to set before them a stimulating example. We may believe that the compilers of the Analects, the sage's immediate disciples, did not think of him so extravagantly as later men have done. It is to be wished, however, that he had been more definite and diffuse in his account of himself. 1. The "learning," to which, at the age of fifteen, Confucius gave himself, is to be understood of the subjects of the "Superior Learning." See Chou He's preliminary essay to the Ta Hëŏ. 2. The "standing firm" probably indicates that he no more needed to bend his will. 3. The "no doubts" may have been concerning what was proper in all circumstances and events. 4. "The decrees of Heaven," the constitution of things making what was proper to be so. 5. "The ear obedient" is the mind receiving, as by intuition, the truth from the ear.

5. FILIAL PIETY MUST BE SHOWN ACCORDING TO THE RULES OF PROPRIETY. 1. Măng I was a great officer of the state of Loo, by name Ho-ke, and the chief of one of the three great families by which in the

3. Fan Ch'e said, "What did you mean?" The Master replied, "That parents, when alive, should be served according to propriety; that when dead, they should be buried according to propriety; and that they should be sacrificed to according to propriety."

VI. Mǎng Woo asked what filial piety was. The Master said, "Parents are anxious lest their children should be sick."

VII. Tsze-yew asked what filial piety was. The Master said, "The filial piety of now-a-days means the support of one's parents. But dogs and horses likewise are able to do something in the way of support;—without reverence, what is there to distinguish the one support given from the other?"

VIII. Tsze-hea asked what filial piety was. The Master said, "The difficulty is with the countenance. If, when *their elders* have any *troublesome* affairs, the young take the toil of them, and if, when *the young* have wine and food, they set them before their elders, is THIS to be considered filial piety?"

time of Confucius the authority of that state was grasped. Those families were descended from three brothers, the sons by a concubine of the Duke Hwan (B.C. 710—693). E, which means "mild and virtuous," was the posthumous honorary title given to Ho-ke. Fan Ch'e was a minor disciple of the sage. Confucius repeated his remark to Fan, that he might report the explanation of it to his friend Mǎng E, and thus prevent him from supposing that all the sage intended was disobedience to parents.

6. THE ANXIETY OF PARENTS ABOUT THEIR CHILDREN AN ARGUMENT FOR FILIAL PIETY. This enigmatical sentence has been interpreted in two ways. Choo He takes it thus:—" Parents have the sorrow of thinking anxiously about their—i. e. their children's—being unwell. Therefore children should take care of their persons." The old commentators interpreted differently: in the sense of "only." "Let parents have only the sorrow of their children's illness. Let them have no other occasion for sorrow. This will be filial piety." Mǎng Woo (the hon. epithet= "Bold and of straightforward principle,") was the son of Mǎng E, of the last chapter.

7. HOW THERE MUST BE REVERENCE IN FILIAL DUTY. Tsze-yew was the designation of Yen Yen, a native of Woo, and distinguished among the disciples of Confucius for his knowledge of the rules of propriety, and for his learning. He is now among the "wise ones." Choo He gives a different turn to the sentiment. "But dogs and horses likewise manage to get their support." The other and older interpretation is better.

8. THE DUTIES OF FILIAL PIETY MUST BE PERFORMED WITH A CHEERFUL COUNTENANCE. To the different interrogatories here recorded about filial duty, the sage, we are told, made answer according to the character of the questioner, as each one needed instruction.

IX. The Master said, "I have talked with Hwuy for a whole day, and he has not made any objection to anything I said;—as if he were stupid. He has retired, and I have examined his conduct when away from me, and found him able to illustrate my teachings. Hwuy! He is not stupid."

X. 1. The Master said, "See what a man does.
2. "Mark his motives.
3. "Examine in what things he rests.
4. "How can a man conceal his character!
5. "How can a man conceal his character!"

XI. The Master said, "If a man keeps cherishing his old knowledge so as continually to be acquiring new, he may be a teacher of others."

XII. The Master said, "The accomplished scholar is not an utensil."

XIII. Tsze-kung asked what constituted the superior man. The Master said, "He acts before he speaks, and afterwards speaks according to his actions."

XIV. The Master said, "The superior man is catholic and no partizan. The mean man is a partizan and not catholic."

XV. The Master said, "Learning without thought is labour lost; thought without learning is perilous."

XVI. The Master said, "The study of strange doctrines is injurious indeed!"

9. THE QUIET RECEPTIVITY OF THE DISCIPLE HWUY. Yen Hwuy was Confucius' favourite disciple, and is now honoured with the first place east among his four assessors in his temples, with the title of "The second sage, the philosopher Yen." At the age of twenty-nine, his hair was entirely white; and at thirty-three, he died, to the excessive grief of the sage.
10. HOW TO DETERMINE THE CHARACTERS OF MEN.
11. TO BE ABLE TO TEACH OTHERS ONE MUST FROM HIS OLD STORES BE CONTINUALLY DEVELOPING THINGS NEW.
12. THE GENERAL APTITUDE OF THE SUPERIOR MAN. This is not like our English saying, that "such a man is a machine,"—a blind instrument. An utensil has its particular use. It answers for that and no other. Not so with the superior man, who is *ad omnia paratus*.
13. HOW WITH THE SUPERIOR MAN WORDS FOLLOW ACTIONS. The reply is literally: "He first acts his words, and afterwards follows them."
14. THE DIFFERENCE BETWEEN THE SUPERIOR MAN AND THE SMALL MAN. The sentence is this—"With the superior man, it is principles not men; with the small man, the reverse."
15. IN LEARNING, READING AND THOUGHT MUST BE COMBINED.
16. STRANGE DOCTRINES ARE NOT TO BE STUDIED. In Confucius' time

XVII. The Master said, "Yew, shall I teach you what knowledge is? When you know a thing, to hold that you know it; and when you do not know a thing, to allow that you do not know it;—this is knowledge."

XVIII. 1. Tsze-chang was learning with a view to official emolument.

2. The Master said, "Hear much and put aside the points of which you stand in doubt, while you speak cautiously at the same time of the others:—then you will afford few occasions for blame. See much and put aside the things which seem perilous, while you are cautious at the same time in carrying the others into practice:—then you will have few occasions for repentance. When one gives few occasions for blame in his words, and few occasions for repentance in his conduct, he is in the way to get emolument."

XIX. The Duke Gae asked, saying, "What should be done in order to secure the submission of the people?" Confucius replied, "Advance the upright and set aside the crooked, then the people will submit. Advance the crooked and set aside the upright, then the people will not submit."

Buddhism was not in China, and we can hardly suppose him to intend Taouism. Indeed, we are ignorant to what doctrines he referred, but his maxim is of general application.

17. THERE SHOULD BE NO PRETENCE IN THE PROFESSION OF KNOWLEDGE, OR THE DENIAL OF IGNORANCE. Yew, by surname Chung, and generally known by his designation of Tsze-loo, was one of the most famous disciples of Confucius, and now occupies in the temples the fourth place east in the sage's own hall, among the "wise ones." He was noted for his courage and forwardness, a man of impulse rather than reflection. Confucius had foretold that he would come to an untimely end, and so it happened. He was killed through his own rashness in a revolution in the state of Wei. The tassel of his cap being cut off when he received his death-wound, he quoted a saying:—"The superior man must not die without his cap," tied on the tassel, adjusted the cap, and expired.

18. THE END IN LEARNING SHOULD BE ONE'S OWN IMPROVEMENT, AND NOT EMOLUMENT. Tsze-chang, named See, with the double surname Chuen-sun, a native of Ch'in, was not undistinguished in the Confucian school. Tsze-kung praised him as a man of merit without boasting, humble in a high position, and not arrogant to the helpless. From this chapter, however, it would appear that inferior motives did sometimes rule him.

19. HOW A PRINCE BY THE RIGHT EMPLOYMENT OF HIS OFFICERS MAY SECURE THE REAL SUBMISSION OF HIS SUBJECTS. Gae was the honorary epithet of Tseang, Duke of Loo (B.C. 494—467). Confucius died in his sixteenth year. According to the laws for posthumous titles, Gae denotes

XX. Ke K'ang asked how to cause the people to reverence *their ruler*, to be faithful to him, and to urge themselves to virtue. The Master said, "Let him preside over them with gravity;—then they will reverence him. Let him be filial and kind to all;—then they will be faithful to him. Let him advance the good and teach the incompetent;—then they will eagerly seek to be virtuous."

XXI. 1. Some one addressed Confucius, saying, "Sir, why are you not engaged in the government?"

2. The Master said, "What does the Shoo-king say of filial piety?—'You are filial, you discharge your brotherly duties. These qualities are displayed in government.' This then also constitutes the exercise of government. Why must there be THAT to make one be in the government?"

XXII. The Master said, "I do not know how a man without truthfulness is to get on. How can a large carriage be made to go without the cross bar for yoking the oxen to, or a small carriage without the arrangement for yoking the horses?"

XXIII. 1. Tsze-chang asked whether *the affairs of* ten ages *after* could be known.

" the respectful and benevolent, early cut off," and Duke Gne, " The to-be-lamented duke."

20. EXAMPLE IN SUPERIORS IS MORE POWERFUL THAN FORCE. K'ang, "easy and pleasant, people-soother," was the honorary epithet of Ke-sun Fei, the head of one of the three great families of Loo; see ch. 5. His idea is seen in " to cause," the power of force ; that of Confucius appears in " then," the power of influence.

21. CONFUCIUS' EXPLANATION OF HIS NOT BEING IN ANY OFFICE. 1. "Confucius" is here "K'ung, the philosopher," the surname indicating that the questioner was not a disciple. He had his reason for not being in office at the time, but it was not expedient to tell. He replied, therefore, as in par. 2. See the Shoo-king, v. xxi. 1. But the text is neither correctly applied nor exactly quoted. A western may think that the philosopher might have made a happier evasion.

22. THE NECESSITY TO A MAN OF BEING TRUTHFUL AND SINCERE.

23. THE GREAT PRINCIPLES GOVERNING SOCIETY ARE UNCHANGEABLE. 1. Confucius made no pretension to supernatural powers, and all commentators are agreed that the things here asked about were not what we would call contingent or indifferent events. He merely says that the great principles of morality and relations of society had continued the same, and would ever do so. 2. The Hea, Yin, and Chow, are now spoken of as the "Three dynasties," literally, " The three Changes." The first emperor of the Hea was " The great Yu," B.C. 2204; of the Yin, T'ang, B.C. 1765; and of Chow, Woo, B.C. 1121.

2. Confucius said, "The Yin dynasty followed the regulations of the Hea: wherein it took from or added to them may be known. The Chow dynasty has followed the regulations of the Yin; wherein it took from or added to them may be known. Some other may follow the Chow, but though it should be at the distance of a hundred ages, its affairs may be known."

XXIV. 1. The Master said, "For a man to sacrifice to a spirit which does not belong to him is flattery."

2. "To see what is right and not to do it, is want of courage."

BOOK III.

CHAPTER I. Confucius said of the head of the Ke family, who had eight rows of pantomimes in his area, "If he can bear to do this, what may he not bear to do?"

II. The three families used the yung ode, while the vessels were being removed, at the conclusion of the sac-

24. NEITHER IN SACRIFICE NOR IN OTHER PRACTICE MAY A MAN DO ANYTHING BUT WHAT IS RIGHT. The spirits of which a man may say that they are his, are those only of his ancestors, and to them only he may sacrifice. The ritual of China provides for sacrifices to three classes of objects—"Spirits of heaven, of the earth, of men." This chapter is not to be extended to all the three. It has reference only to the manes of departed men.

HEADING AND SUBJECTS OF THIS BOOK. The last book treated of the practice of government, and therein no things, according to Chinese ideas, are more important than ceremonial rites and music. With those topics, therefore, the twenty-six chapters of this book are occupied, and "eight rows," the principal words in the first chapter, are adopted as its heading.

1. CONFUCIUS' INDIGNATION AT THE USURPATION OF IMPERIAL RITES. These dancers, or pantomimes rather, kept time in the temple services, in the front space before the raised portion in the principal hall, moving or brandishing feathers, flags, or other articles. In his ancestral temple, the Emperor had eight rows, each row consisting of eight men; a duke or prince had six, and a great officer only four. For the Ke, therefore, to use eight rows was a usurpation, for though it may be argued, that to the ducal family of Loo imperial rites were conceded, and that the offshoots of it might use the same, still great officers were confined to the ordinances proper to their rank. Confucius' remark may also be translated, "If this be endured, what may not be endured?"

2. AGAIN AGAINST USURPED RITES. The three families assembled together as being the descendants of Duke Hwan in one temple. To

rites. The Master said, "'Assisting are the princes;—
the Emperor looks profound and grave:'—what application can these words have in the hall of the three
families?"

III. The Master said, "If a man be without the virtues proper to humanity, what has he to do with the rites
of propriety? If a man be without the virtues proper to
humanity, what has he to do with music?"

IV. 1. Lin Fang asked what was the first thing to
be attended to in ceremonies.

2. The Master said, "A great question indeed!"

3. "In festive ceremonies it is better to be sparing than
extravagant. In the ceremonies of mourning it is better
that there be deep sorrow than a minute attention to
observances."

V. The Master said, "The rude tribes of the east and
north have their princes, and are not like the States of our
great land which are without them."

VI. The chief of the Ke family was about to sacrifice
to the T'ae mountain. The Master said to Yen Yew,
"Can you not save him from this?" He answered, "I
cannot." Confucius said. "Alas! will you say that the
T'ae mountain is not so discerning as Lin Fang?"

---

this temple belonged the aros in the last chapter, which is called the area
of the Ke, because circumstances had concurred to make the Ke the chief of
the three families. For the Yung ode, see the She-king, V. Bk II. vii. 1.
It was properly sung in the imperial temples of the Chow dynasty, at the
"clearing away" of the sacrificial apparatus, and contains the lines quoted
by Confucius, which of course were quite inappropriate to the circumstances of the three families.

3. CEREMONIES AND MUSIC VAIN WITHOUT VIRTUE.

4. THE OBJECT OF CEREMONIES SHOULD REGULATE THEM. AGAINST
FORMALISM. Lin Fang was a man of Loo, supposed to have been a disciple of Confucius, and whose tablet is now placed in the outer court of
the temples. He is known only by the question in this chapter.

5. THE ANARCHY OF CONFUCIUS' TIME.

6. ON THE FOLLY OF USURPED SACRIFICES. The T'ae mountain is the
first of the "five mountains" which are celebrated in Chinese literature,
and have always received religious honours. It was in Loo, or rather on
the borders between Loo and Ts'e, about two miles north of the present
district city of T'ae-gan, in the department of Tse-nan, in Shan-tung.
According to the ritual of China, sacrifice could only be offered to
these mountains by the emperor, and princes in whose States any of
them happened to be. For the chief of the Ke family, therefore, to
sacrifice to the T'ae mountain was a great usurpation. Yen Yew

VII. The Master said, "The student of virtue has no contentions. If it be said he cannot avoid them, shall this be in archery? But he bows complaisantly to his competitors; thus he ascends the platform, descends, and exacts the forfeit of drinking. In his contention, he is still the Keun-tsze."

VIII. 1. Tsze-hea asked, saying, "What is the meaning of the passage—'The loveliness of her artful smile! The well-defined black and white of her fine eyes! The plain ground for the colours'?"

2. The Master said, "The business of laying on the colours follows the preparation of the plain ground."

3. "Ceremonies then are a subsequent thing!" The Master said, "It is Shang who can bring out my meaning! Now I can begin to talk about the odes with him."

IX. The Master said, "I am able to describe the ceremonies of the Hea dynasty, but Ke cannot sufficiently attest my words. I am able to describe the ceremonies of the Yin dynasty, but Sung cannot sufficiently attest my words. They cannot do so because of the insufficiency of their records and wise men. If those were sufficient, I could adduce them in support of my words."

was one of the disciples of Confucius, and is now third among the "wise ones" on the west. He was a man of ability and resources, and on one occasion proved himself a brave soldier.

7. THE SUPERIOR MAN AVOIDS ALL CONTENTIOUS STRIVING. In Confucius' time there were three principal exercises of archery:—the great archery, under the eye of the emperor; the guests' archery, at the visits of the princes among themselves or at the imperial court; and the festive archery. The regulations for the archers were substantially the same in them all. Every stage of the trial was preceded by "bowings and yieldings," making the whole an exhibition of courtesies and not of contention.

8. CEREMONIES ARE SECONDARY AND ORNAMENTAL. The sentences quoted by Tsze-hea are from an old ode, one of those which Confucius did not admit into the She-king. The two first lines, however, are found in it, I. v. 3. The disciple's inquiry turns on the meaning of the last line, which he took to be: "The plain ground is to be regarded as the colouring;" but Confucius, in his reply, corrects his error.

9. THE DECAY OF THE MONUMENTS OF ANTIQUITY. Of Hea and Yin, see II. 23. In the small state of Ke (what is now the district of the same name in K'ae-fung department in Ho-nan), the sacrifices to the emperors of the Hea dynasty were maintained by their descendants. So with the Yin dynasty and Sung, also a part of the present Ho-nan. But the "literary monuments" of those countries, and their "wise men" had become few. Had Confucius therefore delivered all his knowledge about the two dy-

X. The Master said, "At the great sacrifice, after the pouring out of the libation, I have no wish to look on."

XI. Some one asked the meaning of the great sacrifice. The Master said, "I do not know. He who knew its meaning would find it as easy to govern the empire as to look on this;"—pointing to his palm.

XII. 1. He sacrificed *to the dead*, as if they were present. He sacrificed to the spirits, as if the spirits were present.

2. The Master said, "I consider my not being present at the sacrifice, as if I did not sacrifice."

XIII. 1. Wang-sun Kea asked, saying, "What is the meaning of the saying, 'It is better to pay court to the furnace than to the south-west corner'?"

2. The Master said, "Not so. He who offends against Heaven has none to whom he can pray."

nasties, he would have exposed his truthfulness to suspicion, which he would not do. We see from the chapter how in the time of Confucius many of the records of antiquity had perished.

10. THE SAGE'S DISSATISFACTION AT THE WANT OF PROPRIETY OF AND IN CEREMONIES. The "great sacrifice" here spoken of could properly be celebrated only by the emperor. The individual sacrificed to in it was the remotest ancestor from whom the founder of the reigning dynasty traced his descendant. As to who were his assessors in the sacrifice, and how often it was offered;—these are disputed points. An imperial rite, its use in Loo was wrong (see next chapter), but there was something in the service after the early act of libation inviting the descent of the spirits, which more particularly moved the anger of Confucius.

11. THE PROFOUND MEANING OF THE GREAT SACRIFICE. This chapter is akin to ii. 21. Confucius evades replying to his questioner, it being contrary to Chinese propriety to speak in a country of the faults of its government or rulers. If he had entered into an account of the sacrifice, he must have condemned the use of an imperial rite in Loo.

12. CONFUCIUS' OWN SINCERITY IN SACRIFICING. By "the dead" we are to understand Confucius' own forefathers, by "the spirits" other spirits to whom in his official capacity he had to sacrifice.

13. THAT THERE IS NO RESOURCE AGAINST THE CONSEQUENCES OF VIOLATING THE RIGHT. 1. Kea was a great officer of Wei, and having the power of the state in his hands, insinuated to Confucius that it would be for his advantage to pay court to him. The south-west corner was from the structure of ancient houses the coolest nook, and the place of honour. Choo He explains the proverb by reference to the customs of sacrifice. The furnace was comparatively a mean place, but when the spirit of the furnace was sacrificed to, then the rank of the two places was changed for the time, and the proverb quoted was in vogue. But there does not seem much force in this explanation. The *dew*, or *well*, or any other of the

XIV. The Master said, "Chow had the advantage of viewing the two past dynasties. How complete and elegant are its regulations! I follow Chow."

XV. The Master, when he entered the grand temple, asked about everything. Some said, "Who will say that the son of the man of Tsow knows the rules of propriety? He has entered the grand temple and asks about everything." The Master heard the remark, and said, "This is a rule of propriety."

XVI. The Master said, "In archery it is not *going through* the leather which is the principal thing;—because people's strength is not equal. This was the old way."

XVII. 1. Tsze-kung wished to do away with the offering of a sheep connected with the inauguration of the first day of each month.

2. The Master said, "Tsze, you love the sheep; I love the ceremony."

five things in the regular sacrifices, might take the place of the *furnace*. 2. Confucius' reply was in a high tone. Choo Ho says, "Heaven means principle." But why should Heaven mean principle, if there were not in such a use of the term an instinctive recognition of a supreme government of intelligence and righteousness? We find the term explained by "The lofty one who is on high."

14. THE COMPLETENESS AND ELEGANCE OF THE INSTITUTIONS OF THE CHOW DYNASTY.

15. CONFUCIUS IN THE GRAND TEMPLE. "The grand temple" was the temple dedicated to the famous Duke of Chow, and where he was worshipped with imperial rites. The thing is supposed to have taken place at the beginning of Confucius' official service in Loo, when he went into the temple with other officers to assist at the sacrifice. He had studied all about ceremonies, and was famed for his knowledge of them, but he thought it a mark of sincerity and earnestness to make minute inquiries about them on the occasion spoken of. Tsow was the name of the town in Loo, of which Confucius' father had been governor, who was known therefore as "the man of Tsow." We may suppose that Confucius would be styled as in the text, only in his early life, or by very ordinary people.

16. HOW THE ANCIENTS MADE ARCHERY A DISCIPLINE OF VIRTUE.

17. HOW CONFUCIUS CLEAVED TO ANCIENT RITES. The emperor in the last month of the year gave out to the princes a calendar for the first days of the twelve months of the year ensuing. This was kept in their ancestral temples, and on the first of every month they offered a sheep and announced the day, requesting sanction for the duties of the month. The dukes of Loo neglected now their part of this ceremony, but the sheep was still offered;—a meaningless formality, it seemed to Tsze-kung. Confucius, however, thought that while any part of the ceremony was retained, there was a better chance of restoring the whole.

XVIII. The Master said, "The full observance of the rules of propriety in serving one's prince is accounted by people to be flattery."

XIX. The Duke Ting asked how a prince should employ his ministers, and how ministers should serve their prince. Confucius replied, "A prince should employ his ministers according to the rules of propriety; ministers should serve their prince with faithfulness."

XX. The Master said, "The Kwan Ts'eu is expressive of enjoyment without being licentious, and of grief without being hurtfully excessive."

XXI. 1. The Duke Gae asked Tsae Wo about the altars of the spirits of the land. Tsae Wo replied, "The Hea sovereign used the pine tree; the man of the Yin used the cypress; and the man of the Chow used the chestnut tree, meaning thereby to cause the people to be in awe."

2. When the Master heard it, he said, "Things that are done, it is needless to speak about; things that have had their course, it is needless to remonstrate about; things that are past, it is needless to blame."

XXII. 1. The Master said, "Small indeed was the capacity of Kwan Chung!"

18. HOW PRINCES SHOULD BE SERVED. AGAINST THE SPIRIT OF THE TIMES.

19. THE GUIDING PRINCIPLES IN THE REGULATION OF PRINCE AND MINISTER. Ting. "Greatly anxious, tranquilliser of the people," was the posthumous epithet of Sung, Prince of Loo, B.C. 508—494.

20. THE PRAISE OF THE FIRST OF THE ODES. Kwan Ts'eu is the name of the first ode in the She-king, and may be translated,—"Kwan Kwan go the King-ducks."

21. A RASH REPLY OF TSAE WO ABOUT THE ALTARS TO THE SPIRITS OF THE LAND, AND LAMENT OF CONFUCIUS THEREON. 1. King tha, see II. xix. Tsae Wo was an eloquent disciple of the sage, a native of Loo. His place is among the "wise ones." He tells the duke that the founders of the several dynasties planted such and such trees about the altars. The reason was that the soil suited such trees; but as the word for the chestnut tree, the tree of the existing dynasty, is used in the sense of "to be afraid," he suggested a reason for its planting which might lead the duke to severe measures against his people to be carried into effect at the altars. Compare Shoo-king, III. ii. 5, "I will put you to death before the altar to the spirit of the land." 2. This is all directed against Wo's reply. He had spoken, and his words could not be recalled.

22. CONFUCIUS' OPINION OF KWAN CHUNG;—AGAINST HIM. 1. Kwan Chung is one of the most famous names in Chinese history. He was chief minister to the Duke Hwan of Ts'e (B.C. 683—642), the first and greatest of the five pa leaders of the princes of the empire under the Chow

2. Some one said, "Was Kwan Chung parsimonious?" "Kwan," was the reply, "had the San Kwei, and his officers performed no double duties; how can he be considered parsimonious?"

3. "Then, did Kwan Chung know the rules of propriety?" The Master said, "The princes of States have a screen intercepting the view at their gates. Kwan had likewise a screen at his gate. The princes of States on any friendly meeting between two of them, had a stand on which to place their inverted cups. Kwan had also such a stand. If Kwan knew the rules of propriety, who does not know them?"

XXIII. The Master instructing the Grand music-master of Loo said, "How to play music may be known. At the commencement of the piece, all the parts should sound together. As it proceeds, they should be in harmony, while severally distinct and yet flowing without break; and thus on to the conclusion."

XXIV. The border-warden at E requested to be introduced to the Master, saying, "When men of superior virtue have come to this, I have never been denied the privilege of seeing them." The followers of *the sage* introduced him, and when he came out from the interview, he said, "My friends, why are you distressed by your master's loss of office? The empire has long been without the principles *of truth and right;* Heaven is going to use your master as a bell with its wooden tongue."

XXV. The Master said of the Shaou that it was per-

dynasty. In the times of Confucius and Mencius, people thought more of Kwan than those sages, no hero-worshippers, would allow. Most foreign readers, however, in studying the history of Kwan's times, will hesitate in adopting the sage's judgment about him. He rendered great services to his State and to China.

23. ON THE PLAYING OF MUSIC.

24. A STRANGER'S VIEW OF THE VOCATION OF CONFUCIUS. E was a small town on the borders of Wei, referred to a place in the present district of Lan-Yang, department K'ae-fung, Honan province. Confucius was retiring from Wei, the prince of which could not employ him. The "wooden-tongued bell" was a metal bell with a wooden tongue, shaken to call attention to announcements, or along the ways to call people together. Heaven, the warden thought, would employ Confucius to proclaim and call men's attention to the truth and right.

25. THE COMPARATIVE MERITS OF THE MUSIC OF SHUN AND WOO. Shaou was the name of the music made by Shun, perfect in melody and

fectly beautiful and also perfectly good. He said of the Woo that it was perfectly beautiful but not perfectly good.

XXVI. The Master said, "High station filled without indulgent generosity; ceremonies performed without reverence; mourning conducted without sorrow;—wherewith should I contemplate such ways?"

BOOK IV.

CHAPTER I. The Master said, "It is virtuous manners which constitute the excellence of a neighbourhood. If a man in selecting a residence do not fix on one where such prevail, how can he be wise?"

II. The Master said, "Those who are without virtue cannot abide long either in a condition of poverty and hardship, or in a condition of enjoyment. The virtuous rest in virtue; the wise desire virtue."

III. The Master said, "It is only the truly virtuous man who can love, or who can hate, others."

IV. The Master said, "If the will be set on virtue, there will be no practice of wickedness."

V. 1. The Master said, "Riches and honours are what men desire. If it cannot be obtained in the proper way, they should not be held. Poverty and meanness are what

---

sentiment. Woo was the music of King Woo, also perfect in melody, but breathing the martial air, indicative of its author.

26. THE DISREGARD OF WHAT IS ESSENTIAL VITIATES ALL SERVICES.

HEADING AND SUBJECTS OF THIS BOOK.—"Virtue in a neighbourhood." The book is mostly occupied with the subject of *jin*, which is generally translated by "benevolence." That sense, however, will by no means suit many of the chapters here, and we must render it by "perfect virtue" or "virtue." See II. i. 2. The embodiment of virtue demands an acquaintance with ceremonies and music, and this is the reason, it is said, why the one subject immediately follows the other.

1. RULES FOR THE SELECTION OF A RESIDENCE.

2. ONLY TRUE VIRTUE ADAPTS A MAN FOR THE VARIED CONDITIONS OF LIFE.

3. ONLY IN THE GOOD MAN ARE EMOTIONS OF LOVE AND HATRED RIGHT. This chapter, containing an important truth, is incorporated with the Great Learning, comm. X. 15.

4. THE VIRTUOUS WILL PRESERVE FROM ALL WICKEDNESS. Compare the apostle's sentiment, 1 John III. 9, "Whosoever is born of God doth not commit sin."

5. THE DEVOTION OF THE KEUN-TSZE TO VIRTUE.

men dislike. If it cannot be obtained in the proper way, they should not be avoided.

2. "If a superior man abandon virtue, how can he fulfil the requirements of that name?

3. "The superior man does not, even for the space of a single meal, act contrary to virtue. In moments of haste, he cleaves to it. In seasons of danger, he cleaves to it."

VI. 1. The Master said, "I have not seen a person who loved virtue, or one who hated what was not virtuous. He who loved virtue would esteem nothing above it. He who hated what is not virtuous, would practise virtue in such a way that he would not allow anything that is not virtuous to approach his person.

2. "Is any one able for one day to apply his strength to virtue? I have not seen the case in which his strength would be insufficient.

3. "Should there possibly be any such case, I have not seen it."

VII. The Master said, "The faults of men are characteristic of the class to which they belong. By observing a man's faults, it may be known that he is virtuous."

VIII. The Master said, "If a man in the morning hear the right way, he may die in the evening without regret."

IX. The Master said, "A scholar, whose mind is set

---

6. A LAMENT BECAUSE OF THE RARITY OF THE LOVE OF VIRTUE, AND ENCOURAGEMENT TO PRACTISE VIRTUE.

7. A MAN IS NOT TO BE UTTERLY CONDEMNED BECAUSE HE HAS FAULTS. Such is the sentiment found in this chapter, in which we may say, however, that Confucius is liable to the charge brought against Tszehea, I. vii. The faults are the excesses of the general tendencies. Compare Goldsmith's line, "And even his failings leant to virtue's side."

8. THE IMPORTANCE OF KNOWING THE RIGHT WAY. One is perplexed to translate the "way," or "right way," here spoken. One calls it "the path,"—i.e. *of action*—which is in accordance with our nature. Man is formed for this, and if he die without coming to the knowledge of it, his death is no better than that of a beast. One would fain recognize in such sentences as this a vague apprehension of some higher truth or way than Chinese sages have been able to propound.—Ho An takes a different view of the whole chapter, and makes it a lament of Confucius that he was likely to die without hearing of right principles prevailing in the world.— "Could I once hear of the prevalence of right principles, I could die the same evening."

9. THE PURSUIT OF TRUTH SHOULD RAISE A MAN ABOVE BEING ASHAMED OF POVERTY.

on truth, and who is ashamed of bad clothes and bad food, is not fit to be discoursed with."

X. The Master said, " The superior man, in the world, does not set his mind either for anything, or against anything; what is right he will follow."

XI. The Master said, "The superior man thinks of virtue; the small man thinks of comfort. The superior man thinks of the sanctions of law; the small man thinks of favours *which he may receive.*"

XII. The Master said, "He who acts with a constant view to his own advantage will be much murmured against."

XIII. The Master said, "Is *a prince* able to govern his kingdom with the complaisance proper to the rules of propriety, what difficulty will he have? If he cannot govern it with that complaisance, what has he to do with the rules of propriety?"

XIV. The Master said, "*A man should say*, I am not concerned that I have no place,—I am concerned how I may fit myself for one. I am not concerned that I am not known,—I seek to be worthy to be known."

XV. 1. The Master said, "Sin, my doctrine is that of an all-pervading unity." Tsăng the philosopher replied, "Yes."

10. RIGHTEOUSNESS IS THE RULE OF THE KEUN-TSZE'S PRACTICE.
11. THE DIFFERENT MINDINGS OF THE SUPERIOR AND THE SMALL MAN.
12. THE CONSEQUENCE OF SELFISH CONDUCT.
13. THE INFLUENCE IN GOVERNMENT OF CEREMONIES OBSERVED IN THEIR PROPER SPIRIT.
14. ADVISING TO SELF-CULTIVATION. Compare I. xvi.
15. CONFUCIUS' DOCTRINE THAT OF A PERVADING UNITY. This chapter is said to be the most profound in the *Lun Yu*. To myself it occurs to translate "my doctrines have one thing which goes through them," but such an exposition has not been approved by any Chinese commentator. The second paragraph shows us clearly enough what the one thing or unity intended by Confucius was. It was the heart, man's nature, of which all the relations and duties of life are only the development and outgoings. What I have translated by "being true to the principles of our nature," and "exercising those principles benevolently," are in the original only two characters both formed from *sin*, "the heart." The former is compounded of *chung*, "middle," "centre," and *sin*, and the latter of *joo*, "as," and *sin*. The "centre heart " = I, the *ego*, and the "as heart"=the "I in sympathy" with others. One is duty-doing, on a consideration, or from the impulse, of one's own self; the other is duty-doing, on the principle of reciprocity. The chapter is important, showing

2. The Master went out, and the *other* disciples asked, saying, "What do his words mean?" Tsáng said, "The doctrine of our Master is to be true to the principles of our nature and the benevolent exercise of them to others,—this and nothing more."

XVI. The Master said, "The mind of the superior man is conversant with righteousness; the mind of the mean man is conversant with gain."

XVII. The Master said, "When we see men of worth, we should think of equalling them; when we see men of a contrary character, we should turn inwards and examine ourselves."

XVIII. The Master said, "In serving his parents, a son may remonstrate with them, but gently; when he sees that they do not incline to follow *his advice*, he shows an increased degree of reverence, but does not abandon *his purpose*; and should they punish him, he does not allow himself to murmur."

XIX. The Master said, "While his parents are alive, *the son* may not go abroad to a distance. If he does go abroad, he must have a fixed place to which he goes."

XX. The Master said, "If the son for three years does not alter from the way of his father, he may be called filial."

XXI. The Master said, "The years of parents may by no means not be kept in the memory, as an occasion at once for joy and for fear."

XXII. The Master said, "The reason why the ancients did not readily give utterance to their words, was

that Confucius only claimed to unfold and enforce duties indicated by man's mental constitution. He was simply a moral philosopher.

16. HOW RIGHTEOUSNESS AND SELFISHNESS DISTINGUISH THE SUPERIOR MAN AND THE SMALL MAN.

17. THE LESSONS TO BE LEARNED FROM OBSERVING MEN OF DIFFERENT CHARACTERS.

18. HOW A SON MAY REMONSTRATE WITH HIS PARENTS ON THEIR FAULTS. See the Lê Kê, XII. i. 15.

19. A SON OUGHT NOT TO GO TO A DISTANCE WHERE HE WILL NOT BE ABLE TO PAY THE DUE SERVICES TO HIS PARENTS.

20. A REPETITION OF PART OF L. XI.

21. WHAT EFFECT THE AGE OF THE PARENTS SHOULD HAVE ON THEIR CHILDREN.

22. THE VIRTUE OF THE ANCIENTS SEEN IN THEIR SLOWNESS TO SPEAK.

that they feared lest their actions should not come up to them."

XXIII. The Master said, "The cautious seldom err."

XXIV. The Master said, "The superior man wishes to be slow in his words and earnest in his conduct."

XXV. The Master said, "Virtue is not left to stand alone. *He who practises it* will have neighbours."

XXVI. Tsze-yew said, "In serving a prince, frequent remonstrances lead to disgrace. Between friends, frequent reproofs make the friendship distant."

BOOK V.

CHAPTER I. 1. The Master said of Kung-yay Ch'ang that he might be wived; although he was put in bonds, he had not been guilty of any crime. *Accordingly*, he gave him his own daughter to wife.

2. Of Nan Yung he said that if the country were well governed, he would not be out of office, and if it were ill governed, he would escape punishment and disgrace. He gave him the daughter of his own elder brother to wife.

23. ADVANTAGE OF CAUTION. Collie's version, which I have adopted, is here happy.

24. RULE OF THE KEUN-TSZE ABOUT HIS WORDS AND ACTIONS.

25. THE VIRTUOUS ARE NOT LEFT ALONE;—AN ENCOURAGEMENT TO VIRTUE.

26. A LESSON TO COUNSELLORS AND FRIENDS.

HEADING AND SUBJECTS OF THIS BOOK.—"Kung-yay Ch'ang," the surname and name of the first individual spoken of in it, heads this book, which is chiefly occupied with the judgment of the sage on the character of several of his disciples and others. As the decision frequently turns on their being possessed of that *jin*, or perfect virtue, which is so conspicuous in the last book, this is the reason, it is said, why the one immediately follows the other. As Tsze-kung appears in the book several times, some have fancied that it was compiled by his disciples.

1. CONFUCIUS IN MARRIAGE-MAKING WAS GUIDED BY CHARACTER, AND NOT BY FORTUNE. Of Kung-yay Ch'ang, though the son-in-law of Confucius, nothing certain is known, and his tablet is only third on the west among the οἱ πολλοί. Silly legends are told of his being put in prison from his bringing suspicion on himself by his knowledge of the language of birds. Nan Yung, another of the disciples, is now fourth, east, in the outer hall. The discussions about who he was, and whether he is to be identified with Nan-Kung Kwoh, and several other *aliases*, are very perplexing. We cannot tell whether Confucius is giving his impression of Yung's character, or referring to events that had taken place.

II. The Master said, of Tsze-tseen, " Of superior virtue indeed is such a man! If there were not virtuous men in Loo, how could this man have acquired this character?"

III. Tsze-kung asked, "What do you say of me, Ts'ze?" The Master said, " You are an utensil." "What utensil?" " A gemmed sacrificial utensil."

IV. 1. Some one said, "Yung is truly virtuous, but he is not ready with his tongue."

2. The Master said, " What is the good of being ready with the tongue? They who meet men with smartnesses of speech, for the most part procure themselves hatred. I know not whether he be truly virtuous, but why should he show readiness of the tongue?"

V. The Master was wishing Tseih-teaou K'ae to enter on official employment. He replied, "I am not yet able to rest in the assurance of THIS." The Master was pleased.

VI. The Master said, "My doctrines make no way. I will get upon a raft, and float about on the sea. He that will accompany me will be Yew, I dare to say."

2. THE KEUN-TSZE FORMED BY INTERCOURSE WITH OTHER KEUN-TSZE. Tsze-tseen, by surname Fuh, and named Puh-ts'e, appears to have been of some note among the disciples of Confucius, both as an administrator and writer, though his tablet is now only second, west, in the outer hall. What chiefly distinguished him, as appears here, was his cultivation of the friendship of men of ability and virtue.

3. WHERETO TSZE-KUNG HAD ATTAINED. See I. x.; II. xii. While the sage did not grant to Tsze that he was a *Keun-tsze* (II. xii.), he made him " a vessel of honour," valuable and fit for use on high occasions.

4. OF YEN YUNG. READINESS WITH THE TONGUE NO PART OF VIRTUE. Yen Yung, styled Chung-Kung, has his tablet the second on the east of Confucius' own tablet, among the " wise ones." His father was a worthless character (see VI. iv.), but he himself was the opposite.

5. TSEIH-TEAOU K'AE'S OPINION OF THE QUALIFICATIONS NECESSARY TO TAKING OFFICE. Tseih-teaou, now sixth on the east, in the outer hall, was styled Tsze-jŏ. His name originally was K'e, changed into Ka'e, on the accession of the Emperor Heaou-King, A. D. 155, whose name was also K'e. In the chapter about the disciples in the "Family Sayings," it is said that K'ae was reading in the Shoo-king, when Confucius spoke to him about taking office, and he pointed to the book, or some particular passage in it, saying, "I am not yet able to rest in the assurance of *this*." It may have been so.

6. CONFUCIUS PROPOSING TO WITHDRAW FROM THE WORLD:—A LESSON TO TSZE-LOO. Tsze-loo supposed his master really meant to leave the world, and the idea of floating along the coasts pleased his ardent temper, while he was delighted with the compliment paid to himself. But Confucius

Tsze-loo hearing this was glad, upon which the Master said, "Yew is fonder of daring than I am; but he does not exercise his judgment upon matters."

VII. 1. Măng Woo asked about Tsze-loo, whether he was perfectly virtuous. The Master said, "I do not know."

2. He asked again, when the Master replied, "In a kingdom of a thousand chariots, Yew might be employed to manage the military levies, but I do not know whether he is perfectly virtuous."

3. "And what do you say of K'ew?" The Master replied, "In a city of a thousand families, or a House of a hundred chariots, K'ew might be employed as governor, but I do not know whether he is perfectly virtuous."

4. "What do you say of Ch'ih?" The Master replied, "With his sash girt and standing in a court, Ch'ih might be employed to converse with the visitors and guests, but I do not know whether he is perfectly virtuous."

VIII. 1. The Master said to Tsze-kung, "Which do you consider superior, yourself or Hwuy?"

2. Tsze-kung replied, "How dare I compare myself with Hwuy? Hwuy hears one point and knows all about a subject; I hear one point and know a second."

3. The Master said, "You are not equal to him. I grant you, you are not equal to him."

IX. 1. Tsae Yu being asleep during the day time, the Master said, "Rotten wood cannot be carved; a wall of dirty earth will not receive the trowel. This Yu!—what is the use of my reproving him?"

2. The Master said, "At first, my way with men was to hear their words, and give them credit for their con-

only expressed in this way his regret at the backwardness of men to receive his doctrines.

7. OF TSZE-LOO, TSZE-YEW, AND TSZE-HWA. Măng Woo, see II. vi. 3. K'ew, see III. vi. "A house of a hundred chariots," in opposition to "A State of a thousand chariots," was the secondary fief, the territory appropriated to the highest nobles or officers in a State, supposed also to comprehend 1000 families. 4. Ch'ih, surnamed Kung-se, and styled Tsze-hwa, having now the fourteenth place, west, in the outer hall, was famous among the disciples for his knowledge of rules of ceremony, and those especially relating to dress and intercourse.

8. SUPERIORITY OF YEN HWUY TO TSZE-KUNG.

9. THE IDLENESS OF TSAE YU AND ITS REPROOF. Tsae Yu is the same individual as Tsae-wo in III. xxi.

duct. Now my way is to hear their words, and look at their conduct. It is from Yu that I have learned to make this change."

X. The Master said, "I have not seen a firm and unbending man." Some one replied, "There is Shin Ch'ang." "Ch'ang," said the Master, "is under the influence of his lusts, how can he be firm and unbending?"

XI. Tsze-kung said, "What I do not wish men to do to me, I also wish not to do to men." The Master said, "Ts'ze, you have not attained to that."

XII. Tsze-kung said, "The Master's *personal* displays *of his principles* and *ordinary* descriptions of them may be heard. His discourses about *man's* nature, and the way of Heaven, cannot be heard."

XIII. When Tsze-loo heard anything, if he had not yet carried it into practice, he was only afraid lest he should hear *something else*.

XIV. Tsze-kung asked saying, "On what ground did

10. UNBENDING VIRTUE CANNOT CO-EXIST WITH INDULGENCE OF THE PASSIONS. Shin Ch'ang (there are several *aliases*, but they are disputed,) was one of the minor disciples, of whom little or nothing is known. He was styled Tsze-chow, and his place is thirty-first, east, in the outer ranges.

11. THE DIFFICULTY OF ATTAINING TO THE NOT WISHING TO DO TO OTHERS AS WE WISH THEM NOT TO DO TO US. It is said, "This chapter shows that the 'no I' (freedom from selfishness) is not easily reached." In the Doctrine of the Mean, XIII. 3, it is said, "What you do not like when done to yourself, do not do to others." The difference between it and the sentence here is said to be that of "reciprocity," and "benevolence," or the highest virtue, apparent in the two adverbs used, the one prohibitive, and the other a simple, unconstrained, negation. The golden rule of the Gospel is higher than both,—"Do ye unto others as ye would that others should do unto you."

12. THE GRADUAL WAY IN WHICH CONFUCIUS COMMUNICATED HIS DOCTRINES. So the lesson of this chapter is summed up; but there is hardly another more perplexing to a translator. The commentators make the subject of the former clause to be the deportment and manners of the sage and his ordinary discourses, but the verb "to hear" is an inappropriate term with reference to the former. These things, however, were level to the capacity of the disciples generally, and they had the benefit of them. As to his views about man's nature, the gift of Heaven, and the way of Heaven generally;—these he only communicated to those who were prepared to receive them; and Tsze-kung is supposed to have expressed himself thus, after being on some occasion so privileged.

13. THE ARDOUR OF TSZE-LOO IN PRACTISING THE MASTER'S INSTRUCTIONS.

14. AN EXAMPLE OF THE PRINCIPLE ON WHICH HONORARY POSTHU-

Kung-wăn get that title of wăn?" The Master said, "He was of an active nature and yet fond of learning, and he was not ashamed to ask and learn of his inferiors!— On these grounds he has been styled wăn."

XV. The Master said of Tsze-ch'an that he had four of the characteristics of a superior man:—in his conduct of himself, he was humble; in serving his superiors, he was respectful; in nourishing the people, he was kind; in ordering the people, he was just.

XVI. The Master said, "Gan Ping knew well how to maintain friendly intercourse. The acquaintance might be long, but he showed the same respect as at first."

XVII. The Master said, "Tsang Wăn kept a large tortoise in a house, on the capitals of the pillars of which he had hills made, with representations of duckweed on the small pillars above the beams supporting the rafters.— Of what sort was his wisdom?"

XVIII. 1. Tsze-chang asked, saying, "The minister

OUR TITLES WERE CONFERRED. "Wăn," corresponding nearly to our "accomplished," was the posthumous title given to Tsze-yu, an officer of the state of Wei, and a contemporary of Confucius. Many of his actions had been of a doubtful character, which made Tsze-kung stumble at the application to him of so honourable an epithet. But Confucius shows that, whatever he might otherwise be, he had those qualities, which justified his being so denominated. The rule for posthumous titles in China has been, and is very much—" De mortuis nil nisi bonum."

15. THE EXCELLENT QUALITIES OF TSZE-CH'AN. Tsze-ch'an, named Kung-sun K'iaou, was the chief minister of the state of Chĭng—the ablest perhaps, and most upright, of all the statesmen among Confucius' contemporaries. The sage wept when he heard of his death.

16. HOW TO MAINTAIN FRIENDSHIP. "Familiarity breeds contempt," and with contempt friendship ends. It was not so with Gan Ping, another of the worthies of Confucius' times. He was a principal minister of Ts'e, by name Ying. Ping ("Ruling and averting calamity") was his posthumous title.

17. THE SUPERSTITION OF TSANG WĂN. Tsang Wăn (Wăn is the honorary epithet) had been a great officer in Loo, and left a reputation for wisdom, which Confucius did not think was deserved. He was descended from the Duke Hsiaou (B.C. 794—767), whose son was styled Tsze-Tsang. This Tsang was taken by his descendants as their surname. This is mentioned to show one of the ways in which surnames were formed among the Chinese. The old interpreters make the keeping such a tortoise an act of usurpation on the part of Tsang Wăn. Choo He finds the point of Confucius' words, in the keeping it in such a style, as if to flatter it.

18. THE PRAISE OF PERFECT VIRTUE IS NOT TO BE LIGHTLY ACCORDED. 1. Tsze-wăn, the chief minister of the State of Tsoo, had been

Tsze-wăn, thrice took office, and manifested no joy in his countenance. Thrice he retired from office, and manifested no displeasure. He made it a point to inform the new minister of the way in which he had conducted the government;—what do you say of him?" "The Master replied, "He was loyal." "Was he perfectly virtuous?" "I do not know. How can he be pronounced perfectly virtuous?"

2. *Tsze-chang* proceeded, "When the officer Ts'uy killed the prince of Ts'e, Ch'in Wăn, though he was the owner of forty horses, abandoned them and left the country. Coming to another state, he said, 'They are here like our great officer, Ts'uy,' and left it. He came to a second state, and with the same observation left it also;—what do you say of him?" The Master replied, "Ho was pure." "Was he perfectly virtuous?" "I do not know. How can he be pronounced perfectly virtuous?"

XIX. Ke Wăn thought thrice, and then acted. When the Master was informed of it, he said, "Twice may do."

XX. The Master said, "When good order prevailed in his country, Ning Woo acted the part of a wise man. When his country was in disorder, he acted the part of a stupid man. Others may equal his wisdom, but they cannot equal his stupidity."

XXI. When the Master was in Ch'in, he said, "Let me return! Let me return! The little children of my

noted for the things mentioned by Tsze-chang, but the sage would not concede that he was therefore perfectly virtuous. 2. Ts'uy was a great officer of Ts'e. Gan P'ing (ch. xvi.), distinguished himself on the occasion of the murder (B.C. 547) here referred to. Ch'in Wăn was likewise an officer of Ts'e.

19. PROMPT DECISION GOOD. Wăn was the posthumous title of Ke Hing-foo, a faithful and disinterested officer of Loo. Compare Robert Hall's remark,—" In matters of conscience first thoughts are best."

20. THE UNCOMMON BUT ADMIRABLE STUPIDITY OF NING WOO. Ning Woo (Woo, hon. ep. See II. vi.), was an officer of Wei in the times of Wăn (B. C. 635—627), the second of the five *p's* (See on III. xxii.). In the first part of his official life, the State was quiet and prosperous, and he "wisely" acquitted himself of his duties. Afterwards came confusion. The prince was driven from the throne, and Ning Woo might, like other wise men, have retired from the danger. But he "foolishly," as it seemed, chose to follow the fortunes of his prince, and yet adroitly brought it about in the end, that the prince was reinstated and order restored.

21. THE ANXIETY OF CONFUCIUS ABOUT THE TRAINING OF HIS DISCIPLES. Confucius was thrice in Ch'in. It must have been the third time

school are ambitious and too hasty. They are accomplished and complete so far, but they do not know how to restrict and shape themselves."

XXII. The Master said, "Pih-e and Shuh-ts'e did not keep the former wickedness of men in mind, and hence the resentments directed towards them were few."

XXIII. The Master said, "Who says of Wei-shang Kaou that he is upright? One begged some vinegar of him, and he begged it of a neighbour and gave it him."

XXIV. The Master said, "Fine words, an insinuating appearance, and excessive respect;—Tso-k'ew Ming was ashamed of them. I also am ashamed of them. To conceal resentment against a person, and appear friendly with him;—Tso-k'ew Ming was ashamed of such conduct. I also am ashamed of it."

XXV. 1. Yen Yuen and Ke Loo being by his side,

when he thus expressed himself. He was then over sixty years, and being convinced that he was not to see for himself the triumph of his principles, he became the more anxious about their transmission, and the training of the disciples in order to that. Such is the common view of the chapter. Some say, however, that it is not to be understood of all the disciples. Compare Mencius, VII. Pt II. xxxvii. By an affectionate way of speaking of the disciples, he calls them his "little children."

22. THE GENEROSITY OF PIH-E AND SHUH-TS'E, AND ITS EFFECTS. These were ancient worthies of the closing period of the Shang dynasty. Compare Mencius, II. Pt I. ix., et al. They were brothers, sons of the king of Koo-chuh, named respectively Yun and Cha. E and Ts'e are their honourable epithets, and Pih and Shuh only indicate their relation to each other as elder and younger. Pih-e and Shuh-ts'e, however, are in effect their names in the mouths and writings of the Chinese. Koochuh was a small state, included in the present department of Yungp'ing, in Pih-chih-le. Their father left his kingdom to Shuh-ts'e, who refused to take the place of his elder brother. Pih-e in turn declined the throne, so they both abandoned it, and retired into obscurity. When King Woo was taking his measures against the tyrant Chow, they made their appearance, and remonstrated against his course. Finally, they died of hunger, rather than live under the new dynasty. They were celebrated for their purity, and aversion to men whom they considered bad, but Confucius here brings out their generosity.

23. SMALL MEANNESSES INCONSISTENT WITH UPRIGHTNESS. It is implied that Kaou gave the vinegar as from himself.

24. PRAISE OF SINCERITY, AND OF TSO-K'EW MING. Compare I. iii., "excessive respect." The discussions about Tso-k'ew Ming are endless. It is sufficient for us to rest in the judgment of the commentator, Ch'ing, that "he was an ancient of reputation." It is not to be received that he was a disciple of Confucius, or the author of the Tso-chuen.

25. THE DIFFERENT WISHES OF YEN YUEN, TSZE-LOO, AND CON-

the Master said to them, "Come, let each of you tell his wishes."

2. Tsze-loo said, "I should like, having chariots and horses, and light fur dresses, to share them with my friends, and though they should spoil them, I would not be displeased."

3. Yen Yuen said, "I should like not to boast of my excellence, nor to make a display of my meritorious deeds."

4. Tsze-loo then said, "I should like, sir, to hear your wishes." The Master said, "*They are*, in regard to the aged, to give them rest; in regard to friends, to show them sincerity; in regard to the young, to treat them tenderly."

XXVI. The Master said, "It is all over! I have not yet seen one who could perceive his faults, and inwardly accuse himself."

XXVII. The Master said, "In a hamlet of ten families, there may be found one honourable and sincere as I am, but not so fond of learning."

BOOK VI.

CHAPTER I. 1. The Master said, "There is Yung!— He might occupy the place of a prince."

FUCIUS. The Master and the disciples, it is said, agreed in being devoid of selfishness. Hwuy's, however, was seen in a higher style of mind and object than Yew's. In the sage, there was an unconsciousness of self, and without any effort, he proposed acting in regard to his classification of men just as they ought severally to be acted to.

26. A LAMENT OVER MEN'S PERSISTENCE IN ERROR. The remark affirms a fact, inexplicable on Confucius' view of the nature of man. But perhaps such an exclamation should not be pressed too closely.

27. THE HUMBLE CLAIM OF CONFUCIUS FOR HIMSELF. Confucius thus did not claim higher natural and moral qualities than others, but sought to perfect himself by learning.

HEADING AND SUBJECTS OF THIS BOOK. "There is Yung!" commences the first chapter, and stands as the title of the book. Its subjects are much akin to those of the preceding book, and therefore, it is said, they are in juxtaposition.

1. THE CHARACTERS OF YEN YUNG AND TSZE-SANG PIH-TSZE, AS REGARDS THEIR ADAPTATION FOR GOVERNMENT. 1. "Might occupy the place of a prince," is literally "Might be employed with his face to the

2. Chung-kung asked about Tsze-sang Pih-tsze. The Master said, "He may pass. He does not mind small matters."

3. Chung-kung said, "If a man cherish in himself a reverential feeling *of the necessity of attention to business*, though he may be easy in small matters in his government of the people, that may be allowed. But if he cherish in himself that easy feeling, and also carry it out in his practice, is not such an easy mode of procedure excessive?"

4. The Master said, "Yung's words are right."

II. The Duke Gae asked which of the disciples loved to learn. Confucius replied to him, "There was Yen Hwuy; HE loved to learn. He did not transfer his anger; he did not repeat a fault. Unfortunately, his appointed time was short and he died; and now there is not *such another*. I have not yet heard of any one who loves to learn *as he did*."

III. 1. Tsze-hwa being employed on a mission to Ts'e, the disciple Yen requested grain for his mother. The Master said, "Give her a *foo*." Yen requested more. "Give her an *yu*," said the Master. Yen gave her five *ping*.

south." In China, the emperor sits facing the south. So did the princes of the states in their several courts in Confucius' time. An explanation of the practice is attempted in the Yih-King. "The diagram Le conveys the idea of brightness, when all things are exhibited to one another. It is the diagram of the south. The custom of the sages (i. e. monarchs) to sit with their faces to the south, *and listen to the representations* of the empire, governing towards the bright region, was taken from this." 2. Observe, Chung-kung was the designation of Yen Yung; see V. iv. 3. Of Tsze-sang Pih-tsze, we know nothing certain but what is here stated. Choo He seems to be wrong in approving the identification of him with a Tsze-sang Hoo.—"To dwell in respect," to have the mind imbued with it.

2. THE RARITY OF A TRUE LOVE TO LEARN. HWUY'S SUPERIORITY TO THE OTHER DISCIPLES. "He did not transfer his anger," i. e. his anger was no tumultuary passion in the mind, but was excited by some specific cause, to which alone it was directed. The idea of "learning," with the duke and the sage, was a practical obedience to the lessons given.

3. DISCRIMINATION OF CONFUCIUS IN REWARDING OR SALARYING OFFICERS. 1. Choo He says the commission was a private one from Confucius, but this is not likely. The old interpretation makes it a public one from the court of Loo. "Yen, the disciple;" see III. vi. Yen is here styled "the philosopher," like Yew, in I. ii., but only in narrative, not as introducing any wise utterance. A *foo* contained 6 *tow* and 4 *shing*, or

2. The Master said, "When Ch'ih was proceeding to Ts'e, he had fat horses to his carriage, and wore light furs. I have heard that a superior man helps the distressed, but does not add to the wealth of the rich."

3. Yuen Sze being made governor *of his town by the Master,* he gave him nine hundred measures of grain, but Sze declined them.

4. The Master said, "Do not decline them. May you not give them away in the neighbourhoods, hamlets, towns, and villages?"

IV. The Master, speaking of Chung-kung, said, "If the calf of a brindled cow be red and horned, although man may not wish to use it, would *the spirits of* the mountains and rivers refuse it?"

V. The Master said, "Such was Hwuy that for three months there would be nothing in his mind contrary to perfect virtue. The others may attain to this once a day or once a month, but nothing more."

VI. Ke K'ang asked, "Is Chung-yew fit to be employed as an officer of government?" The Master said, "Yew is a man of decision; what difficulty would he find in being an officer of government?" *K'ang* asked, "Is Ts'ze fit to be employed as an officer of government?"

64 *shing.* The *yu* contained 160 *shing,* and the *ping* 16 *hŏ,* or 1600 *shing.* A *shing* of the present day is about one-fourth less than an English pint. 2. Ch'ih, i. e. Tsze-hwa; see V. vii. 4. 3. Yuen Sze, named Hëen, is now the third, east, in the outer hall of the temples. He was noted for his pursuit of truth, and carelessness of worldly advantages. After the death of Confucius, he withdrew into retirement in Wei. It is related that Tszekung, high in official station, came one day in great style to visit him. Sze received him in a tattered coat, and Tsze-kung asking him if he were ill, he replied, "I have heard that to have no money is to be poor, and that to study truth and not be able to find it is to be ill." This answer sent Tsze-kung away in confusion.—The 900 measures (whatever they were) was the proper allowance for an officer of Sze's station.

4. THE VICES OF A FATHER SHOULD NOT DISCREDIT A VIRTUOUS SON. "The father of Chung-kung (see V. iv.) was a man of bad character," and some would have visited this upon his son, which drew forth Confucius' remark. The rules of the Chow dynasty required that sacrificial victims should be red, and have good horns. An animal with those qualities, though it might spring from one not possessing them, would certainly not be unacceptable on that account to the spirits sacrificed to.

5. THE SUPERIORITY OF HWUY TO THE OTHER DISCIPLES.

6. THE QUALITIES OF TSZE-LOO, TSZE-KUNG, AND TSZE-YEW, AND THEIR COMPETENCY TO ASSIST IN GOVERNMENT. The prince is called

and was answered, Ts'ze is a man of intelligence; what difficulty would he find in being an officer of government?" And to the same question about K'ew, the Master gave the same reply, saying, "K'ew is a man of various ability."

VII. The chief of the Ke family sent to ask Min Tsze-k'een to be governor of Pe. Min Tsze-k'een said, "Decline the offer for me politely. If any one come again to me with a second invitation, I shall be *obliged to go and live* on the banks of the Wăn."

VIII. Pih-new being sick, the Master went to ask for him. He took hold of his hand through the window, and said, "It is killing him. It is the appointment *of Heaven*, alas! That such a man should have such a sickness! That such a man should have such a sickness!"

IX. The Master said, "Admirable indeed was the virtue of Hwuy! With a single bamboo dish of rice, a single gourd dish of drink, and living in his mean narrow lane, while others could not have endured the distress, he did not allow his joy to be affected by it. Admirable indeed was the virtue of Hwuy!"

"the *doer* of government;" his ministers and officers are styled "the *followers* (officers) of government."

7. MIN TSZE-K'EEN REFUSES TO SERVE THE KE FAMILY. The tablet of Tsze-k'een (his name was Sun) is now the first on the east among "the wise ones" of the temple. He was among the foremost of the disciples. Confucius praises his filial piety; and we see here, how he could stand firm in his virtue, and refuse the proffers of powerful but unprincipled families of his time. *Pi* was a place belonging to the Ke family. Its name is still preserved in a district of the department of K-chow, in Shantung. The Wăn stream divides Ts'e and Loo. Tsze-k'een threatens, if he should be troubled again, to retreat to Ts'e, where the Ke family could not reach him.

8. LAMENT OF CONFUCIUS OVER THE MORTAL SICKNESS OF PIH-NEW. Pih-new, "elder or uncle New," was the denomination of Yen Kăng, who had an honourable place among the disciples of the sage. In the old interpretation, his sickness is said to have been "an evil disease," by which some leprosy is intended. Suffering from such a disease, Pih-new would not see people, and Confucius took his hand through the window. A different explanation of that circumstance is given by Choo He. He says that sick persons were usually placed on the north side of the apartment, but when the prince visited them, in order that he might appear to them with his face to the south (see ch. I.), they were moved to the south. On this occasion, Pih-new's friends wanted to receive Confucius after this royal fashion, which he avoided by not entering the house.

9. THE HAPPINESS OF HWUY INDEPENDENT OF POVERTY.

X. Yen K'ew said, "It is not that I do not delight in your doctrines, but my strength is insufficient." The Master said, "Those whose strength is insufficient give over in the middle of the way, but now you limit yourself."

XI. The Master said to Tsze-hea, "Do you be a scholar after the style of the superior man, and not after that of the mean man."

XII. Tsze-yew being governor of Woo-shing, the Master said to him, "Have you got *good men there?*" He answered, "There is Tan-t'ae Mĕĕ-ming, who never in walking takes a short cut, and never comes to my office, excepting on public business."

XIII. The Master said, "Măng Che-fan does not boast of his merit. Being in the rear on an occasion of flight, when they were about to enter the gate, he whipt up his horse, saying, 'It is not that I dare to be last. My horse would not advance.'"

XIV. The Master said, "Without the specious speech of the litanist T'o, and the beauty of *the prince* Chaou of Sung, it is difficult to escape in the present age."

10. A HIGH AIM AND PERSEVERANCE PROPER TO A STUDENT. Confucius would not admit K'ew's apology for not attempting more than he did. "Give over in the middle of the way," i. e. they go as long and as far as they can, they are pursuing when they stop; whereas K'ew was giving up when he might have gone on.

11. HOW LEARNING SHOULD BE PURSUED.

12. THE CHARACTER OF TAN-T'AE MĔĔ-MING. The chapter shows, according to Chinese commentators, the advantage to people in authority of their having good men about them. In this way, after their usual fashion, they seek for a profound meaning in the remark of Confucius. Tan-t'ae Mĕĕ-ming, who was styled Tsze-yu, has his tablet the second east outside the hall. The accounts of him are very conflicting. According to one, he was very good-looking, while another says he was so bad-looking that Confucius at first formed an unfavourable opinion of him, an error which he afterwards confessed on Mĕĕ-ming's becoming eminent. He travelled southwards with not a few followers, and places near Soo-chow and elsewhere retain names indicative of his presence.

13. THE VIRTUE OF MANG CHE-FAN IN CONCEALING HIS MERIT. But where was his virtue in deviating from the truth? And how could Confucius commend him for doing so? These questions have never troubled the commentators. Măng Che-fan was an officer of Loo. The defeat, after which he thus distinguished himself, was in the 11th year of Duke Gae, B.C. 483.

14. THE DEGENERACY OF THE AGE REQUIRING GLIBNESS OF TONGUE AND BEAUTY OF PERSON. To, the officer charged with the prayers in the

XV. The Master said, "Who can go out but by the door? How is it that men will not walk according to these ways?"

XVI. The Master said, "Where the solid qualities are in excess of accomplishments, we have rusticity; where the accomplishments are in excess of the solid qualities, we have the manners of a clerk. When the accomplishments and solid qualities are equally blended, we then have the man of complete virtue."

XVII. The Master said, "Man is born for uprightness. If a man lose his uprightness, and yet live, his escape *from death* is the effect of mere good fortune."

XVIII. The Master said, "They who know *the truth* are not equal to those who love it, and they who love it are not equal to those who find delight in it."

XIX. The Master said, "To those whose talents are above mediocrity, the highest subjects may be announced. To those who are below mediocrity, the highest subjects may not be announced."

XX. Fan Ch'e asked what constituted wisdom. The Master said, "To give one's-self earnestly to the duties due to men, and, while respecting spiritual beings, to keep aloof from them, may be called wisdom." He asked

ancestral temple. I have coined the word *literatist*, to come as near to the meaning as possible. He was an officer of the state of Wei, styled Tsze-yu. Prince Ch'aou had been guilty of incest with his sister Nan-tsze (see ch. 26), and afterwards, when she was married to the Duke Ling of Wei, he served as an officer there, carrying on his wickedness. He was celebrated for his beauty of person.

15. A LAMENT OVER THE WAYWARDNESS OF MEN'S CONDUCT. "These ways,"—in a moral sense;—not deep doctrines, but rules of life.

16. THE EQUAL BLENDING OF SOLID EXCELLENCE AND ORNAMENTAL ACCOMPLISHMENTS IN A COMPLETE CHARACTER.

17. LIFE WITHOUT UPRIGHTNESS IS NOT TRUE LIFE, AND CANNOT BE CALCULATED ON. "No more serious warning than this," says one commentator, "was ever addressed to men by Confucius." We long here, as elsewhere, for more perspicuity and fuller development of view. An important truth struggles for expression, but only finds it imperfectly. Without uprightness, the end of man's existence is not fulfilled, but his preservation in such case is not merely a fortunate accident.

18. DIFFERENT STAGES OF ATTAINMENT.

19. TEACHERS MUST BE GUIDED IN COMMUNICATING KNOWLEDGE BY THE SUSCEPTIVITY OF THE LEARNERS.

20. CHIEF ELEMENTS IN WISDOM AND VIRTUE. We may suppose from the second clause that Fan Ch'e was striving after what was uncommon

about perfect virtue. The Master said, "The man of virtue makes the difficulty *to be overcome* his first business, and success only a subsequent consideration;—this may be called perfect virtue."

XXI. The Master said, "The wise find delight in water; the virtuous find delight in hills. The wise are active; the virtuous are tranquil. The wise are joyful; the virtuous are long-lived."

XXII. The Master said, "Ts'e, by one change, would come to the state of Loo. Loo, by one change, would come to a state where true principles predominated."

XXIII. The Master said, "A cornered vessel without corners.—A strange cornered vessel! A strange cornered vessel!"

XXIV. Tsae Wo asked, saying, "A benevolent man, though it be told him,—'There is a man in the well,' will go in after him, I suppose." Confucius said, "Why should he do so? A superior man may be made to go *to the well*, but he cannot be made to go down into it. He may be imposed upon, but he cannot be befooled."

and superhuman. The sage's advice therefore is—"attend to what are plainly human duties, and do not be superstitious."

21. CONTRASTS OF THE WISE AND THE VIRTUOUS. The wise or knowing are active and restless, like the waters of a stream, ceaselessly flowing and advancing. The virtuous are tranquil and firm, like the stable mountains. The pursuit of knowledge brings joy. The life of the virtuous may be expected to glide calmly on and long. After all, the saying is not very comprehensible.

22. THE CONDITION OF THE STATES TS'E AND LOO. Ts'e and Loo were both within the present Shan-tung. Ts'e lay along the coast on the north, embracing the present department of Ts'ing Chow and other territory. Loo was on the south, the larger portion of it being formed by the present department of Yen-chow. At the rise of the Chow dynasty, King Woo invested "the great Duke Wang" with the principality of Ts'e; while his successor, King Ch'ing, constituted the son of his uncle, the famous duke of Chow, prince of Loo. In Confucius' time, Ts'e had degenerated more than Loo.

23. THE NAME WITHOUT THE REALITY IS FOLLY. This was spoken with reference to the governments of the time, retaining ancient names without ancient principles. The vessel spoken of was made with corners, as appears from the composition of the character, which is formed from Këŏ, "a horn," "a sharp corner." In Confucius' time, the form was changed, while the name was kept.

24. THE BENEVOLENT EXERCISE THEIR BENEVOLENCE WITH PRUDENCE. Tsae Wo could see no limitation to acting on the impulse of

XXV. The Master said, "The superior man, extensively studying all learning, and keeping himself under the restraint of the rules of propriety, may thus likewise not overstep what is right."

XXVI. The Master having visited Nan-tsze, Tsze-loo was displeased, on which the Master swore, saying, "Wherein I have done improperly, may Heaven reject me! may Heaven reject me!"

XXVII. The Master said, "Perfect is the virtue which is according to the Constant Mean! Rare for a long time has been its practice among the people."

XXVIII. 1. Tsze-kung said, "Suppose the case of a man extensively conferring benefits on the people, and able to assist all, what would you say of him? Might he be called perfectly virtuous?" The Master said, "Why speak only of virtue in connection with him? Must he not have the qualities of a sage? Even Yaou and Shun were still solicitous about this.

2. "Now the man of perfect virtue, wishing to be established himself, seeks also to establish others; wishing to be enlarged himself, he seeks also to enlarge others.

3. "To be able to judge of others by what is nigh in ourselves;—this may be called the art of virtue."

benevolence. We are not to suppose, with modern commentators, that he wished to show that benevolence was impracticable.

25. THE HAPPY EFFECT OF LEARNING AND PROPRIETY COMBINED.

26. CONFUCIUS VINDICATES HIMSELF FOR VISITING THE UNWORTHY NAN-TSZE. Nan-tsze was the wife of the duke of Wei, and sister of Prince Chaou, mentioned chapter xiv. Her lewd character was well known, and hence Tsze-loo was displeased, thinking an interview with her was disgraceful to the Master. Great pains are taken to explain the incident. "Nan-tsze," says one, "sought the interview from the stirrings of her natural conscience." "It was a rule," says another, "that officers in a state should visit the prince's wife." "Nan-tsze," argues a third, "had all influence with her husband, and Confucius wished to get currency by her means for his doctrine."

27. THE DEFECTIVE PRACTICE OF THE PEOPLE IN CONFUCIUS' TIME. See the Doctrine of the Mean, III.

28. THE TRUE NATURE AND ART OF VIRTUE. There are no higher sayings in the Analects than we have here. 1. Tsze-kung appears to have thought that great doings were necessary to virtue, and propounds a case which would transcend the achievements of Yaou and Shun. From such extravagant views the Master recalls him. 2. This is the description of "the mind of the perfectly virtuous man" as void of all selfishness. 3. It is to be wished that the idea intended by "being able to judge of others

BOOK VII.

CHAPTER I. The Master said, "A transmitter and not a maker, believing in and loving the ancients, I venture to compare myself with our old P'ang."

II. The Master said, "The silent treasuring up of knowledge; learning without satiety; and instructing others without being wearied:—what one of these things belongs to me?"

III. The Master said, "The leaving virtue without proper cultivation; the not thoroughly discussing what is learned; not being able to move towards righteousness of which a knowledge is gained; and not being able to change what is not good:—these are the things which occasion me solicitude."

IV. When the Master was unoccupied with business, his manner was easy, and he looked pleased.

by what is nigh in ourselves," had been more clearly expressed. Still we seem to have here a near approach to a positive enunciation of "the golden rule."

HEADING AND SUBJECTS OF THIS BOOK.—" A transmitter, and——." We have in this book much information of a personal character about Confucius, both from his own lips and from the descriptions of his disciples. The two preceding books treat of the disciples and other worthies, and here, in contrast with them, we have the sage himself exhibited.

1. CONFUCIUS DISCLAIMS BEING AN ORIGINATOR OR MAKER. Commentators say the master's language here is from his extreme humility. But we must hold that it expresses his true sense of his position and work. Who the individual called endearingly " our old P'ang " was, can hardly be ascertained. Choo He adopts the view that he was a worthy officer of the Shang dynasty. But that individual's history is a mass of fables. Others make him to be Laou-tsze, the founder of the Taou sect, and others again make two individuals—one this Laou-tsze, and the other that P'ang.

2. CONFUCIUS' HUMBLE ESTIMATE OF HIMSELF. " The language," says Choo He, " is that of humility upon humility." Some insert, " besides me," in their explanations before " what."—" Besides these, what is there in me?" But this is quite arbitrary. The profession may be inconsistent with what we find in other passages, but the inconsistency must stand rather than violence be done to the language.

3. CONFUCIUS' ANXIETY ABOUT HIS SELF-CULTIVATION:—ANOTHER HUMBLE ESTIMATE OF HIMSELF. Here, again, commentators find only the expressions of humility, but there can be no reason why we should not admit that Confucius was anxious lest these things, which are only put forth as possibilities, should become in his case actual facts.

4. THE MANNER OF CONFUCIUS WHEN UNOCCUPIED.

V. The Master said, "Extreme is my decay. For a long time I have not dreamed, as I was wont to do, that I saw the Duke of Chow."

VI. 1. The Master said, "Let the will be set on the path of duty.

2. "Let every attainment in what is good be firmly grasped.

3. "Let perfect virtue be accorded with.

4. "Let relaxation and enjoyment be found in the polite arts."

VII. The Master said, "From the man bringing his bundle of dried flesh *for my teaching* upwards, I have never refused instruction to any one."

5. HOW THE DISAPPOINTMENT OF CONFUCIUS' HOPES AFFECTED EVEN HIS DREAMS. Chow was the name of the seat of the family from which the dynasty so called sprang, and on the enlargement of this territory, King Wăn divided the original seat between his sons, Tan and Shih. Tan was "the duke of Chow," in wisdom and politics what his elder brother, the first emperor, Woo, was in arms. Confucius had longed to bring the principles and institutions of Chow-kung into practice, and in his earlier years, while hope animated him, had often dreamt of the former sage. The original territory of Chow was what is now the district of K'e-shan, department of Fung-ts'eang, in Shen-se.

6. RULES FOR THE FULL MATURING OF CHARACTER. See a note on "The polite arts," I. vi. A full enumeration makes "six arts," viz. ceremonies, music, archery, charioteering, the study of characters or language, and figures or arithmetic. The ceremonies were ranged in five classes: lucky or sacrifices, unlucky or the mourning ceremonies, military, those of host and guest, and festive. Music required the study of the music of Hwang-te, of Yaou, of Shun, of Yu, of T'ang, and of Woo. Archery had a five-fold classification. Charioteering had the same. The study of the characters required the examination of them, to determine whether there predominated in their formation resemblance to the object, combination of ideas, indication of properties, a phonetic principle, a principle of contrariety, or metaphorical accommodation. Figures were managed according to nine rules, as the object was the measurement of land, capacity, &c. These six subjects were the business of the highest and most liberal education: but we need not suppose that Confucius had them all in view here.

7. THE READINESS OF CONFUCIUS TO IMPART INSTRUCTION. It was the rule anciently that when one party waited on another, he should carry some present or offering with him. Pupils did so when they first waited on their teacher. Of such offerings, one of the lowest was a bundle of "dried flesh." The wages of a teacher are now called "the money of the dried flesh." However small the offering brought to the sage, let him only see the indication of a wish to learn, and he imparted his instructions.

VIII. The Master said, "I do not open up the truth to one who is not eager *to get knowledge,* nor help out any one who is not anxious to explain himself. When I have presented one corner of a subject to any one, and he cannot from it learn the other three, I do not repeat my lesson."

IX. 1. When the Master was eating by the side of a mourner, he never ate to the full.

2. He did not sing on the same day in which he had been weeping.

X. 1. The Master said to Yen Yuen, "When called to office, to undertake its duties; when not so called, to lie retired;—it is only I and you who have attained to this."

2. Tsze-loo said, "If you had the conduct of the armies of a great State, whom would you have to act with you?"

3. The Master said, "I would not have him to act with me, who will unarmed attack a tiger, or cross a river without a boat, dying without any regret. My associate must be the man who proceeds to action full of solicitude, who is fond of adjusting his plans, and then carries them into execution."

XI. The Master said, "If the search for riches is sure to be successful, though I should become a servant with whip in hand to get them, I will do so. As the search may not be successful, I will follow after that which I love."

8. CONFUCIUS REQUIRED A REAL DESIRE AND ABILITY IN HIS DISCIPLES. The last chapter tells of the sage's readiness to teach, which shows that he did not teach where his teaching was likely to prove of no avail.

9. CONFUCIUS' SYMPATHY WITH MOURNERS. The weeping is understood to be on occasion of offering his condolences to a mourner.

10. THE ATTAINMENTS OF HWUY LIKE THOSE OF CONFUCIUS. THE EXCESSIVE BOLDNESS OF TSZE-LOO. The words "unarmed to attack a tiger; without a boat to cross a river," are from the She King, Pt II., Bk V. i. 6. Tsze-loo, it would appear, was jealous of the praise conferred on Hwuy, and pluming himself on his bravery, put in for a share of the Master's approbation. But he only brought on himself rebuke.

11. THE UNCERTAINTY AND FOLLY OF THE PURSUIT OF RICHES. It occurs to a student to understand the first clause—"If it be *proper* to search for riches," and the third—"I will do it." But the translation is according to the modern commentary, and the conclusion agrees better with it. In explaining the words about "whip in hand," some refer us to the attendants who cleared the street with their whips when the prince went abroad, but we need not seek any particular allusion of the kind.

XII. The things in reference to which the Master exercised the greatest caution were—fasting, war, and sickness.

XIII. When the Master was in Ts'e, he heard the Shaou, and for three months did not know the taste of flesh. "I did not think," he said, "that music could have been made so excellent as this."

XIV. 1. Yen Yew said, "Is our Master for the prince of Wei?" Tsze-kung said, "Oh! I will ask him."

2. He went in *accordingly*, and said, "What sort of men were Pih-e and Shuh-ts'e?" "They were ancient worthies," said the Master. "Did they have any repinings *because of their course?*" The Master again replied, "They sought to act virtuously, and they did so; what

---

An objection to the pursuit of wealth may be made on the ground of righteousness (as in chapter xiv.) or on that of its uncertainty. It is the latter on which Confucius here rests.

12. WHAT THINGS CONFUCIUS WAS PARTICULARLY CAREFUL ABOUT. The word used here for "*fasting*" denotes the whole religious adjustment, enjoined before the offering of sacrifice, and extending over the ten days previous to the great sacrificial seasons. Properly it means "to equalize," and the effect of those previous exercises was "to adjust what was not adjusted, to produce a perfect adjustment." Sacrifices presented in such a state of mind were sure to be acceptable. Other people, it is said, might be heedless in reference to sacrifices, to war, and to sickness, but not so the sage.

13. THE EFFECT OF MUSIC ON CONFUCIUS. The *shaou*,—see III. 25. This incident must have happened in the 36th year of Confucius, when he followed the Duke Ch'aou in his flight from Loo to Ts'e. As related in the "Historical Records," before the words "three months," we have "he learned it," which may relieve us from the necessity of extending the three months over all the time in which he did not know the taste of his food. In Ho An's compilation, the "did not know" is explained by "he was careless about and forgot."

14. CONFUCIUS DID NOT APPROVE OF A SON OPPOSING HIS FATHER. 1. The eldest son of Duke Ling of Wei had planned to kill his mother (?,stepmother), the notorious Nau-tsze (VI. xxvi.). For this he had to flee the country, and his son, on the death of Ling, became duke, and subsequently opposed his father's attempts to wrest the sovereignty from him. This was the matter argued among the disciples,—Was Confucius for the son, the reigning duke? 2. In Wei it would not have been according to *propriety* to speak by name of its ruler, and therefore Tsze-kung put the case of Pih-e and Shuh-ts'e, see V. xxii. They having given up a throne, and finally their lives, rather than do what they thought wrong, and Confucius fully approving of their conduct, it was plain he could not approve of a son's holding by force what was the rightful inheritance of the father.

was there for them to repine about?" On this, Tsze-kung went out and said, "Our Master is not for him."

XV. The Master said, "With coarse rice to eat, with water to drink, and my bended arm for a pillow;—I have still joy in the midst of these things. Riches and honours acquired by unrighteousness are to me as a floating cloud."

XVI. The Master said, "If some years were added to my life, I would give fifty to the study of the YIH, and then I might come to be without great faults."

XVII. The Master's frequent themes of discourse were —the Odes, the Book of History, and the maintenance of the Rules of propriety. On all these he frequently discoursed.

XVIII. 1. The duke of Shê asked Tsze-loo about Confucius, and Tsze-loo did not answer him.

2. The Master said, "Why did you not say to him,— He is simply a man, who in his eager pursuit of knowledge forgets his food, who in the joy *of its attainment* forgets his sorrows, and who does not perceive that old age is coming on?"

XIX. The Master said, "I am not one who was born in

15. THE JOY OF CONFUCIUS INDEPENDENT OF OUTWARD CIRCUMSTANCES, HOWEVER STRAITENED.

16. THE VALUE WHICH CONFUCIUS SET UPON THE STUDY OF THE YIH. Choo He supposes that this was spoken when Confucius was about seventy, as he was in his 68th year when he ceased his wanderings, and settled in Loo to the adjustment and compilation of the Yih and other *king*. If the remark be referred to that time, an error may well be found in the number fifty, for he would hardly be speaking at seventy of having fifty years added to his life. Choo also mentions the report of a certain individual that he had seen a copy of the Lun Yu, which made the passage read:—"If I had some more years to finish the study of the Yih," &c. Ho An interprets the chapter quite differently. Referring to the saying, II. iv. 4, "At fifty, I knew the decrees of heaven," he supposes this to have been spoken when Confucius was forty-seven, and explains—"In a few years more I will be fifty, and have finished the Yih, when I may be without great faults."—One thing remains upon both views :—Confucius never claimed what his followers do for him, to be a perfect man.

17. CONFUCIUS' MOST COMMON TOPICS.

18. CONFUCIUS' DESCRIPTION OF HIS CHARACTER AS BEING SIMPLY A MOST EARNEST LEARNER. Shê was a district of Ts'oo, the governor or prefect of which had usurped the title of duke. Its name is still preserved in a district of the department of Nan-yung, in the south of Ho-nan.

19. CONFUCIUS' KNOWLEDGE NOT CONNATE, BUT THE RESULT OF HIS

the possession of knowledge; I am one who is fond of antiquity, and earnest in seeking it *there*."

XX. The subjects on which the Master did not talk, were,—prodigious things, feats of strength, disorder, and spiritual beings.

XXI. The Master said, "When I walk along with two others, they may serve me as my teachers. I will select their good qualities and follow them, their bad qualities and avoid them."

XXII. The Master said, "Heaven produced the virtue that is in me. Hwan T'uy—what can he do to me?"

XXIII. The Master said, "Do you think, my disciples, that I have any concealments? I conceal nothing from you. There is nothing which I do that is not shown to you, my disciples;—that is my way."

XXIV. There were four things which the Master taught,—letters, ethics, devotion of soul, and truthfulness.

XXV. 1. The Master said, "A sage it is not mine to

STUDY OF ANTIQUITY. Here again, according to commentators, is a wonderful instance of the sage's humility disclaiming what he really had. The comment of Yun Ho-tsing, subjoined to Choo He's own, is to the effect that the knowledge born with a man is only "righteousness" and "reason," while ceremonies, music, names of things, history, &c., must be learned. This would make what we may call connate or innate knowledge the moral sense, and those intuitive principles of reason, on and by which all knowledge is built up. But Confucius could not mean to deny his being possessed of these.

20. SUBJECTS AVOIDED BY CONFUCIUS IN CONVERSATION. By "disorder" are meant rebellious disorder, parricide, regicide, and such crimes. For an instance of Confucius avoiding the subject of spiritual beings, see XI. xi.

21. HOW A MAN MAY FIND INSTRUCTORS FOR HIMSELF.

22. CONFUCIUS CALM IN DANGER, THROUGH THE ASSURANCE OF HAVING A DIVINE MISSION. According to the historical accounts, Confucius was passing through Sung on his way from Wei to Ch'in, and was practising ceremonies with his disciples under a large tree, when they were set upon by emissaries of Hwan Tuy, a high officer of Sung. These pulled down the tree, and wanted to kill the sage. His disciples urged him to make haste and escape, when he calmed their fears by these words. At the same time, he disguised himself till he had got past Sung. This story may be apocryphal, but the saying remains,—a remarkable one.

23. CONFUCIUS PRACTISED NO CONCEALMENT WITH HIS DISCIPLES.

24. THE COMMON SUBJECTS OF CONFUCIUS' TEACHING. I confess to apprehend but vaguely the two latter subjects as distinguished from the second.

25. THE PAUCITY OF TRUE MEN IN, AND THE PRETENTIOUSNESS OF CONFUCIUS' TIME. We have in the chapter a climax of character:—

see; could I see a man of real talent and virtue, that would satisfy me."

2. The Master said, "A good man it is not mine to see; could I see a man possessed of constancy, that would satisfy me.

3. "Having not and yet affecting to have, empty and yet affecting to be full, straitened and yet affecting to be at ease:—it is difficult with such characteristics to have constancy."

XXVI. The Master angled,—but did not use a net. He shot,—but not at birds perching.

XXVII. The Master said, "There may be those who act without knowing why. I do not do so. Hearing much and selecting what is good and following it, seeing much and keeping it in memory:—this is the second style of knowledge."

XXVIII. 1. It was difficult to talk with the people of Hoo-heang, and a lad of that place having had an interview with the Master, the disciples doubted.

2. The Master said, "I admit people's approach to me without committing myself *as to what they may do* when they have retired. Why must one be so severe? If a man purify himself to wait upon me, I receive him so purified, without guaranteeing his past conduct."

XXIX. The Master said, "Is virtue a thing remote? I wish to be virtuous, and lo! virtue is at hand."

XXX. 1. The Minister of crime of Ch'in asked whether

the man of constancy, or the single-hearted, steadfast man; the good man, who on his single-heartedness has built up his virtue; the *keun-tsze*, the man of virtue in large proportions, and intellectually able besides; and the sage, or highest style of man. Compare Mencius, VII. Pt II. xxv.

26. THE HUMANITY OF CONFUCIUS. Confucius would only destroy what life was necessary for his use, and in taking that he would not take advantage of the inferior creatures. This chapter is said to be descriptive of him in his early life.

27. AGAINST ACTING NEEDLESSLY. Paou Heen, in Ho An, says that this was spoken with reference to heedless compilers of records; but this is unnecessary. The paraphrasts make the latter part descriptive of Confucius—"I hear much," &c. This is not necessary, and the translation had better be as indefinite as the original.

28. THE READINESS OF CONFUCIUS TO MEET APPROACHES TO HIM THOUGH MADE BY THE UNLIKELY.

29. VIRTUE IS NOT FAR TO SEEK.

30. HOW CONFUCIUS ACKNOWLEDGED HIS ERROR. 1. Ch'in, one of

the Duke Ch'aou knew propriety, and Confucius said, "He knew propriety."

2. Confucius having retired, the minister bowed to Woo-ma K'e to come forward, and said, "I have heard that the superior man is not a partisan. May the superior man be a partisan also? The prince married a daughter of *the house of* Woo, of the same surname with himself, and called her,—'The elder *lady* Tsze of Woo.' If the prince knew propriety, who does not know it?"

3. Woo-ma K'e reported these remarks, and the Master said, "I am fortunate! If I have any errors, people are sure to know them."

XXXI. When the Master was in company with a person who was singing, if he sang well, he would make him repeat the song, while he accompanied it with his own voice.

XXXII. The Master said, "In letters I am perhaps equal to other men, but *the character of* the superior man, carrying out in his conduct what he professes, is what I have not yet attained to."

XXXIII. The Master said, "The sage and the man of perfect virtue;—how dare I *rank myself with them?* It may simply be said of me, that I strive to become such without satiety, and teach others without weariness." Kung-se Hwa said, "This is just what we, the disciples, cannot imitate you in."

the States of China in Confucius' time, is to be referred probably to the present department of Ch'in-chow in Ho-nan province. Ch'aou was the honorary epithet of Chow, duke of Loo, B.C. 541—509. He had a reputation for the knowledge and observance of ceremonies, and Confucius answered the minister's question accordingly, the more readily that he was speaking to the officer of another State, and was bound, therefore, to hide any failings that his own sovereign might have had. 2. With all his knowledge of proprieties, the Duke Ch'aou had violated an important rule,—that which forbids the intermarriage of parties of the same surname. The ruling houses of Loo and Woo were branches of the imperial house of Chow, and consequently had the same surname, *Ke*. To conceal his violation of the rule. Ch'aou called his wife by the surname *Tsze*, as if she had belonged to the ducal house of Sung. Woo-ma K'e was one of the minor disciples of Confucius. 3. Confucius takes the criticism of his questioner very lightly.

31. THE GOOD FELLOWSHIP OF CONFUCIUS.
32. ACKNOWLEDGMENT OF CONFUCIUS IN ESTIMATING HIMSELF.
33. WHAT CONFUCIUS DECLINED TO BE CONSIDERED, AND WHAT HE CLAIMED.

XXXIV. The Master being very sick, Tsze-loo asked leave to pray for him. He said, " May such a thing be done ?" Tsze-loo replied, " It may. In the Prayers it is said, ' Prayer has been made to you, the spirits of the upper and lower worlds.' " The Master said, " My praying has been for a long time."

XXXV. The Master said, " Extravagance leads to insubordination, and parsimony to meanness. It is better to be mean than to be insubordinate."

XXXVI. The Master said, " The superior man is satisfied and composed; the mean man is always full of distress."

XXXVII. The Master was mild, and yet dignified; majestic, and yet not fierce ; respectful, and yet easy.

BOOK VIII.

CHAPTER I. The Master said, " T'ae-pih may be said to have reached the highest point of virtuous action.

34. CONFUCIUS DECLINES TO BE PRAYED FOR. The word here rendered " prayers " means " to write a eulogy, and confer the posthumous honorary title ;" also " to eulogize in prayer," *i.e.* to recite one's excellencies as the ground of supplication. Tsze-loo must have been referring to some well-known collection of such prayers. Choo Ho says, " Prayer is the expression of repentance and promise of amendment, to supplicate the help of the spirits. If there be not those things, then there is no need for praying. In the case of the sage, he had committed no errors, and admitted of no amendment. In all his conduct he had been in harmony with the spiritual intelligences, and therefore he said,—' *my praying has been for a long time.*' " We may demur to some of these expressions, but the declining to be prayed for, and concluding remark, do indicate the satisfaction of Confucius with himself. Here, as in other places, we wish that our information about him were not so stinted and fragmentary.

35. MEANNESS NOT SO BAD AS INSUBORDINATION.

36. CONTRAST IN THEIR FEELINGS BETWEEN THE KEUN-TSZE AND THE MEAN MAN.

37. HOW VARIOUS ELEMENTS MODIFIED ONE ANOTHER IN THE CHARACTER OF CONFUCIUS.

HEADING AND SUBJECTS OF THIS BOOK.—" T'ae-pih." As in other cases, the first words of the book give name to it. The subjects of the book are miscellaneous, but it begins and ends with the character and deeds of ancient sages and worthies ; and on this account it follows the seventh book, where we have Confucius himself described.

1. THE EXCEEDING VIRTUE OF T'AE-PIH. T'ae-pih was the eldest son of King Tae, the grandfather of Wǎn, the founder of the Chow dynasty.

Thrice he declined the empire, and the people *in ignorance of his motives* could not express their approbation of his conduct."

II. 1. The Master said, "Respectfulness, without the rules of propriety, becomes laborious bustle; carefulness, without the rules of propriety, becomes timidity; boldness, without the rules of propriety, becomes insubordination; straightforwardness, without the rules of propriety, becomes rudeness.

2. "When those who are in high stations perform well all their duties to their relations, the people are aroused to virtue. When old ministers and friends are not neglected by them, the people are preserved from meanness."

III. Tsăng the philosopher being sick, he called to him the disciples of his school, and said, "Uncover my feet, uncover my hands. It is said in the Book of Poetry,

T'ae had formed the intention of upsetting the Yin dynasty, of which T'ae-pih disapproved. T'ae, moreover, because of the sage virtues of his grandson Ch'ang, who afterwards became King Wăn, wished to hand down his principality to his third son, Ch'ang's father. T'ae-pih observing this, and to escape opposing his father's purpose, retired with his second brother among the barbarous tribes of the south, and left their youngest brother in possession of the state. The motives of his conduct T'ae-pih kept to himself, so that the people "could not find how to praise him." There is a difficulty in making out the refusal of the empire *three times*, there being different accounts of the times and ways in which he did so. Choo He cuts the knot, by making "thrice" = "firmly," in which solution we may acquiesce. There is as great difficulty to find out a declining of the *empire* in T'ae-pih's withdrawing from the petty state of Chow. It may be added that King Woo, the first emperor of the Chow dynasty, subsequently conferred on T'ae-pih the posthumous title of Chief of Woo, the country to which he had withdrawn, and whose rude inhabitants gathered round him. His second brother succeeded him in the government of them, and hence the ruling house of Woo had the same surname as the imperial house of Chow, that namely of Tsze. See VII. xxx.

2. THE VALUE OF THE RULES OF PROPRIETY; AND OF EXAMPLE IN THOSE IN HIGH STATIONS. 1. We must bear in mind that the ceremonies, or rules of propriety, spoken of in these books, are not mere conventionalities, but the ordinations of man's moral and intelligent nature in the line of what is *proper*. 2. There does not seem any connection between the former paragraph and this, and hence this is by many considered to be a new chapter, and assigned to the philosopher Tsăng.

3. THE PHILOSOPHER TSĂNG'S FILIAL PIETY SEEN IN HIS CARE OF HIS PERSON. We get our bodies perfect from our parents, and should so preserve them to the last. This is a great branch of filial piety with the Chinese, and this chapter is said to illustrate how Tsăng-tsze had made this

'We should be apprehensive and cautious, as if on the brink of a deep gulf, as if treading on thin ice,' *and so have I been*. Now and hereafter, I know my esape *from all injury to my person*, O ye, my little children."

IV. 1. Tsăng the philosopher being sick, Mang King went to ask how he was.

2. Tsăng said to him, "When a bird is about to die, its notes are mournful; when a man is about to die, his words are good.

3. "There are three principles of conduct which the man of high rank should consider specially important:— that in his deportment and manner he keep from violence and heedlessness; that in regulating his countenance he keep near to sincerity; and that in his words and tones he keep far from lowness and impropriety. As to such matters as attending to the sacrificial vessels, there are the proper officers for them."

V. Tsăng the philosopher said, "Gifted with ability, and yet putting questions to those who were not so; possessed of much, and yet putting questions to those possessed of little; having, as though he had not; full, and yet counting himself as empty; offended against, and yet entering into no altercation:—formerly I had a friend who pursued this style of conduct."

VI. Tsăng the philosopher said, "Suppose that there is an individual who can be entrusted with the charge of a young orphan *prince*, and can be commissioned with authority over *a State of* a hundred *le*, and whom no emergency however great can drive from his principles:— is such a man a superior man? He is a superior man indeed."

his life-long study. He made the disciples uncover his hands and feet, to show them in what preservation those members were. The passage quoted from the poetry is in Pt II. Bk V. i. 8.

4. THE PHILOSOPHER TSĂNG'S DYING COUNSELS TO A MAN OF HIGH RANK. King was the honorary epithet of Chung-sun Tsĕĕ, a great officer of Loo, and son of Mang-woo, II. vi. From the conclusion of this chapter, we may suppose that he descended to small matters below his rank.

5. THE ADMIRABLE SIMPLICITY AND FREEDOM FROM EGOTISM OF A FRIEND OF THE PHILOSOPHER TSĂNG. This friend is supposed to have been Yen Yuen.

6. A COMBINATION OF TALENTS AND VIRTUE CONSTITUTING A KEUN-TSZE.

VII. 1. Tsäng the philosopher said, "The scholar may not be without breadth of mind and vigorous endurance. His burden is heavy and his course is long.
2. "Perfect virtue is the burden which he considers it is his to sustain; is it not heavy? Only with death does his course stop;—is it not long?"
VIII. 1. The Master said, "It is by the Odes that the mind is aroused.
2. "It is by the Rules of propriety that the character is established.
3. "It is from Music that the finish is received."
IX. The Master said, "The people may be made to follow a path of action, but they may not be made to understand it."
X. The Master said, "The man who is fond of daring and is dissatisfied with poverty, will proceed to insubordination. So will the man who is not virtuous, when you carry your dislike of him to an extreme."
XI. The Master said, "Though a man have abilities as admirable as those of the duke of Chow, yet if he be proud and niggardly, those other things are really not worth being looked at."
XII. The Master said, "It is not easy to find a man who has learned for three years without coming to be good."

7. THE NECESSITY TO THE SCHOLAR OF COMPASS AND VIGOUR OF MIND. The designation "scholar" here might also be translated "officer." Scholar is the primary meaning; but in all ages learning has been the qualification for, and passport to, official employment in China, hence it is also a general designation for "an officer."
8. THE EFFECTS OF POETRY, PROPRIETIES, AND MUSIC.
9. WHAT MAY, AND WHAT MAY NOT, BE ATTAINED TO WITH THE PEOPLE. This chapter has a very doubtful merit; and the sentiment is much too broadly expressed. Some commentators say, however, that all which is meant is that a knowledge of the reasons and principles of what they are called to do need not be required from the people.
10. DIFFERENT CAUSES OF INSUBORDINATION—A LESSON TO RULERS.
11. THE WORTHLESSNESS OF TALENT WITHOUT VIRTUE.
12. HOW QUICKLY LEARNING LEADS TO GOOD. I have translated here according to the old interpretation of K'ung Gan-kwŏ. Choo He takes the term for "good" in the sense of "emolument," which it also has, and would change the character for "coming to," into another of the same sound and tone, meaning "setting the mind on," thus making the whole a lamentation over the rarity of the disinterested pursuit of learning. But we are not at liberty to admit alterations of the text, unless, as received, it be absolutely unintelligible.

XIII. 1. The Master said, "With sincere faith he unites the love of learning; holding firm to death, he is perfecting the excellence of his course.

2. "*Such an one* will not enter a tottering state, nor dwell in a disorganized one. When right principles of government prevail in the empire, he will show himself; when they are prostrated, he will keep concealed.

3. "When a country is well governed, poverty and a mean condition are things to be ashamed of. When a country is ill governed, riches and honour are things to be ashamed of."

XIV. The Master said, "He who is not in any particular office, has nothing to do with plans for the administration of its duties."

XV. The Master said, "When the music-master, Che, first entered on his office, the finish with the Kwan Ts'eu was magnificent;—how it filled the ears!"

XVI. The Master said, "Ardent and yet not upright; stupid and yet not attentive; simple and yet not sincere: —such persons I do not understand."

XVII. The Master said, "Learn as if you could not reach your object, and were *always* fearing also lest you should lose it."

XVIII. The Master said, "How majestic was the man-

13. THE QUALIFICATIONS OF AN OFFICER, WHO WILL ALWAYS ACT RIGHT IN ACCEPTING AND DECLINING OFFICE. 1. This paragraph is to be taken as descriptive of character, the effects of whose presence we have in the next, and of its absence in the last.—The whole chapter seems to want the warmth of generous principle and feeling. In fact, I doubt whether its parts bear the relation and connection which they are supposed to have.

14. EVERY MAN SHOULD MIND HIS OWN BUSINESS. So the sentiment of this chapter is generalized by the paraphrasts, and perhaps correctly. Its letter, however, has doubtless operated to prevent the spread of right notions about political liberty in China.

15. THE PRAISE OF THE MUSIC-MASTER CHE.

16. A LAMENTATION OVER MORAL ERROR ADDED TO NATURAL DEFECT. "I do not understand them," that is, say commentators, natural defects of endowment are generally associated with certain redeeming qualities, as hastiness with straightforwardness, &c. In the parties Confucius had in view, those redeeming qualities were absent. He did not understand them, and could do nothing for them.

17. WITH WHAT EARNESTNESS AND CONTINUOUSNESS LEARNING SHOULD BE PURSUED.

18. THE LOFTY CHARACTER OF SHUN AND YU. Shun received the

ner in which Shun and Yu held possession of the empire, as if it were nothing to them!"

XIX. 1. The Master said, "Great indeed was Yaou as a sovereign! How majestic was he! It is only Heaven that is grand, and only Yaou corresponded to it. How vast *was his virtue!* The people could find no name for it.

2. "How majestic was he in the works which he accomplished! How glorious in the elegant regulations which he instituted!"

XX. 1. Shun had five ministers, and the empire was well governed.

2. King Woo said, "I have ten able ministers."

3. Confucius said, "Is not *the saying* that talents are difficult to find, true? *Only* when *the dynasties* of T'ang and Yu met, were they more abundant than in this *of* Chow; yet there was a woman among *its able ministers.* There were no more than nine men."

4. "King *Wăn* possessed two of the three parts of the empire, and with those he served the dynasty of Yin. The virtue of the house of Chow may be said to have reached the highest point indeed."

empire from Yaou, B.C. 2254, and Yu received it from Shun, B.C. 2204. The throne came to them not by inheritance. They were called to it by their talents and virtue. And yet the possession of empire did not seem to affect them at all.

19. THE PRAISE OF YAOU. 1. No doubt Yaou, as he appears in Chinese annals, is a fit object of admiration, but if Confucius had had a right knowledge of, and reverence for, Heaven, he could not have spoken as he does here. Grant that it is only the visible heaven overspreading all, to which he compares Yaou, even that is sufficiently absurd.

20. THE SCARCITY OF MEN OF TALENT, AND PRAISE OF THE HOUSE OF CHOW. 1. Shun's five ministers were Yu, superintendent of works, Tseih, superintendent of agriculture, Sëĕ, minister of instruction, Kaou-yaou, minister of justice, and P'ih-yih, warden of woods and marshes. Those five, as being eminent above all their compeers, are mentioned. 2. See the Shoo-king, V. Bk I. ii. 6. Of the ten ministers, the most distinguished of course was the duke of Chow. One of them, it is said in the next paragraph, was a woman, but whether she was the mother of King Wăn, or his wife, is much disputed. 3. Instead of the usual "The Master said," we have here "K'ung the philosopher said." This is accounted for on the ground that the words of *king* Woo having been quoted immediately before, it would not have done to crown the sage with his usual title of "the *Master*." The style of the whole chapter, however, is different from that of any previous one, and we may suspect that it is corrupted. "The dynasties of T'ang and Yu" were those of Yaou and Shun. Yaou is called T'ang, having ascended the throne from the mar-

XXI. The Master said, "I can find no flaw in the character of Yu. He used himself coarse food and drink; but displayed the utmost filial piety towards the spirits. His ordinary garments were poor, but he displayed the utmost elegance in his sacrificial cap and apron. He lived in a low mean house, but expended all his strength on the ditches and water-channels. I can find nothing like a flaw in Yu."

BOOK IX.

CHAPTER I. The subjects of which the Master seldom spoke were—profitableness, and also the appointments *of Heaven*, and perfect virtue.

II. 1. A man of the village of Tã-heang said, "Great indeed is the philosopher K'ung! His learning is extensive, and yet he does not render his name famous by any *particular* thing."

2. The Master heard the observation, and said to his disciples, "What shall I practise? Shall I practise charioteering, or shall I practise archery? I will practise charioteering."

III. 1. The Master said, "The linen cap is that prequisite of that name, and Yu became the accepted surname or style of Shun.

21. THE PRAISE OF YU.
HEADING AND SUBJECTS OF THIS BOOK. "The Master seldom." The thirty chapters of this book are much akin to those of the seventh. They are mostly occupied with the doctrine, character, and ways of Confucius himself.

1. SUBJECTS SELDOM SPOKEN OF BY CONFUCIUS. "Profitableness" is taken here in a good sense;—not as selfish gain, but as it is defined under the first of the diagrams in the Yih-king, "the harmoniousness of all that is righteous;" that is, how what is right is really what is truly profitable. Compare Mencius, I. Pt I. i. Yet even in this sense Confucius seldom spoke of it, as he would not have the consideration of the profitable introduced into conduct at all. With his not speaking of "perfect virtue," there is a difficulty which I know not how to solve. The IVth book is nearly all occupied with it, and it was a prominent topic in Confucius' teachings.

2. AMUSEMENT OF CONFUCIUS AT THE REMARK OF AN IGNORANT MAN ABOUT HIM. Commentators, old and new, say that the chapter shows the exceeding humility of the sage, educed by his being praised, but his observation on the man's remark was evidently ironical.

3. SOME COMMON PRACTICES INDIFFERENT AND OTHERS NOT. 1. The

scribed by the rules of ceremony, but now a silk one is worn. It is economical, and I follow the common practice.

2. "The rules of ceremony prescribe the bowing below *the hall*, but now the practice is to bow *only after* ascending it. That is arrogant. I *continue to* bow below the hall, though I oppose the common practice."

IV. There were four things from which the Master was entirely free. He had no foregone conclusions, no arbitrary predeterminations, no obstinacy, and no egoism.

V. 1. The Master was put in fear in K'wang.

2. He said, "After the death of king Wăn, was not the cause of truth lodged here *in me*?

3. "If Heaven had wished to let this cause of truth perish, then I, a future mortal, should not have got such a relation to that cause. While Heaven does not let the cause of truth perish, what can the people of K'wang do to me?"

cap here spoken of was that prescribed to be worn in the ancestral temple, and made of very fine linen dyed of a deep dark colour. It had fallen into disuse, and was superseded by a simpler one of silk. Rather than be singular, Confucius gave in to a practice, which involved no principle of right, and was economical. 2. "In the ceremonial intercourse between ministers and their prince, it was proper for them to bow below the raised hall. This the prince declined, on which they ascended and completed the homage." The prevailing disregard of the first part of the ceremony Confucius considered inconsistent with the proper distance to be observed between prince and minister, and therefore he would be singular in adhering to the rule.

4. FRAILTIES FROM WHICH CONFUCIUS WAS FREE.

5. CONFUCIUS ASSURED IN A TIME OF DANGER BY HIS CONVICTION OF A DIVINE MISSION. Compare VII. xxii., but the adventure to which this chapter refers is placed in the sage's history before the other, and seems to have occurred in his fifty-seventh year, not long after he had resigned office, and left Loo. There are different opinions as to what state K'wang belonged to. The most likely is that it was a border town of Ch'ing, and its site is now to be found in the department of K'ae-fung in Ho-nan. The account is that K'wang had suffered from Yang Foo, an officer of Loo, to whom Confucius bore a resemblance. As he passed by the place, moreover, a disciple who had been associated with Yang Foo in his operations against K'wang, was driving him. These circumstances made the people think that Confucius was their old enemy, so they attacked him, and kept him prisoner for five days. The accounts of his escape vary, some of them being evidently fabulous. The disciples were in fear. The text would indicate that Confucius himself was so, but this is denied. He here identifies himself with the line of the great sages, to whom Heaven has intrusted the instruction of men. In all the six

VI. 1. A high officer asked Tsze-kung saying, "May we not say that your Master is a sage? How various is his ability!"

2. Tsze-kung said, "Certainly, Heaven has endowed him unlimitedly;—he is about a sage. And, moreover, his ability is various."

3. The Master heard of the conversation and said, "Does the high officer know me? When I was young, my condition was low, and therefore I acquired my ability in many things, but they were mean matters. Must the superior man have such variety of ability? He does not need variety of ability."

4. Laou said, "The Master said, 'Having no official employment, I acquired many arts.'"

VII. The Master said, "Am I indeed possessed of knowledge? I am not knowing. But if a mean person, who appears quite empty-like, ask anything of me, I set it forth from one end to the other, and exhaust it."

VIII. The Master said, "The fung bird does not come; the river sends forth no map:—it is all over with me."

centuries between himself and King Wăn, he does not admit of such another.

6. ON THE VARIOUS ABILITY OF CONFUCIUS:—HIS SAGEHOOD NOT THEREIN. The officer had found the sagehood of Confucius in his various ability. Tsze-kung, positively, and yet with some appearance of hesitancy, affirms the sagehood, and makes that ability only an additional circumstance. Confucius explains his possession of various ability, and repudiates its being essential to the sage, or even to the *keun-tsze*. Laou was a disciple, by surname K'in, and styled Tsze-k'ae, or Tsze-chang. It is supposed that when these conversations were being digested into their present form, some one remembered that Laou had been in the habit of mentioning the remark given, and accordingly it was appended to the chapter.

7. CONFUCIUS DISCLAIMS THE KNOWLEDGE ATTRIBUTED TO HIM, AND DECLARES HIS EARNESTNESS IN TEACHING. The first sentence here was probably an exclamation with reference to some remark upon himself as having extraordinary knowledge.

8. FOR WANT OF AUSPICIOUS OMENS, CONFUCIUS GIVES UP THE HOPE OF THE TRIUMPH OF HIS DOCTRINES. The *fung* is the male of a fabulous bird, which has been called the Chinese phœnix, said to appear when a sage ascends the throne, or when right principles are going to triumph through the empire. The female is called *hwang*. In the days of Shun, they gambolled in his hall, and were heard singing on mount Ke—in the time of King Wăn. The river and the map carry us farther back still, to the time of Fuh-he, to whom a monster with the head

IX. When the Master saw a person in a mourning dress, or any one with the cap and upper and lower garments of full dress, or a blind person, on observing them *approaching*, though they were younger than himself, he would rise up, and if he had to pass by them, he would do so hastily.

X. 1. Yen Yuen, *in admiration of the Master's doctrines*, sighed and said, " I looked up to them, and they *seemed to become* more high; I tried to penetrate them, and they *seemed to become* more firm; I looked at them before me, and suddenly they *seemed to be* behind.

2. "The Master, by orderly method, skilfully leads men on. He enlarged my mind with learning, and taught me the restraints of propriety.

3. "When I wish to give over *the study of his doctrines*, I cannot do so, and having exerted all my ability, there seems something to stand right up before me ; but though I wish to follow *and lay hold of it*, I really find no way to do so."

XI. 1. The Master being very ill, Tsze-loo wished the disciples to act as ministers to him.

2. During a remission of his illness, he said, "Long has the conduct of Yew been deceitful ! By pretending to have ministers when I have them not, whom should I impose upon ? Should I impose upon Heaven ?

3. " Moreover, than that I should die in the hands of ministers, is it not better that I should die in the hands of you, my disciples ? And though I may not get a great burial, shall I die upon the road ? "

XII. Tsze-kung said, " There is a beautiful gem here. Should I lay it up in a case and keep it ? or should I seek

the body of a horse, rose from the water, being so marked on the back as to give that first of the sages the idea of his diagrams. Confucius endorses these fables.

9. CONFUCIUS' SYMPATHY WITH SORROW, RESPECT FOR RANK, AND PITY FOR MISFORTUNE.

10. YEN YUEN'S ADMIRATION OF HIS MASTER'S DOCTRINES, AND HIS OWN PROGRESS IN THEM.

11. CONFUCIUS' DISLIKE OF PRETENSION, AND CONTENTMENT WITH HIS CONDITION. Confucius had been a great officer, and had enjoyed the services of ministers, as in a petty court. Tsze-loo would have surrounded him in his great sickness with the illusions of his former state, and brought on himself this rebuke.

12. HOW THE DESIRE FOR OFFICE SHOULD BE QUALIFIED BY SELF-

for a good price and sell it?" The Master said, "Sell it! Sell it! But I would wait till the price was offered."

XIII. 1. The Master was wishing to go and live among the nine wild tribes of the east.

2. Some one said, "They are rude. How can you do such a thing?" The Master said, "If a superior man dwelt among them, what rudeness would there be?"

XIV. The Master said, "I returned from Wei to Loo, and then the music was reformed, and the pieces in the Correct Odes and Praise Songs found all their proper place."

XV. The Master said, "Abroad, to serve the high ministers and officers; at home, to serve one's father and elder brother; in all duties to the dead, not to dare not to exert one's-self; and not to be overcome of wine:— what one of these things do I attain to?"

XVI. The Master standing by a stream, said, "It passes on just like this, not ceasing day or night!"

XVII. The Master said, "I have not seen one who loves virtue as he loves beauty."

RESPECT. The disciple wanted to elicit from Confucius why he declined office so much, and insinuated the subject in this way.

13. HOW BARBARIANS CAN BE CIVILIZED. This chapter is to be understood, it is said, like V. vi., not as if Confucius really wished to go among the E (barbarians), but that he thus expressed his regret that his doctrine did not find acceptance in China.

14. CONFUCIUS' SERVICES IN CORRECTING THE MUSIC OF HIS NATIVE STATE AND ADJUSTING THE BOOK OF POETRY. Confucius returned from Wei to Loo in his sixty-ninth year, and died five years after. The "Correct Odes" and "Praise Songs" are the names of two, or rather three, of the divisions of the she-king, the former being the "elegant" or "correct" odes, to be used with music mostly at imperial festivals, and the latter, celebrating principally the virtues of the founders of different dynasties, to be used in the services of the ancestral temple.

15. CONFUCIUS' VERY HUMBLE ESTIMATE OF HIMSELF. Compare VII. ii.; but the things which Confucius here disclaims are of a still lower character than those there mentioned. Very remarkable is the last, as from the sage.

16. HOW CONFUCIUS WAS AFFECTED BY A RUNNING STREAM. What does the *it* in the translation refer to? The construction of the sentence indicates something in the sage's mind, suggested by the ceaseless movement of the water. Choo Ho makes it "our course of nature." Others say "events," "the things of time." Probably Choo He is correct. Compare Mencius, IV. Pt II. xviii.

17. THE RARITY OF A SINCERE LOVE OF VIRTUE.

XVIII. The Master said, "*The prosecution of learning* may be compared to what may happen in raising a mound. If there want but one basket *of earth* to complete the work, and I stop, the stopping is my own work. It may be compared to *throwing down the earth* on the level. ground. Though *but* one basketful is thrown *at a time*, the advancing with it is my own going forward."

XIX. The Master said, "Never flagging when I set forth anything to him ;—ah! that is Hwuy."

XX. The Master said of Yen Yuen, "Alas! I saw his constant advance. I never saw him stop in his progress."

XXI. The Master said, "There are cases in which the blade springs, but the plant does not go on to flower! There are cases where it flowers, but no fruit is subsequently produced!"

XXII. The Master said, "A youth is to be regarded with respect. How do we know that his future will not be equal to *our* present? If he reach the age of forty or fifty, and has not made himself heard of, then indeed he will not be worth being regarded with respect."

XXIII. The Master said, "Can men refuse to assent to the words of strict admonition? But it is reforming the conduct because of them which is valuable. Can men

18. THAT LEARNERS SHOULD NOT CEASE NOR INTERMIT THEIR LABOURS. This is a fragment, like many other chapters, of some conversation, and the subject thus illustrated must be supplied, after the modern commentators, as in the translation; or, after the old, by " the following of virtue." See the Shoo-king, Pt V. Bk V. ix., where the subject is virtuous consistency. The lesson of the chapter is—that repeated acquisitions individually small will ultimately amount to much, and that the learner is never to give over.

19. HWUY THE EARNEST STUDENT.

20. CONFUCIUS' FOND RECOLLECTION OF HWUY AS A MODEL STUDENT.

21. IT IS THE END WHICH CROWNS THE WORK.

22. HOW AND WHY A YOUTH SHOULD BE REGARDED WITH RESPECT. The same person is spoken of throughout the chapter. With Confucius' remark compare that of John Trebonius, Luther's schoolmaster at Eisenach, who used to raise his cap to his pupils on entering the schoolroom, and gave as the reason —" There are among these boys men of whom God will one day make burgomasters, chancellors, doctors, and magistrates. Although you do not yet see them with the badges of their dignity, it is right that you should treat them with respect."

23. THE HOPELESSNESS OF THE CASE OF THOSE WHO ASSENT AND APPROVE WITHOUT REFORMATION OR SERIOUS THOUGHT.

refuse to be pleased with words of gentle advice? But it is unfolding their aim which is valuable. If a man be pleased with these words, but does not unfold their aim, and assents to those, but does not reform his conduct, I can really do nothing with him."

XXIV. The Master said, " Hold faithfulness and sincerity as first principles. Have no friends not equal to yourself. When you have faults, do not fear to abandon them."

XXV. The Master said, " The commander of the forces of a large State may be carried off, but the will of even a common man cannot be taken from him."

XXVI. 1. The Master said, " Dressed himself in a tattered robe quilted with hemp, yet standing by the side of men dressed in furs, and not ashamed;—ah! it is Yew who is equal to this.

2. "' He dislikes none, he covets nothing!—what does he do which is not good?'"

3. Tsze-loo kept continually repeating these *words of the ode*, when the Master said, " Those ways are by no means sufficient to constitute perfect excellence."

XXVII. The Master said, " When the year becomes cold, then we know how the pine and the cypress are the last to lose their leaves."

XXVIII. The Master said, " The wise are free from perplexities; the virtuous from anxiety; and the bold from fear."

XXIX. The Master said, " There are some with whom we may study in common, but we shall find them unable to go along with us to principles. *Perhaps* we may go on with them to principles, but we shall find them unable to

24. This is a repetition of part of I. viii.
25. THE WILL UNSUBDUABLE.
26. TSZE-LOO'S BRAVE CONTENTMENT IN POVERTY, BUT FAILURE TO SEEK THE HIGHEST AIMS. 2. See the She-king, Pt I. Bk III. viii. 4. Tsze-loo was a man of impulse, with many fine points, but not sufficiently reflective.
27. MEN ARE KNOWN IN TIMES OF ADVERSITY. " The last to lose their leaves," may be regarded as a meiosis for their being evergreens.
28. SEQUENCES OF WISDOM, VIRTUE, AND BRAVERY.
29. HOW DIFFERENT INDIVIDUALS STOP AT DIFFERENT STAGES OF PROGRESS. More literally rendered, this chapter would be — " It may be possible with *some parties* together to study, *but* it may not yet be possible with them to go on to principles," &c.

got established in those along with us. Or if we may get so established along with them, we shall find them unable to weigh occurring events along with us."

XXX. 1. How the flowers of the aspen-plum flutter and turn! Do I not think of you? But your house is distant.

2. The Master said, "It is the want of thought about it. How is it distant?"

BOOK X.

CHAPTER I. 1. Confucius, in his village, looked simple and sincere, and as if he were one who was not able to speak.

2. When he was in the prince's ancestorial temple, or in the court, he spoke minutely on every point, but cautiously.

II. 1. When he was waiting at court, in speaking with the officers of the lower grade, he spake freely, but in a

---

30. THE NECESSITY OF REFLECTION. 1. This is from one of the pieces of poetry which were not admitted into the She-king, and no more of it being preserved than what we have here, it is not altogether intelligible. 2. With this paragraph Choo He compares VII, 30.—The whole chapter is like the 20th of the last book, and suggests the thought of its being an addition by another hand to the original compilation.

HEADING AND SUBJECTS OF THIS BOOK. "The village." This book is different in its character from all the others in the work. It contains hardly any sayings of Confucius, but is descriptive of his ways and demeanour in a variety of places and circumstances. It is not uninteresting, but, as a whole, it does not heighten our veneration for the sage. We seem to know him better from it, and to Western minds, after being viewed in his bed-chamber, his undress, and at his meals, he becomes divested of a good deal of his dignity and reputation. There is something remarkable about the style. Only in one passage is Confucius styled "The Master." He appears either as "K'ung the philosopher," or as "The superior man." A suspicion is thus raised that the chronicler had not the same relation to him as the compilers of the other books. Anciently, the book formed only one chapter, but it is now arranged under seventeen divisions. Those divisions, for convenience in the translation, I continue to denominate chapters, which is done also in some native editions.

1. DEMEANOUR OF CONFUCIUS IN HIS VILLAGE, IN THE ANCESTRAL TEMPLE, AND IN THE COURT.

2. DEMEANOUR OF CONFUCIUS AT COURT WITH OTHER OFFICERS, AND BEFORE THE PRINCE. It was the custom for all the officers to repair at

straightforward manner; in speaking with the officers of the higher grade, he did so blandly, but precisely.

2. When the prince was present, his manner displayed respectful uneasiness; it was grave, but self-possessed.

III. 1. When the prince called him to employ him in the reception of a visitor, his countenance appeared to change, and his legs to bend beneath him.

2. He inclined himself to the *other officers* among whom he stood, moving his left or right arm, *as their position required*, but keeping the skirts of his robe before and behind evenly adjusted.

3. He hastened forward, *with his arms* like the wings of a bird.

4. When the guest had retired, he would report to the prince, "The visitor is not turning round any more."

daybreak to the court, and wait for the prince to give them audience. "Great officer" was a general name, applicable to all the higher ministers in a court. At the imperial court they were divided into three classes,— "highest," "middle," and "lowest," but the various princes had only the first and third. Of the first order there were properly three, the *king* or nobles of the state, who were in Loo the chiefs of the "three families." Confucius belonged himself to the lower grade.

3. DEMEANOUR OF CONFUCIUS AT THE OFFICIAL RECEPTION OF A VISITOR. 1. The visitor is supposed to be the prince of another state. On the occasion of two princes meeting there was much ceremony. The visitor having arrived, remained outside the front gate, and the host inside his reception-room, which was in the ancestral temple. Messages passed between them by means of a number of officers called *hsei*, on the side of the visitor, and *pin*, on the side of the host, who formed a zigzag line of communication from the one to the other, and passed their question and answers along, till an understanding about the visit was thus officially effected. 2. This shows Confucius' manner when engaged in the transmission of the messages between the prince and his visitor. He must have occupied an intermediate place in the row of his prince's *pin*, bowing to them on the right or the left, as he transmitted the messages to and from the prince. 3. The host having come out to receive his visitor, proceeded in with him, it is said, followed by all their internuncios in a line, and to his manner in this movement this paragraph is generally referred. But the duty of seeing the guest off, the subject of the next paragraph, belonged to the *pin* who had been nearest to the prince, and was of higher rank than Confucius sustained. Hence arises a difficulty. Either it is true that Confucius was at one time raised to the rank of the highest dignitaries of the state, or he was temporarily employed, for his knowledge of ceremonies, after the first act in the reception of visitors, to discharge the duties of one. Assuming this, the "hastening forward" is to be explained of some of his movements in the reception-room. How could he hurry forward when walking in file with the other internuncios?

IV. 1. When he entered the palace gate, he seemed to bend his body, as if it were not sufficient to admit him.

2. When he was standing, he did not occupy the middle of the gate-way; when he passed in or out, he did not tread upon the threshold.

3. When he was passing the vacant place *of the prince*, his countenance appeared to change, and his legs to bend under him, and his words came like those of one who hardly had breath to utter them.

4. He ascended the dais, holding up his robe with both his hands, and his body bent; holding in his breath also, as if he dared not breathe.

5. When he came out *from the audience*, as soon as he had descended one step, he began to relax his countenance, and had a satisfied look. When he had got to the bottom of the steps, he advanced rapidly to his place, *with his arms* like wings, and on occupying it, his manner *still* showed respectful uneasiness.

V. 1. When he was carrying the sceptre *of his prince*, he seemed to bend his body, as if he were not able to bear its weight. He did not hold it higher than the position of the hands in making a bow, nor lower than their

---

The ways of China, it appears, were much the same anciently as now. A guest turns round and bows repeatedly in leaving, and the host can't return to his place till these salutations are ended.

4. DEMEANOUR OF CONFUCIUS IN THE COURT AT AN AUDIENCE. 1. The imperial court consisted of five divisions, each having its peculiar gate. That of a prince of a State consisted only of three, whose gates were named *foo*, *che*, and *loo*. The "gate" in the text is any one of these. The bending his body when passing through, high as the gate was, is supposed to indicate the great reverence which Confucius felt. 2. Each gate had a post in the centre, by which it was divided into two halves, appropriated to ingress and egress. The prince only could stand in the centre of either of them, and he only could tread on the threshold or sill. 3. At the early formal audience at daybreak, when the prince came out of the inner apartment, and received the homage of the officers, he occupied a particular spot. This is the "place," now empty, which Confucius passes in his way to the audience in the inner apartment. 4. He is now ascending the steps to the "dais" or raised platform in the inner apartment, where the prince held his council, or gave entertainments, and from which the family rooms of the palace branched off. 5. The audience is now over, and Confucius is returning to his usual place at the formal audience.

5. DEMEANOUR OF CONFUCIUS WHEN EMPLOYED ON A FRIENDLY EMBASSY. 1. "Sceptre" here is in the sense simply of "a badge of

position in giving anything to another. His countenance seemed to change, and looked apprehensive, and he dragged his feet along as if they were held by something to the ground.

2. In presenting the presents *with which he was charged*, he wore a placid appearance.

3. At his private audience, he looked highly pleased.

VI. 1. The superior man did not use a deep purple, or a puce colour, in the ornaments of his dress.

2. Even in his undress, he did not wear anything of a red or reddish colour.

3. In warm weather, he had a single garment either of coarse or fine texture, but he wore it displayed over an inner garment.

4. Over lamb's fur he wore a garment of black; over fawn's fur one of white; and over fox's fur one of yellow.

5. The fur robe of his undress was long, with the right sleeve short.

authority." It was a precious stone, conferred by the emperor on the princes, and differed in size and shape, according to their rank. They took it with them when they attended the imperial court, and, according to Choo He, and the old interpretation, it was carried also by their representatives, as their voucher, on occasions of embassies among themselves. 2. The preceding paragraph describes Confucius' manner in the friendly court, at his first interview, showing his credentials, and delivering his message. That done, he had to deliver the various presents with which he was charged. After all the public presents were delivered, the ambassador had others of his own to give, and his interview for that purpose is here spoken of.—Choo He remarks that there is no record of Confucius ever having been employed on such a mission, and supposes that this chapter and the preceding are simply summaries of the manner in which he used to say duties referred to in them ought to be discharged.

6. RULES OF CONFUCIUS IN REGARD TO HIS DRESS. 1. The title of "Superior Man," used here to denote Confucius, can hardly have come from the hand of a disciple. "The ornaments," *i.e.* the collar and sleeves. The first colour, it is said, by Choo He, after K'ung Gan-kwŏ, was worn in fasting, and the other in mourning, on which account Confucius would not use them. 2. There are five colours which go by the name of "correct," viz., "azure, yellow, carnation, white, and black;" others, among which are red, and red-drop, go by the name "intermediate." Confucius would use only the correct colours; and moreover, Choo He adds, red and reddish-blue are liked by women and girls. 3. This single garment was made from the fibres of a creeping plant, the *dolichos*. See the She-king, Pt I. Bk I. ii. 4. The lamb's fur belonged to the court dress, the fawn's was worn on embassies, the fox's on occasions of sacrifice, &c. The fur and the thin garment over it were of the same colour. This was winter wear. 5. Confucius knew how to blend comfort

6. He required his sleeping dress to be half as long again as his body.

7. When staying at home, he used thick furs of the fox or the badger.

8. When he put off mourning, he wore all the appendages of the girdle.

9. His under garment, except when it was required to be of the curtain shape, was made of silk cut narrow above and wide below.

10. He did not wear lamb's fur, or a black cap, on a visit of condolence.

11. On the first day of the month, he put on his court robes, and presented himself at court.

VII. 1. When fasting, he thought it necessary to have his clothes brightly clean, and made of linen cloth.

2. When fasting, he thought it necessary to change his food, and also to change the place where he commonly sat in the apartment.

VIII. 1. He did not dislike to have his rice finely cleaned, nor to have his minced meat cut quite small.

2. He did not eat rice which had been injured by heat or damp and turned sour, nor fish or flesh which was gone. He did not eat what was discoloured; nor what was of a bad flavour; nor anything which was badly cooked; nor that which was not in season.

and convenience. 6. This paragraph, it is supposed, belongs to the next chapter, in which case it is not the usual sleeping garment of Confucius that is spoken of, but the one he used in fasting. 7. These are the furs of paragraph 5. 8. The appendages of the girdle were—the handkerchief, a small knife, a spike for opening knots, &c. Being ornamental, they were laid aside in mourning. 9. The lower garment reached below the knees like a kilt or petticoat. For court and sacrificial dress, it was made curtain-like, as wide at top as at bottom. In that worn on other occasions, Confucius saved the cloth in the way described. So, at least, says K'ung Gan-kwŏ. 10. Lamb's fur was worn black (paragraph 4), but white is the colour of mourning in China, and Confucius would not visit mourners but in a sympathising colour. 11. This was Confucius' practice, after he had ceased to be in office.

7. RULES OBSERVED BY CONFUCIUS WHEN FASTING. 1. The sixth paragraph of last chapter should come in as the second here. 2. The fasting was not from all food, but only from wine or spirits, and from strong-flavoured vegetables.

8. RULES OF CONFUCIUS ABOUT HIS FOOD. 1. The "minced meat," according to the commentators, was made of beef, mutton, or fish, uncooked. One hundred *shing* of paddy were reduced to thirty, to bring it to the state

3. He did not eat meat which was not cut properly, nor what was served without its proper sauce.

4. Though there might be a large quantity of meat, he would not allow what he took to exceed the due proportion for the rice. It was only in wine that he laid down no limit for himself, but he did not allow himself to be confused by it.

5. He did not partake of wine and dried meat bought in the market.

6. He was never without ginger when he ate.

7. He did not eat much.

8. When he had been *assisting* at the ducal sacrifice, he did not keep the flesh *which he received* over night. The flesh of his *family* sacrifice he did not keep over three days. If kept over three days, people could not eat it.

9. When eating, he did not converse. When in bed, he did not speak.

10. Although his food might be coarse rice and vegetable soup, he would offer *a little of it* in sacrifice with a grave respectful air.

IX. If his mat was not straight, he did not sit on it.

X. 1. When the villagers were drinking together, on those who carried staves going out, he went out immediately after.

2. When the villagers were going through their cere-

of finely-cleaned rice. 4. It is said, that in other things he had a limit, but the use of wine being to make glad, he could not beforehand set a limit to the quantity of it. 8. The prince, anciently (and it is still a custom), distributed among the assisting ministers the flesh of his sacrifices. Each would only get a little, and so it could be used at once. 10. The "sacrificing" refers to a custom something like our saying grace. The Master took a few grains of rice, or part of the other provisions, and placed them on the ground, among the sacrificial vessels, a tribute to the worthy or worthies who first taught the art of cooking. The Buddhist priests in their monasteries have a custom of this kind ; and on public occasions, as when K'e-ying gave an entertainment in Hongkong in 1845, something like it is sometimes observed, but any such ceremony is unknown among the common habits of the people. However poor might be his fare, Confucius always observed it.

9. RULE OF CONFUCIUS ABOUT HIS MAT.

10. OTHER WAYS OF CONFUCIUS IN HIS VILLAGE. 1. At sixty, people carried staves. Confucius here showed his respect for age. He would not go out before the "fathers." 2. There were three of these ceremonies every year, but that in the text was called "the great *no*," being observed in the winter season, when the officers led all the

monies to drive away pestilential influences, he put on his court robes and stood on the eastern steps.

XI. 1. When he was sending complimentary inquiries to any one in another state, he bowed twice as he escorted the messenger away.

2. Ke K'ang having sent him a present of physic, he bowed and received it, saying, "I do not know it. I dare not taste it."

XII. The stable being burned down, when he was at court, on his return he said, "Has any man been hurt?" He did not ask about the horses.

XIII. 1. When the prince sent him a gift of *cooked* meat, he would adjust his mat, *first* taste it, *and then give it away to others*. When the prince sent him a gift of undressed meat, he would have it cooked, and offer it *to the spirits of his ancestors*. When the prince sent him a gift of a living animal, he would keep it alive.

2. When he was in attendance on the prince and joining in the entertainment, the prince only sacrificed; but he first tasted everything.

3. When he was sick and the prince came to visit him, he had his head to the east, made his court robes be spread over him, and drew his girdle across them.

people of a village about, searching every house to expel demons, and drive away pestilence. It was conducted with great uproar, and little better than a play, but Confucius saw a good old idea in it, and when the mob was in his house, he stood on the eastern steps (the place of a host receiving guests) in full dress. Some make the steps those of his ancestral temple, and his standing there to be to assure the spirits of his shrine.

11. TRAITS OF CONFUCIUS' INTERCOURSE WITH OTHERS. 1. The two bows, it is said, were not to the messenger, but intended for the distant friend to whom he was being sent. 2. K'ang was Ke K'ang-tsze of II. xx. *et al*. Confucius accepted the gift, but thought it necessary to let the donor know he could not, for the present at least, avail himself of it.

12. HOW CONFUCIUS VALUED HUMAN LIFE. A "stable" was fitted to accommodate 216 horses. The term may be used indeed for a private stable, but it is more natural to take it here for the State kew. This is the view in the Family Sayings.

13. DEMEANOUR OF CONFUCIUS IN RELATION TO HIS PRINCE. 1. He would not offer the cooked meat to the spirits of his ancestors, not knowing but it might previously have been offered by the prince to the spirits of his. But he reverently tasted it, as if he had been in the prince's presence. He "honoured" the gift of cooked food, "glorified" the

4. When the prince's order called him, without waiting for his carriage to be yoked, he went at once.

XIV. When he entered the ancestral temple of the state, he asked about everything.

XV. 1. When any of his friends died, if he had no relations who could be depended on for the necessary offices, he would say, "I will bury him."

2. When a friend sent him a present, though it might be a carriage and horses, he did not bow. The only present for which he bowed was that of the flesh of sacrifice.

XVI. 1. In bed, he did not lie like a corpse. At home, he did not put on any formal deportment.

2. When he saw any one in a mourning dress, though it might be an acquaintance, he would change countenance; when he saw any one wearing the cap of full dress, or a blind person, though he might be in his undress, he would salute them in a ceremonious manner.

3. To any person in mourning he bowed forward to the crossbar of his carriage; he bowed in the same way to any one bearing the tables of population.

4. When he was at an entertainment where there was

---

undressed, and "was kind" to the living animal. 2. The sacrifice here is that in chapter viii. 10. Among parties of equal rank all performed the ceremony, but Confucius, with his prince, held that the prince sacrificed for all. He tasted everything, as if he had been a *cook*, it being the cook's duty to taste every dish before the prince partook of it. 3. The head to the east was the proper position for a person in bed; a sick man might for comfort be lying differently, but Confucius would not see the prince but in the correct position, and also in the court dress, so far as he could accomplish it. 4. He would not wait a moment, but let his carriage follow him.

14. A repetition of part of III. xv. Compare also chapter ii. These two passages make the explanation, given at III. xv., of the questioning being on his first entrance on office very doubtful.

15. TRAITS OF CONFUCIUS IN THE RELATION OF A FRIEND. 2. Between friends there should be a community of goods. "The flesh of sacrifice," however, was that which had been offered by his friend to the spirits of his parents or ancestors. That demanded acknowledgment.

16. CONFUCIUS IN BED, AT HOME, HEARING THUNDER, &c. 2. Compare IX. ix., which is here repeated, with heightening circumstances. 3. The carriage of Confucius's time was hardly more than what we call a cart. In saluting when riding, parties bowed forward to the front bar. 4. He showed these signs, with reference to the generosity of the provider.

an abundance of provisions set before him, he would change countenance and rise up.

5. On a sudden clap of thunder, or a violent wind, he would change countenance.

XVII. 1. When he was about to mount his carriage, he would stand straight, holding the cord.

2. When he was in the carriage, he did not turn his head quite round, he did not talk hastily, he did not point with his hands.

XVIII. 1. *Seeing* the countenance, it instantly rises. It flies round, and by-and-by settles.

2. *The Master* said, "There is the hen-pheasant on the hill bridge. At its season! At its season!" Tsze-loo made a motion to it. Thrice it smelt him and then rose.

BOOK XI.

CHAPTER I. 1. The Master said, "The men of former times, in the matters of ceremonies and music, were rustics, *it is said*, while the men of *these* latter times, in ceremonies and music, are accomplished gentlemen.

2. "If I have occasion to use these things, I follow the men of former times."

II. 1. The Master said, "Of those who were with me

17. CONFUCIUS AT AND IN HIS CARRIAGE. 1. The strap or cord was attached to the carriage to assist in mounting it.

18. A fragment, which seemingly has no connection with the rest of the book. Various corrections of characters are proposed, and various views of the meaning given. Ho An's view of the conclusion is this. "Tsze-loo took it and served it up. The Master thrice smelt it and rose."

HEADING AND SUBJECTS OF THIS BOOK.—"The former men—No. XI." With this Book there commences the second part of the Analects, commonly called the *Hea Lun*. There is, however, no classical authority for this division. It contains twenty-five chapters, treating mostly of various disciples of the Master, and deciding the point of their worthiness. Min Tsze-K'een appears in it four times, and on this account some attribute the compilation of it to his disciples. There are indications in the style of a peculiar hand.

1. CONFUCIUS' PREFERENCE OF THE SIMPLER WAYS OF FORMER TIMES.

2. CONFUCIUS' REGRETFUL MEMORY OF HIS DISCIPLES' FIDELITY. CHARACTERISTICS OF TEN OF THE DISCIPLES. 1. This utterance must have been made towards the close of Confucius' life, when many of his

in Ch'in and Ts'ae, there are none to be found to enter my door."

2. Distinguished for their virtuous principles and practice, there were Yen Yuen, Min Tsze-k'een, Yen Pih-new, and Chung-kung; for their ability in speech, Tsae Wo and Tsze-kung; for their administrative talents, Yen Yew and Ke Loo; for their literary acquirements, Tsze-yew and Tsze-hea.

III. The Master said, "Hwuy gives me no assistance. There is nothing that I say in which he does not delight."

IV. The Master said, "Filial indeed is Min Tsze-k'een! Other people say nothing of him different from the report of his parents and brothers."

V. Nan Yung was frequently repeating the *lines about a white sceptre-stone.* Confucius gave him the daughter of his elder brother to wife.

VI. Ke K'ang asked which of the disciples loved to learn. Confucius replied to him, "There was Yen Hwuy; he loved to learn. Unfortunately his appointed time was short, and he died. Now there is no one *who loves to learn,* as he did."

disciples had been removed by death, or separated from him by other causes. In his sixty-second year or thereabouts, as the accounts go, he was passing, in his wanderings from Ch'in to Ts'ae, when the officers of Ch'in, afraid that he would go on into Tsoo, endeavoured to stop his course, and for several days he and the disciples with him were cut off from food. Both Ch'in and Ts'ae were in the present province of Ho-nan, and are referred to the departments of Ch'in-Chow and Joo-ning. 2. This paragraph is to be taken as a note by the compilers of the book, enumerating the principal followers of Confucius on the occasion referred to, with their distinguishing qualities. They are arranged in four classes, and, amounting to ten, are known as the ten wise ones. The "four classes" and "ten wise ones" are often mentioned in connection with the sage's school.

3. HWUY'S SILENT RECEPTION OF THE MASTER'S TEACHINGS. A teacher is sometimes *helped* by the doubts and questions of learners, which lead him to explain himself more fully. Compare III. viii. 3.

4. THE FILIAL PIETY OF MIN TSZE-K'EEN.

5. CONFUCIUS' APPROBATION OF NAN YUNG. Nan Yung, see V. I. For the lines, see the She-king, Pt III. Bk III. ii. 5. They are — " A flaw in a white sceptre-stone may be ground away; but for a flaw in speech, nothing can be done." In his repeating of these lines, we have, perhaps, the ground-virtue of the character for which Yung is commended in V. I.

6. HOW HWUY LOVED TO LEARN. See VI. ii., where the same question is put by the Duke Gae, and the same answer is returned, only in a more extended form.

VII. 1. When Yen Yuen died, Yen Loo begged the carriage of the Master to get an outer shell for his son's coffin.

2. The Master said, "Every one calls his son his son, whether he has talents or has not talents. There was Le; when he died, he had a coffin, but no outer shell. I would not walk on foot to get a shell for him, because, following after the great officers, it was not proper that I should walk on foot."

VIII. When Yen Yuen died, the Master said, "Alas! Heaven is destroying me! Heaven is destroying me!"

IX. 1. When Yen Yuen died, the Master bewailed him exceedingly; and the disciples who were with him said, "Sir, your grief is excessive?"

2. "Is it excessive?" said he.

3. "If I am not to mourn bitterly for this man, for whom should I mourn?"

X. 1. When Yen Yuen died, the disciples wished to give him a great funeral, and the Master said, "You may not do so."

2. The disciples did bury him in great style.

3. The Master said, "Hwuy behaved towards me as his father. I have not been able to treat him as my

---

7. HOW CONFUCIUS WOULD NOT SELL HIS CARRIAGE TO BUY A SHELL FOR YEN YUEN. 1. In the Family Sayings and in the History of Records, Hwuy's death is represented as taking place before the death of Le. It is difficult to understand how such a view could ever have been adopted, if the authors were acquainted with this chapter. 2. "I follow in rear of the great officers." This is said to be an expression of humility. Confucius, retired from office, might still present himself at court, in the robes of his former dignity, and would still be consulted on emergencies. He would no doubt have a foremost place on such occasions.

8. CONFUCIUS FELT HWUY'S DEATH AS IF IT HAD BEEN HIS OWN. The old interpreters make this simply the exclamation of bitter sorrow. The modern, perhaps correctly, make the chief ingredient to be grief that the man was gone to whom he looked most for the transmission of his doctrines.

9. CONFUCIUS VINDICATES HIS GREAT GRIEF FOR THE DEATH OF HWUY.

10. CONFUCIUS' DISSATISFACTION WITH THE GRAND WAY IN WHICH HWUY WAS BURIED. The old interpreters take the disciples here as being the disciples of Yen Yuen. This is not natural, and yet we can hardly understand how the disciples of Confucius would act so directly contrary to his express wishes. Confucius objected to a grand funeral as inconsistent with the poverty of the family (see chapter vii.).

son. The fault is not mine; it belongs to you, O disciples."

XI. Ke Loo asked about serving the spirits *of the dead*. The Master said, "While you are not able to serve men, how can you serve *their* spirits?" Ke Loo added, "I venture to ask about death?" He was answered, "While you do not know life, how can you know about death?"

XII. 1. The disciple Min was standing by his side, looking bland and precise; Tsze-loo, looking bold and soldierly; Yen Yew and Tsze-kung, with a free and straightforward manner. The Master was pleased.

2. He said, "Yew there!—he will not die a natural death."

XIII. 1. Some parties in Loo were going to take down and rebuild the Long treasury.

2. Min Tsze-k'een said, "Suppose it were to be repaired after its old style;—why must it be altered, and made anew?"

3. The Master said, "This man seldom speaks; when he does, he is sure to hit the point."

XIV. 1. The Master said, "What has the harpsichord of Yew to do in my door?"

2. The other disciples *began* not to respect Tsze-loo. The Master said, "Yew has ascended to the hall, though he has not yet passed into the inner apartments."

11. CONFUCIUS AVOIDS ANSWERING QUESTIONS ABOUT SERVING SPIRITS, AND ABOUT DEATH. Two views of the replies here are found in commentators. The older ones say—"Confucius put off Ke Loo, and gave him no answer, because spirits and death are obscure, and unprofitable subjects to talk about." With this some modern writers agree, but others, and the majority, say—"Confucius answered the disciple profoundly, and showed him how he should prosecute his inquiries in the proper order. The service of the dead must be in the same spirit as the service of the living. Obedience and sacrifice are equally the expression of the filial heart. Death is only the natural termination of life. We are born with certain gifts and principles, which carry us on to the end of our course." This is ingenious refining; but, after all, Confucius avoids answering the important questions proposed to him.

12. CONFUCIUS HAPPY WITH HIS DISCIPLES ABOUT HIM. HE WARNS TSZE-LOO.

13. WISE ADVICE OF MIN SUN AGAINST USELESS EXPENDITURE.

14. CONFUCIUS' ADMONITION AND DEFENCE OF TSZE-LOO. 1. The form of the harpsichord seems to come nearer to that of the *shĭh* than any other of our instruments. The *shĭh* is a kindred instrument with the *k'in*, commonly called "the scholar's lute." See the Chinese Repository, vol.

XV. 1. Tsze-kung asked which of the two, Sze or Shang, was the superior. The Master said, "Sze goes beyond *the due Mean*, and Shang does not come up to it."

2. "Then," said Tsze-kung, "the superiority is with Sze, I suppose."

3. The Master said, "To go beyond is as wrong as to fall short."

XVI. 1. The head of the Ke family was richer than the duke of Chow had been, and yet K'ew collected his imposts for him, and increased his wealth.

2. The Master said, "He is no disciple of mine. My little children, beat the drum and assail him."

XVII. 1. Ch'ae is simple.
2. Sin is dull.
3. Sze is specious.
4. Yew is coarse.

XVIII. 1. The Master said, "There is Hwuy! He has nearly attained *to perfect virtue*. He is often in want."

2. "Tsze does not acquiesce in the appointments *of Heaven*, and his goods are increased by him. Yet his judgments are often correct."

VIII. p. 38. The music made by Yew was more martial in its air than befitted the peace-inculcating school of the sage. 2. This contains a defence of Yew, and an illustration of his real attainments.

15. COMPARISON OF SZE AND SHANG. EXCESS AND DEFECT EQUALLY WRONG.

16. CONFUCIUS' INDIGNATION AT THE SUPPORT OF USURPATION AND EXTORTION BY ONE OF HIS DISCIPLES. "Beat the drum and assail him;" this refers to the practice of executing criminals in the market-place, and by beat of drum collecting the people to hear their crimes. Commentators, however, say that the Master only required the disciples here to tell K'ew of his faults and recover him.

17. CHARACTERS OF THE FOUR DISCIPLES—CH'AE, SIN, SZE, AND YEW. It is supposed "The Master said," is missing from the beginning of this chapter. Admitting this, the sentences are to be translated in the present tense, and not in the past, which would be required, if the chapter were simply the record of the compilers. Ch'ae, by surname Kaou, and styled Tsze-Kaou, has his tablet now the fifth, west, in the outer court of the temples. He was small and ugly, but distinguished for his sincerity, filial piety, and justice. Such was the conviction of his impartial justice, that in a time of peril he was saved by a man whom he had formerly punished with cutting off his feet.

18. HWUY AND TSZE CONTRASTED. Hwuy's being brought often to this state is mentioned merely as an additional circumstance about him,

XIX. Tsze-chang asked what were the characteristics of the GOOD man. The Master said, "He does not tread in the footsteps of others, but, moreover, he does not enter the chamber *of the sage."*

XX. The Master said, "If, because a man's discourse appears solid and sincere, we allow him *to be a good man*, is he *really* a superior man? or is his gravity only in appearance?"

XXI. 1. Tsze-loo asked whether he should immediately carry into practice what he heard. The Master said, "There are your father and elder brothers *to be consulted;* —why should you act on that principle of immediately carrying into practice what you hear?" Yen Yew asked the same, whether he should immediately carry into practice what he heard, and the Master answered, "Immediately carry into practice what you hear." Kung-se Hwa said, "Yew asked whether he should carry immediately into practice what he heard, and you said, 'There are your father and elder brothers *to be consulted.*' K'ew asked whether he should immediately carry into practice what he heard, and you said, 'Carry it immediately into practice.' I, Ch'ih, am perplexed, and venture to ask you for an explanation." The Master said, "K'ew is retiring and slow; therefore I urged him forward. Yew has more than his own share of energy; therefore I kept him back."

XXII. The Master was put in fear in K'wang and Yen Yuen fell behind. The Master, *on his rejoining him,*

---

intended to show that he was happy in his deep poverty. Ho An preserves the comment of some one, which is worth giving here, and according to which, "empty-hearted," free from all vanities and ambitions, was the formative element of Hwuy's character.

19. THE GOOD MAN. Compare VII. xxv. By a "good man" Choo He understands "one of fine natural capacity, but who has not learned." Such a man will in many things be a law to himself, and needs not to follow in the wake of others, but after all his progress will be limited. The text is rather enigmatical.

20. WE MAY NOT HASTILY JUDGE A MAN TO BE GOOD FROM HIS DISCOURSE.

21. AN INSTANCE IN TSZE-LOO AND YEN YEW OF HOW CONFUCIUS DEALT WITH HIS DISCIPLES ACCORDING TO THEIR CHARACTERS.

22. YEN YUEN'S ATTACHMENT TO CONFUCIUS, AND CONFIDENCE IN HIS MISSION. See IX. v. If Hwuy's answer was anything more than pleasantry, we must pronounce it foolish. The commentators, however,

said, "I thought you had died." *Hwuy* replied, "While you were alive, how should I presume to die?"

XXIII. 1. Ke Tsze-jen asked whether Chung-yew and Yen K'ew could be called great ministers.

2. The Master said, "I thought you would ask about some extraordinary individuals, and you only ask about Yew and K'ew!

3. "What is called a great minister, is one who serves his prince according to what is right, and when he finds he cannot do so, retires."

4. "Now, as to Yew and K'ew, they may be called ordinary ministers."

5. Tsze-jen said, "Then they will always follow their chief;—will they?"

6. The Master said, "In an act of parricide or regicide, they would not follow him."

XXIV. 1. Tsze-loo got Tsze-kaou appointed governor of Pe.

2. The Master said, "You are injuring a man's son."

3. Tsze-loo said, "There are (there) common people and officers; there are the altars of the spirits of the land and grain. Why must one read books before he can be considered to have learned?"

expand it thus:—"I knew that you would not perish in this danger, and therefore I would not rashly expose my own life, but preserved it rather, that I might continue to enjoy the benefit of your instructions." If we inquire how Hwuy knew that Confucius would not perish, we are informed that he shared his master's assurance that he had a divine mission. See VII. xxii., IX. v.

23. A GREAT MINISTER. CHUNG-YEW AND YEN K'EW ONLY ORDINARY MINISTERS. The paraphrasts sum up the contents thus:—"Confucius represses the boasting of Ke Tsze-jen, and indicates an acquaintance with his traitorous purposes." This Ke Tsze-jen was a younger brother of Ke Hwan, who was the head of the Ke family spoken of in III. i. Having an ambitious purpose on the dukedom of Loo, he was increasing his officers, and having got the two disciples to enter his service, he boastingly speaks to Confucius about them.

24. HOW PRELIMINARY STUDY IS NECESSARY TO THE EXERCISE OF GOVERNMENT:—A REPROOF OF TSZE-LOO. 1. Pe,—see VI. vii. This commandantship is probably what Min Sun there refused. Tsze-loo had entered into the service of the Ke family (see last chapter), and recommended Tsze-kaou as likely to keep the turbulent Pe in order, thereby withdrawing him from his studies with the Master. 2. By denominating Tsze-kaou "a man's son," Confucius intimates, I suppose, that the father was injured as well. His son ought not to be so dealt with. 3. The absurd defence of Tsze-loo. It is to this effect:—"The whole duty of

4. The Master said, "It is on this account that I hate your glib-tongued people."

XXV. 1. Tsze-loo, Tsăng Sih, Yen Yew, and Kung-se Hwa, were sitting by *the Master*.

2. He said to them, though I am a day or so older than you, don't think of that.

3. "From day to day you are saying, 'We are not known.' If some *prince* were to know you, what would you do?"

4. Tsze-loo hastily and lightly replied, "Suppose the case of a state of ten thousand chariots; let it be straitened between *other* large states; let it be suffering from invading armies; and to this let there be added a famine in corn and in all vegetables;—if I were intrusted with the government of it, in three years' time I could make the people to be bold, and to recognize the rules of righteous conduct." The Master smiled at him.

5. *Turning to Yen Yew, he said*, "K'ew, what are your wishes?" K'ew replied, "Suppose a state of sixty or seventy *le* square, or one of fifty or sixty, and let me have the government of it;—in three years' time I could make plenty to abound among the people. As to *teaching them* the principles of propriety and music, I must wait for the rise of a superior man *to do that*."

6. "What are your wishes, Ch'ih, *said the Master next to Kung-se Hwa*. Ch'ih replied, I do not say that my ability extends to these things, but I should wish to learn them. At the services of the ancestral temple, and at the audiences of the princes with the emperor, I should like, dressed in the dark square-made robe and the black linen cap, to act as a small assistant."

7. *Last of all, the Master asked T'săng Sih*, "Teen, what are your wishes?" *Teen*, pausing as he was playing on his harpsichord, while it was yet twanging, laid the in-

man is in treating other men right, and rendering what is due to spiritual beings, and it may be learned practically without the study you require." "On this account,"—with reference to Tsze-loo's reply.

25. THE AIMS OF TSZE-LOO, TSANG SIH, YEN YEW, AND KUNG-SE HWA; AND CONFUCIUS' REMARKS ABOUT THEM. Compare V. vii. and xxv. 1. The disciples mentioned here are all familiar to us excepting Tsăng Sih. He was the father of the more celebrated Tsăng Sin, and himself by name Teen. The four are mentioned in the order of their age, and Teen would have answered immediately after Tsze-loo, but that Con-

strument aside, and rose. " My wishes," he said, " are different from the cherished purposes of these three gentlemen." " What harm is there in that ?" said the Master; " do you also, as well as they, speak out your wishes." *Teen* then said, " In *this*, the last month of spring, with the dress of the season all complete, along with five or six young men who have assumed the cap, and six or seven boys, I would wash in the E, enjoy the breeze among the rain-altars, and return home singing." The Master heaved a sigh and said, " I give my approval to Teen."

8. The three others having gone out, Tsăng Sih remained behind, and said, " What do you think of the words of these three friends ?" The Master replied, " They simply told each one his wishes."

9. *Teen* pursued, " Master, why did you smile at Yew ?"

10. He was answered, " The management of a state demands the rules of propriety. His words were not humble; therefore I smiled at him."

11. *Teen again said*, " But was it not a state which K'ew proposed for himself ?" *The reply was*, " Yes; did you ever see a territory of sixty or seventy *le*, or one of fifty or sixty, which was not a state ? "

12. *Once more Teen inquired*, " And was it not a state which Ch'ih proposed for himself ?" *The Master again replied*, "Yes; who but princes have to do with ancestral temples, and audiences with the emperor ? If Ch'ih were to be a small *assistant* in these *services*, who could be a great one ? "

BOOK XII.

Chapter I. 1. Yen Yuen asked about perfect virtue. The Master said, " To subdue one's self and return to

fucius passed him by, as he was occupied with his harpsichord. It does not appear whether Teen, even at the last, understood why Confucius had laughed at Tsze-loo, and not at the others. " It was not," say the commentators, " because Tsze-loo was extravagant in his aims. They were all thinking of great things, yet not greater than they were able for. Tsze-loo's fault was in the levity with which he had proclaimed his wishes. That was his offence against *propriety*."

Heading and subjects of this book. "Yen Yuen." It contains twenty-four chapters, conveying lessons on perfect virtue, government,

propriety, is perfect virtue. If a man can for one day subdue himself and return to propriety, all under heaven will ascribe perfect virtue to him. Is the practice of perfect virtue from a man himself, or is it from others?"

2. Yen Yuen said, "I beg to ask the steps of that process." The Master replied, "Look not at what is contrary to propriety; listen not to what is contrary to propriety; speak not what is contrary to propriety; make no movement which is contrary to propriety." Yen Yuen *then* said, "Though I am deficient in intelligence and vigour, I will make it my business to practise this lesson."

II. Chung-kung asked about perfect virtue. The Master said, "*It is*, when you go abroad, *to behave to every one*

and other questions of morality and policy, addressed in conversation by Confucius chiefly to his disciples. The different answers, given about the same subject to different questioners, show well how the sage suited his instructions to the characters and capacities of the parties with whom he had to do.

1. HOW TO ATTAIN TO PERFECT VIRTUE:—A CONVERSATION WITH YEN YUEN. 1. In Ho An, "to subdue one's self" is explained by "to restrain the body." Choo He defines the "subdue" by "to overcome," and the "self" by "the selfish desires of the body." In one commentary it is said "self here is not exactly selfishness, but selfishness is what abides by being attached to the body, and hence it is said that selfishness is self." And again, "To subdue one's self is not subduing and putting away the *self*, but subduing and putting away the selfish desires *in the self*." This "selfishness in the self" is of a three-fold character:—first, what is said by Morrison to be "a person's natural constitution and disposition of mind:" it is, I think, very much the ψυχικὸς ἄνθρωπος, or "animal man;" second, "the desires of the ears, the eyes, the mouth, the nose, *i.e.*, the dominating influences of the senses; and third, "Thou and I," *i.e.*, the lust of superiority. More concisely, the self is said to be "the mind of man" in opposition to the "mind of reason." See the Shoo-king II. Bk II. xv. This refractory "mind of man," it is said, is "innate," or perhaps "connate." In all these statements, there is an acknowledgment of the fact—the morally abnormal condition of human nature—which underlies the Christian doctrine of original sin. With reference to the above three-fold classification of selfish desires, the second paragraph shows that it was the second order of them—the influence of the senses, which Confucius especially intended. We turn to propriety, see note on VIII. ii. The thing is not here *ceremonies*. Choo He defines it "the specific divisions and graces of heavenly principle or reason." This is continually being departed from, on the impulse of selfishness, but there is an ideal of it as *proper* to man, which is to be sought—"returned to"—by overcoming that.

2. WHEREIN PERFECT VIRTUE IS REALIZED:—A CONVERSATION WITH CHUNG-KUNG. From this chapter, it appears that reverence and reciprocity, on the largest scale, are perfect virtue. "Ordering the people" is

as if you were receiving a great guest; to employ the people as if you were assisting at a great sacrifice; not to do to others as you would not wish done to yourself; to have no murmuring against you in the country, and none in the family." Chung-kung said, "Though I am deficient in intelligence and vigour, I will make it my business to practise this lesson."

III. 1. Sze-ma New asked about perfect virtue.

2. The Master said, "The man of perfect virtue is cautious and slow in his speech."

3. "Cautious and slow in his speech!" said New;—"is this what is meant by perfect virtue?" The Master said, "When a man feels the difficulty of doing, can he be other than cautious and slow in speaking?"

IV. 1. Sze-ma New asked about the superior man. The Master said, "The superior man has neither anxiety nor fear."

2. "Being without anxiety or fear!" said New;—"does this constitute what we call the superior man?"

3. The Master said, "When internal examination discovers nothing wrong, what is there to be anxious about, what is there to fear?"

V. 1. Sze-ma New, full of anxiety, said, "*Other* men all have their brothers, I only have not."

apt to be done with haughtiness. This part of the answer may be compared with the apostle's precept—"Honour all men," only the "all men" is much more comprehensive there.—The answer, the same as that of Hway in last chapter, seems to betray the hand of the compiler.

3. CAUTION IN SPEAKING A CHARACTERISTIC OF PERFECT VIRTUE:— A CONVERSATION WITH TSZE-NEW. Tsze-new was the designation of Sze-ma Kang, whose tablet is now the seventh, east, in the outer range of the temples. He belonged to Sung, and was a brother of Hwan T'uy, VII. xxii. Their ordinary surname was Heang, but that of Hwan could also be used by them, as they were descended from the duke so called. The office of "Master of the horse" had long been in the family, and that title appears here as if it were New's surname.

4. HOW THE KEUN-TSZE HAS NEITHER ANXIETY NOR FEAR, CONSCIOUS RECTITUDE FREEING FROM THESE.

5. CONSOLATION OFFERED BY TSZE-HEA TO TSZE-NEW ANXIOUS ABOUT THE PERIL OF HIS BROTHER. 1. Tsze-new's anxiety was occasioned by the conduct of his eldest brother, Hwan T'uy, who, he knew, was contemplating rebellion, which would probably lead to his death. ."All have their brothers,"—*i.e.*, all can rest quietly without anxiety in their relation. 2. It is naturally supposed that the author of the observation was Confucius. 4. One writer says that the expression:—"all within the

2. Tsze-hea said to him, "There is the following saying which I have heard:—

3. "'Death and life have their determined appointment; riches and honours depend upon Heaven.'

4. "Let the superior man never fail reverentially to order his own conduct, and let him be respectful to others and observant of propriety:—then all within the four seas will be his brothers. What has the superior man to do with being distressed because he has no brothers?"

VI. Tsze-chang asked what constituted intelligence. The Master said, "He with whom neither slander that gradually soaks *into the mind*, nor statements that startle like a wound in the flesh, are successful, may be called intelligent indeed. Yea, he with whom neither soaking slander, nor startling statements, are successful, may be called far-seeing."

VII. 1. Tsze-kung asked about government. The Master said, "*The requisites of government* are that there be sufficiency of food, sufficiency of military equipment, and the confidence of the people in their ruler."

2. Tsze-kung said, "If it cannot be helped, and one of

four seas are brothers," "does not mean that all under heaven have the same genealogical register." Choo He's interpretation is that, when a man so acts, other men will love and respect him as a brother. This, no doubt, is the extent of the saying. I have found no satisfactory gloss on the phrase—"the four seas." It is found in the Shoo-king, the She-king, and the Le-ke. In the Urh Ya, a sort of Lexicon, very ancient, which was once reckoned among the *king*, it is explained as a territorial designation, the name of the dwelling-place of all the barbarous tribes. But the great Yu is represented as having made the four seas as four ditches, to which he drained the waters inundating "the middle kingdom." Plainly, the ancient conception was of their own country as the great habitable tract, north, south, east, and west of which were four seas or oceans, between whose shores and their own borders the intervening space was not very great, and occupied by wild hordes of inferior races. Commentators consider Tsze-hea's attempt at consolation altogether wide of the mark.

6. WHAT CONSTITUTES INTELLIGENCE:—ADDRESSED TO TSZE-CHANG. Tsze-chang, it is said, was always seeking to be wise about things lofty and distant, and therefore Confucius brings him back to things near at hand, which it was more necessary for him to attend to.

7. REQUISITES IN GOVERNMENT:—A CONVERSATION WITH TSZE-CHANG. 3. The difficulty here is with the concluding clause which is literally, "No faith, not stand." Transferring the meaning of faith or confidence from paragraph 1, we naturally render as in the translation, "the state will not stand." This is the view, moreover, of the old interpreters.

these must be dispensed with, which of the three should be foregone first?" "The military equipment," said the Master.

3. Tsze-kung *again* asked, "If it cannot be helped, and one of the remaining two must be dispensed with, which of them should be foregone?" The Master answered, "Part with the food. From of old, death has been the lot of all men; but if the people have no faith *in their rulers*, there is no standing *for the State.*"

VIII. 1. Kih Tsze-shing said, "In a superior man it is only the substantial qualities which are wanted;—why should we seek for ornamental accomplishments?"

2. Tsze-kung said, "Alas! Your words, sir, show you to be a superior man, but four horses cannot overtake the tongue.

"Ornament is as substance; substance is as ornament. The hide of a tiger or leopard stript of its hair is like the hide of a dog or goat stript of its hair."

IX. 1. The Duke Gae inquired of Yew Jŏ, saying, "The year is one of scarcity, and *the returns for* expenditure are not sufficient;—what is to done?"

2. Yew Jŏ replied to him, "Why not simply tithe the people."

Choo He and his followers, however, seek to make much more of "faith." On the first paragraph he comments,—"The granaries being full, and the military preparation complete, then let the influence of instruction proceed. So shall the people have faith in their ruler, and will not leave him or rebel." On the third paragraph he says,—"If the people be without food, they must die, but death is the inevitable lot of men. If they are without faith, though they live, they have not wherewith to establish themselves. It is better for them in such case to die. Therefore it is better for the ruler to die, not losing faith to his people, so that the people will prefer death rather than lose faith to him."

8. SUBSTANTIAL QUALITIES AND ACCOMPLISHMENTS IN THE KEUN-TSZE. 1. Tsze-shing was an officer of the state of Wei, and, distressed by the pursuit in the times of what was merely external, made this not sufficiently well-considered remark, to which Tsze-kung replied, in, according to Choo He, an equally one-sided manner. 3. The modern commentators seem hypercritical in condemning Tsze-kung's language here. He shows the desirableness of the ornamental accomplishments, but does not necessarily put them on the same level with the substantial qualities.

9. LIGHT TAXATION THE BEST WAY TO SECURE THE GOVERNMENT FROM EMBARRASSMENT FOR WANT OF FUNDS. 2. By the statutes of the Chow dynasty, the ground was divided into allotments cultivated in common by the families located upon them, and the produce was divided

3. "With two tenths," said the duke, "I find them not enough;—how could I do with that system of one tenth?"

4. Yew Jŏ answered, "If the people have plenty, their prince will not be left to want alone. If the people are in want, their prince cannot enjoy plenty alone."

X. 1. Tsze-chang having asked how virtue was to be exalted, and delusions to be discovered, the Master said, "Hold faithfulness and sincerity as first principles, and be moving continually to what is right;—this is the way to exalt one's virtue.

2. "You love a man and wish him to live; you hate him and wish him to die. Having wished him to live, you also wish him to die. This is a case of delusion.

3. "'It may not be on account of his being rich, yet you come to make a difference.'"

XI. 1. The Duke King, of Ts'e, asked Confucius about government.

2. Confucius replied, "*There is government,* when the

equally, nine tenths being given to the farmers, and one tenth being reserved as a contribution to the state. 3. A former duke of Loo, Seuen (B.C. 601—590), had imposed an additional tax of another tenth from each family's portion. 4. The meaning of this paragraph is given in the translation. Literally rendered it is,—"The people having plenty, the prince—with whom not plenty? The people not having plenty, with whom can the prince have plenty?" Yew Jŏ wished to impress on the duke, that a sympathy and common condition should unite him and his people. If he lightened his taxation to the regular tithe, then they would cultivate their allotments with so much vigour, that his receipts would be abundant. They would be able, moreover, to help their kind ruler in any emergency.

10. HOW TO EXALT VIRTUE AND DISCOVER DELUSIONS. 2. The Master says nothing about the "discriminating," or "discovering," of delusions, but gives an instance of a twofold delusion. Life and death, it is said, are independent of our wishes. To desire for a man either the one or the other, therefore, is one delusion. And on the change of our feelings to change our wishes in reference to the same person, is another. But in this Confucius hardly appears to be the sage. 3. See the She-king, Pt II. Bk IV. iv. 3. I have translated according to the meaning in the She-king. The quotation may be twisted into some sort of accordance with the preceding paragraph, as a case of delusion, but the commentator Ch'ing is probably correct in supposing that it should be transferred to XVI. xii.

11. GOOD GOVERNMENT OBTAINS ONLY WHEN ALL THE RELATIVE DUTIES ARE MAINTAINED. 1. Confucius went to Ts'e in his thirty-sixth year, and finding the reigning duke—styled King after his death—overshadowed by his ministers, and thinking of setting aside his eldest son

prince is prince, and the minister is minister; when the father is father, and the son is son."

3. "Good!" said the duke; "if, indeed, the prince be not prince, the minister not minister, the father not father, and the son not son, although I have my revenue, can I enjoy it?"

XII. 1. The Master said, "Ah! it is Yew, who could with half a word settle litigations!"

2. Tsze-loo never slept over a promise.

XIII. The Master said, "In hearing litigations, I am like any other body. What is necessary, is to cause *the people* to have no litigations."

XIV. Tsze-chang asked about government. The Master said, "*The art of governing* is to keep *its affairs* before the mind without weariness, and to practise them with undeviating consistency."

XV. The Master said, "By extensively studying all learning, and keeping himself under the restraint of the rules of propriety, *one* may thus likewise not err from what is right."

XVI. The Master said, "The superior man *seeks* to perfect the admirable qualities of men, and does not *seek* to perfect their bad qualities. The mean man does the opposite of this."

XVII. Ke K'ang asked Confucius about government. Confucius replied, "To govern means to rectify. If you lead on *the people* with correctness, who will dare not to be correct?"

from the succession, he shaped his answer to the question about government accordingly.

12. WITH WHAT EASE TSZE-LOO COULD SETTLE LITIGATIONS. 1. We translate here—"could," and not—"can," because Confucius is not referring to facts, but simply praising the disciple's character. 2. This paragraph is a note by the compilers, stating a fact about Tsze-loo, to illustrate what the Master said of him.

13. TO PREVENT BETTER THAN TO DETERMINE LITIGATIONS. See the Great Learning, Commentary, IV. Little stress is to be laid on the "I." The meaning simply—"One man is as good as another." Much stress is to be laid on " to cause " as—" to influence to."

14. THE ART OF GOVERNING.

15. HARDLY DIFFERENT FROM VI. xxv.

16. OPPOSITE INFLUENCE UPON OTHERS OF THE SUPERIOR MAN AND THE MEAN MAN.

17. GOVERNMENT MORAL IN ITS END, AND EFFICIENT BY EXAMPLE.

XVIII. Ke K'ang distressed about the number of thieves *in the State*, inquired of Confucius *about how to do away with them*. Confucius said, "If you, sir, were not covetous, although you should reward them to do it, they would not steal.

XIX. Ke K'ang asked Confucius about government, saying, "What do you say to killing the unprincipled for the good of the principled?" Confucius replied, "Sir, in carrying on your government, why should you use killing at all? Let your *evinced* desires be for what is good, and the people will be good. The relation between superiors and inferiors is like that between the wind and the grass. The grass must bend when the wind blows across it."

XX. 1. Tsze-chang asked, "What must the officer be, who may be said to be distinguished?"

2. The Master said, "What is it you call being distinguished?"

3. Tsze-chang replied, "It is to be heard of through the State, to be heard of through the Family."

4. The Master said, "That is notoriety, not distinction.

5. "Now, the man of distinction is solid and straightforward, and loves righteousness. He examines people's words, and looks at their countenances. He is anxious to humble himself to others. Such a man will be distinguished in the country; he will be distinguished in the Family.

6. "As to the man of notoriety, he assumes the appearance of virtue, but his actions are opposed to it, and he rests in this character without any doubts *about himself*. Such a man will be heard of in the country; he will be heard of in the Family."

XXI. 1. Fan-ch'e rambling with the Master under

---

18. THE PEOPLE ARE MADE THIEVES BY THE EXAMPLE OF THEIR RULERS. This is a good instance of Confucius' boldness in reproving men in power. Ke K'ang had confirmed himself as head of the Ke family, and entered into all its usurpations, by taking off the infant nephew, who should have been its rightful chief.

19. KILLING NOT TO BE TALKED OF BY RULERS; THE EFFECT OF THEIR EXAMPLE.

20. THE MAN OF TRUE DISTINCTION, AND THE MAN OF NOTORIETY.

21. HOW TO EXALT VIRTUE, CORRECT VICE, AND DISCOVER DELUSIONS. Compare chapter x. Here, as there, under the last point of the inquiry,

the trees about the rain-altars, said, "I venture to ask how to exalt virtue, to correct cherished evil, and to discover delusions."

2. The Master said, "Truly a good question!

3. "If doing what is to be done be made the first business, and success a secondary consideration;—is not this the way to exalt virtue? To assail one's own wickedness and not assail that of others;—is not this the way to correct cherished evil? For a morning's anger, to disregard one's own life, and involve that of one's parents;—is not this a case of delusion?"

XXII. 1. Fan Ch'e asked about benevolence. The Master said, "It is to love *all* men." He asked about knowledge. The Master said, "It is to know *all* men."

2. Fan Ch'e did not immediately understand *these answers.*

3. The Master said, "Employ the upright and put aside all the crooked;—in this way, the crooked can be made to be upright."

4. Fan Ch'e retired, and seeing Tsze-hea, he said to him, "A little ago, I had an interview with our Master, and asked him about knowledge. He said, 'Employ the upright, and put aside all the crooked;—in this way, the crooked can be made to be upright.' What did he mean?"

5. Tsze-hea said, "Truly rich is his saying!

6. "Shun, being in possession of the empire, selected from among all the people, and employed Kaou-yaou, on which all who were devoid of virtue disappeared. T'ang being in possession of the empire, selected from among all the people, and employed E-Yin, and all who were devoid of virtue disappeared."

XXIII. Tsze-kung asked about friendship. The Master

Confucius simply indicates a case of delusion, and perhaps this is the best way to teach how to discover delusions generally.

22. ABOUT BENEVOLENCE AND WISDOM;—HOW KNOWLEDGE SUBSERVES BENEVOLENCE. Fan Ch'e might well deem the Master's replies enigmatical, and, with the help of Tsze-hea's explanations, the student still finds it difficult to understand the chapter.—Shun and T'ang showed their wisdom—their knowledge of men—in the selection of those ministers. That was their employment of the upright, and therefore all devoid of virtue disappeared. That was their making the crooked upright;—and so their love reached to all.

23. PRUDENCE IN FRIENDSHIP.

said, "Faithfully admonish *your friend*, and kindly try to lead him. If you find him impracticable, stop. Do not disgrace yourself."

XXIV. The philosopher Tsăng said, "The superior man on literary grounds meets with his friends, and by their friendship helps his virtue."

BOOK XIII.

Chapter I. 1. Tsze-loo asked about government. The Master said, "Go before the people *with your example*, and be laborious in their affairs."

2. He requested further instruction, and was answered, "be not weary in these things."

II. 1. Chung-kung, being chief minister to the head of the Ke family, asked about government. The Master said, "Employ first the services of your various officers, pardon small faults, and raise to office men of virtue and talents."

2. *Chung-kung* said, "How shall I know the men of virtue and talent, so that I may raise them to office?"

---

24. THE FRIENDSHIP OF THE KEUN-TSZE. "On literary grounds," —literally, "by means of letters," *i.e.*, common literary studies and pursuits.

HEADING AND SUBJECTS OF THIS BOOK.—"Tsze-loo." Here, as in the last book, we have a number of subjects touched upon, all bearing more or less directly on the government of the state, and the cultivation of the person. The book extends to thirty chapters.

1. THE SECRET OF SUCCESS IN GOVERNING IS THE UNWEARIED EXAMPLE OF THE RULERS:—A LESSON TO TSZE-LOO. 1. To what understood antecedents do the *Che* refer? For the first, we may suppose to "people;" "precede the people," or "lead the people," that is, do so by the example of your personal conduct. But we cannot in the second clause bring *Che* in the same way under the regimen of *laou*, "to be laborious for them;" that is, to set them the example of diligence in agriculture, &c. It is better, however, according to the idiom I have several times pointed out, to take *Che* as giving a sort of neuter and general force to the preceding words, so that the expressions are— "example and laboriousness."—K'ung Gan-kwŏ understands the meaning differently:—"set the people an example, and then you may make them labour." But this is not so good.

2. THE DUTIES CHIEFLY TO BE ATTENDED TO BY A HEAD MINISTER: —A LESSON TO YEN YUNG. 1. Compare VIII. iv. 3. A head minister should assign to his various officers their duties, and not be inter-

He was answered, "Raise to office those whom you know. As to those whom you do not know, will others neglect them?"

III. 1. Tsze-loo said, "The prince of Wei has been waiting for you, in order with you to administer the government. What will you consider the first thing to be done?"

2. The Master replied, "What is necessary is to rectify names."

3. "So, indeed!" said Tsze-loo. "You are wide of the mark. Why must there be such rectification?"

4. The Master said, "How uncultivated you are, Yew! A superior man, in regard to what he does not know, shows a cautious reserve."

5. "If names be not correct, language is not in accordance with the truth of things. If language be not in accordance with the truth of things, affairs cannot be carried on to success.

6. "When affairs cannot be carried on to success, proprieties and music will not flourish. When proprieties and music do not flourish, punishments will not be properly

---

fering in them himself. His business is to examine into the manner in which they discharge them. And in doing so, he should overlook small faults. 2. Confucius' meaning is, that Chung-kung need not trouble himself about *all* men of worth. Let him advance those he knew. There was no fear that the others would be neglected. Compare what is said on "knowing men," in XII. xxii.

3. THE SUPREME IMPORTANCE OF NAMES BEING CORRECT. 1. This conversation is assigned by Choo He to the eleventh year of the Duke Gae of Loo, when Confucius was sixty-nine, and he returned from his wanderings to his native state. Tsze-loo had then been some time in the service of the Duke Ch'uh of Wei, who it would appear had been wishing to get the services of the sage himself, and the disciple did not think that his Master would refuse to accept office, as he had not objected to *his* doing so. 2. "Names" must have here a special reference, which Tsze-loo did not apprehend. Nor did the old interpreter, for Ma Yung explains the counsel "to rectify the names of all things." On this view, the reply would indeed be "wide of the mark." The answer is substantially the same as the reply to Duke King of Ts'e about government in XII. xi., that it obtains when the prince is prince, the father father, &c.; that is, when each man in his relations is what the *name* of his relation would require. Now, the Duke Ch'uh held the rule of Wei against his father; see VII. xiv. Confucius, from the necessity of the case and peculiarity of the circumstances, allowed his disciples, notwithstanding that, to take office in Wei; but at the time of this conversation, Ch'uh had been duke for

awarded. When punishments are not properly awarded, the people do not know how to move hand or foot.

7. "Therefore, a superior man considers it necessary that the names he uses may be spoken *appropriately*, and also that what he speaks may be carried out *appropriately*. What the superior man requires, is just that in his words there may be nothing incorrect."

IV. 1. Fan Ch'e requested to be taught husbandry. The Master said, "I am not so good for that as an old husbandman." He requested *also* to be taught gardening, and was answered, "I am not so good for that as an old gardener."

2. Fan Ch'e having gone out, the Master said, "A small man, indeed, is Fan Seu!"

3. "If a superior man love propriety, the people will not dare not to be reverent. If he love righteousness, the people will not dare not to submit *to his example*. If he love good faith, the people will not dare not to be sincere. Now, when these things obtain, the people from all quarters will come to him, bearing their children on their backs. What need has he of a knowledge of husbandry?"

V. The Master said, "Though a man may be able to recite the three hundred odes, yet if, when intrusted with a governmental charge, he knows not how to act, or if, when sent to any quarter on a mission, he cannot give his replies unassisted, notwithstanding the extent *of his learning*, of what practical use is it?"

nine years, and ought to have been so established that he could have taken the course of a filial son without subjecting the state to any risks. On this account, Confucius said he would begin with rectifying the name of the duke, that is, with requiring him to resign the dukedom to his father, and be what his name of *son* required him to be. This view enables us to understand better the climax that follows, though its successive steps are still not without difficulty.

4. A RULER HAS NOT TO OCCUPY HIMSELF WITH WHAT IS PROPERLY THE BUSINESS OF THE PEOPLE. It is to be supposed that Fan Ch'e was at this time in office somewhere, and thinking of the Master, as the villager and high officer did, IX. ii. and vi., that his knowledge embraced almost every subject, he imagined that he might get lessons from him on the two subjects he specifies, which he might use for the benefit of the people. The last paragraph shows what people in office should learn. Confucius intended that it should be repeated to Fan Ch'e.

5. LITERARY ACQUIREMENTS USELESS WITHOUT PRACTICAL ABILITY.

VI. The Master said, "When a prince's personal conduct is correct, his government is effective without the issuing of orders. If his personal conduct is not correct, he may issue orders, but they will not be followed."

VII. The Master said, "The governments of Loo and Wei are brothers."

VIII. The Master said of King, a scion of the ducal family of Wei, that he knew the economy of a family well. When he began to have means, he said, "Ha! here is a collection!" when they were a little increased, he said, "Ha! this is complete!" when he had become rich, he said, "Ha! this is admirable!"

IX. 1. When the Master went to Wei, Yen Yew acted as driver of his carriage.

2. The Master observed, "How numerous are the people!"

3. Yew said, "Since they are thus numerous, what more shall be done for them?" "Enrich them," was the reply.

4. "And when they have been enriched, what more shall be done?" The Master said, "Teach them."

X. The Master said, "If there were any of the princes who would employ me, in the course of twelve months, I should have done something considerable. In three years, the *government* would be perfected."

XI. The Master said, "'If good men were to govern a country in *succession* for a hundred years, they would be

---

6. HIS PERSONAL CONDUCT ALL IN ALL TO A RULER.

7. THE SIMILAR CONDITION OF THE STATES OF LOO AND WEI. Compare VI. xxii. Loo's state had been so from the influence of Chow-kung, and Wei was the fief of his brother Fung, commonly known as K'ang-shuh. They had, similarly, maintained an equal and brotherly course in their progress, or, as it was in Confucius' time, in their degeneracy. That portion of the present Ho-nan, which runs up and lies between Shan-se and Pih-chih-le, was the bulk of Wei.

8. THE CONTENTMENT OF THE OFFICER KING, AND HIS INDIFFERENCE IN GETTING RICH. The commentators say that it is not to be understood that King really made these utterances, but that Confucius thus vividly represents how he felt.

9. A PEOPLE NUMEROUS, WELL-OFF, AND EDUCATED, IS THE GREAT ACHIEVEMENT OF GOVERNMENT.

10. CONFUCIUS' ESTIMATE OF WHAT HE COULD DO, IF EMPLOYED TO ADMINISTER THE GOVERNMENT OF A STATE.

11. WHAT A HUNDRED YEARS OF GOOD GOVERNMENT COULD EFFECT. Confucius quotes here a saying of his time, and approves of it.

able to transform the violently bad, and dispense with capital punishments.' True indeed is this saying!"

XII. The Master said, "If a truly royal ruler were to arise, it would *still* require a generation, and then virtue would prevail."

XIII. The Master said, "If a minister make his own conduct correct, what difficulty will he have in assisting in government? If he cannot rectify himself, what has he to do with rectifying others?"

XIV. The disciple Yen returning from the court, the Master said to him, "How are you so late?" He replied, "We had government business." The Master said, "It must have been *Family* affairs. If there had been government business, though I am not *now* in office, I should have been consulted about it."

XV. 1. The Duke Ting asked whether there was a single sentence which could make a country prosperous. Confucius replied, "Such an effect cannot be expected from one sentence.

2. "There is a saying, however, which people have— 'To be a prince is difficult; to be a minister is not easy.'

12. IN WHAT TIME A ROYAL RULER COULD TRANSFORM THE EMPIRE. The character denoting "a king," "a royal ruler," is formed by three straight lines representing the three powers of Heaven, Earth, and Man, and a perpendicular line going through and uniting them, and thus conveys the highest idea of power and influence. Here it means the highest wisdom and virtue in the highest place.—To save Confucius from the charge of vanity in what he says, in chapter x., that he could accomplish in three years, it is said that the perfection which he predicates there would only be the foundation for the virtue here realized.

13. THAT HE BE PERSONALLY CORRECT ESSENTIAL TO AN OFFICER OF GOVERNMENT.

14. AN IRONICAL ADMONITION TO YEN YEW ON THE USURPING TENDENCIES OF THE KE FAMILY. The point of the chapter turns on the opposition of the phrases "government business," and "family affairs;"—at the court of the Kĕ family, that is, they had really been discussing matters of government, affecting the State, and proper only for the prince's court. Confucius affects not to believe it, and says that at the chief's court they could only have been discussing the affairs of his house. Superannuated officers might go to court on occasions of emergency, and might also be consulted on such, though the general rule was to allow them to retire at seventy. See the Le Ke, I. i. 28.

15. HOW THE PROSPERITY AND RUIN OF A COUNTRY MAY DEPEND ON THE RULER'S VIEW OF HIS POSITION, HIS FEELING ITS DIFFICULTY, OR ONLY CHERISHING A HEADSTRONG WILL. 1. I should suppose that these

"If *a ruler* knows this,—the difficulty of being a prince,—may there not be expected from this one sentence the prosperity of his country?"

4. The *duke then* said, "Is there a single sentence which can ruin a country?" Confucius replied, "Such an effect as that cannot be expected from one sentence. There is, *however*, the saying which people have—'I have no pleasure in being a prince, only in that no one offer any opposition to what I say!'

5. "If *a ruler's* words be good, is it not also good that no one oppose them? But if they are not good, and no one opposes them, may there not be expected from this one sentence the ruin of his country?"

XVI. 1. The duke of Shĕ asked about government.

2. The Master said, "*Good government obtains, when* those who are near are made happy, and those who are far off are attracted."

XVII. Tsze-hea, being governor of Keu-foo, asked about government. The Master said, "Do not be desirous to have things done quickly; do not look at small advantages. Desire to have things done quickly prevents their being done thoroughly. Looking at small advantages prevents great affairs from being accomplished."

XVIII. 1. The duke of Shĕ informed Confucius, saying, "Among us here there are those who may be styled upright in their conduct. If their father have stolen a sheep, they will bear witness to the fact."

2. Confucius said, "Among us, in our part of the country, those who are upright are different from this. The

---

were commentators' sayings, about which the duke asks, in a way to intimate his disbelief of them.

16. GOOD GOVERNMENT SEEN FROM ITS EFFECTS. 1. Shĕ;—see VII. xviii. 2. Confucius is supposed to have in view the oppressive and aggressive government of Tsoo, to which Shĕ belonged.

17. HASTE AND SMALL ADVANTAGES NOT TO BE DESIRED IN GOVERNING. Keu-foo was a small city in the western borders of Loo.

18. NATURAL DUTY AND UPRIGHTNESS IN COLLISION. 1. We cannot say whether the duke is referring to one or more actual cases, or giving his opinion of what his people would do. Confucius' reply would incline us to the latter view. Accounts are quoted of such cases, but they are probably founded on this chapter. *Ching* seems to convey here the idea of accusation, as well as of witnessing. 2. The concluding expression does not absolutely affirm that this is upright, but that in this there is a better principle than in the other conduct.—Anybody but a

father conceals the misconduct of the son, and the son conceals the misconduct of the father. Uprightness is to be found in this."

XIX. Fan Ch'e asked about perfect virtue. The Master said, "It is, in retirement, to be sedately grave; in the management of business, to be reverently attentive; in intercourse with others, to be strictly sincere. Though a man go among rude uncultivated tribes, these *qualities* may not be neglected."

XX. 1. Tsze-kung asked, saying, "What qualities must a man possess to entitle him to be called an officer?" The Master said, "He who in his conduct of himself maintains a sense of shame, and when sent to any quarter will not disgrace his prince's commission, deserves to be called an officer."

2. *Tsze-kung* pursued, "I venture to ask who may be placed in the next lower rank?" and he was told, "He whom the circle of his relatives pronounce to be filial, whom his fellow-villagers and neighbours pronounce to be fraternal."

3. *Again the disciple* asked, "I venture to ask about the class still next in order." *The Master* said, "They are determined to be sincere in what they say, and to carry out what they do. They are obstinate little men. Yet perhaps they may make the next class."

4. *Tsze-kung finally* inquired, "Of what sort are those of the present day, who engage in government?" The Master said, "Pooh! they are so many pecks and hampers, not worth being taken into account."

XXI. The Master said, "Since I cannot get men pursuing the due medium, to whom I might communicate *my instructions*, I must find the ardent and the cautiously-decided. The ardent will advance and lay hold *of truth*;

Chinese will say that both the duke's view of the subject and the sage's were incomplete.

19. CHARACTERISTICS OF PERFECT VIRTUE, EVEN WHEN ASSOCIATING WITH BARBARIANS.

20. DIFFERENT CLASSES OF MEN WHO IN THEIR SEVERAL DEGREES MAY BE STYLED OFFICERS, AND THE INFERIORITY OF THE MASS OF THE OFFICERS OF CONFUCIUS' TIME.

21. CONFUCIUS OBLIGED TO CONTENT HIMSELF WITH THE ARDENT AND CAUTIOUS AS DISCIPLES. Compare V. xxi., and Mencius, VII. Bk II. xxxvii.

the cautiously-decided will keep themselves from what is wrong."

XXII. 1. The Master said, "The people of the south have a saying—'A man without constancy cannot be either a wizard or a doctor.' Good!

2. "Inconstant in his virtue, he will be visited with disgrace."

3. The Master said, "This arises simply from not prognosticating."

XXIII. The Master said, "The superior man is affable, but not adulatory; the mean adulatory, but not affable."

XXIV. Tsze-kung asked saying, "What do you say of a man who is loved by all the people of his village?" The Master replied, "We may not for that accord our approval of him." "And what do you say of him who is hated by all the people of his village?" The Master said, "We may not for that conclude that he is bad. It is better than either of these cases that the good in the village love him, and the bad hate him."

XXV. The Master said, "The superior man is easy to serve and difficult to please. If you try to please him in any way which is not accordant with right, he will not be pleased. But in his employment of men, he uses them according to their capacity. The mean man is difficult to serve, and easy to please. If you try to please him, though it be in a way which is not accordant with right, he may be pleased. But in his employment of men, he wishes them to be equal to everything."

XXVI. The Master said, "The superior man has a dignified ease without pride. The mean man has pride without a dignified ease."

XXVII. The Master said, "The firm, the enduring, the simple, and the modest, are near to virtue."

XXVIII. Tsze-loo asked saying, "What qualities must a man possess to entitle him to be called a scholar?" The Master said, "He must be thus,—earnest, urgent, and bland:—among his friends, earnest and urgent; among his brethren, bland."

XXIX. The Master said, "Let a good man teach the people seven years, and they may then likewise be employed in war."

XXX. The Master said, "To lead an uninstructed people to war is to throw them away."

26. THE DIFFERENT AIR AND BEARING OF THE SUPERIOR AND THE MEAN MAN.
27. NATURAL QUALITIES WHICH ARE FAVOURABLE TO VIRTUE.
28. QUALITIES THAT MARK THE SCHOLAR IN SOCIAL INTERCOURSE. This is the same question as in chapter xx. 1, but the subject is here "the scholar," the gentleman of education, without reference to his being in office or not.
29. HOW THE GOVERNMENT OF A GOOD RULER WILL PREPARE THE PEOPLE FOR WAR. "A good man,"—spoken with reference to him as a ruler. The teaching is not to be understood of military training, but of the duties of life and citizenship; a people so taught are morally fitted to fight for their government. What military training may be included in the teaching, would merely be the hunting and drilling during the people's repose from the toils of agriculture.
30. THAT PEOPLE MUST BE TAUGHT, TO PREPARE THEM FOR WAR. Compare the last chapter. The language is very strong, and the instruction being understood as in that chapter, shows how Confucius valued education for all classes.

BOOK XIV.

CHAPTER I. Hëen asked what might be considered shameful. The Master said, "When good government prevails in a State, *to be thinking only of his salary;* and, when bad government prevails, *to be thinking in the same way, only of his salary;*—this is shameful."

II. 1. "When the love of superiority, boasting, resentments, and covetousness are repressed, may this be deemed perfect virtue?"

2. The Master said, "This may be regarded as the achievement of what is difficult. But I do not know that it is to be deemed perfect virtue."

III. The Master said, "The scholar who cherishes the love of comfort, is not fit to be deemed a scholar."

IV. The Master said, "When good government prevails in a State, language may be lofty and bold, and actions the same. When bad government prevails, the actions may be lofty and bold, but the language may be with some reserve."

HEADING AND SUBJECTS OF THIS BOOK.—The glossarist Hing P'ing says, "In this Book we have the characters of the *Three Kings*, and *Two Chiefs*, the courses proper for princes and great officers, the practice of virtue, the knowledge of what is shameful, personal cultivation, and the tranquillizing of the people;—all subjects of great importance in government. They are therefore collected together, and arranged after the last chapter which commences with an inquiry about government." Some writers are of opinion that the whole book was compiled by Hëen or Yuen Sze, who appears in the first chapter.

1. IT IS SHAMEFUL IN AN OFFICER TO BE CARING ONLY ABOUT HIS EMOLUMENT. Hëen is the Yuen Sze of VI. III.; and if we suppose Confucius' answer designed to have a practical application to Hëen himself, it is not easily reconcilable with what appears of his character in that other place.

2. THE PRAISE OF PERFECT VIRTUE IS NOT TO BE ALLOWED FOR THE REPRESSION OF BAD FEELINGS. In Ho An, this chapter is joined to the preceding, and Choo He also takes the first paragraph to be a question of Yuen Hëen.

3. A SCHOLAR MUST BE AIMING AT WHAT IS HIGHER THAN COMFORT OR PLEASURE. Compare IV. xi.

4. WHAT ONE DOES MUST ALWAYS BE RIGHT; WHAT ONE FEELS NEED NOT ALWAYS BE SPOKEN:—A LESSON OF PRUDENCE.

V. The Master said, "The virtuous will be sure to speak correctly, but those whose speech is good may not always be virtuous. Men of principle are sure to be bold, but those who are bold may not always be men of principle."

VI. Nan-kung Kwŏh, submitting an inquiry to Confucius, said, " E was skilful at archery, and Ngaou could move a boat along upon the land, but neither of them died a natural death. Yu and Tseih personally wrought at the toils of husbandry, and they became possessors of the empire." The Master made no reply, but when Nan-kung Kwŏh went out, he said, "A superior man indeed is this! An esteemer of virtue indeed is this!"

VII. The Master said, "Superior men, and yet not *always* virtuous, there have been, alas! But there never has been a mean man, and, *at the same time*, virtuous."

VIII. The Master said, "Can there be love which does not lead to strictness with its object? Can there be loyalty which does not lead to the instruction of its object?"

5. WE MAY PREDICATE THE EXTERNAL FROM THE INTERNAL, BUT NOT VICE VERSÂ.

6. EMINENT PROWESS CONDUCTING TO RUIN, EMINENT VIRTUE LEADING TO EMPIRE. THE MODESTY OF CONFUCIUS. Nan-kung Kwŏh is said by Choo He to have been the same as Nan Yung in V. i.; but this is doubtful. See on Nan Yung there. Kwŏh, it is said, insinuated in his remark an inquiry, whether Confucius was not like Yu or Tseih, and the great men of the time so many E's and Ngaous, and the sage was modestly silent upon the subject. E and Ngaou carry us back to the twenty-second century before Christ. The first belonged to a family of princelets, famous, from the time of the Emperor Kuh (B.C. 2432), for their archery, and dethroned the Emperor How Seang, B.C. 2145. E was afterwards slain by his minister, Han Tsuh, who then married his wife, and one of their sons was the individual here named Ngaou, who was subsequently destroyed by the Emperor Shaou-k'ang, the posthumous son of How-seang. Tseih was the son of the Emperor Kuh, of whose birth many prodigies are narrated, and appears in the Shoo-king as the minister of agriculture to Yaou and Shun, by name K'e. The Chow family traced their descent lineally from him, so that though the empire only came to his descendants more than a thousand years after his time, Nan-kung Kwŏh speaks as if he had got it himself, as Yu did.

7. THE HIGHEST VIRTUE NOT EASILY ATTAINED TO, AND INCOMPATIBLE WITH MEANNESS. Compare IV. iv. We must supply the "always," to bring out the meaning.

8. A LESSON FOR PARENTS AND MINISTERS, THAT THEY MUST BE STRICT AND DECIDED.

IX. The Master said, "In preparing the governmental notifications, P'e Shin first made the rough draught; She-shuh examined and discussed its contents; Tsze-yu, the manager of Foreign intercourse, then improved and polished it; and, finally, Tsze-ch'an of Tung-le gave it the proper softness and finish."

X. 1. Some one asked about Tsze-ch'an. The Master said, "He was a kind man."

2. He asked about Tsze-se. The Master said, "That man! That man!"

3. He asked about Kwan Chung. "For him," said the Master, "the city of Pëen, with three hundred families, was taken from the chief of the Pih family, who did not utter a murmuring word, though, till he was toothless, he had only coarse rice to eat."

XI. The Master said, "To be poor without murmuring is difficult. To be rich without being proud is easy."

XII. The Master said, "Măng Kung-ch'ö is more than fit to be chief officer in the Families of Chaou

9. THE EXCELLENCE OF THE OFFICIAL NOTIFICATIONS OF CH'ING, OWING TO THE ABILITY OF FOUR OF ITS OFFICERS. The state of Ch'ing, small and surrounded by powerful neighbours, was yet fortunate in having able ministers, through whose mode of conducting its government it enjoyed considerable prosperity. Tsze-ch'an (see V. xv.) was the chief minister of the State, and in preparing such documents first used the services of P'e Shin, who was noted for his wise planning of matters. "She-shuh" shows the relation of the officer indicated to the ruling family. His name was Yew-keih.

10. THE JUDGMENT OF CONFUCIUS CONCERNING TSZE-CH'AN, TSZE-SE, AND KWAN CHUNG. 1. See V. xv. 2. Tsze-se was the chief minister of Tsoo. He had refused to accept the nomination to the sovereignty of the State in preference to the rightful heir, but did not oppose the usurping tendencies of the rulers of Tsoo. He had moreover opposed the wish of King Ch'aou to employ the sage. 3. Kwan Chung,—see III. xxii. To reward his merits, the Duke Hwan conferred on him the domain of the officer mentioned in the text, who had been guilty of some offence. His submitting, as he did, to his changed fortunes was the best tribute to Kwan's excellence.

11. IT IS HARDER TO BEAR POVERTY ARIGHT THAN TO CARRY RICHES. This sentiment may be controverted.

12. THE CAPACITY OF MĂNG KUNG-CH'Ö. Kung-ch'ö was the head of the Măng, or Chung-sun family, and according to the "Historical Records," was valued by Confucius more than any other great man of the times in Loo. His estimate of him, however, as appears here, was not very high. In the sage's time, the government of the State of Tsin was in the hands of the three Families, Chaou, Wei, and Han, which after-

and Wei, but he is not fit to be minister to either of the States T'ăng or Sëĕ."

XIII. 1. Tsze-loo asked what constituted a COMPLETE man. The Master said, "Suppose a man with the knowledge of Tsang Woo-chung, the freedom from covetousness of Kung-ch'ŏ, the bravery of Chwang of Peen, and the varied talents of Yen K'ew; add to these the accomplishments of the rules of propriety and music:—such an one might be reckoned a COMPLETE man."

2. He then added, "But what is the necessity for a complete man of the present day to have all these things? The man, who in the view of gain thinks of righteousness; who in the view of danger is prepared to give up his life; and who does not forget an old agreement, however far back it extends:—such a man may be reckoned a COMPLETE man."

XIV. 1. The Master asked Kung-ming Kea about Kung-shuh Wăn, saying, " Is it true that your master speaks not, laughs not, and takes not ? "

2. Kung-ming Kea replied, "This has arisen from the reporters going beyond *the truth*.—My master speaks when it is the time to speak, and so men do not get tired of his speaking. He laughs when there is occasion to be joyful, and so men do not get tired of his laughing. He takes when it is consistent with righteousness to do so,

wards divided the territory among themselves, and became, as we shall see, in the times of Mencius, three independent principalities. T'ang was a small state, the place of which is seen in the district of the same name in the department of Yen-chow, Shan-tung. Sëĕ was another small state adjacent to it.

13. OF THE COMPLETE MAN:—A CONVERSATION WITH TSZE-LOO. 1. Tsang Woo-chung had been an officer of Loo in the reign anterior to that in which Confucius was born. So great was his reputation for wisdom that the people gave him the title of "sage." Woo was his honorary epithet, and Chung denotes his family place, among his brothers. Chwang, it is said, by Choo He, after Chow, one of the oldest commentators, whose surname only has come down to us, was "great officer of the city of Peen." In the "Great Collection of Surnames," a secondary branch of a family of the state of Tsaou having settled in Loo, and being gifted with Peen, its members took their surname thence.

14. THE CHARACTER OF KUNG-SHUH WĂN, WHO WAS SAID NEITHER TO SPEAK, NOR LAUGH, NOR TAKE. 1. Wăn was the honorary epithet of the individual in question, by name Che, or, as some say, Fă, an officer of the state of Wei. He was descended from the Duke Hëen, and was himself the founder of the Kung-shuh family, being so designated, I

and so men do not get tired of his taking." The Master said, " So ! But is it so with him ?"

XV. The Master said, " Tsang Woo-chung, keeping possession of Fang, asked of *the duke of* Loo to appoint a successor to him *in his Family*. Although it may be said that he was not using force with his sovereign, I believe he was."

XVI. The Master said, " The Duke Wăn of Tsin was crafty and not upright. The Duke Hwan of Ts'e was upright and not crafty."

XVII. 1. Tsze-loo said, " The Duke Hwan caused his brother Kew to be killed, when Shaou Hwŭh died *with his master*, but Kwan Chung did not do so. May not I say that he was wanting in virtue?"

2. The Master said, " The Duke Hwan assembled all the princes together, and that not with weapons of war

---

suppose, because of his relation to the reigning duke. Of Kung-ming Kea nothing seems to be known.

15. CONDEMNATION OF TSANG WOO-CHUNG FOR FORCING A FAVOUR FROM HIS PRINCE. Woo-chung (see chapter xiii.) was obliged to fly from Loo, by the animosity of the Măng family, and took refuge in Choo. As the head of the Tsang family, it devolved on him to offer the sacrifices in the ancestral temple, and he wished one of his half-brothers to be made the head of the family, in his room, that those might not be neglected. To strengthen the application for this, which he contrived to get made, he returned himself to the city of Fang, which belonged to his family, and thence sent a message to the court, which was tantamount to a threat that if the application were not granted, he would hold possession of the place. This was what Confucius condemned,—in a matter which should have been left to the duke's grace.

16. THE DIFFERENT CHARACTERS OF THE DUKES WĂN OF TSIN AND HWAN OF TS'E. Hwan and Wăn were the two first of the five leaders of the princes of the empire, who play an important part in Chinese history, during the period of the Chow dynasty known as the Ch'un Ts'ew. Hwan ruled in Ts'e, B.C. 683—640, and Wăn in Tsin B.C. 635—627. Of Duke Hwan, see the next chapter. The attributes mentioned by Confucius are not to be taken absolutely, but as respectively predominating in the two chiefs.

17. THE MERIT OF KWAN CHUNG:—A CONVERSATION WITH TSZE-LOO. 1. " The duke's son Kew," but, to avoid the awkwardness of that rendering, I say—" his brother." Hwan and Kew had both been refugees in different States, the latter having been carried into Loo, away from the troubles and dangers of Ts'e, by the ministers Kwan Chung and Shaou Hwuh. On the death of the prince of Ts'e, Hwan anticipated Kew, got to Ts'e, and took possession of the State. Soon after, he required the duke of Loo to put his brother to death, and to deliver up the two ministers,

and chariots :—it was all through the influence of Kwan Chung. Whose beneficence was like his? Whose beneficence was like his?"

XVIII. 1. Tsze-kung said, "Kwan Chung, I apprehend, was wanting in virtue. When the Duke Hwan caused his brother Kew to be killed, Kwan Chung was not able to die with him. Moreover, he became prime minister to Hwan."

2. The Master said, "Kwan Chung acted as prime minister to the Duke Hwan, made him leader of all the princes, and united and rectified the whole empire. Down to the present day, the people enjoy the gifts which he conferred. But for Kwan Chung, we should now be wearing our hair dishevelled, and the lappets of our coats buttoning on the left side.

3. "Will you require from him the small fidelity of common men and common women, who would commit suicide in a stream or ditch, no one knowing anything about them?"

when Shaou Hwuh chose to dash his brains out, and die with his master, while Kwan Chung returned gladly to Ts'e, took service with Hwan, became his prime minister, and made him supreme arbiter among the various chiefs of the empire. Such conduct was condemned by Tsze-loo. 2. Confucius defends Kwan Chung, on the ground of the services which he rendered.

18. THE MERIT OF KWAN CHUNG :—A CONVERSATION WITH TSZE-KUNG. 1. Tsze-loo's doubts about Kwan Chung arose from his not dying with the Prince Kew; Tsze-kung's turned principally on his subsequently becoming premier to Hwan. 2. Anciently the right was the position of honour, and the right hand, moreover, is the more convenient for use, but the practice of the barbarians was contrary to that of China in both points. The sentence of Confucius is, that but for Kwan Chung, his countrymen would have sunk to the state of the rude tribes about them. 3. By "small fidelity" is intended the faithfulness of a married couple of the common people, where the husband takes no concubine in addition to his wife. The argument is this:—"Do you think Kwan Chung should have considered himself bound to Kew, as a common man considers himself bound to his wife? And would you have had him commit suicide, as common people will do on any slight occasion?" Commentators say that there is underlying the vindication this fact:—that Kwang Chung's and Shaou Hwuh's adherence to Kew was wrong in the first place, Kew being the younger brother. Chung's conduct therefore was not to be judged as if Kew had been the senior. There is nothing of this, however, in Confucius' words. He vindicates Chung simply on the ground of his subsequent services, and his reference to "the small fidelity" of husband and wife among the common people is very unhappy.

XIX. 1. The officer, Seen, who had been family-minister to Kung-shuh Wăn, ascended to the prince's court in company with Wăn.

2. The Master having heard of it, said, "He deserves to be considered WĂN."

XX. 1. The Master was speaking about the unprincipled course of the Duke Ling of Wei, when Kí K'ang said, "Since he is of such a character, how is it he does not lose his throne?"

2. Confucius said, "The Chung-shuh, Yu, has the superintendence of his guests and of strangers; the litanist, T'o, has the management of his ancestral temple; and Wang-sun Kea has the direction of the army and forces:—with such officers as these, how should he lose his throne?"

XXI. The Master said, "He who speaks without modesty will find it difficult to make his words good."

XXII. 1. Ch'in Ch'ing murdered the Duke Këen of Ts'e.

2. Confucius bathed, went to court, and informed the Duke Gae, saying, "Ch'in Hăng has slain his sovereign. I beg that you will undertake to punish him."

19. THE MERIT OF KUNG-SHUH WĂN IN RECOMMENDING TO OFFICE A MAN OF WORTH. Kung-shuh Wăn, see chapter xiv. The paragraph is to be understood as intimating that Kung-shuh, seeing the worth and capacity of his minister, had recommended him to his sovereign, and afterwards was not ashamed to appear in the same rank with him at court.

20. THE IMPORTANCE OF GOOD AND ABLE MINISTERS:—SEEN IN THE STATE OF WEI. 1. *Ling* was the honorary epithet of Yuen, duke of Wei, B.C. 533—492. He was the husband of Nan-tsze. VI. xxvi. 2. The Chung-shuh, Yu, is the K'ung Wăn of V. xiv. Chung-shuh expresses his family position, according to the degrees of kindred. "The litanist, T'o,"—see VI. xiv. Wang-sun Kea,—see III. xiii.

21. EXTRAVAGANT SPEECH HARD TO BE MADE GOOD. Compare IV. xxii.

22. HOW CONFUCIUS WISHED TO AVENGE THE MURDER OF THE DUKE OF TS'E:—HIS RIGHTEOUS AND PUBLIC SPIRIT. 1. *K'en*,—"indolent in not a single virtue," and "tranquil, not speaking unadvisedly," are the meanings attached to this as an honorary epithet; while *Ch'ing* indicates "tranquillizer of the people, and establisher of government." The murder of the Duke Këen by his officer, Ch'in Hăng, took place B.C. 480, barely two years before Confucius' death. 2. "Bathing" implies all the fasting and other solemn preparation, as for a sacrifice or other great occasion. According to the account of this matter in the Tso Ch'wen, Confucius meant that the Duke Gae should himself, with the forces of Loo, undertake the punishment of the regicide. Some modern commentators cry

3. The duke said, "Inform the chiefs of the three families of it."

4. Confucius *retired*, and said, "Following, *as I do*, in the rear of the great officers, I did not dare not to represent such a matter, and my prince says, 'Inform the chiefs of the three families of it.'"

5. He went to the chiefs, and informed them, but they would not act. Confucius *then* said, "Following in the rear of the great officers, I did not dare not to represent such a matter."

XXIII. Tsze-loo asked how a sovereign should be served. The Master said, "Do not impose on him, and, moreover, withstand him to his face."

XXIV. The Master said, "The progress of the superior man is upwards; the progress of the mean man is downwards."

XXV. The Master said, "In ancient times, men learned with a view to their own improvement. Now-a-days, men learn with a view to the approbation of others."

XXVI. 1. Keu Pih-yuh sent a messenger *with friendly inquiries* to Confucius.

2. Confucius sat with him, and questioned him. "What," said he, "is your master engaged in?" The messenger replied, "My master is anxious to make his faults few, but he has not yet succeeded." He then went out, and the Master said, "A messenger indeed! A messenger indeed!"

out against this. The sage's advice, they say, would have been that the duke should report the thing to the emperor, and with his authority associate other princes with himself to do justice on the offender. 5. This is taken as the remark of Confucius, or his colloquy with himself, when he had gone out from the duke. The last observation was spoken to the chiefs, to reprove them for their disregard of a crime, which concerned every public man.

23. How the minister of a prince must be sincere and boldly upright.

24. The different progressive tendencies of the superior man and the mean man.

25. The different motives of learners in old times, and in the times of Confucius.

26. An admirable messenger. Pih-yuh was the designation of Keu Yuen, an officer of the state of Wei, and a disciple of the sage. His place is now first, east, in the outer court of the temples. Confucius had lodged with him when in Wei, and it was after his return to Loo, that Pih-yuh sent to inquire for him.

XXVII. The Master said, "He who is not in any particular office has nothing to do with plans for the administration of its duties."

XXVIII. 1. The philosopher Tsäng said, "The superior man, in his thoughts, does not go out of his place."

XXIX. The Master said, "The superior man is modest in his speech, but exceeds in his actions."

XXX. 1. The Master said, "The way of the superior man is threefold, but I am not equal to it. Virtuous, he is free from anxieties; wise, he is free from perplexities; bold, he is free from fear."

2. Tsze-kung said, "Master, that is what you yourself say."

XXXI. Tsze-kung was in the habit of comparing men together. The Master said, "Ts'ze must have reached a high pitch of excellence! Now, I have not leisure for this."

XXXII. The Master said, "I will not be concerned at man's not knowing me; I will be concerned at my own want of ability."

XXXIII. The Master said, "He who does not anticipate attempts to deceive him, nor think beforehand of

27. A repetition of VIII. xiv.

28. THE THOUGHTS OF A SUPERIOR MAN IN HARMONY WITH HIS POSITION. Tsäng here quotes from the illustration of the fifty-second diagram of the Yih-king, but he leaves out a character, and thereby alters the meaning somewhat. What is said in the Yih, is—"The superior man is thoughtful, and so does not go out of his place."—The chapter, it is said, is inserted here, from its analogy with the preceding.

29. THE SUPERIOR MAN MORE IN DEEDS THAN IN WORDS.

30. CONFUCIUS' HUMBLE ESTIMATE OF HIMSELF, WHICH TSZE-KUNG DENIES.

31. ONE'S WORK IS WITH ONE'S SELF:—AGAINST MAKING COMPARISONS.

32. CONCERN SHOULD BE ABOUT OUR PERSONAL ATTAINMENT, AND NOT ABOUT THE ESTIMATION OF OTHERS. See I. xvi., et al. A critical canon is laid down here by Choo He:—"All passages, the same in meaning and in words, are to be understood as having been spoken only once, and their recurrence is the work of the compilers. Where the meaning is the same and the language a little different, they are to be taken as having been repeated by Confucius himself, with the variations." According to this rule, the sentiment in this chapter was repeated by the master in four different utterances.

33. QUICK DISCRIMINATION WITHOUT SUSPICIOUSNESS IS HIGHLY MERITORIOUS.

his not being believed, and yet apprehends these things readily when they occur;—is he not a man of superior worth?"

XXXIV. 1. Wei-shang Mow said to Confucius, "K'ew, how is it that you keep roosting about? Is it not that you are an insinuating talker?"

2. Confucius said, "I do not dare to play the part of such a talker, but I hate obstinacy."

XXXV. The Master said, "A horse is called a *k'e*, not because of its strength, but because of its *other* good qualities."

XXXVI. 1. Some one said, "What do you say concerning the principle that injury should be recompensed with kindness?"

2. The Master said, "With what then will you recompense kindness?

3. "Recompense injury with justice, and recompense kindness with kindness."

XXXVII. 1. The Master said, "Alas! there is no one that knows me."

34. CONFUCIUS NOT SELF-WILLED, AND YET NO GLIB-TONGUED TALKER:—DEFENCE OF HIMSELF FROM THE CHARGE OF AN AGED REPROVER. From Wei-shang's addressing Confucius by his name, it is presumed that he was an old man. Such a liberty in a young man would have been impudence. It is presumed, also, that he was one of those men who kept themselves retired from the world in disgust. "Rooster-er," as a bird, is used contemptuously with reference to Confucius going about among the princes, and wishing to be called to office.

35. VIRTUE, AND NOT STRENGTH, THE FIT SUBJECT OF PRAISE. K'e was the name of a famous horse of antiquity who could run 1000 *le* in one day. See the dictionary in voc. It is here used generally for "a good horse."

36. GOOD IS NOT TO BE RETURNED FOR EVIL; EVIL IS TO BE MET SIMPLY WITH JUSTICE. 1. The phrase "Recompense injury with kindness" is found in Laou-tsze; but it is likely that Confucius' questioner simply consulted him about it as a saying which he had heard and was inclined to approve himself. 2. How far the ethics of Confucius fall below the Christian standard is evident from this chapter. The same expressions are attributed to Confucius in the Le-ke, XXXII. 11, and it is there added,—"He who returns good for evil is a man who is careful of his person," *i. e.*, will try to avert danger from himself by such a course. One author says, that the injuries intended by the questioner were only trivial matters, which perhaps might be dealt with in the way he mentioned, but great offences, as those against a sovereign, a father, may not be dealt with by such an inversion of the principles of justice. The Master himself, however, does not fence his deliverance in any way.

37. CONFUCIUS, LAMENTING THAT MEN DID NOT KNOW HIM, REsts

2. Tsze-kung said, "What do you mean by thus saying—that no one knows you?" The Master replied, "I do not murmur against Heaven. I do not grumble against men. My studies lie low, and my penetration rises high. But there is Heaven;—that knows me!"

XXXVIII. 1. The Kung-pih, Leaou, having slandered Tsze-loo to Ke-sun, Tsze-fuh King-pih informed Confucius of it, saying, "Our Master is certainly being led astray by the Kung-pih, Leaou, but I have still power enough left to cut *Leaou* off, and expose his corpse in the market and in the court."

2. The Master said, "If *my* principles are to advance, it is so ordered. If they are to fall to the ground, it is so ordered. What can the Kung-pih, Leaou, do, where such ordering is concerned?"

XXXIX. 1. The Master said, "*Some* men of worth retire from the world.

2. "Some retire from *particular* countries.

3. "Some retire because of *disrespectful* looks.

4. "Some retire because of *contradictory* language."

IN THE THOUGHT THAT HEAVEN KNEW HIM. Confucius referred in his complaint, commentators say, to the way in which he pursued his course, simply, out of his own conviction of duty, and for his own improvement, without regard to success, or the opinions of others. 2. "My studies lie low, and my penetration rises high" is literally—"beneath I learn, above I penetrate;"—the meaning appears to be that he contented himself with the study of men and things, common matters as more ambitious spirits would deem them, but from those he rose to understand the high principles involved in them,—"the appointments of Heaven," according to one commentator.

38. HOW CONFUCIUS RESTED, AS TO THE PROGRESS OF HIS DOCTRINES, ON THE ORDERING OF HEAVEN:—ON OCCASION OF TSZE-LOO'S BEING SLANDERED. Leaou, called Kung-pih (literally, duke's uncle), probably from an affinity with the ducal house, is said by some to have been a disciple of the sage, but that is not likely, as we find him here slandering Tsze-loo, that he might not be able, in his official connection with the Ke family, to carry the Master's lessons into practice. Tsze-fuh King-pih was an officer of Loo. Exposing the bodies of criminals was a sequel of their execution. The bodies of "great officers" were so exposed in the court, and those of meaner criminals in the market-place. "The market-place and the court" came to be employed together, though the exposure could take place only in one place.

39. DIFFERENT CAUSES WHY MEN OF WORTH WITHDRAW FROM PUBLIC LIFE, AND DIFFERENT EXTENTS TO WHICH THEY SO WITHDRAW THEMSELVES.

XL. The Master said, "Those who have done this are seven men."

XLI. Tsze-loo happening to pass the night in Shihmun, the gate-keeper said to him, "Whom do you come from?" Tsze-loo said, "From Mr K'ung." "It is he, —is it not?"—said the other, "who knows the impracticable nature of the times, and yet will be doing in them."

XLII. 1. The Master was playing, *one day*, on a musical stone in Wei, when a man, carrying a straw basket, passed the door of the house where Confucius was, and said, "His heart is full who so beats the musical stone."

2. A little while after he added, "How contemptible is the one-idea obstinacy *those sounds display!* When one is taken no notice of, he has simply at once to give over *his wish for public employment.* 'Deep water must be crossed with the clothes on; shallow water may be waded through with the clothes rolled up.'"

3. The Master said, "How determined is he in his purpose! *But* this is not difficult."

XLIII. 1. Tsze-chang said, "What is meant when the shoo says that Kaou-tsung, while observing the usual imperial mourning, was for three years without speaking?"

2. The Master said, "Why must Kaou-tsung *be referred to as an example of this?* The ancients all did so. When the sovereign died, the officers all attended to their

---

40. THE NUMBER OF MEN OF WORTH WHO HAD WITHDRAWN FROM PUBLIC LIFE IN CONFUCIUS' TIME. This chapter is understood, both by Choo He and the old commentators, in connection with the preceding, as appears in the translation. Some also give the names of the seven men, which, according to Choo, is "chiselling," i. e., forging out an illustration of the text.

41. CONDEMNATION OF CONFUCIUS' COURSE IN SEEKING TO BE EMPLOYED, BY ONE WHO HAD WITHDRAWN FROM PUBLIC LIFE. The site of Shih-mun is referred to the district of Ch'ang-ts'ing, department of Ts'e-nan, in Shan-tung. The keeper was probably one of the seven worthies, spoken of in the preceding chapter. We might translate Shih-mun by "Stony-gate." It seems to have been one of the frontier passes between Ts'e and Loo.

42. THE JUDGMENT OF A RETIRED WORTHY ON CONFUCIUS' COURSE, AND REMARK OF CONFUCIUS THEREON.

43. HOW GOVERNMENT WAS CARRIED ON DURING THE THREE YEARS OF SILENT MOURNING BY THE EMPEROR. See the Shoo-king, IV. viii. 1, but the passage there is not exactly as in the text. It is there said that

several duties, taking instructions from the prime minister for three years."

XLIV. The Master said, "When rulers love *to observe* the rules of propriety, the people respond readily to the calls on them for service."

XLV. Tsze-loo asked what constituted the superior man. The Master said, "The cultivation of himself in reverential carefulness." "And is this all?" said *Tsze-loo*. "He cultivates himself so as to give rest to others," was the reply. "And is this all?" *again* asked *Tsze-loo*. The *Master* said, "He cultivates himself so as to give rest to all the people. He cultivates himself so as to give rest to all the people:—even Yaou and Shun were still solicitous about this."

XLVI. Yuen Jang was squatting on his heels, and so waited *the approach of* the Master, who said to him: "In youth, not humble as befits a junior; in manhood, doing nothing worthy of being handed down; and living on to old age:—this is to be a pest." With this he hit him on the shank with his staff.

Kaou-tsung, *after* the three years' mourning, still did not speak. Kaou-tsung was the honorary epithet of the Emperor Woo-ting, B.C. 1323—1263. —Tsze-chang was perplexed to know how government could be carried on during so long a period of silence.

44. HOW A LOVE OF THE RULES OF PROPRIETY IN RULERS FACILITATES GOVERNMENT.

45. REVERENT SELF-CULTIVATION THE DISTINGUISHING CHARACTERISTIC OF THE KEUN-TSZE. "All the people" is literally, "the hundred surnames," which, as a designation for the mass of the people, occurs as early as in the first Book of the Shoo. It is — "the surnames of the hundred families," into which number the families of the people were perhaps divided at a very early time. The surnames of the Chinese now amount to several hundreds. A small work, made in the Sung dynasty, contains nearly 450. We find a ridiculous reason given for the surnames being a hundred, to the effect that the ancient sages gave a surname for each of the five notes of the scale in music, and of the five great relations of life and of the four seas; consequently, $5 \times 5 \times 4 = 100$." It is to be observed, that in the Shoo-king, we find "a hundred surnames," interchanged with "ten thousand surnames," and it would seem needless, therefore, to seek to attach a definite explanation to the number. On the concluding remark,—see VI. xxviii.

46. CONFUCIUS' CONDUCT TO AN UNMANNERLY OLD MAN OF HIS ACQUAINTANCE. Yuen Jang was an old acquaintance of Confucius, but had adopted the principles of Laou-tsze, and gave himself extraordinary license in his behaviour.—See an instance in the Le-ke, II. Pt II. iii. 24. The address of Confucius might be translated in the second person, but it

XLVII. 1. A lad of the village of K'euĕh was employed by *Confucius* to carry the messages between him and his visitors. Some one asked about him, saying, " I suppose he has made great progress."

2. The Master said, " I observe that he is fond of occupying the seat *of a full-grown man;* I observe that he walks shoulder to shoulder with his elders. He is not one who is seeking to make progress *in learning.* He wishes quickly to become a man."

BOOK XV.

CHAPTER I. 1. The Duke Ling of Wei asked Confucius about tactics. Confucius replied, " I have heard all about sacrificial vessels, but I have not learned military matters." On this, he took his departure the next day.

2. When he was in Ch'in, their provisions were exhausted, and his followers became so ill that they were unable to rise.

3. Tsze-loo, with evident dissatisfaction, said, " Has the superior man likewise to endure *in this way?* " The

---

is perhaps better to keep to the third, leaving the application to be understood.

47. CONFUCIUS' EMPLOYMENT OF A FORWARD YOUTH. 1. There is a tradition that Confucius lived and taught in the village of K'euĕh ; but it is much disputed. The inquirer supposed that Confucius' employment of the lad was to distinguish him for the progress which he had made. According to the rules of ceremony, a youth must sit in the corner, the body of the room being reserved for full-grown men. See the Lǐ-kǐ, II. Pt I. i. 17. In walking with an elder, a youth was required to keep a little behind him. See the Lǐ-kǐ, III. v. 15. Confucius' employment of the lad, therefore, was to teach him the courtesies required by his years, as he would not dare to give himself his usual airs with the sage's visitors.

HEADING AND SUBJECTS OF THIS BOOK. " The duke, Ling, of Wei." The contents of the Book, contained in forty chapters, are as miscellaneous as those of the former. Rather they are more so, some chapters bearing on the public administration of government, several being occupied with the superior man, and others containing lessons of practical wisdom. " All the subjects," says Hing Ping, " illustrate the feeling of the sense of shame and consequent pursuit of the correct course, and therefore the Book immediately follows the preceding one."

1. CONFUCIUS REFUSES TO TALK ON MILITARY AFFAIRS. IN THE MIDST OF DISTRESS, HE SHOWS THE DISCIPLES HOW THE SUPERIOR MAN IS ABOVE DISTRESS. 1. " About sacrificial vessels " is literally, "about

Master said, "The superior man may indeed have to endure want, but the mean man, when he is in want, gives way to unbridled license."

II. 1. The Master said, "Ts'ze, you think, I suppose, that I am one who learns many things and keeps them in memory?"

2. Tsze-kung replied, "Yes,—but perhaps it is not so?"

3. "No," was the answer; "*I seek a unity all-pervading.*"

III. The Master said, "Yew, those who know virtue are few."

IV. The Master said, "May not Shun be instanced as having governed efficiently without exertion? What did he do? He did nothing but gravely and reverently occupy his imperial seat."

V. 1. Tsze-chang asked how a man might conduct himself, *so as to be everywhere appreciated.*

---

the 'che' and 'tow,'" vessels with which Confucius, when a boy, was fond of playing. He wished, by his reply and departure, to teach the duke that the rules of propriety, and not war, were essential to the government of a State. 2. From Wei, Confucius proceeded to Ch'in, and there met with the distress here mentioned. It is probably the same which is referred to in XI. ii. 1, though there is some chronological difficulty about the subject.

2. HOW CONFUCIUS AIMED AT THE KNOWLEDGE OF AN ALL PERVADING UNITY. This chapter is to be compared with IV. xv.; only, says Choo Hsi, "that is spoken with reference to practice, and this with reference to knowledge." But the design of Confucius was probably the same in them both; and I understand the first paragraph here as meaning—"Tsze, do you think that I am aiming, by the exercise of memory, to acquire a varied and extensive knowledge?" Then the third paragraph is equivalent to:—"I am not doing this. My aim is to know myself,—the mind which embraces all knowledge, and regulates all practice."

3. FEW REALLY KNOW VIRTUE. This is understood as spoken with reference to the dissatisfaction manifested by Tsze-loo in chapter I. If he had possessed a right knowledge of virtue, he would not have been so affected by distress.

4. HOW SHUN WAS ABLE TO GOVERN WITHOUT PERSONAL EFFORT. "Made himself reverent" and "He gravely and reverently occupied his imperial seat" is literally, "he correctly adjusted his southward face;" see VI. i. Shun succeeding Yaou, there were many ministers of great virtue and ability, to occupy all the offices of the government. All that Shun did, was by his grave and sage example. This is the lesson—the influence of a ruler's personal character.

5. CONDUCT THAT WILL BE APPRECIATED IN ALL PARTS OF THE

2. The Master said, "Let his words be sincere and truthful, and his actions honourable and careful;—such conduct may be practised among the rude tribes of the South or the North. If his words be not sincere and truthful, and his actions not honourable and careful, will he, with such conduct, be appreciated, even in his neighbourhood?

3. "When he is standing, let him see those two things, as it were fronting him. When he is in a carriage, let him see them attached to the yoke. Then may he subsequently carry them into practice."

4. Tsze-chang wrote these counsels on the end of his sash.

VI. 1. The Master said, "Truly straightforward was the historiographer Yu. When good government prevailed in his state, he was like an arrow. When bad government prevailed, he was like an arrow.

2. "A superior man indeed is Keu Pih-yuh! When good government prevails in his state, he is to be found in office. When bad government prevails, he can roll his principles up, and keep them in his breast."

VII. The Master said, "When a man may be spoken with, not to speak to him is to err in reference to the man. When a man may not be spoken with, to speak to him is to err in reference to our words. The wise err neither in regard to their man nor to their words."

VIII. The Master said, "The determined scholar and the man of virtue will not seek to live at the expense of

WORLD. 1. We must supply a good deal to bring out the meaning here. Choo He compares the question with that other of Tsze-chang about the scholar who may be called "distinguished," see XII. xx.

6. THE ADMIRABLE CHARACTERS OF TSZE-YU AND KEU PIH-YUH. 1. Tsze-yu was the historiographer of Wei. On his death-bed, he left a message for his prince, and gave orders that his body should be laid out in a place and manner likely to attract his attention when he paid the visit of condolence. It was so, and the message then delivered had the desired effect. Perhaps it was on hearing this that Confucius made this remark. 2. Keu Pih-yuh,—see XIV. xxvi. Commentators say that Tsze-yu's uniform straightforwardness was not equal to Pih-yuh's rightly adapting himself to circumstances.

7. THERE ARE MEN WITH WHOM TO SPEAK, AND MEN WITH WHOM TO KEEP SILENCE. THE WISE KNOW THEM.

8. HIGH NATURES VALUE VIRTUE MORE THAN LIFE. "They will sacrifice their lives" may be translated—"They will kill themselves." No

injuring their virtue. They will even sacrifice their lives to preserve their virtue complete."

IX. Tsze-kung asked about the practice of virtue. The Master said, "The mechanic, who wishes to do his work well, must first sharpen his tools. When you are living in any state, take service with the most worthy among its great officers, and make friends of the most virtuous among its scholars."

X. 1. Yen Yuen asked how the government of a country should be administered.

2. The Master said, "Follow the seasons of Hea.

3. "Ride in the state carriage of Yin.

4. "Wear the ceremonial cap of Chow.

5. "Let the music be the Shaou with its pantomimes.

6. "Banish the songs of Ch'ing, and keep far from specious talkers. The songs of Ch'ing are licentious; specious talkers are dangerous."

doubt michle is included in the expression (see the amplification of Ho An's commentary), and Confucius here justifies that act, as in certain cases expressive of high virtue.

9. HOW INTERCOURSE WITH THE GOOD AIDS THE PRACTICE OF VIRTUE. Compare Proverbs xxvii. 17, "Iron sharpeneth iron; so a man sharpeneth the countenance of his friend."

10. CERTAIN RULES, EXEMPLIFIED IN THE ANCIENT DYNASTIES, TO BE FOLLOWED IN GOVERNING:—A REPLY TO YEN YUEN. 1. The disciple modestly put his question with reference to the government of a State, but the Master answers it according to the disciple's ability, as if it had been about the ruling of the empire. 2. The three great ancient dynasties began the year at different times. According to an ancient tradition, "Heaven was opened at the time tsze; Earth appeared at the time ch'ow; and Man was born at the time yin. Tsze commences in our December, at the winter solstice; ch'ow a month later; and yin a month after ch'ow. The Chow dynasty began its year with tsze; the Shang with ch'ow; and the Hea with yin. As human life then commenced, the year in reference to human labours, naturally proceeds from the spring, and Confucius approved the rule of the Hea dynasty. His decision has been the law of all dynasties since the Ts'in. See the " Discours Préliminaire, Chapter I.," in Gaubil's Shoo King. 3. The state carriage of the Yin dynasty was plain and substantial, which Confucius preferred to the more ornamented ones of Chow. 4. Yet he does not object to the more elegant cap of that dynasty, "the cap," says Choo He, " being a small thing, and placed over all the body." 5. The shaou was the music of Shun; see III. xxv.; the "dancers," or "pantomimes," kept time to the music. See the Shoo-king II. Bk II. 21. 6. "The sounds of Ch'ing," meaning both the songs of Ch'ing and the appropriate music to which they were sung. Those songs form the seventh book of the first division of the She-king, and are here characterised justly.

XI. The Master said, "If a man take no thought about what is distant, he will find sorrow near at hand."

XII. The Master said, "It is all over! I have not seen one who loves virtue as he loves beauty."

XIII. The Master said, "Was not Tsang Wăn like one who had stolen his situation? He knew the virtue and the talents of Hwuy of Lew-hea, and yet did not *procure that he should stand* with him in *court*."

XIV. The Master said, "He who requires much from himself and little from others, will keep himself from *being the object of* resentment."

XV. The Master said, "When a man is not *in the habit of* saying—'What shall I think of this? What shall I think of this?' I can indeed do nothing with him!"

XVI. The Master said, "When a number of people are together, for a whole day, without their conversation turning on righteousness, and when they are fond of carrying out *the suggestions of* a small shrewdness;—theirs is indeed a hard case."

XVII. The Master said, "The superior man in *everything* considers righteousness to be essential. He performs it according to the rules of propriety. He brings it forth in humility. He completes it with sincerity. This is indeed a superior man."

11. THE NECESSITY OF FORETHOUGHT AND PRECAUTION.

12. THE RARITY OF A TRUE LOVE OF VIRTUE. "It is all over,"—see V. xxvi.; the rest is a repetition of IX. xvii., said to have been spoken by Confucius when he was in Wei, and saw the duke riding out openly in the same carriage with Nan-tsze.

13. AGAINST JEALOUSY OF OTHERS' TALENTS;—THE CASE OF TSANG WĂN, AND HWUY OF LEW-HEA. Tsang Wăn-ching,—see V. xvii. Tsang Wăn would not recommend Hwuy, because he was an abler and better man than himself. Hwuy is a famous name in China. He was an officer of Loo, styled Hwuy after death, and derived his revenue from a town called Lew-hea, though some say that it was a *lew* or willow tree, overhanging his house, which made him to be known as Lew-hea Hwuy—"Hwuy that lived under the willow tree." See Mencius II. Bk. I. ix.

14. THE WAY TO WARD OFF RESENTMENTS.

15. NOTHING CAN BE MADE OF PEOPLE WHO TAKE THINGS EASILY, NOT GIVING THEMSELVES THE TROUBLE TO THINK. Compare VII. viii.

16. AGAINST FRIVOLOUS TALKERS AND SUPERFICIAL SPECULATORS. "A hard case." *i. e.*, they will make nothing out, and nothing can be made of them.

17. THE CONDUCT OF THE SUPERIOR MAN IS RIGHTEOUS, COURTEOUS, HUMBLE, AND SINCERE.

XVIII. The Master said, "The superior man is distressed by his want of ability. He is not distressed by men's not knowing him."

XIX. The Master said, "The superior man dislikes the thought of his name not being mentioned after his death."

XX. The Master said, "What the superior man seeks, is in himself. What the mean man seeks, is in others."

XXI. The Master said, "The superior man is dignified, but does not wrangle. He is sociable, but not a partisan."

XXII. The Master said, "The superior man does not promote a man *simply* on account of his words, nor does he put aside *good* words because of the man."

XXIII. Tsze-kung asked, saying, "Is there one word which may serve as a rule of practice for all one's life?" The Master said, "Is not RECIPROCITY such a word? What you do not want done to yourself, do not do to others."

XXIV. 1. The Master said, "In my *writing or speaking of* men, whose evil do I blame, whose goodness do I praise, beyond what is proper? If I do sometimes exceed in praise, there must be ground for it in my examination *of the individual.*

18. OUR OWN INCOMPETENCY, AND NOT OUR REPUTATION, THE PROPER BUSINESS OF CONCERN TO US. See XIV. xxxii., *et al.*

19. THE SUPERIOR MAN WISHES TO BE HAD IN REMEMBRANCE. Not, say the commentators, that the superior man cares about fame, but fame is the invariable concomitant of merit. He can't have been the superior man, if he be not remembered.

20. HIS OWN APPROBATION IS THE SUPERIOR MAN'S RULE. THE APPROBATION OF OTHERS IS THE MEAN MAN'S. Compare XIV. xxv.

21. THE SUPERIOR MAN IS DIGNIFIED AND AFFABLE, WITHOUT THE FAULTS TO WHICH THOSE QUALITIES OFTEN LEAD. Compare II. xiv., and VII. xxx.

22. THE SUPERIOR MAN IS DISCRIMINATING IN HIS EMPLOYMENT OF MEN AND JUDGING OF STATEMENTS.

23. THE GREAT PRINCIPLE OF RECIPROCITY IS THE RULE OF LIFE. Compare V. xi. It is singular that Tsze-kung professes there to act on the principle here recommended to him.

24. CONFUCIUS SHOWED HIS RESPECT FOR MEN BY STRICT TRUTHFULNESS IN AWARDING PRAISE OR CENSURE. The meaning of this chapter seems to be this:—First, Confucius was very careful in according praise or blame. If he ever seemed to go beyond the truth, it was on the side of praise; and even then he saw something in the individual which made him believe that his praise of him would in the future be justified. Second, In this matter, Confucius acted as the founders of the three great dynasties

2. "This people supplied the ground why the *founders of the three dynasties* pursued the path of straightforwardness."

XXV. The Master said, "Even in my *early* days, a historiographer would leave a blank in his text, and he who had a horse would lend him to another to ride. Now, alas! there are no such things."

XXVI. The Master said, "Specious words confound virtue. Want of forbearance in small matters confounds great plans."

XXVII. The Master said, "When the multitude hate a man, it is necessary to examine into the case. When the multitude like a man, it is necessary to examine into the case."

XXVIII. The Master said, "A man can enlarge the principles *which he follows;* those principles do not enlarge the man."

---

bad done. Third, Those founders and himself were equally influenced by a regard to the truth-approving nature of man. This was the rule for the former in their institutions, and for him in his judgments.

25. INSTANCES OF THE DEGENERACY OF CONFUCIUS' TIMES. The appointment of the historiographer is referred to Hwang-te or "The Yellow emperor," the inventor of the cycle. The statutes of Chow mention no fewer than five classes of such officers. They were attached also to the feudal courts, and what Confucius says, is, that, in his early days, a historiographer, on any point about which he was not sure, would leave a blank; so careful were they to record only the truth. This second sentence is explained in Ho An.—"If any one had a horse which he could not tame, he would lend it to another to ride and exercise it!"—The commentator Hoo says well that the meaning of the chapter must be left in uncertainty.

26. THE DANGER OF SPECIOUS WORDS AND OF IMPATIENCE. The subject of the second sentence is not "a little impatience," but impatience in little things; "the hastiness," it is said, "of women and small people."

27. IN JUDGING OF A MAN WE MUST NOT BE GUIDED BY HIS BEING GENERALLY LIKED OR DISLIKED. Compare XIII. xxiv.

28. PRINCIPLES OF DUTY AN INSTRUMENT IN THE HAND OF MAN. This sentence is quite mystical in its sententiousness. One writer says— "The subject here is the path of duty, which all men, in their various relations, have to pursue, and man has the three virtues of knowledge, benevolence, and fortitude, wherewith to pursue that path, and so he enlarges it. That virtue, remote, occupying an empty place, cannot enlarge man, needs not to be said." That writer's account of the subject here is probably correct, and "duty unapprehended," "in an empty place," can have no effect on any man; but this is a mere truism. Duty apprehended is constantly enlarging, elevating, and energizing multitudes who had pre-

XXIX. The Master said, "To have faults and not to reform them,—this, indeed, should be pronounced having faults."

XXX. The Master said, "I have been the whole day without eating, and the whole night without sleeping:—occupied with thinking. It was of no use. The better plan is to learn."

XXXI. The Master said, "The object of the superior man is truth. Food is not his object. There is ploughing;—even in that there is *sometimes* want. So with learning;—emolument may be found in it. The superior man is anxious lest he should not get truth; he is not anxious lest poverty should come upon him."

XXXII. 1. The Master said, "When a man's knowledge is sufficient to attain, and his virtue is not sufficient to enable him to hold, whatever he may have gained, he will lose again.

2. "When his knowledge is sufficient to attain, and he has virtue enough to hold fast, if he cannot govern with dignity, the people will not respect him.

---

viously been uncognizant of it. The first clause of the chapter may be granted; but the second is not in accordance with truth.

29. THE CULPABILITY OF NOT REFORMING KNOWN FAULTS. Compare I. viii. Choo He's commentary appears to make the meaning somewhat different. He says:—"If one having faults can change them, he comes back to the condition of having no faults. But if he do not change them, then they go on to their completion, and will never come to be changed."

30. THE FRUITLESSNESS OF THINKING WITHOUT READING. Compare II. xv., where the dependence of acquisition and reflection on each other is set forth.—Many commentators say that Confucius merely transfers the things which he here mentions to himself for the sake of others, not that it ever was really thus with himself.

31. THE SUPERIOR MAN SHOULD NOT BE MERCENARY, BUT HAVE TRUTH FOR HIS OBJECT. "Want may be in the midst of ploughing,"—*i.e.*, husbandry is the way to plenty, and yet despite the labours of the husbandman, a famine or scarcity sometimes occurs. The application of this to the case of learning, however, is not very apt. Is the emolument that sometimes comes with learning a calamity like famine?—Ch'ing K'ang-shing's view is:—"Although a man may plough, yet, not learning, he will come to hunger. If he learn, he will get emolument, and though he do not plough, he will not be in want. This is advising men to learn!"

32. HOW KNOWLEDGE WITHOUT VIRTUE IS NOT LASTING, AND TO KNOWLEDGE AND VIRTUE A RULER SHOULD ADD DIGNITY AND THE RULES OF PROPRIETY.

3. "When his knowledge is sufficient to attain, and he has virtue enough to hold fast; when he governs also with dignity, yet if he try to move the people contrary to the rules of propriety:—full excellence is not reached."

XXXIII. The Master said, "The superior man cannot be known in little matters; but he may be intrusted with great concerns. The small man may not be intrusted with great concerns, but he may be known in little matters."

XXXIV. The Master said, "Virtue is more to man than either water or fire. I have seen men die from treading on water and fire, but I have never seen a man die from treading the course of virtue."

XXXV. The Master said, "Let every man consider virtue as what devolves on himself. He may not yield the performance of it *even* to his teacher."

XXXVI. The Master said, "The superior man is correctly firm, and not firm merely."

XXXVII. The Master said, "*A minister*, in serving his prince, reverently discharges his duties, and makes his emolument a secondary consideration."

33. HOW TO KNOW THE SUPERIOR MAN AND THE MEAN MAN; AND THEIR CAPACITIES. Choo He says, "The knowing here *is* our knowing the individuals." The "little matters" are ingenious but trifling arts and accomplishments, in which a really great man may sometimes be deficient while a small man will be familiar with them. The "knowing" is not, that the parties are *keun-tsze* and *small men*, but what attainments they have, and for what they are fit. The difficulty, on this view, is with the conclusion. Ho An gives the view of Wang Shub:—" The way of the *keun-tsze* is profound and far-reaching. He may not let his knowledge be small, and he may receive what is great. The way of the *seaou-jin* is shallow and near. He may let his knowledge be small, and he may not receive what is great."

34. VIRTUE MORE TO MAN THAN WATER OR FIRE, AND NEVER HURTFUL TO HIM. "The people's relation to, or dependence on, virtue." The case is easily conceivable of men's suffering death on account of their virtue. There have been martyrs for their loyalty and other virtues, as well as for their religious faith. Choo He provides for this difference in his remarks:—"The want of fire and water is hurtful only to man's body, but to be without virtue is to lose one's mind (the higher nature), and so it is more to him than water or fire." See on IV. viii.

35. VIRTUE PERSONAL AND OBLIGATORY ON EVERY MAN.

36. THE SUPERIOR MAN'S FIRMNESS IS BASED ON RIGHT.

37. THE FAITHFUL MINISTER.

XXXVIII. The Master said, "There being instruction, there will be no distinction of classes."

XXXIX. The Master said, "Those whose courses are different cannot lay plans for one another."

XL. The Master said, "In language it is simply required that it convey the meaning."

XLI. 1. The Music-master, Meën, having called upon him, when they came to the steps, the Master said, "Here are the steps." When they came to the mat *for the guest* to sit upon, he said, "Here is the mat." When all were seated, the Master informed him, saying, "So and so is here; so and so is here."

2. The Music-master, Meën, having gone out, Tsze-chang asked, saying, "Is it the rule to tell those things to the Music-masters?"

3. The Master said, "Yes. This is certainly the rule for those who lead the blind."

BOOK XVI.

CHAPTER I. 1. The head of the Ke family was going to attack Chuen-vu.

38. THE EFFECT OF TEACHING. Choo He says on this:—"The nature of all men is good, but we find among them the different classes of good and bad. This is the effect of physical constitution and of practice. The superior man, in consequence, employs his teaching, and all may be brought back to the state of good, and there is no necessity of speaking any more of the badness of some." This is very extravagant. Teaching is not so omnipotent.—The old interpretation is simply that in teaching there should be no distinction of classes.

39. AGREEMENT IN PRINCIPLE NECESSARY TO CONCORD IN PLANS.

40. PERSPICUITY THE CHIEF VIRTUE OF LANGUAGE.

41. CONSIDERATION OF CONFUCIUS FOR THE BLIND. Anciently, the blind were employed in the offices of music, partly because their sense of hearing was more than ordinarily acute, and partly that they might be made of some use in the world. Meën had come to Confucius' house, under the care of a guide, but the sage met him, and undertook the care of him himself.

HEADING AND SUBJECTS OF THIS BOOK. "The chief of the Ke." Throughout this book, Confucius is spoken of as "K'ung, the philosopher," and never by the designation, "The Master." Then, the style of several of the chapters (IV.—XI.) is not like the utterances of Confucius to which we have been accustomed. From these circumstances, one commentator, Hung Kwŏh, supposed that it belonged to the Ts'e *recensus* of

2. Yen Yew and Ke Loo had an interview with Confucius, and said, "Our chief, Ke, is going to commence operations against Chuen-yu."

3. Confucius said, "K'ew, is it not you who are in fault here?

4. "Now, in regard to Chuen-yu, long ago, a former king appointed it to preside over *the sacrifices to* the eastern Mung; moreover, it is in the midst of the territory of our State; and its ruler is a minister in direct connection with the emperor:—What has *your chief* to do with attacking it?"

5. Yen Yew said, "Our master wishes the thing; neither of us two ministers wishes it."

6. Confucius said, "K'ew, there are the words of Chow Jin,—'When he can put forth his ability, he takes his place in the ranks *of office*; when he finds himself unable to do so, he retires from it. How can he be used as a guide to a blind man, who does not support him when tottering, nor raise him up when fallen?'

these analects; the other books belonging to the Loo *recensus*. This supposition, however, is not otherwise supported.

1. CONFUCIUS EXPOSES THE PRESUMPTUOUS AND IMPOLITIC CONDUCT OF THE CHIEF OF THE KE FAMILY IN PROPOSING TO ATTACK A MINOR STATE, AND REBUKES YEN YEW AND TSZE-LOO FOR ABETTING THE DESIGN. 1. Chuen-yu was a small territory in Loo, whose ruler was of the fourth order of nobility. It was one of the States called "attached," whose chiefs could not appear in the presence of the emperor, excepting in the train of the prince within whose jurisdiction they were embraced. Their existence was not from a practice like the sub-infeudation, which belonged to the feudal system of Europe. They held of the lord paramount or emperor, but with the restriction which has been mentioned, and with a certain subservience also to their immediate superior. Its particular position is fixed by its proximity to Pe, and to the Mung hill. The word "to attack" is not merely "to attack," but "to attack and punish," —an exercise of judicial authority, which could emanate only from the emperor. The term is used here, to show the nefarious and presumptuous character of the contemplated operations. 2. There is some difficulty here, as, according to the "Historical Records," the two disciples were not in the service of the Ke family at the same time. We may suppose, however, that Tsze-loo, returning with the sage from Wei on the invitation of Duke One, took service a second time, and for a short period, with the Ke family, of which the chief was then Ke K'ang. This brings the time of the transaction to B.C. 483, or 482. 3. Confucius addresses himself only to K'ew, as he had been a considerable time, and very active, in the Ke service. 4. It was the prerogative of the princes to sacrifice to the hills and rivers within their jurisdictions;—here was the chief of Chuen-

7. "And further, you speak wrongly. When a tiger or wild bull escapes from his cage; when a tortoise or gem is injured in its repository:—whose is the fault?"

8. Yen Yew said, "But at present, Chuen-yu is strong and near to Pe; if our chief do not now take it, it will hereafter be a sorrow to his descendants."

9. Confucius said, "K'ow, the superior man hates that declining to say—'I want such and such a thing,' and framing explanations *for the conduct*.

10. "I have heard that rulers of states and chiefs of families are not troubled lest their people should be few, but are troubled lest they should not keep their several places; that they are not troubled with fears of poverty, but are troubled with fears of a want of contented repose *among the people in their several places*. For when the people keep their several places, there will be no poverty; when harmony prevails, there will be no scarcity of people; and when there is such a contented repose, there will be no rebellious upsettings.

11. "So it is. Therefore, if remoter people are not submissive, all the influences of civil culture and virtue are to be cultivated to attract them to be so; and when they have been so attracted, they must be made contented and tranquil.

yu, imperially appointed (the "former king" is probably Ch'ing, the second emperor of the Chow dynasty) to be the lord of the Mung mountain, that is, to preside over the sacrifices offered to it. This raised him high above any mere ministers or officers of Loo. The mountain Mung is in the present district of Pe, in the department of E-chow. It was called eastern, to distinguish it from another of the same name in Shen-se, which was the western Mung. "It is in the midst of the territory of our State,"—this is mentioned, to show that Chuen-yu was so situated as to give Loo no occasion for apprehension. "Its ruler is a minister in direct connection with the emperor" is, literally, "a minister of the altars to the spirits of the land and grain." To those spirits only, the prince had the prerogative of sacrificing. The chief of Chuen-yu having this, how dared an officer of Loo to think of attacking him? The term "minister" is used of his relation to the emperor. Choo He makes the phrase = "a minister of the ducal house," saying that the three families had usurped all the dominions proper of Loo, leaving only the chiefs of the "attached" States to appear in the ducal court. I prefer the former interpretation.
6. Chow Jin is by Choo He simply called—"a good historiographer of ancient times." Some trace him back to the Shang dynasty, and others only to the early times of the Chow. There are other weighty utterances of his in vogue, besides that in the text. From this point, Confucius

12. "Now, here are you, Yew and K'ow, assisting your chief. Remoter people are not submissive, and, *even with your help*, he cannot attract them to him. In his own territory there are divisions and downfalls, leavings and separations, and, *with your help*, he cannot preserve it.

13. "And yet he is planning these hostile movements within our State.—I am afraid that the sorrow of the Ke-sun *family* will not be on account of Chuen-yu, but will be found within the screen of their own court."

II. 1. Confucius said, "When good government prevails in the empire, ceremonies, music, and punitive military expeditions, proceed from the emperor. When bad government prevails in the empire, ceremonies, music, and punitive military expeditions proceed from the princes. When these things proceed from the princes, as a rule, the cases will be few in which they do not lose their power in ten generations. When they proceed from the great officers *of the princes, as a rule*, the cases will be few in which they do not lose their power in five generations. When the subsidiary ministers *of the great officers* hold in their grasp the orders of the kingdom, *as a rule*, the cases will be few in which they do not lose their power in three generations.

2. "When right principles prevail in the empire, government will not be in the hands of the great officers.

3. "When right principles prevail in the empire, there will be no discussions among the common people."

speaks of the general disorganization of Loo under the management of the three families, and especially of the Ke. 12. All this is to be understood of the head of the Ke family, as controlling the government of Loo, and *as being assisted by the two disciples*, so that the reproof falls heavily on them. 13. "Within the screen of their own court" is, literally, "in the inside of the wall of reverence." "Officers, on reaching the screen, which they had only to pass, to find themselves in the presence of their head, were supposed to become more reverential;" and hence the expression in the text—" among his own immediate officers."

2. THE SUPREME AUTHORITY OUGHT EVER TO MAINTAIN ITS POWER. THE VIOLATION OF THIS RULE ALWAYS LEADS TO RUIN, WHICH IS SPEEDIER AS THE RANK OF THE VIOLATOR IS LOWER. In these utterances, Confucius had reference to the disorganized state of the empire, when "the son of Heaven" was fast becoming an empty name, the princes of States were in bondage to their great officers, and those again at the mercy of their family ministers.

III. Confucius said, "The revenue of the State has left the ducal house, now for five generations. The government has been in the hands of the great officers for four generations. On this account, the descendants of the three Hwan are much reduced."

IV. Confucius said, "There are three friendships which are advantageous, and three which are injurious. Friendship with the upright; friendship with the sincere; and friendship with the man of much observation:—these are advantageous. Friendship with the man of specious airs; friendship with the insinuatingly soft; and friendship with the glib-tongued:—these are injurious."

V. Confucius said, "There are three things men find enjoyment in which are advantageous, and three things they find enjoyment in which are injurious. To find enjoyment in the discriminating study of ceremonies and music; to find enjoyment in speaking of the goodness of others; to find enjoyment in having many worthy friends:—these are advantageous. To find enjoyment in extravagant pleasures; to find enjoyment in idleness and sauntering; to find enjoyment in the pleasures of feasting:—these are injurious."

VI. Confucius said, "There are three errors to which they who stand in the presence of a man of virtue and station are liable. They may speak when it does not come to them to speak;—this is called rashness. They

3. ILLUSTRATION OF THE PRINCIPLES OF THE LAST CHAPTER. In the year B.C. 608, at the death of Duke Wăn, his rightful heir was killed, and the son of a concubine raised to the dukedom. He is in the annals as Duke Seuen, and after him came Shing, Seang, Ch'aou, and Ting, in whose time the dukes have been spoken. These dukes were but shadows, pensionaries of their great officers, so that it might be said the revenue had gone from them. "The three Hwan" are the three families, as being all descended from Duke Hwan; see on II. v. Choo He appears to have fallen into a mistake in enumerating the four heads of the Ke family who had administered the government of Loo as Woo, Tseu, P'ing, and Hwan, as Taou died before his father, and would not be said therefore to have the government in his hands. The right enumeration is Wăn, Woo, P'ing, and Hwan.

4. THREE FRIENDSHIPS ADVANTAGEOUS, AND THREE INJURIOUS.

5. THREE SOURCES OF ENJOYMENT ADVANTAGEOUS, AND THREE INJURIOUS.

6. THREE ERRORS IN REGARD TO SPEECH TO BE AVOIDED IN THE PRESENCE OF THE GREAT. "Without looking at the countenance,"—i.e.,

may not speak when it comes to them to speak;— this is called concealment. They may speak without looking at the countenance *of their superior;*—this is called blindness."

VII. Confucius said, "There are three things which the superior man guards against. In youth, when the physical powers are not yet settled, he guards against lust. When he is strong, and the physical powers are full of vigour, he guards against quarrelsomeness. When he is old, and the animal powers are decayed, he guards against covetousness."

VIII. 1. Confucius said, "There are three things of which the superior man stands in awe. He stands in awe of the ordinances of Heaven. He stands in awe of great men. He stands in awe of the words of sages.

2. "The mean man does not know the ordinances of Heaven, and *consequently* does not stand in awe of them. He is disrespectful to great men. He makes sport of the words of sages."

IX. Confucius said, "Those who are born with the possession of knowledge are the highest class of men. Those who learn, and so, *readily,* get possession of know-

to see whether he is paying attention or not.—The general principle is that there is a time to speak. Let that be observed, and these three errors will be avoided.

7. THE VICES WHICH YOUTH, MANHOOD, AND AGE HAVE TO GUARD AGAINST. As to what causal relation Confucius may have supposed to exist between the state of the physical powers and the several vices indicated, that is not developed. Hing Ping explains the first caution thus:— "Youth embraces all the period below 29. Then, the physical powers are still weak, and the sinews and bones have not reached their vigour, and indulgence in lust will injure the body."

8. CONTRAST OF THE SUPERIOR AND THE MEAN MAN IN REGARD TO THE THREE THINGS OF WHICH THE FORMER STANDS IN AWE. "The ordinances of Heaven," according to Choo He, means the moral nature of man, conferred by Heaven. High above the nature of other creatures, it lays him under great responsibility to cherish and cultivate himself. The old interpreters take the phrase to indicate Heaven's moral administration by rewards and punishments. The "great men" are men high in position and great in wisdom and virtue, the royal instructors, who have been raised up by Heaven for the training and ruling of mankind. So, the commentators; but the verb employed suggests at once a more general and a lower view of the phrase.

9. FOUR CLASSES OF MEN IN RELATION TO KNOWLEDGE. On the first clause, see on VII. xix., where Confucius disclaims for himself being

lodge, are the next. Those who are dull and stupid, and yet compass the learning, are another class next to these. As to those who are dull and stupid and yet do not learn;—they are the lowest of the people."

X. Confucius said, "The superior man has nine things which are subjects with him of thoughtful consideration. In regard to the use of his eyes, he is anxious to see clearly. In regard to the use of his ears, he is anxious to hear distinctly. In regard to his countenance, he is anxious that it should be benign. In regard to his demeanour, he is anxious that it should be respectful. In regard to his speech, he is anxious that it should be sincere. In regard to his doing of business, he is anxious that it should be reverently careful. In regard to what he doubts about, he is anxious to question others. When he is angry, he thinks of the difficulties his anger may involve him in. When he sees gain to be got, he thinks of righteousness."

XI. 1. Confucius said, "Contemplating good, *and pursuing it,* as if they could not reach it; contemplating evil, *and shrinking from it,* as they would from thrusting the hand into boiling water:—I have seen such men, as I have heard such words.

2. "Living in retirement to study their aims, and practising righteousness to carry out their principles:—I have heard these words, but I have not seen such men."

---

ranked in the first of the classes here mentioned. In the concluding words, "They are the lowest of the people," I suppose "the people"— *men.* The term is elsewhere so used.

10. NINE SUBJECTS OF THOUGHT TO THE SUPERIOR MAN:—VARIOUS INSTANCES OF THE WAY IN WHICH HE REGULATES HIMSELF. The conciseness of the text contrasts here with the verbosity of the translation, and yet the many words of the latter seem necessary.

11. THE CONTEMPORARIES OF CONFUCIUS COULD ESCHEW EVIL, AND FOLLOW AFTER GOOD, BUT NO ONE OF THE HIGHEST CAPACITY HAD APPEARED AMONG THEM. 1. The two first clauses here, and in the next paragraph also, are quotations of old sayings, current in Confucius' time. Such men were several of the sage's own disciples. 2. "To study their aims" is, literally, "seeking for their aims;" *i.e.,* meditating on them, studying them, fixing them, to be prepared to carry them out, as in the next clause. Such men among the ancients were the great ministers E-Yin and T'ae-kung. Such might the disciple Yen Hwuy have been, but an early death snatched him away before he could have an opportunity of showing what was in him.

XII. 1. The Duke King of Ts'e had a thousand teams, each of four horses, but on the day of his death, the people did not praise him for a single virtue. P'ih-o and Shuh-ts'e died of hunger at the foot of the Show-yang mountain, and the people, down to the present time, praise them.

2. "Is not that saying illustrated by this?"

XIII. 1. Ch'in K'ang asked Pih-yu, saying, "Have you heard any lessons *from your father* different *from what we have all heard?*"

2. Pih-yu replied, "No. He was standing alone once, when I passed below the hall with hasty steps, and said to me, 'Have you learned the Odes?' On my replying 'Not yet,' *he added*, 'If you do not learn the Odes, you will not be fit to converse with.' I retired and studied the Odes.

3. "Another day, he was in the same way standing alone, when I passed by below the hall with hasty steps, and he said to me, 'Have you learned the rules of Propriety?' On my replying 'Not yet,' *he added*, 'If you do not learn the rules of Propriety, your character cannot be established.' I then retired, and studied the rules of Propriety.

4. "I have heard only these two things from him."

5. Ch'in K'ang retired, and, quite delighted, said, "I asked one thing, and I have got three things. I have heard about the Odes. I have heard about the rules of Propriety. I have also heard that the superior man maintains a distant reserve towards his son."

12. WEALTH WITHOUT VIRTUE AND VIRTUE WITHOUT WEALTH:—THEIR DIFFERENT APPRECIATIONS. This chapter is plainly a fragment. As it stands, it would appear to come from the compilers and not from Confucius. Then the second paragraph implies a reference to something which has been lost. Under XII. x., I have referred to the proposal to transfer to this place the last paragraph of that chapter, which might be explained so as to harmonize with the sentiment of this.—The Duke King of Ts'e,—see XII. xi. Pih-e and Shuh-ts'e,—see VI. xxii. The mountain Show-yang is to be found probably in the department of P'oo-chow in Shan-se.

13. CONFUCIUS' INSTRUCTION OF HIS SON NOT DIFFERENT FROM HIS INSTRUCTION OF HIS DISCIPLES GENERALLY. Ch'in K'ang is the Tsze-k'in of I. x. When Confucius' eldest son was born, the duke of Loo sent the philosopher a present of a carp, on which account he named the child Le (the carp), and afterwards gave him the designation of Pih-yu (Fish, the elder).

XIV. The wife of the prince of a State is called by him FOO-JIN. She calls herself SEAOU T'UNG. The people of the State call her KEUN FOO-JIN, and, to the people of other States, they call her K'WA SEAOU KEUN. The people of other States also call her KEUN FOO-JIN.

BOOK XVII.

CHAPTER I. 1. Yang Ho wished to see Confucius, but Confucius would not go to see him. *On this*, he sent a present of a pig to Confucius, who, having chosen a time when Ho was not at home, went to pay his respects *for the gift*. He met him, *however*, on the way.

2. *Ho* said to Confucius, "Come, let me speak with you." He then asked, "Can he be called benevolent who keeps his jewel in his bosom, and leaves his country to confusion?" *Confucius* replied, "No." "Can he be

14. APPELLATIONS FOR THE WIFE OF A PRINCE. This chapter may have been spoken by Confucius to rectify some disorder of the times, but there is no intimation to that effect. The different appellations may be thus explained:—"Wife" is equivalent to "she who is her husband's equal." The designation *foo-jin* is equivalent to "help-meet." The wife modestly calls herself *Seaou-t'ung*, "the little girl." The old interpreters take—most naturally—*keun foo-jin* as = "our prince's help-meet," but the modern commentators take *keun* to be a verb, with reference to the office of the wife to "preside over the internal economy of the palace." On this view *keun foo-jin* is "the domestic help-meet." The ambassador of a prince spoke of him by the style of k'wa-keun, "my prince of small virtue." After that example of modesty, his wife was styled to the people of other States, "our small prince of small virtue." The people of other States had no reason to imitate her subjects in that, and so they styled her—"your prince's help-meet," or "the domestic help-meet."

HEADING AND SUBJECTS OF THIS BOOK. "Yang Ho." As the last book commenced with the presumption of the head of the Ke family, who kept his prince in subjection, this begins with an account of an officer, who did for the head of the Ke what he did for the duke of Loo. For this reason—some similarity in the subject matter of the first chapters—this book, it is said, is placed after the former. It contains twenty-six chapters.

1. CONFUCIUS' POLITE BUT DIGNIFIED TREATMENT OF A POWERFUL, BUT USURPING AND UNWORTHY, OFFICER. Yang Ho, known also as Yang Hoo, was nominally the principal minister of the Ke family; but its chief was entirely in his hands, and he was scheming to arrogate the whole authority of the state of Loo to himself. He first appears in the Chronicles of Loo about the year B.C. 514, acting against the exiled

called wise who is anxious to be engaged in public employment, and yet is constantly losing the opportunity of being so?" Confucius again said, "No." "The days and months are passing away; the years do not wait for us." Confucius said, "Right; I will go into office."

II. The Master said, "By nature, men are nearly alike; by practice, they get to be wide apart."

III. The Master said, "There are only the wise of the highest class, and the stupid of the lowest class, who cannot be changed."

IV. 1. The Master having come to Woo-shing, heard there the sound of stringed instruments and singing.

2. Well-pleased and smiling, he said, "Why use an ox-knife to kill a fowl?"

3. Tsze-yew replied, "Formerly, Master, I heard you

Duke Ch'aou; in B.C. 504, we find him keeping his own chief, Ka Hwan, a prisoner, and, in B.C. 501, he is driven out, on the failure of his projects, a fugitive into Ts'e. At the time when the incidents in this chapter occurred, Yang Ho was anxious to get, or appears to get, the support of a man of Confucius' reputation, and finding that the sage would not call on him, he adopted the expedient of sending him a pig, at the time when Confucius was not at home, the rules of ceremony requiring that when a great officer sent a present to a scholar, and the latter was not in his house on its arrival, he had to go to the officer's house to acknowledge it. See the Le-ke, XIII. iii. 20. Confucius, however, was not to be entrapped. He also timed Hoo's being away from home, and went to call on him.

2. THE DIFFERENCES IN THE CHARACTERS OF MEN ARE CHIEFLY OWING TO HABIT. "Nature," it is contended, is here not the moral constitution of man, absolutely considered, but his complex, actual nature, with its elements of the material, the animal, and the intellectual, by association with which the perfectly good moral nature is continually being led astray. The moral nature is the same in all, and though the material organism and disposition do differ in different individuals, they are, at first, more nearly alike than they subsequently become. No doubt, it is true that many—perhaps most—of the differences among men are owing to habit.

3. ONLY TWO CLASSES WHOM PRACTICE CANNOT CHANGE. This is a sequel to the last chapter, with which it is incorporated in Ho An's edition. The case of the "stupid of the lowest class" would seem to be inconsistent with the doctrine of the perfect goodness of the moral nature of all men. Modern commentators, to get over the difficulty, say that they are the "self violators," "self abandoners," of Mencius, IV. Pt. I. x.

4. HOWEVER SMALL THE SPHERE OF GOVERNMENT, THE RIGHTEST INFLUENCES OF PROPRIETIES AND MUSIC SHOULD BE EMPLOYED. Woo-shing was in the district of Fe. Tsze-yew appears as the commandant of it, in VI. xii. We read, "The town was named M'ao, from its position, precipitous and favourable to military operations, but Tsze-yew had been

say,—"When the man of high station is well instructed, he loves men; when the man of low station is well instructed, he is easily ruled.'"

4. The Master said, "My disciples, Yen's words are right. What I said was only in sport."

V. 1. Kung-shan Fuh-jaou, when he was holding Pe, and in an attitude of rebellion, invited the Master to visit him, who was rather inclined to go.

2. Tsze-loo was displeased, and said, "Indeed you cannot go! Why must you think of going to see Kung-shan?"

3. The Master said, "Can it be without some reason that he has invited ME? If any one employ me, may I not make an eastern Chow?"

VI. 1. Tsze-chang asked Confucius about perfect virtue. Confucius said, "To be able to practise five things everywhere under heaven constitutes perfect virtue." He begged to ask what they were, and was told, "Gravity, generosity *of soul*, sincerity, earnestness, and kindness. If you are grave, you will not be treated with disrespect. If you are generous, you will win all. If you are sincere, people will repose trust in you. If you are earnest, you will accomplish much. If you are kind, this will enable you to employ the services of others."

VII. 1. Peih Heih inviting him to visit him, the Master was inclined to go.

able, by his course, to transform the people, and make them change their mail and helmets for stringed instruments and singing. This was what made the Master glad."

5. THE LENGTHS TO WHICH CONFUCIUS WAS INCLINED TO GO, TO GET HIS PRINCIPLES CARRIED INTO PRACTICE. Kung-shan Fuh-jaou was a confederate of Yang Ho (chapter I.), and, according to K'ung Gan-kwŏ, it was after the imprisonment by them, in common, of Ke Hwan, that Fuh-jaou sent this invitation to Confucius. Others make the invitation subsequent to Ho's discomfiture and flight to Ts'e. We must conclude, with Tsze-loo, that Confucius ought not to have thought of accepting the invitation of such a man. The original seat of the Chow dynasty lay west from Loo, and the revival of the principles and government of Wăn and Woo in Loo, or even in Pe, which was but a part of it, might make an eastern Chow; so that Confucius would perform the part of King Wăn.—After all, the sage did not go to Pe.

6. FIVE THINGS THE PRACTICE OF WHICH CONSTITUTES PERFECT VIRTUE.

7. CONFUCIUS, INCLINED TO RESPOND TO THE ADVANCES OF AN UNWORTHY MAN, PROTESTS AGAINST HIS CONDUCT BEING JUDGED BY

2. Tsze-loo said, "Master, formerly I have heard you say, 'When a man in his own person is guilty of doing evil, a superior man will not associate with him.' Peih Heih is in rebellion, holding possession of Chung-mow; if you go to him, what shall be said?"

3. The Master said, "Yes, I did use these words. But is it not said, that, if a thing be really hard, it may be ground without being made thin? Is it not said, that, if a thing be really white, it may be steeped in a dark fluid without being made black?

4. "Am I a bitter gourd! How can I be hung up out of the way of being eaten?"

VIII. 1. The Master said, "Yew, have you heard the six words to which are attached six becloudings?" Yew replied, "I have not."

2. "Sit down, and I will tell them to you.

3. "There is the love of being benevolent without the love of learning;—the beclouding here leads to a foolish simplicity. There is the love of knowing without the love of learning;—the beclouding here leads to dissipation of mind. There is the love of being sincere without the love of learning;—the beclouding here leads to an injurious disregard of consequences. There is the love of straight-

ORDINARY RULES. Compare chapter V.; but the invitation of Peih Heih was subsequent to that of Kung-shan Fuh-jaou, and after Confucius had given up office in Loo. 1. Peih Heih was commandant of Chung-mow, for *the* chief of the Chaou family, in the State of Tsin. 2. There were two places of the name of Chung-mow, one belonging to the State of Ch'ing, and the other to the State of Tsin, which is that intended here, and is referred to the present district of T'ang-yin, department of Chang-tih, in Ho-nan province. 3. The application of the proverbial sayings is to Confucius himself, as, from his superiority, incapable of being affected by evil communications.

8. KNOWLEDGE, ACQUIRED BY LEARNING, IS NECESSARY TO THE COMPLETION OF VIRTUE, BY PRESERVING THE MIND FROM BEING BECLOUDED. 1. "The six words" are the benevolence, knowledge, sincerity, straight-forwardness, boldness, and firmness, mentioned below, all virtues, but yet each, when pursued without discrimination, tending to becloud the mind. 2. "Sit down."—Tsze-loo had risen, according to the rules of propriety, to give his answer; see the Le-ke, I. Pt I. iii. 21; and Confucius tells him to resume his seat. 3. I give here the paraphrase of the "Daily Lesson," on the first virtue and its beclouding, which may illustrate the manner in which the whole paragraph is deve'oped:—"In all matters, there is a perfect right and unchangeable principle, which men ought carefully to study, till they have thoroughly examined and appre-

forwardness without the love of learning;—the beclouding here leads to rudeness. There is the love of boldness without the love of learning;—the beclouding here leads to insubordination. There is the love of firmness without the love of learning;—the beclouding here leads to extravagant conduct."

IX. 1. The Master said, "My children, why do you not study the Book of Poetry?

2. "*The Odes* serve to stimulate the mind.

3. "They may be used for purposes of self-contemplation.

4. "They teach the art of sociability.

5. "They show how to regulate feelings of resentment.

6. "From them you learn the more immediate duty of serving one's father, and the remoter one of serving one's prince.

7. "From them we become largely acquainted with the names of birds, beasts, and plants."

X. The Master said to Pih-yu, "Do you give yourself to the Chow-nan, and the Shaou-nan. The man, who has not studied the Chow-nan and the Shaou-nan, is like one who stands with his face right against a wall. Is he not so?"

XI. The Master said, "'It is according to the rules of propriety,' they say.—'It is according to the rules of propriety,' they say. Are gems and silk all that is meant

headed it. Then their actions will be without error, and their virtue may be perfected. For instance, loving is what rules in benevolence. It is certainly a beautiful virtue, but if you only set yourself to love men, and do not care to study to understand the principle of benevolence, then your mind will be beclouded by that loving, and you will be following a man into a well to save him, so that both he and you will perish. Will not this be foolish simplicity?"

9. BENEFITS DERIVED FROM STUDYING THE BOOK OF POETRY.

10. THE IMPORTANCE OF STUDYING THE CHOW-NAN AND SHAOU-NAN. Chow-nan and Shaou-nan are the titles of the first two books in the National Songs, or first part of the She-king. For the meaning of the titles, see the She-king, Pt I. Bk I, and Pt I. Bk II. They are supposed to inculcate important lessons about personal virtue and family government. A man "with his face against a wall" cannot advance a step, nor see anything. This chapter in the old editions is incorporated with the preceding one.

11. IT IS NOT THE EXTERNAL APPURTENANCES WHICH CONSTITUTE PROPRIETY, NOR THE SOUND OF INSTRUMENTS WHICH CONSTITUTES MUSIC.

by propriety? 'It is Music,' they say. 'It is Music,' they say. Are bells and drums all that is meant by Music?"

XII. The Master said, "He who puts on an appearance of stern firmness, while inwardly he is weak, is like one of the small, mean people;—yea, is he not like the thief who breaks through or climbs over a wall?"

XIII. The Master said, "Your good careful people of the villages are the thieves of virtue."

XIV. The Master said, "To tell, as we go along, what we have heard on the way, is to cast away our virtue."

XV. 1. The Master said, "There are those mean creatures! How impossible it is along with them to serve one's prince!

2. "While they have not got their aims, their anxiety is how to get them. When they have got them, their anxiety is lest they should lose them.

3. "When they are anxious lest they should be lost, there is nothing to which they will not proceed."

XVI. 1. The Master said, "Anciently, men had three failings, which now perhaps are not to be found.

2. "The high-mindedness of antiquity showed itself in a disregard of small things; the high-mindedness of the present day shows itself in wild license. The stern dignity of antiquity showed itself in grave reserve; the stern dignity of the present day shows itself in quarrelsome perverseness. The stupidity of antiquity showed itself in straightforwardness; the stupidity of the present day shows itself in sheer deceit."

12. THE MEANNESS OF PRESUMPTION AND PUSILLANIMITY CONJOINED. The last clause shows emphatically to whom, among the low, mean people, the individual spoken of is like,—a thief, namely, who is in constant fear of being detected.

13. CONTENTMENT WITH VULGAR WAYS AND VIEWS INJURIOUS TO VIRTUE. See the sentiment of this chapter explained and expanded by Mencius, VII. Pt II. xxxvii. 7, 8.

14. SWIFTNESS TO SPEAK INCOMPATIBLE WITH THE CULTIVATION OF VIRTUE. It is to be understood that what has been heard contains some good lesson. At once to be talking of it without revolving it, and striving to practise it, shows an indifference to our own improvement.

15. THE CASE OF MERCENARY OFFICERS, AND HOW IT IS IMPOSSIBLE TO SERVE ONE'S PRINCE ALONG WITH THEM.

16. THE DEFECTS OF FORMER TIMES BECOME VICES IN THE TIME OF CONFUCIUS.

XVII. The Master said, "Fine words and an insinuating appearance are seldom associated with virtue."

XVIII. The Master said, "I hate the manner in which purple takes away *the lustre of* vermilion. I hate the way in which the songs of Ch'ing confound the music of the Ya. I hate those who with their sharp mouths overthrow kingdoms and families."

XIX. 1. The Master said, "I would prefer not speaking."

2. Tsze-kung said, "If you, Master, do not speak, what shall we, your disciples, have to record?"

3. The Master said, "Does Heaven speak? The four seasons pursue their courses, and all things are *continually* being produced, but does Heaven say anything?"

XX. Joo Pei wished to see Confucius, but Confucius declined, on the ground of being sick, to see him. When the bearer of this message went out at the door, he took his harpsichord, and sang to it, in order that Pei might hear him.

XXI. 1. Tsae Wo asked about the three years' mourning *for parents, saying* that one year was long enough.

17. A repetition of I. iii.

18. CONFUCIUS' INDIGNATION AT THE WAY IN WHICH THE WRONG OVERCAME THE RIGHT. On the first clause,—see X. vi. 2. "The songs or sounds of Ch'ing,"—see XV. x. "The Ya,"—see on IX. xiv.

19. THE ACTIONS OF CONFUCIUS WERE LESSONS AND LAWS, AND NOT HIS WORDS MERELY. Such is the scope of this chapter, according to Choo He and his school. The older commentators say that it is a caution to men to pay attention to their conduct rather than to their words. This interpretation is far-fetched, but on the other hand, it is not easy to defend Confucius from the charge of presumption in comparing himself to Heaven.

20. HOW CONFUCIUS COULD BE NOT AT HOME, AND YET GIVE INTIMATION TO THE VISITOR OF HIS PRESENCE. Of Joo Pei little is known. He was a man of Loo, and had at one time been in attendance on Confucius to receive his instructions. There must have been some reason—some fault in him—why Confucius would not see him on the occasion in the text, and that he might understand that it was on that account, and not that he was really sick, that he declined his visit, the sage acted as we are told. But what was the necessity for sending a false message in the first place? In the notes to the K-le. III. 1, it is said that Joo Pei's fault was in trying to see the master without using the services of an internuncius.

21. THE PERIOD OF THREE YEARS' MOURNING FOR PARENTS; IT MAY NOT ON ANY ACCOUNT BE SHORTENED; THE REASON OF IT. 1. On the three years' mourning, see the 31st book of the Le-ke. Nominally ex-

2. "If the superior man," said he, "abstains for three years from the observances of propriety, those observances will be quite lost. If for three years he abstains from music, music will be ruined.

3. "Within a year, the old grain is exhausted, and the new grain has sprung up, and, in procuring fire by friction, we go through all the changes of wood for that purpose. After a complete year the mourning may stop."

4. The Master said, "If you were, after a year, to eat good rice, and wear embroidered clothes, would you feel at ease?" "I should," replied Wo.

5. The Master said, "If you can feel at ease, do it. But a superior man, during the whole period of mourning, does not enjoy pleasant food which he may eat, nor derive pleasure from music which he may hear. He also does not feel at ease, if he is comfortably lodged. Therefore he does not do what you propose. But now you feel at ease and may do it."

6. Tsae Wo then went out, and the Master said, "This shows Yu's want of virtue. It is not till a child is three years old that it is allowed to leave the arms of its parents. And the three years' mourning is universally observed throughout the empire. Did Yu enjoy the three years' affection for his parents?"

XXII. The Master said, "Hard is the case of him, who will stuff himself with food the whole day, without

---

tending to three years, that period comprehended properly but twenty-five months, and at most twenty-seven months. 2. Tsae Wo finds here a reason for his view in the necessity of "human affairs." 3. He finds here a reason for his view in "the seasons of heaven." Certain woods were assigned to the several seasons, to be employed for getting fire by friction, the elm and willow, for instance, to spring, the date and almond trees to summer, &c., so that Wo says, "In boring to get fire, we have changed from wood to wood through the ones appropriate to the four seasons." 4. Coarse food and coarse clothing were appropriate, though in varying degree, to all the period of mourning. Tsae Wo is strangely insensible to the home-put argument of the Master. 7. "This shows Yu's want of virtue" responds to all that has gone before, and forms a sort of apodosis. Confucius added, it is said, the remarks in this paragraph, that they might be reported to Tsae Wo, lest he should "feel at ease" to go and do as he said he could. Still the reason which the Master finds for the statute-period of mourning for parents must be pronounced puerile. Very

22. THE HOPELESS CASE OF GLUTTONY AND IDLENESS. "Gamesters

applying his mind to anything good! Are there not gamesters and chess-players? To be one of these would still be better than doing nothing at all."

XXIII. Tsze-loo said, "Does the superior man esteem valour?" The Master said, "The superior man holds righteousness to be of highest importance. A man in a superior situation, having valour without righteousness, will be guilty of insubordination; one of the lower people, having valour without righteousness, will commit robbery."

XXIV. 1. Tsze-kung said, "Has the superior man his hatreds also?" The Master said, "He has his hatreds. He hates those who proclaim the evil of others. He hates the man who, being in low station, slanders his superiors. He hates those who have valour merely, and are unobservant of propriety. He hates those who are forward and determined, and, *at the same time*, of contracted understanding."

2. *The Master then* inquired, "Ts'ze, have you also your hatreds?" *Tsze-kung replied*, "I hate those who pry out matters, and ascribe the knowledge to their wisdom. I

---

and chess-players:"—Of the game of chess, the Chinese have two kinds. There is what is called the "surrounding chess," which is played with 361 pieces, and is referred to the Emperor Yaou as its inventor. This is still not uncommon, though I have never seen it played myself. There is also what is called the "elephant chess," played with 32 pieces, and having a great analogy to our game, which indeed was borrowed from the East. "The elephant" is the piece corresponding to our "bishop," though his movement is more like that of a double knight. The invention of this is ascribed to the first emperor of the Chow dynasty (B.C. 1122), though some date it a few hundred years later. "Gamesters" in the text are different from the chess-players. The game specially intended was one played with twelve dice, the invention of which is ascribed to the time of one or other of the tyrants, with whom the dynasties of Hea and Shang terminated. I have also seen it referred to a much later date, and said to have been imported from India. If it were so, then we do not know what game Confucius had in his mind. Commentators are much concerned to defend him from the suspicion of giving in this chapter any sanction to gambling. He certainly expresses his detestation of the idle glutton very strongly.

23. VALOUR TO BE VALUED ONLY IN SUBORDINATION TO RIGHTEOUSNESS; ITS CONSEQUENCES APART FROM THAT.

24. CHARACTERS DISLIKED BY CONFUCIUS AND TSZE-KUNG. Tsze-kung is understood to have intended Confucius himself by "the superior man."

hate those who are *only* not modest, and think that they are valorous. I hate those who make known secrets, and think that they are straightforward."

XXV. The Master said, "Of all people, girls and servants are the most difficult to behave to. If you are familiar with them, they lose their humility. If you maintain a reserve towards them, they are discontented."

XXVI. The Master said, "When a man at forty is the object of dislike, he will always continue what he is."

BOOK XVIII.

CHAPTER I. 1. *The viscount of Wei withdrew from the court. The viscount of Ke became a slave to Chow. Pe-kan remonstrated with him, and died.*

25. THE DIFFICULTY HOW TO TREAT CONCUBINES AND SERVANTS. The text does not speak here of women generally, as Collie has translated, but of girls, *i.e.*, concubines. The commentators find in the chapter a lesson for the great in the ordering of their harems; but there is nothing in the language to make us restrict the meaning in any way.

26. THE DIFFICULTY OF IMPROVEMENT IN ADVANCED YEARS. According to Chinese views, at forty a man is at his best in every way.— Youth is doubtless the season for improvement, but the sentiment of the chapter is too broadly stated.

HEADING AND CONTENTS OF THIS BOOK.—" The viscount of Wei." This book, consisting of only eleven chapters, treats of various individuals famous in Chinese history, as eminent for the way in which they discharged their duties to their sovereign, or for their retirement from public service. It commemorates also some of the worthies of Confucius' days, who lived in retirement rather than be in office in so degenerate times. The object of the whole is to illustrate and vindicate the course of Confucius himself.

1. THE VISCOUNTS OF WEI AND KE, AND PE-KAN:—THREE WORTHIES OF THE YIN DYNASTY. 1. Wei-tsze and Ke-tsze are continually repeated by Chinese, as if they were proper names. But Wei and Ke were the names of two small States, presided over by chiefs of the Tsze, or fourth, degree of nobility, called *viscounts*, for want of a more exact term. They both appear to have been within the limits of the present Shan-se, Wei being referred to the district of Loo-ch'ing, department Loo-gan, and Ke to Yu-shay, department Ltsen-chow. The chief of Wei was an elder brother (by a concubine) of the tyrant Chow, the last emperor of the Yin dynasty, B.C. 1153—1122. The chief of Ke, and Pe-kan, were both, probably, uncles of the tyrant. The first, seeing that remonstrance availed nothing, withdrew from court, wishing to preserve the sacrifices of their family, amid the ruin which he saw was impending. The second

2. Confucius said, "The Yin dynasty possessed these three men of virtue."

II. Hwuy of Lew-hea being chief criminal judge, was thrice dismissed from his office. Some one said to him, "Is it not yet time for you, Sir, to leave this?" He replied, "Serving men in an upright way, where shall I go to, and not experience such a thrice-repeated dismissal? If I choose to serve men in a crooked way, what necessity is there for me to leave the country of my parents?"

III. The Duke King of Ts'e, *with reference to the manner in which* he should treat Confucius, said, "I cannot treat him as I would the chief of the Ke family. I will treat him in a manner between that accorded to the chief of the Ke, and that given to the chief of the Măng family." He *also* said, "I am old; I cannot use *his doctrines.*" Confucius took his departure.

IV. The people of Ts'e sent *to Loo* a present of female

was thrown into prison, and, to escape death, feigned madness. He was used by Chow as a buffoon. Pe-kan, persisting in his remonstrances, was put barbarously to death, the tyrant having his heart torn out, that he might see, he said, a sage's heart.

2. How HWUY OF LEW-HEA, THOUGH OFTEN DISMISSED FROM OFFICE, STILL CLAVE TO HIS COUNTRY. Lew-hea Hwuy,—see XV. xiii. The office which Hwuy held is described in the Chow-le, XXXIV. iii. He was under the minister of Crime, but with many subordinate magistrates under him.—Some remarks akin to that in the text are ascribed to Hwuy's wife. It is observed by the commentator Hoo, that there ought to be another paragraph, giving Confucius' judgment upon Hwuy's conduct, but it has been lost.

3. How CONFUCIUS LEFT TS'E, WHEN THE DUKE COULD NOT APPRECIATE AND EMPLOY HIM. It was in the year B.C. 516, that Confucius went to Ts'e. The remarks about how he should be treated, &c., are to be understood as having taken place in consultation between the duke and his ministers, and being afterwards reported to the sage. The Măng family (see II. v.) was, in the time of Confucius, much weaker than the Ke. The chief of it was only the lowest noble of Loo, while the Ke was the highest. Yet for the duke of Ts'e to treat Confucius better than the duke of Loo treated the chief of the Măng family, was not dishonouring the sage. We must suppose that Confucius left Ts'e, because of the duke's concluding remarks.

4. How CONFUCIUS GAVE UP OFFICIAL SERVICE IN LOO. In the fourteenth year of the Duke Ting, Confucius reached the highest point of his official service. He was minister of Crime, and also, according to the general opinion, acting premier. He effected in a few months a wonderful renovation of the State, and the neighbouring countries began to fear that

musicians, which Ke Hwan received, and for three days no court was held. Confucius took his departure.

V. 1. The madman of Ts'oo, Tsëĕ-yu, passed by Confucius, singing and saying, "Oh Fung! Oh Fung! How is your virtue degenerated! As to the past, reproof is useless; but the future may be provided against. Give up *your vain pursuit.* Give up *your vain pursuit.* Peril awaits those who now engage in affairs of government."

2. Confucius alighted and wished to converse with him, but *Tsëĕ-yu* hastened away, so that he could not talk with him.

VI. 1. Ch'ang-tseu and Këĕ-neih were at work in the field together, when Confucius passed by them, and sent Tsze-loo to inquire for the ford.

2. Ch'ang-tseu said, "Who is he that holds the reins in the carriage there?" Tsze-loo told him, "It is K'ung K'ew." "Is it not K'ung K'ew of Loo?" asked he. "Yes," was the reply, to which the other rejoined, "He knows the ford."

3. *Tsze-loo then* inquired of Këĕ-neih, who said to him, "Who are you, Sir?" He answered, "I am Chung Yew." "Are you not the disciple of K'ung K'ew of Loo?" asked the other. "I am," replied he; and then Këĕ-neih said to him, "Disorder, like a swelling flood, spreads over the whole empire, and who is he that will change it *for you?* Than follow one who merely with-

---

under his administration, Loo would overtop and subdue them all. To prevent this, the duke of Ts'e sent a present to Loo of fine horses and of eighty highly accomplished beauties. The duke of Loo was induced to receive these by the advice of the head of the Ke family, Ke Sze or Ke Hwan. The sage was forgotten; government was neglected. Confucius, indignant and sorrowful, withdrew from office, and for a time, from the country too.

5. CONFUCIUS AND THE MADMAN OF TS'OO, WHO BLAMES HIS NOT RETIRING FROM THE WORLD. 1. Tsëĕ-yu was the designation of one Luh T'ung, a native of Ts'oo, who feigned himself mad, to escape being importuned to engage in public service. It must have been about the year B.C. 489, that the incident in the text occurred. By the *fung* or phœnix, his satirizer or adviser intended Confucius; see IX. viii.

6. CONFUCIUS AND THE TWO RECLUSES, CH'ANG-TSEU AND KËĔ-NEIH; WHY HE WOULD NOT WITHDRAW FROM THE WORLD. 1. The surnames and names of these worthies are not known. It is supposed that they belonged to Ts'oo, like the hero of the last chapter, and that the interview with them occurred about the same time. The designations in the text

draws from this one and that one, had you not better follow those who have withdrawn from the world altogether?" *With this* he fell to covering up the seed, *and proceeded with his work*, without stopping.

4. Tsze-loo went and reported their remarks, when his master observed with a sigh, "It is impossible to associate with birds and beasts, as if they were the same with us. If I associate not with these people,—with mankind,—with whom shall I associate? If right principles prevailed through the empire, there would be no use for me to change its state."

VII. 1. Tsze-loo, following the Master, happened to fall behind, when he met an old man, carrying, across his shoulder on a staff, a basket for weeds. Tsze-loo said to him, "Have you seen my master, Sir!" The old man replied, "Your four limbs are unaccustomed to toil; you cannot distinguish the five kinds of grain:—who is your master?" With this, he planted his staff in the ground, and proceeded to weed.

2. Tsze-loo joined his hands across his breast, and stood *before him.*

3. The old man kept Tsze-loo to pass the night in his house, killed a fowl, prepared millet, and feasted him. He also introduced to him his two sons.

4. Next day, Tsze-loo went on his way, and reported *his adventure.* The Master said, "He is a recluse," and sent Tsze-loo back to see him again, but when he got to the place, the old man was gone.

---

are descriptive of their character, and—"the long Rester," and "the firm Recluse." What kind of field labour is here denoted cannot be determined. 2. The original of "he knows the ford," indicates that "he" is emphatic,—he, going about everywhere, and seeking to be employed, ought to know the ford. The use of "his Master" in the last paragraph is remarkable. It must mean "his Master" and not "the Master." ₵ The compiler of this chapter can hardly have been a disciple of the sage.

7. TSZE-LOO'S RENCONTRE WITH AN OLD MAN, A RECLUSE: HIS VINDICATION OF HIS MASTER'S COURSE. The incident in this chapter was probably nearly contemporaneous with those which occupy the two previous ones. Some say that the old man belonged to Shĕ, which was a part of Ts'oo. "The five grains" are "rice, millet, sacrificial millet, wheat, and pulse." But they are sometimes otherwise enumerated. We have also "the six kinds," "the eight kinds," "the nine kinds," and perhaps other classifications. 2. Tsze-loo, standing with his arms across his breast, indicated his respect, and won upon the old man. 5.

5. Tsze-loo then said *to the family*, "Not to take office is not righteous. If the relations between old and young may not be neglected, how is it that he sets aside the duties that should be observed between sovereign and minister? Wishing to maintain his personal purity, he allows that great relation to come to confusion. A superior man takes office, and performs the righteous duties belonging to it. As to the failure of right principles to make progress, he is aware of that."

VIII. 1. The men who have retired to privacy from the world have been Pih-e, Shŭh-ts'e, Yu-chung, E-yih, Choo-chang, Hwuy of Lew-hea, and Shaou-lëen.

2. The Master said, "Refusing to surrender their wills, or to submit to any taint in their persons;—such, I think, were Pih-e and Shuh-ts'e.

3. "It may be said of Hwuy of Lew-hen, and of Shaou-lëen, that they surrendered their wills, and submitted to taint in their persons, but their words corresponded with reason, and their actions were such as men are anxious to see. This is all that is to be remarked in them.

4. "It may be said of Yu-chung and E-yih, that, while they hid themselves in their seclusion, they gave a license to their words, but in their persons they succeeded in preserving their purity, and in their retirement they acted according to the exigency of the times.

Tsze-loo is to be understood as here speaking the sentiments of the Master, and vindicating his course. By "the relations between old and young," he refers to the manner in which the old man had introduced his sons to him the evening before, and to all the orderly intercourse between old and young, which he had probably seen in the family.

8. CONFUCIUS' JUDGMENT OF FORMER WORTHIES WHO HAD KEPT FROM THE WORLD. HIS OWN GUIDING PRINCIPLE. 1. On the word "retired" with which this chapter commences, it is said:—"Retirement here is not that of seclusion, but is characteristic of men of large souls, who cannot be measured by ordinary rules. They may display their character by retiring from the world. They may display it also in the manner of their discharge of office." The phrase is guarded in this way, I suppose, because of its application to Hwuy of Lew-hea, who did not obstinately withdraw from the world. Pih-e, and Shuh-ts'e,—see V. xxii. Yu-chung should probably be Woo-chung. He was the brother of T'ae-pih, called Chung-yung, and is mentioned in the note on VIII. i. He retired with T'ae-pih among the barbarous tribes, then occupying the country of Woo, and succeeded to the chieftaincy of them on his brother's death.

5. "I am different from all these. I have no course for which I am predetermined, and no course against which I am predetermined."

IX. 1. The grand music-master, Che, went to Ts'e.

2. Kan, *the master of the band at* the second meal, went to Ts'oo. Leaou, *the band-master at* the third meal, went to Ts'ae. Keuĕh, *the band-master* at the fourth meal, went to Ts'in.

3. Fang-shuh, the drum-master, withdrew to *the no th of* the river.

4. Woo, the master of the hand-drum, withdrew to the Han.

5. Yang, the assistant music-master, and Seang, master of the musical stone, withdrew to *an island in* the sea.

X. The duke of Chow addressed *his son*, the duke of Loo, saying, "The virtuous prince does not neglect his relations. He does not cause the great ministers to repine at his not employing them. Without some great

---

"E-yih and Choo-chang," says Choo He, "are not found in the classics and histories. From a passage in the Le-ke, XXI. i. 14, it appears that Shaou-lëen belonged to one of the barbarous tribes on the east, but was well acquainted with, and observant of, the rules of propriety, particularly those relating to mourning. 4. "Living in retirement, they gave a license to their words."—this is intended to show that in this respect they were inferior to Hwuy and Shaou-lëen. 5. Confucius's openness to act according to circumstances is to be understood as being always in subordination to right and propriety.

9. THE DISPERSION OF THE MUSICIANS OF LOO. The dispersion here narrated is supposed to have taken place in the time of Duke Gae. When once Confucius had rectified the music of Loo (IX. xiv.), the musicians would no longer be assisting in the prostitution of their art, and so, as the disorganization and decay proceeded, the chief among them withdrew to other countries, or from society altogether. 1. "The music-master, Che,"—see VIII. xv. 2. The princes of China, it would appear, had music at their meals, and a separate band performed at each meal, or possibly, the band might be the same, but under the superintendence of a separate officer at each meal. The emperor had four meals a day, and the princes of States only three, but it was the prerogative of the duke of Loo to use the ceremonies of the imperial household. Nothing is said here of the band-master at the first meal, perhaps because he did not leave Loo, or nothing may have been known of him. 3. "The river" is of course "the Yellow River." 5. It was from Seang that Confucius learned to play on the lute.

10. INSTRUCTIONS OF CHOW-KUNG TO HIS SON ABOUT GOVERNMENT; A GENEROUS CONSIDERATION OF OTHERS TO BE CHERISHED. See VI. v. It would seem that the duke of Chow was himself appointed to the

cause, he does not dismiss from their offices the members of old families. He does not seek in one man talents for every employment."

XI. To Chow belonged the eight officers, Pih-tă, Pih-kwŏh, Chung-tŭh, Chung-hwŭh, Shuh-yay, Shuh-hea, Ke-suy, and Ke-kwa.

BOOK XIX.

CHAPTER I. Tsze-chang said, "The scholar, *trained for public duty*, seeing threatening danger, is prepared to sacrifice his life. When the opportunity of gain is presented to him, he thinks of righteousness. In sacrificing, his thoughts are reverential. In mourning, his thoughts are about the grief *which he should feel*. Such a man commands our approbation indeed."

II. Tsze-chang said, "When a man holds fast virtue, but without seeking to enlarge it, and believes right prin-

principality of Loo, but being detained at court by his duties to the young Emperor Ch'ing, he sent his son, here called "the duke of Loo," to that State as his representative.

11. THE FRUITFULNESS OF THE EARLY TIME OF THE CHOW DYNASTY IN ABLE OFFICERS. The eight individuals mentioned here are said to have been brothers, four pairs of twins by the same mother. This is intimated in their names, the two first being *primi*, the next pair *secundi*, the third *tertii*, and the last two *ultimi*. One mother, bearing twins four times in succession, and all proving distinguished men, showed the vigour of the early days of the dynasty in all that was good.—It is disputed to what reign these brothers belonged, nor is their surname ascertained.

HEADING AND CONTENTS OF THIS BOOK. "Tsze-chang—No. XIX." Confucius does not appear personally in this book at all. Choo He says:—"This book records the words of the disciples, Tsze-hea being the most frequent speaker, and Tsze-kung next to him. For in the Confucian school, after Yen Yuen there was no one of such discriminating understanding as Tsze-kung, and, after Tsăng Sin no one of such firm sincerity as Tsze-hea." The disciples deliver their sentiments very much after the manner of their master, and yet we can discern a falling off from him.

1. TSZE-CHANG'S OPINION OF THE CHIEF ATTRIBUTES OF THE TRUE SCHOLAR.

2. TSZE-CHANG ON NARROW-MINDEDNESS AND A HESITATING FAITH. Hing Ping interprets this chapter in the following way:—" If a man grasp hold of his virtue, and is not widened and enlarged by it, although he may believe good principles, he cannot be sincere and generous." But

ciples, but without firm sincerity, what account can be made of his existence or non-existence?"

III. The disciples of Tsze-hea asked Tsze-chang about the principles of intercourse. Tsze-chang asked, "What does Tsze-hea say on the subject?" They replied, "Tsze-hea says:—'Associate with those who can *advantage you*. Put away from you those who cannot *do so*.'" Tsze-chang observed, "This is different from what I have learned. The superior man honours the talented and virtuous, and bears with all. He praises the good, and pities the incompetent. Am I possessed of great talents and virtue?—who is there among men whom I will not bear with? Am I devoid of talents and virtue?—men will put me away from them. What have we to do with the putting away of others?"

IV. Tsze-hea said, "Even in inferior studies and employments there is something worth being looked at, but if it be attempted to carry them out to what is remote, there is a danger of their proving inapplicable. Therefore, the superior man does not practise them."

V. Tsze-hea said, "He, who from day to day recognizes what he has not yet, and from month to month does not forget what he has attained to, may be said indeed to love to learn."

it is better to take the clauses as coördinate, and not dependent on each other.

3. THE DIFFERENT OPINIONS OF TSZE-HEA AND TSZE-CHANG ON THE PRINCIPLES WHICH SHOULD REGULATE OUR INTERCOURSE WITH OTHERS. It is strange to me that the disciples of Tsze-hea should begin their answer to Tsze-chang with the designation Tsze-hea, instead of saying "our Master." Hing Ping expounds Tsze-hea's rule thus:—"If the man be worthy, fit for you to have intercourse with, then have it, but if he be not worthy," &c. On the other hand, we find:—"If the man will advantage you, he is a fit person; then maintain intercourse with him," &c. This seems to be merely carrying out Confucius' rule, I. viii. 3. Choo He, however, approves of Tsze-chang's censure of it, while he thinks also that Tsze-chang's own view is defective.—Paou Heen says:—"Our intercourse with friends should be according to Tsze-hea's rule; general intercourse according to Tsze-chang's."

4. TSZE-HEA'S OPINION OF THE INAPPLICABILITY OF SMALL PURSUITS TO GREAT OBJECTS. Gardening, husbandry, divining, and the healing art, are all mentioned by Choo He as instances of the "small ways," here intended, having their own truth in them, but not available for higher purposes, or what is beyond themselves.

5. THE INDICATIONS OF A REAL LOVE OF LEARNING:—BY TSZE-HEA.

VI. Tsze-hea said, "There are learning extensively, and having a firm and sincere aim; inquiring with earnestness, and reflecting with self-application:—virtue is in such a course."

VII. Tsze-hea said, "Mechanics have their shops to dwell in, in order to accomplish their works. The superior man learns, in order to reach to the utmost of his principles."

VIII. Tsze-hea said, "The mean man is sure to gloss his faults."

IX. Tsze-hea said, "The superior man undergoes three changes. Looked at from a distance, he appears stern; when approached, he is mild; when he is heard to speak, his language is firm and decided."

X. Tsze-hea said, "The superior man, having obtained their confidence, may then impose labours on his people. If he have not gained their confidence, they will think that he is oppressing them. Having obtained the confidence *of his prince*, he may then remonstrate with him. If he have not gained his confidence, *the prince* will think that he is vilifying him."

XI. Tsze-hea said, "When a person does not trans-

---

6. HOW LEARNING SHOULD BE PURSUED TO LEAD TO VIRTUE:—BY TSZE-HEA.

7. LEARNING IS THE STUDENT'S WORKSHOP:—BY TSZE-HEA. A certain quarter was assigned anciently in Chinese towns and cities for mechanics, and all of one art were required to have their shops together. A son must follow his father's profession, and, seeing nothing but the exercise of that around him, it was supposed that he would not be led to think of anything else, and would so become very proficient in it.

8. GLOSSING HIS FAULTS THE PROOF OF THE MEAN MAN:—BY TSZE-HEA. Literally, "The faults of the mean man, must gloss," *i.e. he is* sure to gloss.

9. CHANGING APPEARANCES OF THE SUPERIOR MAN TO OTHERS:— BY TSZE-HEA. Tsze-hea probably intended Confucius by the *Kewn-tsze*, but there is a general applicability in his language and sentiments.—The description is about equivalent to our "*fortiter in re, suaviter in modo.*"

10. THE IMPORTANCE OF ENJOYING CONFIDENCE TO THE RIGHT SERVING OF SUPERIORS AND ORDERING OF INFERIORS:—BY TSZE-HEA.

11. THE GREAT VIRTUES DEMAND THE CHIEF ATTENTION, AND THE SMALL ONES MAY BE SOMEWHAT VIOLATED:—BY TSZE-HEA. The sentiment here is very questionable. A different turn, however, is given to the chapter in the older interpreters. Hing Ping, expanding K'ung Gan-kwǒ says:—" Men of great virtue never go beyond the boundary-line: it is enough for those who are virtuous in a less degree to keep near to it,

gress the boundary-line in the great virtues, he may pass and repass it in the small virtues."

XII. 1. Tsze-yew said, "The disciples and followers of Tsze-hea, in sprinkling and sweeping the ground, in answering and replying, in advancing and receding, are sufficiently accomplished. But these are only the branches *of learning*, and they are left ignorant of what is essential. —How can they be acknowledged as sufficiently taught?"

2. Tsze-hea heard of the remark and said, "Alas! Yen Yew is wrong. According to the way of the superior man *in teaching*, what departments are there which he considers of prime importance, and therefore *first* delivers? what are there which he considers of secondary importance, and so allows himself to be idle about? *But* as in the case of plants, which are assorted according to their classes, *so he deals with his disciples*. How can the way of a superior man be such as to make fools of *any of* them? Is it not the sage alone, who can unite in one the beginning and the consummation *of learning?*"

XIII. Tsze-hea said, "The officer, *having discharged all his duties*, should devote his leisure to learning. The student, having completed his learning, should apply himself to be an officer."

XIV. Tsze-hea said, "Mourning, having been carried to the utmost degree of grief, should stop with that."

going beyond and coming back." We adopt the more natural interpretation of Choo He.

12. TSZE-HEA'S DEFENCE OF HIS OWN GRADUATED METHOD OF TEACHING:—AGAINST TSZE-YEW. 1. The sprinkling, &c., are the things boys were supposed anciently to be taught, the rudiments of learning, from which they advanced to all that is inculcated in the "Great Learning." But as Tsze-hea's pupils were not boys, but men, we should understand, I suppose, these specifications as but a contemptuous reference to his instructions, as embracing merely what was external. The general scope of Tsze-hen's reply is sufficiently plain, but the old interpreters and new differ in explaining the several sentences. After dwelling long on it, I have agreed generally with the new school, and followed Choo He in the translation. Tsze-hea did not teach what he taught as being in itself more important than what he for the time left untouched. He communicated knowledge as his disciples were able to bear it.

13. THE OFFICER AND THE STUDENT SHOULD ATTEND EACH TO HIS PROPER WORK IN THE FIRST INSTANCE:—BY TSZE-YEW.

14. THE TRAPPINGS OF MOURNING MAY BE DISPENSED WITH:—BY TSZE-YEW. The sentiment here is perhaps the same as that of Confucius in III. iv., but the sage guards and explains his utterance.—K'ung Gan-

' XV. Tsze-hea said, "My friend Chang can do things which are hard to be done, but yet he is not perfectly virtuous."

XVI. Tsäng the philosopher said, "How imposing is the manner of Chang! It is difficult along with him to practise virtue."

XVII. Tsäng the philosopher said, "I have heard this from our Master:—'Men may not have shown what is in them to the full extent, and yet they will be found to do so, on occasion of mourning for their parents.'"

XVIII. Tsäng the philosopher said, "I have heard this from our Master:—'The filial piety of Mäng Chwang, in other matters, was what other men are competent to, but, as seen in his not changing the ministers of his father, nor his father's mode of government, it is difficult to be attained to.'"

XIX. The chief of the Mäng family having appointed Yang Foo to be chief criminal judge, the latter consulted the philosopher Tsäng. Tsäng said, "The rulers have failed in their duties, and the people have consequently been disorganized, for a long time. When you have found

kwŏ, following an expression in the "Classic of Filial Piety," makes the meaning to be that the mourner may not endanger his health or life by excessive grief and abstinence.

15. TSZE-YEW'S OPINION OF TSZE-CHANG, AS MINDING TOO MUCH HIGH THINGS.

16. THE PHILOSOPHER TSANG'S OPINION OF TSZE-CHANG, AS TOO HIGH-PITCHED FOR FRIENDSHIP.

17. HOW GRIEF FOR THE LOSS OF PARENTS BRINGS OUT THE REAL NATURE OF MAN :—BY TSANG SIN.

18. THE FILIAL PIETY OF MANG CHWANG :—BY TSANG SIN. Chwang was the honorary epithet of Suh, the head of the Mäng family, not long anterior to Confucius. His father, according to Choo He, had been a man of great merit, nor was Chwang inferior to him, but his virtue especially appeared in what the text mentions.—Ho An gives the comment of Ma Yung, that though there were bad men among his father's ministers, and defects in his government, yet Chwang made no change in the one or the other, during the three years of mourning, and that it was this which constituted his excellence.

19. HOW A CRIMINAL JUDGE SHOULD CHERISH COMPASSION IN HIS ADMINISTRATION OF JUSTICE :—BY TSANG SIN. Seven disciples of Tsäng Sin are more particularly mentioned, one of them being this Yang Foo. "Disorganized," literally "scattered," is to be understood of the moral state of the people, and not, physically, of their being scattered from their dwellings.

out the truth *of any accusation*, be grieved for and pity them, and do not feel joy *at your own ability*."

XX. Tsze-kung said, "Chow's wickedness was not so great *as that name implies*. Therefore, the superior man hates to dwell in a low-lying situation, where all the evil of the world will flow in upon him."

XXI. Tsze-kung said, "The faults of the superior man are like the eclipses of the sun and moon. He has his faults, and all men see them; he changes again, and all men look up to him."

XXII. 1. Kung-sun Ch'aóu of Wei asked Tsze-kung, saying, "From whom did Chung-ne get his learning?"

2. Tsze-kung replied, "The doctrines of Wăn and Woo have not yet fallen to the earth. They are to be found among men. Men of talents and virtue remember the great principles of them, and others, not possessing such talents and virtue, remember the smaller. *Thus*, all possess the doctrines of Wăn and Woo. From whom did our Master not learn them? And yet what necessity was there for his having a regular master?"

XXIII. 1. Shuh-sun Woo-shuh observed to the great officers in the court, saying, "Tsze-kung is superior to Chung-ne."

20. THE DANGER OF A BAD NAME:—BY TSZE-KUNG. "Not so bad as the name implies," is, literally, "not so very bad as this;"—the *this* is understood by Hing Ping as referring to the epithet Chow, which cannot be called honorary in this instance. According to the laws for such terms, it means "cruel and unmerciful, injurious to righteousness." If the *this* does not in this way refer to the name, the remark would seem to have occurred in a conversation about the wickedness of Chow.

21. THE SUPERIOR MAN DOES NOT CONCEAL HIS ERRORS, NOR PERSIST IN THEM:—BY TSZE-KUNG. Such is the lesson of this chapter, as expanded in the "Daily Lessons." The sun and the moon being here spoken of together, the term must be confined to "eclipses," but it is also applied to the ordinary waning of the moon.

22. CONFUCIUS' SOURCES OF KNOWLEDGE WERE THE RECOLLECTIONS AND TRADITIONS OF THE PRINCIPLES ON WĂN AND WOO:—BY TSZE-KUNG. 1. Of the questioner here we have no other memorial. His surname indicates that he was a descendant of some of the dukes of Wei. Observe how he calls Confucius by his designation of Chung-ne or "Ne *secundus*." (There was an elder brother, a concubine's son, who was called Pih-ne.) The last clause is taken by modern commentators, as asserting Confucius' connate knowledge, but Gan-kwŏ finds in it only a repetition of the statement that the sage found teachers everywhere.

23. TSZE-KUNG REPUDIATES BEING THOUGHT SUPERIOR TO CONFUCIUS, AND, BY THE COMPARISON OF A HOUSE AND WALL, SHOWS HOW ORDIN-

2. Tsze-fuh King-pih reported the observation to Tsze-kung, who said, "Let me use the comparison of a house and its *encompassing* wall. My wall *only* reaches to the shoulders. One may peep over it, and see whatever is valuable in the apartments.

3. "The wall of my master is several fathoms high. If one do not find the door and enter by it, he cannot see the ancestral temple with its beauties, nor all the officers in their rich array.

4. "But I may assume that they are few who find the door. Was not the observation of the chief only what might have been expected?"

XXIV. Shuh-sun Woo-shuh having spoken revilingly of Chung-ne, Tsze-kung said, "It is of no use doing so. Chung-ne cannot be reviled. The talents and virtue of other men are hillocks and mounds, which may be stept over. Chung-ne is the sun or moon, which it is not possible to step over. Although a man may wish to cut himself off *from the sage*, what harm can he do to the sun or moon? He only shows that he does not know his own capacity."

XXV. 1. Tsze-k'in addressing Tsze-kung, said, "You are too modest. How can Chung-ne be said to be superior to you?"

2. Tsze-kung said to him, "For one word a man is

A RY PEOPLE COULD NOT UNDERSTAND THE MASTER. 1. "Woo" was the honorary epithet of Chow Kew, one of the chiefs of the Shuh-sun family. From a mention of him in the "Family Sayings," we may conclude that he was given to envy and detraction. The term rendered "house" is now the common word for a "palace," but here it is to be taken generally for a house or building. It is a poor house, as representing the disciple, and a ducal mansion, as representing his master. Many commentators make the wall to be the sole object in the comparison; but it is better to take both the house and the wall as members of the comparison. The wall is not a part of the house, but one inclosing it.

24. CONFUCIUS IS LIKE THE SUN OR MOON, HIGH ABOVE THE REACH OF DEPRECIATION :—BY TSZE-KUNG.

25. CONFUCIUS CAN NO MORE BE EQUALLED THAN THE HEAVENS CAN BE CLIMBED:—BY TSZE-KUNG. We find it difficult to conceive of the sage's disciples speaking to one another, as Tsze-k'in does here to Tsze-kung; and Hing Ping says that this was not the disciple Tsze-k'in, but another man of the same surname and designation. But this is inadmissible, especially as we find the same parties, in I. x., talking about the character of their master. I think it likely the conversation took place

often deemed to be wise, and for one word he is *often* deemed to be foolish. We ought to be careful indeed in what we say.

3. "Our Master cannot be attained to, just in the same way as the heavens cannot be gone up to by the steps of a stair.

4. "Were our Master in the position of the prince of a State or the chief of a Family, we should find verified the description *which has been given of a sage's rule*:—he would plant the people, and forthwith they would be established; he would lead them on, and forthwith they would follow him; he would make them happy, and forthwith *multitudes* would resort to *his dominions*; he would stimulate them, and forthwith they would be harmonious. While he lived, he would be glorious. When he died, he would be bitterly lamented. How is it possible for him to be attained to?"

BOOK XX.

CHAPTER I. 1. Yaou said, "Oh! you, Shun, the Heaven-determined order of succession now rests in your person. Sincerely hold fast the due Mean. If there shall be distress and want within the four seas, *your* Heavenly revenue will come to a perpetual end."

2. Shun also used the same language in giving charge to Yu.

after the sage's death, in which case the tenses in the translation would in several cases have to be altered. Unfortunately the Chinese language has no inflexions of any kind, and in concise composition such as that of these Analects the adjunctive indications of mood and tense seldom occur.

HEADING AND CONTENTS OF THIS BOOK.—"Yaou said." Hing Ping says:—"This records the words of the two emperors, the three kings, and Confucius, throwing light on the excellence of the ordinances of Heaven, and the transforming power of government. Its doctrines are all those of sages, worthy of being transmitted to posterity. On this account, it brings up the rear of all the other books, without any particular relation to the one immediately preceding."

1. PRINCIPLES AND WAYS OF YAOU, SHUN, YU, T'ANG, AND WOO. The first five paragraphs here are mostly compiled from different parts of the Shoo-king. But there are many variations of language. The compiler may have thought it sufficient, if he gave the substance of the original in his quotations, without seeking to observe a verbal accuracy,

3. T'ang said, "I, the child Le, presume to use a dark-coloured victim, and presume to announce to Thee, O most great and sovereign God, that the sinner I dare not pardon, and thy ministers, O God, I do not keep in obscurity. The examination of them is by thy mind, O God. If, in my person, I commit offences, they are not to be attributed to you, *the people of* the myriad regions. If you in the myriad regions commit offences, these offences must rest on my person."

4. Chow conferred great gifts, and the good were enriched.

5. "Although he has his near relatives, they are not equal to *my* virtuous men. The people are throwing blame upon me, the one man."

6. He carefully attended to the weights and measures, examined the body of the laws, restored the discarded officers, and the good government of the empire took its course.

7. He revived States that had been extinguished, restored families whose line of succession had been broken, and called to office those who had retired into obscurity, so that throughout the empire the hearts of the people turned towards him.

or, possibly, the Shoo-king, as it was in his days, may have contained the passages as he gives them, and the variations be owing to the burning of most of the classical books by the founder of the Ts'in dynasty, and their recovery and restoration in a mutilated state. 1. We do not find this address of Yaou to Shun in the Shoo-king, Pt I, but the different sentences may be gathered from Pt II. Bk II. 14, 15, 17, where we have the charge of Shun to Yu. Yaou's reign commenced B.C. 2356, and after reigning 73 years, he resigned the administration to Shun. He died, B.C. 2256, and, two years after, Shun occupied the throne, in obedience to the will of the people. "The Heaven-determined order of succession" is, literally, "the represented and calculated numbers of heaven," *i.e.,* the divisions of the year, its terms, months, and days, all described in a calendar, as they succeed one another with determined regularity. Here, ancient and modern interpreters agree in giving to the expression the meaning which appears in the translation. I may observe here, that Choo He differs often from the old interpreters in explaining these passages of the Shoo-king, but I have followed him, leaving the correctness or incorrectness of his views to be considered in the annotations on the Shoo-king. 3. At the commencement of this paragraph we must understand T'ang, the founder of the Shang dynasty. The sentences here may in substance be collected in a measure from the Shoo-king, Pt IV. Bk III. 4, 8. The sinner is Këĕ, the tyrant, and last emperor

8. What he attached chief importance to, were the food of the people, the duties of mourning, and sacrifices.

9. By his generosity, he won all. By his sincerity, he made the people repose trust in him. By his earnest activity, his achievements were great. By his justice, all were delighted.

II. 1. Tsze-chang asked Confucius, saying, "In what way should *a person in authority* act, in order that he may conduct government properly?" The Master replied, "Let him honour the five excellent, and banish away the four bad, things;—then may he conduct government properly." Tsze-chang said, "What are meant by the five excellent things?" The Master said, "When the person in authority is beneficent without great expenditure; when he lays tasks on *the people* without their repining; when he *pursues what he desires* without being covetous; when he maintains a dignified ease without being proud; when he is majestic without being fierce."

2. Tsze-chang said, "What is meant by being beneficent without great expenditure?" The Master replied, "When *the person in authority* makes more beneficial to the people the things from which they naturally derive benefit; is not this being beneficent without *great* expenditure? When he chooses the labours which are proper, and makes them labour on them, who will repine? When his desires are set on benevolent *government*, and he realizes it, who will accuse him of covetousness? Whether he has to do with many people or few, or with things great or small, he does not dare to indicate any disrespect;—is not this to maintain a dignified ease with-

of the Hea dynasty. "The ministers of God" are the able and virtuous men, whom T'ang had called, or would call, to office. 4. In the Shoo-king, Pt V. Bk III. 9, we find King Woo saying, "He distributed great rewards through the empire, and all the people were pleased and submitted." 5. See the Shoo-king, Pt V. Bk I. sect. ii. 8, 7. The subject is Chow, the tyrant of the Yin dynasty. The people found fault with King Woo, because he did not come to save them from their sufferings, by destroying their oppressor. The remaining paragraphs are descriptive of the policy of King Woo, but cannot, excepting the eighth one, be traced in the present Shoo-king.

2. HOW GOVERNMENT MAY BE CONDUCTED WITH EFFICIENCY, BY HONOURING FIVE EXCELLENT THINGS, AND PUTTING AWAY FOUR BAD THINGS:—A CONVERSATION WITH TSZE-CHANG. It is understood that

out any pride? He adjusts his clothes and cap, and throws a dignity into his looks, so that, thus dignified, he is looked at with awe; is not this to be majestic without being fierce?"

3. Tsze-chang then asked, "What are meant by the four bad things?" The Master said, "To put the people to death without having instructed them;—this is called cruelty. To require from them, *suddenly*, the full tale of work, without having given them warning;—this is called oppression. To issue orders as if without urgency, *at first*, and, when the time comes, *to insist on them with severity;* —this is called injury. And, generally speaking, to give *pay or rewards* to men, and yet to do it in a stingy way; —this is called acting the part of a mere official."

III. 1. The Master said, "Without recognizing the ordinances *of Heaven*, it is impossible to be a superior man.

2. "Without an acquaintance with the rules of Propriety, it is impossible for the character to be established.

3. "Without knowing *the force of* words, it is impossible to know men."

this chapter, and the next, give the ideas of Confucius on government, as a sequel to those of the ancient sages and emperors, whose principles are set forth in the last chapter, to show how Confucius was their proper successor.

3. THE ORDINANCES OF HEAVEN, THE RULES OF PROPRIETY, AND THE FORCE OF WORDS, ALL NECESSARY TO BE KNOWN.

THE GREAT LEARNING.

My master, the philosopher Ch'ing, says:—"The Great Learning is a book left by Confucius, and forms the gate by which first learners enter into virtue. That we can now perceive the order in which the ancients pursued their learning, is solely owing to the preservation of this work, the Analects and Mencius coming after it. Learners must commence their course with this, and then it may be hoped they will be kept from error."

THE TEXT OF CONFUCIUS.

1. WHAT the Great Learning teaches, is—to illustrate illustrious virtue; to renovate the people; and to rest in the highest excellence.

TITLE OF THE WORK.—"The Great Learning." I have pointed out, in the prolegomena, the great differences which are found among Chinese commentators on this Work, on almost every point connected with the criticism and interpretation of it. We encounter them here on the very threshold. The name itself is simply the adoption of the two commencing characters of the treatise, according to the custom noticed at the beginning of the Analects; but in explaining those two characters, the old and new schools differ widely. I have contented myself with the title—" The Great Learning," which is a literal translation of the characters.

THE INTRODUCTORY NOTE.—I have thought it well to translate this, and all the other notes and supplements appended by Choo He to the original text, because they appear in nearly all the editions of the work which fall into the hands of students, and his view of the classics is what must be regarded as the orthodox one. The translation, which is here given, is also, for the most part, according to his views, though my own differing opinion will be found freely expressed in the notes. Another version, following the order of the text, before it was transposed by him and his masters, the Ch'ing, and without reference to its interpretations, will be found in the translation of the Le-ke. The Ch'ing here is the

2. The point where to rest being known, the object of pursuit is then determined; and, that being determined, a calm unperturbedness may be attained. To that calmness there will succeed a tranquil repose. In that repose there may be careful deliberation, and that deliberation will be followed by the attainment *of the desired end*.

3. Things have their root and their completion. Affairs have their end and their beginning. To know what is first and what is last will lead near to what is taught in *the Great Learning*.

second of the two brothers, to whom reference is made in the prolegomena. But how can we say that "The Great Learning" is a work left by Confucius? Even Choo He ascribes only a small portion of it to the Master, and makes the rest to be the production of the disciple Tsǎng, and before his time, the whole work was attributed generally to the sage's grandson.

CHAPTER I. THE TEXT OF CONFUCIUS. Such Choo Ho, as will be seen from his concluding note, determines this chapter to be, and it has been divided into two sections, the first containing three paragraphs, occupied with the *heads* of "the Great Learning," and the second containing four paragraphs, occupied with the *particulars* of those.

Par. 1. *The heads of the Great Learning.*—"To illustrate illustrious virtue,"—the illustrious virtue is the virtuous nature which man derives from Heaven. This is perverted as man grows up, through defects of the physical constitution, through inward lusts, and through outward seductions; and the great business of life should be, to bring the nature back to its original purity.—"To renovate the people,"—this object of "the Great Learning" is made out, by changing the character in the text, which means "to love," into another signifying "to renovate." The Ch'ing first proposed the alteration, and Choo He approved of it. When a man has entirely illustrated his own illustrious nature, he has to proceed to bring about the same result in every other man, till "under heaven" there be not an individual, who is not in the same condition as himself.—"The highest excellence" is understood of the two previous matters. It is not a third and different object of pursuit, but indicates a perseverance in the two others, till they are perfectly accomplished.—According to these explanations, the objects contemplated in "the Great Learning," are not three, but two. Suppose them realized, and we should have the whole world of mankind perfectly good, every individual what he ought to be!

Against the above interpretation, we have to consider the older and simpler. "Virtue" is there not the *nature*, but simply virtue, or virtuous conduct, and the first object in "the Great Learning" is the making of one's self more and more illustrious in virtue, or in the practice of benevolence, reverence, filial piety, kindness, and sincerity. There is nothing, of course, of the *renovating of the people*, in this interpretation. The second object of "the Great Learning" is "to love the people."—The third object is said by Ying-tǎ to be "in resting in conduct which is perfectly good," and here, also, there would seem to be only two objects, for what essential distinction can we make between the first and third? "To love the people" is,

4. The ancients who wished to illustrate illustrious virtue throughout the empire, first ordered well their own States. Wishing to order well their States, they first regulated their families. Wishing to regulate their families, they first cultivated their persons. Wishing to cultivate their persons, they first rectified their hearts. Wishing to rectify their hearts, they first sought to be sincere in their thoughts. Wishing to be sincere in their thoughts, they first extended to the utmost their knowledge. Such extension of knowledge lay in the investigation of things.

5. Things being investigated, knowledge became complete. Their knowledge being complete, their thoughts were sincere. Their thoughts being sincere, their hearts were then rectified. Their hearts being rectified, their persons were cultivated. Their persons being cultivated, their families were regulated. Their families being regulated, their States were rightly governed. Their States being rightly governed, the whole empire was made tranquil and happy.

doubtless, the second thing taught by "the Great Learning."—Having the heads of "the Great Learning" now before us, according to both interpretations of it, we feel that the student of it should be an emperor, and not an ordinary man.

Par. 2. *The mental process by which the point of rest may be attained.* I confess that I do not well understand this paragraph, in the relation of its parts in itself, nor in relation to the rest of the chapter. Perhaps it just intimates that the objects of "the Great Learning" being so great, a calm, serious thoughtfulness is required in proceeding to seek their attainment.

Par. 3. *The order of things and methods in the two preceding paragraphs.* So, according to Choo He, does this paragraph wind up the two preceding. "The illustration of virtue," he says, "is the *root*, and the renovation of the people is the *completion* (literally, *the branches*). Knowing where to rest is the *beginning*, and being able to attain is the *end*. The root and beginning are *what is first*. The completion and end are *what is last*."—The adherents of the old commentators say, on the contrary, that this paragraph is introductory to the succeeding ones. They contend that the illustration of virtue and renovation of the people are *doings*, and not *things*. According to them the *things* are the person, heart, thoughts, &c., mentioned below, which are "the root," and the family, kingdom, and empire, which are "the branches." The *affairs* are the various processes put forth on those things.—This, it seems to me, is the correct interpretation.

Par. 4. *The different steps by which the illustration of illustrious virtue throughout the empire may be brought about.* Of the several steps described, the central one is "the cultivation of the person," which, in-

6. From the emperor down to the mass of the people, all must consider the cultivation of the person the root of *everything besides*.

7. It cannot be, when the root is neglected, that what should spring from it will be well ordered. It never has been the case that what was of great importance has been slightly cared for, and, at the same time, that what was of slight importance has been greatly cared for.

The preceding chapter of classical text is in the words of Confucius, handed down by the philosopher Tsăng. The ten chapters of explanation which follow contain the views of Tsăng, and were recorded by his disciples. In the old copies of the work, there appeared considerable confusion in these, from the disarrangement of the tablets. But now, availing myself of the decisions of the philosopher Ch'ing, and having examined anew the classical text, I have arranged it in order, as follows :—

deed, is called " the root." in paragraph 6. This requires "the heart to be correct," and that again " that the thoughts be sincere." "The heart " is the metaphysical part of our nature, all that we comprehend under the terms of mind or soul, heart, and spirit. This is conceived of as quiescent, and when its activity is aroused, then we have thoughts and purposes relative to what affects it. The "being sincere " is explained by " real." The sincerity of the thoughts is to be obtained by "carrying our knowledge to its utmost extent, with the desire that there may be nothing which it shall not embrace." This knowledge finally is realized, through "exhausting by examination the principles of things and affairs, with the desire that their uppermost point may be reached."—We feel that this explanation cannot be correct, or that, if it be correct, the teaching of the Chinese sage is far beyond and above the condition and capacity of men. How can we suppose that, in order to secure sincerity of thought and our self-cultivation, there is necessarily the study of all the phenomena of physics and metaphysics, and of the events of history ?

Par. 5. *The synthesis of the preceding processes.*

Par. 6. *The cultivation of the person is the prime, radical thing required from all.* I have said above that " the Great Learning " is adapted only to an emperor, but it is intimated here that *the people* also may take part in it in their degree.

Par. 7. *Reiteration of the importance of attending to the root.*

CONCLUDING NOTE. It has been shown in the prolegomena that there is no ground for the distinction made here between so much oracular teaching attributed to Confucius, and so much commentary ascribed to his disciple Tsăng. The invention of paper is ascribed to Ts'ae Lun, an officer of the Han dynasty, in the time of the Emperor Ho. A.D. 89—104. Before that time, and long after also, slips of wood and of bamboo were used to write and engrave upon. We can easily conceive how a

COMMENTARY OF THE PHILOSOPHER TSANG.

CHAPTER I. 1. In the Announcement to K'ang it is said, " He was able to make his virtue illustrious."
2. In the T'ae Kĕä, it is said, " He contemplated and studied the illustrious decrees of Heaven."
3. In the Canon of the Emperor Yaou, it is said, " He was able to make illustrious his lofty virtue."
4. These *passages* all *show how those sovereigns* made themselves illustrious.

The above first chapter of commentary explains the illustration of illustrious virtue.

II. 1. On the bathing-tub of T'ang, the following words were engraved:—" If you can one day renovate yourself, do so from day to day. Yea, let there be daily renovation."
2. In the Announcement to K'ang, it is said, " To stir up the new people."
3. In the Book of Poetry, it is said, " Although Chow

collection of them might get disarranged, but whether those containing " the Great Learning" did do so is a question vehemently disputed.

COMMENTARY OF THE PHILOSOPHER TSANG.
1. THE ILLUSTRATION OF ILLUSTRIOUS VIRTUE. 1. See the Shoo-king, Pt V. Bk ix. 3. The words are part of the address of King Woo to his brother Fung, called also K'ang-shuh, on appointing him to the marquisate of Wei. The subject is King Wăn, to whose example K'ang-shuh is referred. 2. See the Shoo-king, Pt IV. Bk V. i. 2. The sentence is part of the address of the premier, E Yin, to T'ae-kĕä, the second emperor of the Shang dynasty, B.C. 1752—1718. The subject of " contemplated " is T'ae-kĕa's grandfather, the great T'ang. 3. See the Shoo-king, Pt I. 2. It is of the Emperor Yaou that this is said.
2. THE RENOVATION OF THE PEOPLE. Here the character " new," " to renovate," occurs five times, and it was to find something corresponding to it at the commencement of the work, which made the Ch'ing change the old text. But the terms here have nothing to do with the renovation of the people. This is self-evident in the first and third paragraphs. The heading of the chapter, as above, is a misnomer. 1. This fact about T'ang's bathing-tub had come down by tradition. At least, we do not now find the mention of it anywhere but here. It was customary among the ancients, as it is in China at the present day, to engrave, all about them, on the articles of their furniture, such moral aphorisms and lessons. 2. See the Book quoted, p. 7, where K'ang-shuh is exhorted to assist the emperor " to settle the decree of Heaven, and to make the bad people of Yin into good people, or to stir up the new people," *i.e., new, as recently subjected to Chow.* 3. See the She-king, Pt III. Bk I. l. 1. The subject of the ode is the praise of King Wăn, whose virtue led to the

was an ancient State, the ordinance which lighted on it was new."

4. Therefore, the superior man in everything uses his utmost endeavours.

The above second chapter of commentary explains the renovating of the people.

III. 1. In the Book of Poetry, it is said, "The imperial domain of a thousand le is where the people rest."

2. In the Book of Poetry, it is said, "The twittering yellow bird rests on a corner of the mound." The Master said, "When it rests, it knows where to rest. Is it possible that a man should not be equal to this bird?"

3. In the Book of Poetry, it is said, "Profound was King Wăn. With how bright and unceasing a feeling of reverence did he regard his resting-places!" As a sovereign, he rested in benevolence. As a minister, he rested in reverence. As a son, he rested in filial piety. As a father, he rested in kindness. In communication with his subjects, he rested in good faith.

4. In the Book of Poetry, it is said, "Look at that winding course of the K'e, with the green bamboos so luxuriant! Here is our elegant and accomplished prince!

possession of the empire by his house, more than a thousand years after its first rise. 3. The " superior man " is here the man of rank and office probably, as well as the man of virtue; but I do not, for my own part, see the particular relation of this to the preceding paragraphs, nor the work which it does in relation to the whole chapter.

3. ON RESTING IN THE HIGHEST EXCELLENCE. 1. See the She-king, Pt IV. Bk III. iii. 4. The ode celebrates the rise and establishment of the Shang or Yin dynasty. A thousand *le* around the capital constituted the imperial demesne. The quotation shows, according to Choo He, that " everything has the place where it ought to rest." But that surely is a very sweeping conclusion from the words. 2. See the She-king, Pt II. Bk VIII. vi. 2, where we have the complaint of a down-trodden man, contrasting his position with that of a bird. " The yellow bird " is known by a variety of names. It seems to be a species of oriole. The " Master said," is worthy of observation. If the first chapter of the classical text, as Choo He calls it, really contains the words of Confucius, we might have expected it to be headed by these characters. 3. See the She-king, Pt III. Bk I. i. 4. 4. See the She-king, Pt I. Bk V. i. 1. The ode celebrates the virtue of the Duke Woo of Wei, in his laborious endeavours to cultivate his person. The transposition of this paragraph by Choo He to this place does seem unhappy. It ought evidently to come in connection with the work of the seventh chapter. 5. See the She-king, Pt

As we cut and then file; as we chisel and then grind: *so has he cultivated himself.* How grave is he and dignified! How majestic and distinguished! Our elegant and accomplished prince never can be forgotten." *That expression*—"as we cut and then file," indicates the work of learning. "As we chisel and then grind," indicates that of self-culture. "How grave is he and dignified!" indicates the feeling of cautious reverence. "How commanding and distinguished," indicates an awe-inspiring deportment. "Our elegant and accomplished prince never can be forgotten," indicates how, when virtue is complete and excellence extreme, the people cannot forget them.

5. In the Book of Poetry, it is said, "Ah! the former kings are not forgotten." *Future* princes deem worthy what they deemed worthy, and love what they loved. The common people delight in what they delighted, and are benefited by their beneficial arrangements. It is on this account that the former kings, after they have quitted the world, are not forgotten.

The above third chapter of commentary explains resting in the highest excellence.

IV. The Master said, "In hearing litigations, I am like any other body. What is necessary is to cause the people to have no litigations?" *So,* those who are devoid of principle find it impossible to carry out their speeches, and a great awe would be struck into men's minds:—this is called knowing the root.

The above fourth chapter of commentary explains the root and the issue.

II. Bk I. Sect. L iv. 3. The former kings are Wăn and Woo, the founders of the Chow dynasty. According to Ying-tă, "this paragraph illustrates the business of having the thoughts sincere." According to Choo He, it tells that how the former kings renovated the people, was by their resting in perfect excellence, so as to be able, throughout the empire and to future ages, to effect that there should not be a single thing but got its proper place.

4. EXPLANATION OF THE ROOT AND THE BRANCHES. See the Analects, XII. xiii., from which we understand that the words of Confucius terminate at "no litigations," and that what follows is from the compiler. According to the old commentators, this is the conclusion of the chapter on having the thoughts made sincere, and that this is the *root*. But

V. 1. This is called knowing the root.
2. This is called the perfecting of knowledge.

The above fifth chapter of commentary explained the meaning of "investigating things and carrying knowledge to the utmost extent," but it is now lost. I have ventured to take the views of the scholar Ch'ing to supply it, as follows:—The meaning of the expression, "The perfecting of knowledge depends on the investigation of things," is this:—If we wish to carry our knowledge to the utmost, we must investigate the principles of all things we come into contact with, for the intelligent mind of man is certainly formed to know, and there is not a single thing in which its principles do not inhere. But so long as all principles are not investigated, man's knowledge is incomplete. On this account, the Learning for Adults, at the outset of its lessons, instructs the learner, in regard to all things in the world, to proceed from what knowledge he has of their principles, and pursue his investigation of them, till he reaches the extreme point. After exerting himself in this way for a long time, he will suddenly find himself possessed of a wide and far-reaching penetration. Then, the qualities of all things, whether external or internal, the subtle or the coarse, will all be apprehended, and the mind, in its entire substance and its relations to things, will be perfectly intelligent. This is called the investigation of things. This is called the perfection of knowledge.

VI. 1. What is meant by "making the thoughts sin-

according to Choo He, it is the illustration of illustrious virtue which is the *root*, while the renovation of the people is the *result* therefrom. Looking at the words of Confucius, we must conclude that *sincerity* was the subject in his mind.

5. ON THE INVESTIGATION OF THINGS, AND CARRYING KNOWLEDGE TO THE UTMOST EXTENT. 1. This is said by one of the Ch'ing to be "superfluous text." 2. Choo He considers this to be the conclusion of a chapter which is now lost. But we have seen that the two sentences come in, as the work stands in the Le-ke, at the conclusion of what is deemed the classical text. It is not necessary to add anything here to what has been said there, and in the prolegomena, on the new dispositions of the work from the time of the Sung scholars, and the manner in which Choo He has supplied this supposed missing chapter.

6. ON HAVING THE THOUGHTS SINCERE. 1. *The sincerity of the*

cere," is the allowing no self-deception, as *when* we hate a bad smell, and as *when* we love what is beautiful. This is called self-enjoyment. Therefore, the superior man must be watchful over himself when he is alone.

2. There is no evil to which the mean man, dwelling retired, will not proceed, but when he sees a superior man, he instantly tries to disguise himself, concealing his evil, and displaying what is good. The other beholds him, as if he saw his heart and reins;—of what use *is his disguise?* This is an instance of the saying—" What truly is within will be manifested without." Therefore, the superior man must be watchful over himself when he is alone.

3. Tsăng the philosopher said, " What ten eyes behold, what ten hands point to, is to be regarded with reverence!"

4. Riches adorn a house, and virtue adorns the person. The mind is expanded, and the body is at ease. Therefore, the superior man must make his thoughts sincere.

The above sixth chapter of commentary explains making the thoughts sincere.

thoughts obtains, when they move without effort to what is right and wrong; and, in order to this, a man must be specially on his guard in his solitary moments. 2. *An enforcement of the concluding clause in the last paragraph.* " His heart and reins " is, literally, " the lungs and liver," but with the meaning which we attach to the expression substituted for it. The Chinese make the lungs the seat of righteousness, and the liver the seat of benevolence. 3. The use of " Tsăng the philosopher " at the beginning of this paragraph (and extending, perhaps, over to the next) should suffice to show that the whole work is not his, as assumed by Choo He. " Ten " is a round number, put for *many.* The recent commentator, Lo Chung-fan, refers Tsăng's expressions to the multitude of spiritual beings, servants of Heaven or God, who dwell in the regions of the air, and are continually beholding men's conduct. But they are probably only an emphatic way of exhibiting what is said in the preceding paragraph. 4. This paragraph is commonly referred to Tsăng Sin, but whether correctly so or not cannot be positively affirmed. It is of the same purport as the two preceding, showing that hypocrisy is of no use. Compare Mencius, VII. Pt. I. xxi. 4. It is only the first of these paragraphs from which we can in any way ascertain the views of the writer on making the thoughts sincere. The other paragraphs contain only illustration or enforcement. Now, the gist of the first paragraph seems to be in "allowing no self-deception." After knowledge has been carried to the utmost, this remains to be done, and it is not true that, when knowledge has been completed, the thoughts become sincere. This fact overthrows Choo He's interpretation of the vexed passages in what he calls the text of Confucius.

VII. 1. What is meant by "The cultivation of the person depends on rectifying the mind," may be thus illustrated:—If a man be under the influence of passion, he will be incorrect in his conduct. He will be the same, if he is under the influence of terror, or under the influence of fond regard, or under that of sorrow and distress.

2. When the mind is not present, we look and do not see; we hear and do not understand; we eat and do not know the taste of what we eat.

3. This is what is meant by saying that the cultivation of the person depends on the rectifying of the mind.

The above seventh chapter of commentary explains rectifying the mind and cultivating the person.

VIII. 1. What is meant by "The regulation of one's family depends on the cultivation of his person," is this: —Men are partial where they feel affection and love; partial where they despise and dislike; partial where they stand in awe and reverence; partial where they feel sorrow and compassion; partial where they are arrogant and rude. Thus it is that there are few men in the world who love, and at the same time know the bad qualities of *the object of their love,* or who hate, and yet know the excellences of *the object of their hatred.*

2. Hence it is said, in the common adage, "A man does not know the wickedness of his son; he does not know the richness of his growing corn."

3. This is what is meant by saying that if the person be not cultivated, a man cannot regulate his family.

The above eighth chapter of commentary explains cultivating the person and regulating the family.

IX. 1. What is meant by "In order rightly to govern

Let the student examine his note appended to this chapter, and he will see that Choo was not unconscious of this pinch of the difficulty.

7. ON PERSONAL CULTIVATION AS DEPENDENT ON THE RECTIFICATION OF THE MIND.

8. THE NECESSITY OF CULTIVATING THE PERSON, IN ORDER TO THE REGULATION OF THE FAMILY. The lesson here is evidently, that men are continually falling into error, in consequence of the partiality of their feelings and affections. How this error affects their personal cultivation, and interferes with the regulating of their families, is not specially indicated.

9. ON REGULATING THE FAMILY AS THE MEANS TO THE WELL-ORDER-

his State, it is necessary first to regulate his family," is this:—It is not possible for one to teach others, while he cannot teach his own family. Therefore, the ruler, without going beyond his family, completes the lessons for the State. There is filial piety:—therewith the sovereign should be served. There is fraternal submission:—therewith elders and superiors should be served. There is kindness:—therewith the multitude should be treated.

2. In the Announcement to K'ang, it is said, "*Act* as if you were watching over an infant." If a mother is really anxious about it, though she may not hit *exactly the wants of her infant*, she will not be far from doing so. There never has been a *girl* who learned to bring up a child, that she might afterwards marry.

3. From the loving *example* of one family, a whole State becomes loving, and from its courtesies, the whole State becomes courteous, while, from the ambition and perverseness of the one man, the whole State may be led to rebellious disorder;—such is the nature of the influence. This verifies the saying, "Affairs may be ruined by a single sentence; a kingdom may be settled by its one man."

4. Yaou and Shun led on the empire with benevolence, and the people followed them. Këë and Chow led on the empire with violence, and the people followed them. The orders which these issued were contrary to the practices which they loved, and so the people did not follow them. On this account, the ruler must himself be possessed of the *good* qualities, and then he may require them

ING OF THE STATE. 1. *There is here implied the necessity of self-cultivation to the rule, both of the family and of the State; and that being supposed to exist, it is shown how the virtues that secure the regulation of the family have their corresponding virtues in the wider sphere of the State.* 2. See the Shoo-king, Pt V. Bk IX. 9. Both in the Shoo-king and here, some verb, like *act*, must be supplied. This paragraph seems designed to show that *the ruler must be carried on to his object by an inward, unconstrained feeling, like that of the mother for her infant.* Lo Chung-fan insists on this as harmonizing with "to love the people," as the second object proposed in the Great Learning. 3. *How certainly and rapidly the influence of the family extends to the State.* The "one man" is the ruler. "I, the one man," is a way in which the emperor speaks of himself; see Analects XX. i. 5. 4. *An illustration of the last part of the last paragraph.* But from the examples cited, the sphere of influence is extended from the State to the empire, and the family, moreover, does not

in the people. He must not have *the bad qualities* in himself, and then he may require that they shall not be in the people. Never has there been a man, who, not having reference to his own character and wishes in dealing with others, was able effectually to instruct them.

5. Thus we see how the government of the State depends on the regulation of the family.

6. In the Book of Poetry, it is said, "That peach tree, so delicate and elegant! How luxuriant is its foliage! This girl is going to her husband's house. She will rightly order her household." Let the household be rightly ordered, and then the people of the State may be taught.

7. In the Book of Poetry, it is said, "They can discharge their duties to their elder brothers. They can discharge their duties to their younger brothers." Let the ruler discharge his duties to his elder and younger brothers, and then he may teach the people of the State.

8. In the Book of Poetry, it is said, "In his deportment there is nothing wrong; he rectifies all the people of the State." Yes; when the ruler, as a father, a son, and a brother, is a model, then the people imitate him.

9. This is what is meant by saying, "The government of his kingdom depends on his regulation of the family."

The above ninth chapter of commentary explains regulating the family, and governing the kingdom.

X. 1. What is meant by "The making the whole empire peaceful and happy depends on the government of

intervene between the empire and the ruler. 6. See the She-king, Pt I. Bk I. vi. 3. The ode celebrates the wife of King Wăn, and the happy influence of their family government. 7. See the She-king, Pt II. Bk II. ix. 3. The ode was sung at entertainments, when the emperor feasted the princes. It celebrates their virtues. 8. See the She-king, Pt I. Bk XIV. iii. 3. It celebrates, according to Choo He, the praises of some *kwn-tsze*, or ruler.

10. ON THE WELL-ORDERING OF THE STATE, AND MAKING THE WHOLE EMPIRE PEACEFUL AND HAPPY. The key to this chapter is in the phrase "a measuring square," the principle of reciprocity, the doing to others as we would that they should do to us, though here, as elsewhere, it is put forth negatively. It is implied in the fifth paragraph of the last chapter, but it is here discussed at length, and shown in its highest application. The following analysis of the chapter is translated freely from a native work:—" This chapter explains the well-ordering of the State, and

his State," is this:—When the sovereign behaves to his aged, as the aged should be behaved to, the people become filial; when the sovereign behaves to his elders, as elders should be behaved to, the people learn brotherly submission; when the sovereign treats compassionately the young and helpless, the people do the same. Thus the ruler has a principle with which, as with a measuring square, he may regulate his conduct.

the tranquillization of the empire. The greatest stress is to be laid on the phrase—*the measuring square*. That, and the expression in the general commentary—*loving and hating what the people love and hate, and not thinking only of the profit*, exhaust the teaching of the chapter. It is divided into five parts. The *first*, embracing the two first paragraphs, teaches, that the way to make the empire tranquil and happy is in the principle of the measuring square. The *second* part embraces three paragraphs, and teaches that the application of the measuring square is seen in loving, and hating, in common sympathy with the people. The consequences of *losing* and *gaining* are mentioned for the first time in the fourth paragraph to wind up the chapter so far, showing that the decree of Heaven goes or remains, according as the people's hearts are lost or gained. The *third* part embraces eight paragraphs, and teaches that the most important result of loving and hating in common with the people is seen in making the *root* the primary subject, and the *branch* only secondary. Here, in paragraph eleven, mention is again made of *gaining* and *losing*, illustrating the meaning of the quotation in it, and showing that to the collection or dissipation of the people the decree of Heaven is attached. The *fourth* part consists of five paragraphs, and exhibits the extreme results of loving and hating, as shared with the people, or on one's own private feeling, and it has special reference to the sovereign's employment of ministers, because there is nothing in the principle more important than that. The nineteenth paragraph speaks of *gaining and losing*, for the third time, showing that from the fourth paragraph downwards, in reference both to the hearts of the people and the decree of Heaven, the application or non-application of the principle of the *measuring square* depends on the mind of the sovereign. The *fifth* part embraces the other paragraphs. Because the root of the evil of a sovereign's not applying that principle, lies in his not knowing how wealth is produced, and employs mean men for that object, the distinction between righteousness and profit is here much insisted on, the former bringing with it all advantages, and the latter leading to all evil consequences. Thus the sovereign is admonished, and it is seen how to be careful of his virtue is the root of the principle of the *measuring square;* and his loving and hating, in common sympathy with the people, is its reality."

1. There is here no progress of thought, but a repetition of what has been insisted on in the two last chapters. But it having been seen that the ruler's example is so influential, it follows that the minds of all men are the same in sympathy and tendency. He has then only to take his own mind, and measure therewith the minds of others. If he act accordingly,

2. What a man dislikes in his superiors, let him not display in the treatment of his inferiors; what he dislikes in inferiors, let him not display in the service of his superiors; what he hates in those who are before him, let him not therewith precede those who are behind him; what he hates in those who are behind him, let him not therewith follow those who are before him; what he hates to receive on the right, let him not bestow on the left; what he hates to receive on the left, let him not bestow on the right:—this is what is called "The principle, with which, as with a measuring square, to regulate one's conduct."

3. In the Book of Poetry, it is said, "How much to be rejoiced in are these princes, the parents of the people!" When *a prince* loves what the people love, and hates what the people hate, then is he what is called the parent of the people.

4. In the Book of Poetry, it is said, "Lofty is that southern hill, with its rugged masses of rocks! Full of majesty are you, O *grand*-teacher Yin, the people all look up to you." Rulers of kingdoms may not neglect to be careful. If they deviate *to a mean selfishness*, they will be a disgrace in the empire.

5. In the Book of Poetry, it is said, "Before the sovereigns of the Yin *dynasty* had lost the *hearts of the* people, they were the mates of God. Take warning from *the house of* Yin. The great decree is not easily *preserved.*" This shows that, by gaining the people, the kingdom is gained, and, by losing the people, the kingdom is lost.

6. On this account, the ruler will first take pains about *his own* virtue. Possessing virtue will give him the people. Possessing the people will give him the territory. Pos-

the grand result—the empire tranquil and happy—will ensue. 2. *A lengthened description of the principle of reciprocity.* 3. See the She-king, Pt II. Bk II. v. 3. The ode is one that was sung at festivals, and celebrates the virtues of the princes present. 4. See the She-king, Pt II. Bk IV. vii. 1. The ode complains of the Emperor Yew, for his employing unworthy ministers. 5. See the She-king, Pt III. Bk I. i. 6. The ode is supposed to be addressed to King Ch'ing, to stimulate him to imitate the virtues of his grandfather Wăn. " Yin,"="the sovereigns of the Yin dynasty." The capital of the Shang dynasty was changed to Yin by P'wan-kang, B.C. 1400, after which the dynasty was so denominated. 6. "Virtue" here, according to Choo He, is the "illustrious virtue" at the beginning of the book. His opponents say that it is the exhibition of virtue; that is, of filial piety, brotherly submission, &c. This is more in

sessing the territory will give him its wealth. Possessing the wealth, he will have resources for expenditure.

7. Virtue is the root; wealth is the result.

8. If he make the root his secondary object, and the result his primary, he will *only* wrangle with his people, and teach them rapine.

9. Hence, the accumulation of wealth is the way to scatter the people; and the letting it be scattered among them is the way to collect the people.

10. And hence, the ruler's words going forth contrary to right, will come back to him in the same way, and wealth, gotten by improper ways, will take its departure by the same.

11. In the Announcement to K'ang, it is said, "The decree indeed may not always rest on *us;*" that is, goodness obtains the decree, and the want of goodness loses it.

12. In the Book of Ts'oo, it is said, "The kingdom of Ts'oo does not consider that to be valuable. It values, *instead*, its good men."

13. *Duke Wăn's* uncle, Fan, said, "Our fugitive does not account that to be precious. What he considers precious, is the affection due to his parent."

14. In the Declaration *of the duke of* Ts'in, it is said, "Let me have but one minister, plain and sincere, not *pretending to* other abilities, but with a simple, upright mind; and possessed of generosity, *regarding* the talents

---

harmony with the first paragraph of the chapter. 10. The "words" are to be understood of governmental orders and enactments. Our proverb—"Goods ill-gotten go ill-spent" might be translated by the characters in the text. 11. See the Book quoted, p. 23. 12. The Book of Ts'oo is found in the "Narratives of the States," a collection purporting to be of the Chow dynasty, and, in relation to the other States, what Confucius' "Spring and Autumn" is to Loo. The exact words of the text do not occur, but they could easily be constructed from the narrative. An officer of Ts'oo being sent on an embassy to Tsin, the minister who received him asked about a famous girdle of Ts'oo, how much it was worth. The officer replied that his country did not look on such things as its treasures, but on its able and virtuous ministers. 13. "Uncle Fan;" that is, uncle to Wăn, the duke of Ts'in. See Analects XIV. xvi. Wăn is the "fugitive." In the early part of his life he was a fugitive, and suffered many vicissitudes of fortune. Once, the duke of Ts'in having offered to help him, when he was in mourning for his father who had expelled him, to recover Tsin, his uncle Fan gave the reply in the text. The *that* in the translation refers to "getting the kingdom." 14. "The declaration *of the duke of*

of others as though he himself possessed them, and, where he finds accomplished and perspicacious men, loving them in his heart more than his mouth expresses, and really showing himself able to bear *and employ them:*—such a minister will be able to preserve my sons and grandsons, and black-haired people, and benefits likewise to the kingdom may well be looked for from him. But *if it be his character,* when he finds men of ability, to be jealous and hate them; and, when he finds accomplished and perspicacious men, to oppose them and not allow their advancement, showing himself really not able to bear them:—such a minister will not be able to protect my sons and grandsons, and black-haired people; and may he not also be pronounced dangerous *to the State?"*

15. It is only the truly virtuous man who can send away such a man and banish him, driving him out among the barbarous tribes around, determined not to dwell along with him in the Middle kingdom. This is in accordance with the saying, "It is only the truly virtuous man who can love or who can hate others."

16. To see men of worth and not be able to raise them to office; to raise them to office, but not to do so quickly:—this is disrespectful. To see bad men and not be able to remove them; to remove them, but not to do so to a distance:—This is weakness.

17. To love those whom men hate, and to hate those whom men love; this is to outrage the natural feeling of men. Calamities cannot fail to come down on him who does so.

18. Thus *we see* that the sovereign has a great course *to pursue.* He must show entire self-devotion and sin-

---

Ts'in is the last book in the Shoo-king. It was made by one of the dukes of Ts'in to his officers, after he had sustained a great disaster, in consequence of neglecting the advice of his most faithful minister. Between the text here, and that which we find in the Shoo-king, there are some differences, but they are unimportant. 17. This is spoken of the ruler not having respect to the common feelings of the people in his employment of ministers, and the consequences thereof to himself. 18. *This paragraph speaks generally of the primal cause of gaining and losing, and shows how the principle of the measuring square must have its root in the ruler's mind.* The great course is explained by Choo He as—" the art of occupying the throne, and therein cultivating himself and governing others." Ying-tă says it is—" the course by which he practises filial piety, fraternal duty,

cerity to attain it, and by pride and extravagance he will fail of it.

19. There is a great course *also* for the production of wealth. Let the producers be many and the consumers few. Let there be activity in the production, and economy in the expenditure. Then the wealth will always be sufficient.

20. The virtuous *ruler*, by means of his wealth, makes himself more distinguished. The vicious ruler accumulates wealth, at the expense of his life.

21. Never has there been a case of the sovereign loving benevolence, and the people not loving righteousness. Never has there been a case where the people have loved righteousness, and the affairs of the sovereign have not been carried to completion. And never has there been a case where the wealth in such a State, collected in the treasuries and arsenals, did not continue in the sovereign's possession.

22. The officer Măng Heen said, "He who keeps horses and a carriage does not look after fowls and pigs. The family which keeps its stores of ice does not rear cattle or sheep. So, the house which possesses a hundred chariots should not keep a minister to look out for imposts that he may lay them on the people. Than to have such a minister, it were better for that house to have one who should rob it *of its revenues.*" This is in accordance with the saying:—"In a State, *pecuniary* gain is not to be considered to be prosperity, but its prosperity *will* be found in righteousness."

benevolence, and righteousness." 19. This is understood by K'ang-shing as requiring the promotion of agriculture; and that is included, but does not exhaust the meaning. The consumers are the salaried officers of the government. The sentiment of the whole is good;—where there is cheerful industry in the people, and an economical administration of the government, the finances will be flourishing. 20. The sentiment here is substantially the same as in paragraphs seven and eight. The old interpretation is different:—"The virtuous man uses his wealth so as to make his person distinguished. He who is not virtuous, toils with his body to increase his wealth." 21. This shows how the people respond to the influence of the ruler, and that benevolence, even to the scattering of his wealth on the part of the latter, is the way to permanent prosperity and wealth. 22. Hëen was the honorary epithet of Chung-sun Mëě, a worthy minister of Loo, under the two dukes, who ruled before the birth of Confucius. His sayings, quoted here, were preserved by tradition or recorded in some

23. When he who presides over a State or a family makes his revenues his chief business, he must be under the influence of some small, mean man. He may consider this man to be good; but when such a person is employed in the administration of a State or family, calamities *from Heaven,* and injuries *from men,* will befall it together, and, though a good man may take his place, he will not be able to remedy the evil. This illustrates *again* the saying, " In a State, gain is not to be considered prosperity, but its prosperity will be found in righteousness."

The above tenth chapter of commentary explains the government of the State, and the making the empire peaceful and happy.

There are thus, in all, ten chapters of commentary, the first four of which discuss, in a general manner, the scope of the principal topic of the Work; while the other six go particularly into an exhibition of the work required in its subordinate branches. The fifth chapter contains the important subject of comprehending true excellence, and the sixth, what is the foundation of the attainment of true sincerity. Those two chapters demand the especial attention of the learner. Let not the reader despise them because of their simplicity.

work which is now lost. On a scholar's being first called to office, he was gifted by his prince with a carriage and four horses. He was then supposed to withdraw from petty ways of getting wealth. The high officers of a State kept ice for use in their funeral rites and sacrifices.

THE DOCTRINE OF THE MEAN.

My master, the philosopher Ch'ing, says, "Being without inclination to either side is called CHUNG; *admitting of no change is called* YUNG." *By* CHUNG *is denoted the correct course to be pursued by all under heaven; by* YUNG *is denoted the fixed principle regulating all under heaven. This work contains the law of the mind, which was handed down from one to another, in the Confucian school, till Tsze-sze, fearing lest in the course of time errors should arise about it, committed it to writing, and delivered it to Mencius. The book first speaks of one principle; it next spreads this out, and embraces all things; finally, it returns and gathers them all up under the one principle. Unroll it, and it fills the universe; roll it up, and it retires and lies hid in mysteriousness. The relish of it is inexhaustible. The whole of it is solid learning. When the skilful reader has explored it with delight till he has apprehended it, he may carry it into practice all his life, and will find that it cannot be exhausted.*

THE TITLE OF THE WORK.—*Chung Yung,* "The Doctrine of the Mean." It is hardly possible amid the conflicting views of native scholars, and the various meanings of which the terms are capable, to decide categorically on the exact force of the terms in the title. The Work treats of the human mind:—in its state of *chung,* absolutely correct, as it is in itself; and in its state of harmony, acting *ad extra,* according to its correct nature. —In the version of the Work, given in the collection of "*Mémoires concernant l'histoire, les sciences, &c., des Chinois.*" vol. L, it is styled—"*Juste Milieu.*" Remusat calls it "*L'invariable Milieu,*" after Ch'ing E. Intorcetta, and his coadjutors, call it—"*Medium constans vel sempiternum.*" The book treats, they say, "*De* MEDIO SEMPITERNO, *sive de aurea medi-*

CHAPTER I. 1. What Heaven has conferred is called THE NATURE; an accordance with this nature is called THE PATH *of duty;* the regulation of this path is called INSTRUCTION.

2. The path may not be left for an instant. If it could be left, it would not be the path. On this account, the superior man does not wait till he sees things, to be cautious, nor till he hears things, to be apprehensive.

3. There is nothing more visible than what is secret, and nothing more manifest than what is minute. Therefore, the superior man is watchful over himself, when he is alone.

4. While there are no stirrings of pleasure, anger, sorrow, or joy, the mind may be said to be in the state of EQUILIBRIUM. When those feelings have been stirred, and they act in their due degree, there ensues what may be

---

acritate illa, quæ est, ut ait Cicero, inter nimium et parvum, constanter et omnibus in rebus tenenda." Morrison says, "*Chung Yung*, the constant (golden) medium." Collie calls it—" The golden medium." The objection which I have to all these names is, that from them it would appear as if the first term were a noun, and the other a qualifying adjective, whereas they are co-ordinate terms.

1. It has been stated, in the prolegomena, that the current division of the Chung Yung into chapters was made by Choo He, as well as their subdivision into paragraphs. The thirty-three chapters, which embrace the work, are again arranged by him in five divisions, as will be seen from his supplementary notes. The first and last chapters are complete in themselves, as the introduction and conclusion of the treatise. The second part contains ten chapters; the third, nine; and the fourth, twelve.

Par. 1. *The principles of duty have their root in the evidenced will of Heaven, and their full exhibition in the teaching of sages.* What is taught seems to be this:—To man belongs a moral nature, conferred on him by Heaven or God, by which he is constituted a law to himself. But as he is prone to deviate from the path in which, according to his nature, he should go, wise and good men—sages—have appeared, to explain and regulate this, helping all by their instructions to walk in it.

Par. 2. *The path indicated by the nature may never be left, and the superior man—he who would embody all principles of right and duty—exercises a most sedulous care that he may attain thereto.*

Par. 3. It seems to me that the secrecy here must be in the recesses of one's own heart, and the minute things, the springs of thought and stirrings of purpose there. The full development of what is intended here is probably to be found in all the subsequent passages about "sincerity."

Par. 4. "This," says Choo He, "speaks of the virtue of the nature and passions, to illustrate the meaning of the statement that the path may not be left." It is difficult to translate the paragraph, because it is difficult to understand it.

called the state of HARMONY. This EQUILIBRIUM is the great root *from which grow all the human actings* in the world, and this HARMONY is the universal path *which they all should pursue.*

5. Let the states of equilibrium and harmony exist in perfection, and a happy order will prevail throughout heaven and earth, and all things will be nourished and flourish.

In the first chapter which is given above, Tsze-sze states the views which had been handed down to him, as the basis of his discourse. First, it shows clearly how the path of duty is to be traced to its origin in Heaven, and is unchangeable, while the substance of it is provided in ourselves, and may not be departed from. Next, it speaks of the importance of preserving and nourishing this, and of exercising a watchful self-scrutiny with reference to it. Finally, it speaks of the meritorious achievements and transforming influence of sage and spiritual men in their highest extent. The wish of Tsze-sze was that hereby the learner should direct his thoughts inwards, and by searching in himself, there find these truths, so that he might put aside all outward tempta-

Par. 5. On this Intorcetta and his colleagues observe:—"*Quis non ridet eo dumtaxat collimasse philosophum, ut hominis naturam, quam ab origine sua rectam, sed deinde lapsam et depravatam passim Sinenses docent, ad primaevum innocentiae statum reducere? Atque ita reliquas res creatas, homini jam rebelles, et in ejusdem ruinam armatas, ad pristinum obsequium veluti revocaret. Hoc f. I. s. I. libri Ta Hëŏ, hoc item hic et alibi non semel indicat. Etsi autem nesciret philosophus nos a prima felicitate propter peccatum primi parentis excidisse, tamen et tot rerum quae adversantur et infestae sunt homini, et ipsius naturae humanae ad deteriora tam pronae, longo usu et contemplatione didicisse videtur, non posse hoc universum, quod homo vitiatus quodam modo vitiarat, connaturali suae integritati et ordini restitui, nisi prius ipse homo per victoriam sui ipsius, eam, quam amiserat, integritatem et ordinem recuperaret.*" I fancied something of the same kind, before reading their note. According to Choo He, the paragraph describes the Work and influence of sage and spiritual men in the highest issues. The subject is developed in the fourth part of the Work, in very extravagant and mystical language. The study of it will modify very much our assent to the views in the above passage. There is in this whole chapter a mixture of sense and mysticism,—of what may be grasped, and what tantalizes and eludes the mind.

CONCLUDING NOTE. The writer Yang, quoted here, was a distinguished scholar and author in the reign of Ying-Tsung, A.D. 1064—1085. He was a disciple of Ch'ing Haou, and a friend both of him and his brother, E.

tions *appealing to his selfishness, and fill up the measure of the goodness which is natural to him.* This chapter is what the writer Yang called it,—" *The sum of the whole work.*" In the ten chapters which follow, Tsze-sze quotes the words of the Master to complete the meaning of this.

II. 1. Chung-ne said, "The superior man *embodies* the course of the Mean; the mean man acts contrary to the course of the Mean.

2. "The superior man's embodying the course of the Mean is because he is a superior man, and so always maintains the Mean. The mean man's acting contrary to the course of the Mean is because he is a mean man, and has no caution."

III. The Master said, "Perfect is the virtue which is according to the Mean! Rare have they long been among the people, who could practise it!"

IV. I. The Master said, "I know how it is that the path *of the Mean* is not walked in:—The knowing go beyond it, and the stupid do not come up to it. I know how it is that the path of the Mean is not understood:—The men of talents and virtue go beyond it, and the worthless do not come up to it.

2. "There is no body but eats and drinks. But they are few who can distinguish flavours."

2. ONLY THE SUPERIOR MAN CAN FOLLOW THE MEAN; THE MEAN MAN IS ALWAYS VIOLATING IT. 1. Why Confucius should here be quoted by his designation, or marriage name, is a moot-point. It is said by some that disciples might in this way refer to their teacher, and a grandson to his grandfather, but such a rule is constituted probable on the strength of this instance, and that in chapter xxx. Others say that it is the honorary designation of the sage, and = the "Father *ne*," which Duke Gae used in reference to Confucius, in eulogizing him after his death. See the Le-ke, II. Pt L iii. 43. This, and the ten chapters which follow, all quote the words of Confucius with reference to the *Chung-yung*, to explain the meaning of the first chapter, and "though there is no connection of composition between them," says Choo He, " they are all related by their meaning."

3. THE RARITY, LONG EXISTING IN CONFUCIUS' TIME, OF THE PRACTICE OF THE MEAN. See the Analects VI. xxvii. K'ang-shing and Ying-tă take the last clause as=" few can practise it long." But the view in the translation is better.

4. HOW IT WAS THAT FEW WERE ABLE TO PRACTISE THE MEAN. 2. We have here not a comparison, but an illustration which may help

V. The Master said, "Alas! How is the path of the Mean untrodden!"

VI. The Master said, "There was Shun:—He indeed was greatly wise! Shun loved to question *others*, and to study their words, though they might be shallow. He concealed what was bad *in them*, and displayed what was good. He took hold of their two extremes, *determined* the Mean, and employed it in *his government of* the people. It was by this that he was Shun!"

VII. The Master said, "Men all say, 'We are wise;' but being driven forward and taken in a net, a trap, or a pitfall, they know not how to escape. Men all say, 'We are wise;' but happening to choose the course of the Mean, they are not able to keep it for a round month."

VIII. The Master said, "This was the manner of

to an understanding of the former paragraph, though it does not seem very apt. People don't know the true flavour of what they eat and drink, but they need not go beyond that to learn it. So, the Mean belongs to all the actions of ordinary life, and might be discerned and practised in them, without looking for it in extraordinary things.

5. Choo He says:—"From not being understood, therefore it is not practised." According to K'ang-shing, the remark is a lament that there was no intelligent sovereign to teach the path. But the two views are reconcileable.

6. HOW SHUN PURSUED THE COURSE OF THE MEAN. This example of Shun, it seems to me, is adduced in opposition to the knowing of chapter iv. Shun, though a sage, invited the opinions of all men, and found truth of the highest value in their simplest sayings, and was able to determine from them the course of the Mean. "The two extremes" are understood by K'ang-shing of the two errors of exceeding and coming short of the Mean. Choo He makes them—"the widest differences in the opinions which he received." I conceive the meaning to be that he examined the answers which he got, in their entirety, from beginning to end. Compare Analects IX. vii. His concealing what was bad, and displaying what was good, was alike to encourage people to speak freely to him. K'ang-shing makes the last sentence to turn on the meaning of Shun when applied as an honorary epithet of the dead, = "Full, all-accomplished;" but Shun was so named when he was alive.

7. THEIR CONTRARY CONDUCT SHOWS MEN'S IGNORANCE OF THE COURSE AND NATURE OF THE MEAN. The first "We are wise" is to be understood with a general reference,—" We are wise," *i.e.*, we can very well take care of ourselves. Yet the presumption of such a profession is seen in men's not being able to take care of themselves. The application of this illustration is then made to the subject in hand, the second "We are wise," being to be specially understood, with reference to the subject of the Mean. The conclusion in both parts is left to be drawn by the reader for himself.

Hwuy:—he made choice of the Mean, and whenever he got hold of what was good, he clasped it firmly, as if wearing it on his breast, and did not lose it."

IX. The Master said, "The empire, its States, and its families may be perfectly ruled; dignities and emoluments may be declined; naked weapons may be trampled under the feet; but the course of the Mean cannot be attained to."

X. 1. Tsze-loo asked about forcefulness.

2. The Master said, "Do you mean the forcefulness of the South, the forcefulness of the North, or the forcefulness which you should cultivate yourself?

3. "To show forbearance and gentleness in teaching others; and not to revenge unreasonable conduct:—this is the forcefulness of Southern regions, and the good man makes it his study.

4. "To lie under arms; and meet death without regret:—this is the forcefulness of Northern regions, and the forceful make it their study.

8. How HWUY HELD FAST THE COURSE OF THE MEAN. Here the example of Hwuy is likewise adduced in opposition to those mentioned in chapter iv.

9. THE DIFFICULTY OF ATTAINING TO THE COURSE OF THE MEAN. "The empire;" we should say—"empires," but the Chinese know only of *one* empire, and hence this name, "all under heaven," for it. The empire is made up of States, and each State, of Families. See the Analects V. vii.; XII. xx.

10. ON FORCEFULNESS IN ITS RELATION TO THE MEAN. In the Analects we find Tsze-loo, on various occasions, putting forward the subject of his valour, and claiming, on the ground of it, such praise as the Master awarded to Hwuy. We may suppose, with the old interpreters, that hearing Hwuy commended, as in chapter viii., he wanted to know whether Confucius would not allow that he also could, with his forceful character, seize and hold fast the Mean. 1. I have ventured to coin the term "forcefulness." Choo He defines the original term correctly—"the name of strength, sufficient to overcome others." 3. That climate and situation have an influence on character is not to be denied, and the Chinese notions on the subject may be seen in the amplification of the ninth of K'ang-he's celebrated maxims. But to speak of their effects, as Confucius here does, is extravagant. The barbarism of the south, according to the interpretation mentioned above, could not have been described by him in these terms. The forcefulness of mildness and forbearance, thus described, is held to come short of the Mean; and therefore "the good man" is taken with a low and light meaning, far short of what it has in paragraph five. 4. This forcefulness of the north, it is said, is in excess of the Mean, and the "therefore," at the beginning of paragraph five, —

5. "Therefore, the superior man cultivates *a friendly* harmony, without being weak. How firm is he in his forcefulness! He stands erect in the middle, without inclining to either side.—How firm is he in his forcefulness! When good principles prevail in the government of his country, he does not change from what he was in retirement.—How firm is he in his forcefulness!" When bad principles prevail in the country, he maintains his course to death without changing.—How firm is he in his forcefulness!"

XI. 1. The Master said, "To live in obscurity, and yet practise wonders, in order to be mentioned with honour in future ages;—this is what I do not do.

2. "The good man tries to proceed according to the right path, but when he has gone half-way, he abandons it;—I am not able *so* to stop.

3. "The superior man accords with the course of the Mean. Though he may be all unknown, unregarded by the world, he feels no regret.—It is only the sage who is able for this."

"these two kinds of forcefulness being thus respectively in defect and excess." This illustrates the forcefulness which is in exact accord with the Mean, in the individual's treatment of others, in his regulation of himself, and in relation to public affairs.

11. ONLY THE SAGE CAN COME UP TO THE REQUIREMENTS OF THE MEAN. 3. The name *Keun-tsze* has here its very highest signification, and = the "sage," in the last clause. It will be observed how Confucius declines saying that he had himself attained to this highest style.— "With this chapter," says Choo He, "the quotations by Tsze-sse of the Master's words, to explain the meaning of the first chapter, stop. The great object of the work is to set forth wisdom, benevolent virtue, and valour, as the three grand virtues whereby entrance is effected into the path of the Mean, and therefore, at its commencement, they are illustrated by reference to Shun, Yen Yuen, and Tsze-loo, Shun possessing the wisdom, Yen Yuen the benevolence, and Tsze-loo the valour. If one of these virtues be absent, there is no way of advancing to the path, and perfecting the virtue. This will be found fully treated of in the twentieth chapter." So, Choo He. The student forming a judgment for himself, however, will not see very distinctly any reference to these cardinal virtues. The utterances of the sage illustrate the phrase *Chung-Yung*, showing that the course of the Mean had fallen out of observance, some overshooting it, and others coming short of it. When we want some precise directions how to attain to it, we come finally to the conclusion that only the sage is capable of doing so. We greatly want teaching more practical and precise.

XII. 1. The way which the superior man pursues, reaches wide and far, and yet is secret.

2. Common men and women, however ignorant, may intermeddle with the knowledge of it; yet in its utmost reaches, there is that which even the sage does not know. Common men and women, however much below the ordinary standard of character, can carry it into practice; yet in its utmost reaches, there is that which even the sage is not able to carry into practice. Great as heaven and earth are, men still find some things in them with which to be dissatisfied. Thus it is, that were the superior man to speak of his way in all its greatness, nothing in the world would be found able to embrace it; and were he to speak of it in its minuteness, nothing in the world would be found able to split it.

3. It is said in the Book of Poetry, "The hawk flies up to heaven; the fishes leap in the deep." This expresses how this *way* is seen above and below.

4. The way of the superior man may be found, in its simple elements, in the intercourse of common men and women; but in its utmost reaches, it shines brightly through heaven and earth.

The twelfth chapter above contains the words of Tsze-sze, and is designed to illustrate what is said in the first

12. THE COURSE OF THE MEAN REACHES FAR AND WIDE, BUT YET IS SECRET. With this chapter the third part of the work commences, and the first sentence may be regarded as its text. Mysteries have been found in the terms of it; but I believe that the author simply intended to say, that the way of the superior man reaching everywhere,—embracing all duties,—yet had its secret spring and seat in the Heaven-gifted nature, the individual consciousness of duty in every man. 2. I confess to be all at sea in the study of this paragraph. Choo He quotes from the scholar How, that what the superior man fails to know, was exemplified in Confucius having to ask about ceremonies, and about offices; and what he fails to practise, was exemplified in Confucius not being on the throne, and in Yaou and Shun's being dissatisfied that they could not make every individual enjoy the benefits of their rule. He adds his own opinion, that wherein men complained of Heaven and Earth, was the partiality of their operations in overshadowing and supporting, producing and completing, the heat of summer, the cold of winter, &c. If such things were intended by the writer, we can only regret the vagueness of his language, and the want of coherence in his argument. See the She-king, Pt III. Bk I. v. 3. The ode is in praise of the virtue of King Wăn. The application of the words of the ode does appear strange.

chapter, that "The path may not be left." In the eight chapters which follow, he quotes, in a miscellaneous way, the words of Confucius to illustrate it.

XIII. 1. The Master said, "The path is not far from man. When men try to pursue a course, which is far from the common indications of consciousness, this course cannot be considered THE PATH.

2. "In the Book of Poetry, it is said, 'In hewing an axe-handle, in hewing an axe-handle, the pattern is not far off.' We grasp one axe-handle to hew the other, and yet, if we look askance from the one to the other, we may consider them as apart. Therefore, the superior man governs men, according to their nature, with what is proper to them, and as soon as they change *what is wrong*, he stops.

3. "When one cultivates to the utmost the principles of his nature, and exercises them on the principle of reciprocity, he is not far from the path. What you do not like, when done to yourself, do not do to others.

4. "In the way of the superior man there are four things, to not one of which have I as yet attained.—To serve my father as I would require my son to serve me: to this I have not attained; to serve my prince as I would require my minister to serve me: to this I have not attained; to serve my elder brother as I would require my younger brother to serve me: to this I have not attained; to set the example in behaving to a friend as I would require him to behave to me: to this I have not attained. Earnest in practising the ordinary virtues, and careful in speaking about them, if, in his practice, he

---

13. THE PATH OF THE MEAN IS NOT FAR TO SEEK. EACH MAN HAS THE LAW OF IT IN HIMSELF. AND IT IS TO BE PURSUED WITH EARNEST SINCERITY. 1. Literally we should read,—"When men practise a course, and wish to be far from men." The meaning is as in the translation. 2. See the She-king, Pt I. Bk XV. v. 2. The object of the paragraph seems to be to show that the rule for dealing with men, according to the principles of the Mean, is nearer to us than the axe in the hand is to the one which is to be cut down with, and fashioned after, it. The branch is hewn, and its form altered from its natural one. Not so with man. The change in him only brings him to his proper state. 3. Compare Analects, IV. xv. 4. Compare Analects, VII. i., ii., xix., *et al.* The admissions made by Confucius here are important to those who find it necessary, in their intercourse with the Chinese, to insist on his having been, like other men, compassed with

has anything defective, the superior man dares not but exert himself; and if, in his words, he has any excess, he dares not allow himself such license. Thus his words have respect to his actions, and his actions have respect to his words; is it not just an entire sincerity which marks the superior man?"

XIV. 1. The superior man does what is proper to the station in which he is: he does not desire to go beyond this.

2. In a position of wealth and honour, he does what is proper to a position of wealth and honour. In a poor and low position, he does what is proper to a poor and low position. Situated among barbarous tribes, he does what is proper to a situation among barbarous tribes. In a position of sorrow and difficulty, he does what is proper to a position of sorrow and difficulty. The superior man can find himself in no situation in which he is not himself.

3. In a high situation, he does not treat with contempt his inferiors. In a low situation, he does not court the favour of his superiors. He rectifies himself, and seeks for nothing from others, so that he has no dissatisfactions. He does not murmur against heaven, nor grumble against men.

4. Thus it is that the superior man is quiet and calm, waiting for the appointments *of Heaven*, while the mean man walks in dangerous paths, looking for lucky occurrences.

5. The Master said, "In archery we have something like the way of the superior man. When the archer misses the centre of the target, he turns round and seeks for the cause of his failure in himself."

XV. 1. The way of the superior man may be compared

infirmity. It must be allowed, however, that the cases, as put by him, are in a measure hypothetical, his father having died when he was a child. In the course of the paragraph, he passes from speaking of himself by his name, to speak of the *keun-tsze*, and the change is most naturally made after the last "I have not attained."

14. HOW THE SUPERIOR MAN, IN EVERY VARYING SITUATION, PURSUES THE MEAN, DOING WHAT IS RIGHT, AND FINDING HIS RULE IN HIMSELF.

15. IN THE PRACTICE OF THE MEAN THERE IS AN ORDERLY ADVANCE FROM STEP TO STEP. 2. See the She-king, Pt II. Bk L iv. 7, 8. The old

to what takes place in travelling, when to go to a distance we must first traverse the space that is near, and in ascending a height, when we must begin from the lower ground.

2. It is said in the Book of Poetry, " Happy union with wife and children is like the music of lutes and harps. When there is concord among brethren, the harmony is delightful and enduring. *Thus* may you regulate your family, and enjoy the pleasure of your wife and children."

3. The Master said, " In such a state of things, parents have entire complacence ! "

XVI. 1. The Master said, " How abundantly do spiritual beings display the powers that belong to them !

2. " We look for them, but do not see them; we listen to, but do not hear them; yet they enter into all things, and there is nothing without them.

celebrates, in a regretful tone, the dependence of brethren on one another, and the beauty of brotherly harmony. Maou says :—" Although there may be the happy union of wife and children, like the music of lutes and harps, yet there must also be the harmonious concord of brethren, with its exceeding delight, and then may wife and children be regulated and enjoyed. Brothers are near to us, while wife and children are more remote. Thus it is, that from what is near we proceed to what is remote." He adds that anciently the relationship of husband and wife was not among the five relationships of society, because the union of brothers is from heaven, and that of husband and wife is from man ! 3. This is understood to be a remark of Confucius on the ode. From wife, and children, and brothers, parents at last are reached, illustrating how from what is low we ascend to what is high.—But all this is far-fetched and obscure.

16. AN ILLUSTRATION, FROM THE OPERATION AND INFLUENCE OF SPIRITUAL BEINGS, OF THE WAY OF THE MEAN. What is said of the *kwei-shin*, or " ghosts and spirits " = spiritual beings, in this chapter, is only by way of illustration. There is no design on the part of the sage to develope his views on those beings or agencies. The key of it is to be found in the last paragraph, where the language evidently refers to that of paragraph 3, in chapter i. This paragraph, therefore, should be separated from the others, and not interpreted specially of the *kwei-shin*. I think that Dr Medhurst, in rendering it (Theology of the Chinese, p. 22) —" How great then is the manifestation of *their* abstruseness ! Whilst displaying their sincerity, they are not to be concealed," was wrong, notwithstanding that he may be defended by the example of many Chinese commentators. The second clause of paragraph 5 appears altogether synonymous with the " what truly is within will be manifested without," in the Commentary of the Great Learning, chapter vi. 2, to which chapter we have seen that the whole of chapter i. pp. 2, 3, has a remarkable similarity. However we may be driven to find a recondite, mystical meaning for " *sincerity*," in the fourth part of this work, there is no ne-

3. "They cause all the people in the empire to fast and purify themselves, and array themselves in their richest dresses, in order to attend at their sacrifices. Then, like overflowing water, they seem to be over the heads, and on the right and left *of their worshippers.*

4. "It is said in the Book of Poetry, 'The approaches of the spirits, you cannot surmise;—and can you treat them with indifference?'

5. "Such is the manifestness of what is minute! Such is the impossibility of repressing the outgoings of sincerity!"

cessity to do so here. With regard to what is said of the *kwei-shin*, it is only the first two paragraphs which occasion difficulty. In the third paragraph the sage speaks of the spiritual beings that are sacrificed to. The same is the subject of the fourth paragraph; or rather, spiritual beings generally, whether sacrificed to or not, invisible themselves and yet able to behold our conduct. See the She-king, Pt III. Bk IV. ii. 7. The ode is said to have been composed by one of the dukes of Wei, and was repeated daily in his hearing for his admonition. In the context of the quotation, he is warned to be careful of his conduct, when alone as when in company. For in truth we are never alone. "Millions of spiritual beings walk the earth," and can take note of us. What now are the *kwei-shin* in the first two paragraphs? Are we to understand by them something different from what they are in the third paragraph, to which they run on from the first as the nominative or subject of the verb "to cause"? I think not. The precise meaning of what is said of "their entering into all things," and "there being nothing without them," cannot be determined. The old interpreters say that the meaning of the whole is—"that of all things there is not a single thing which is not produced by the breath (or energy) of the *kwei-shin.*" This is all that we learn from them. The Sung school explain the terms with reference to their physical theory of the universe, derived, as they think, from the *Yih-king.* Choo He's master, Ch'ing, explains:—"The *kwei-shin* are the energetic operations of Heaven and Earth, and the traces of production and transformation." The scholar Chang says:—"The *kwei-shin* are the easily acting powers of the two breaths of nature." Choo He's own account is: "If we speak of two breaths, then by *kwei* is denoted the efficaciousness of the secondary or inferior one, and by *shin*, that of the superior one. If we speak of one breath, then by *shin* is denoted its advancing and developing, and by *kwei*, its returning and reverting. They are really only one thing." It is difficult—not to say impossible—to conceive to one's-self what is meant by such descriptions. And nowhere else in the Four Books is there an approach to this meaning of the phrase.

Rémusat translates the first paragraph:—"*Que les vertus des esprits sont sublimes!*" His Latin version is:—"*spirituum geniorumque est virtus: ea capax!*" Intorcetta renders:—"*spiritibus inest operativa virtus et efficacitas, et hæc o quam præstans est! quam multiplex! quam sublimis!*" In a note, he and his friends say that the dignitary of the

XVII. 1. The Master said, "How greatly filial was Shun! His virtue was that of a sage; his dignity was the imperial throne; his riches were all within the four seas. He offered his sacrifices in his ancestral temple, and his descendants preserved the sacrifices to himself.

2. "Therefore having such great virtue, it could not but be that he should obtain the throne, that he should obtain those riches, that he should obtain his fame, that he should attain to his long life.

3. "Thus it is that Heaven, in the production of things, is surely bountiful to them, according to their qualities. Hence the tree that is flourishing, it nourishes, while that which is ready to fall, it overthrows.

4. "In the Book of Poetry, it is said, 'The admirable, amiable, prince, Displayed conspicuously his excelling virtue, Adjusting his people, and Adjusting his officers. *Therefore*, he received from Heaven the emoluments of dignity. It protected him, assisted him, decreed him the throne; Sending from heaven these favours, *as it were* repeatedly.'

empire who assisted them, rejecting other interpretations, understood by *kwei-shin* here—"those spirits for the veneration of whom and imploring their help, sacrifices were instituted." *Shin* signifies "spirits," "a spirit," "spirit;" and *kwei* "a ghost," or "demon." The former is used for the *animus*, or intelligent soul separated from the body, and the latter for the *anima*, or animal, grosser, soul, so separated. In the text, however, they blend together, and are not to be separately translated. They are together equivalent to *shin* alone in paragraph four, "spirits," or "spiritual beings."

17. THE VIRTUE OF FILIAL PIETY, EXEMPLIFIED IN SHUN AS CARRIED TO THE HIGHEST POINT, AND REWARDED BY HEAVEN. 1. One does not readily see the connection between Shun's great filial piety, and all the other predicates of him that follow. The paraphrasts, however, try to trace it in this way:—"A son without virtue is insufficient to distinguish his parents. But Shun was born with all knowledge, and acted without any effort:—in virtue, a sage. How great was the distinction which he thus conferred on his parents!" And so with regard to the other predicate. 2. The whole of this is to be understood with reference to Shun. He died at the age of one hundred years. The word "virtue" takes here the place of "filial piety," in the last paragraph, according to Maou, because that is the root, the first and chief, of all virtues. 4. See the She-king. Pt III. Bk II. v. 1. The prince spoken of is king Wăn, who is thus brought forward to confirm the lesson taken from Shun. That lesson, however, is stated much too broadly in the last paragraph. It is well to say that only virtue is a solid title to eminence; but to hold forth the certain attainment of wealth and position as an

5. "We may say therefore that he who is greatly virtuous will be sure to receive the appointment of Heaven."

XVIII. 1. The Master said, "It is only king Wăn of whom it can be said that he had no cause for grief! His father was king Ke, and his son was king Woo. His father laid the foundations of his dignity, and his son transmitted it.

2. "King Woo continued the enterprise of king T'ae, king Ke, and king Wăn. He *only* once buckled on his armour, and got possession of the empire. He did not lose the distinguished personal reputation which he had throughout the empire. His dignity was the imperial throne. His riches were the possession of all within the four seas. He offered his sacrifices in his ancestral temple, and his descendants maintained the sacrifices to himself.

3. "It was in his old age that king Woo received the appointment *to the throne*, and the duke of Chow completed the virtuous course of Wăn and Woo. He carried up the title of king to T'ae and Ke, and sacrificed to all the former dukes above them with the imperial ceremonies. And this rule he extended to the princes of the empire, the great officers, the scholars, and the common people. Was the father a great officer, and the son a scholar, then the burial was that due to a great officer,

inducement to virtue is not favourable to morality. The case of Confucius himself, who attained neither to power nor to long life, may be adduced as inconsistent with these teachings.

18. ON KING WĂN, KING WOO, AND THE DUKE OF CHOW. 1. Shun's father was bad, and the fathers of Yaou and Yu were undistinguished. Yaou and Shun's sons were both bad, and Yu's not remarkable. But to Wăn neither father nor son gave occasion but for satisfaction and happiness. King Ke was the Duke Ke-leih, the most distinguished by his virtues and prowess of all the princes of his time. He prepared the way for the elevation of his family. 2. King T'ae—this was the Duke T'anfoo, the father of Ke-leih, a prince of great eminence, and who, in the decline of the Yin dynasty, drew to his family the thoughts of the people. "He did not lose his distinguished reputation;" that is, though he proceeded against his rightful sovereign, the people did not change their opinion of his virtue. 3. "When old;"—Woo was eighty-seven when he became emperor, and he only reigned seven years. His brother Tan, the duke of Chow (see Analects, VI. xxii., VII. v.), acted as his chief minister. The house of Chow traced their lineage up to the Emperor Kuh, B.C. 2432; but in various passages of the Shoo-king, king T'ae and king K'e are spoken of, as if the conference of those titles had been by king Woo.

and the sacrifice that due to a scholar. Was the father a scholar, and the son a great officer, then the burial was that due to a scholar, and the sacrifice that due to a great officer. The one year's mourning was made to extend *only* to the great officers, but the three years' mourning extended to the emperor. In the mourning for a father or mother, he allowed no difference between the noble and the mean."

XIX. 1. The Master said, "How far extending was the filial piety of king Woo and the duke of Chow!

2. "Now filial piety is seen in the skilful carrying out of the wishes of our forefathers, and the skilful carrying forward of their undertakings.

3. "In spring and autumn, they repaired and beautified the temple-halls of their fathers, set forth their an-

On this there are very long discussions. The truth seems to be, that Chow-kung, carrying out his brother's wishes by laws of state, confirmed the titles, and made the general rule about burials and sacrifices which is described. From "this rule," &c., to the end, we are at first inclined to translate in the present tense, but the past with a reference to Chow-kung is more correct. The "year's mourning" is that principally for uncles and cousins, and it does not extend beyond the great officers, because their uncles, &c., being the subjects of the princes and of the emperor, feelings of kindred must not be allowed to come into collision with the relation of governor and governed. On the "three years' mourning," see Analects XVII. xxi.

19. THE FAR-REACHING FILIAL PIETY OF KING WOO, AND OF THE DUKE OF CHOW. 2. This definition of "filial piety" is worthy of notice. Its operation ceases not with the lives of parents and parents' parents 3. In spring and autumn; the emperors of China sacrificed, as they still do, to their ancestors every season. Though spring and autumn only are mentioned in the text, we are to understand that what is said of the sacrifices in those seasons applies to all the others. 4. It was an old interpretation that the sacrifices and accompanying services, spoken of here, were not the seasonal services of every year, which are the subject of the preceding paragraph, but the still greater sacrifices (see one of them spoken of in Analects, III. x., xi.); and to that view I would give in my adhesion. The emperor had seven shrines, or apartments, in the hall of the ancestral temple. One belonged to the remote ancestor to whom the dynasty traced its origin. At the great sacrifices, his spirit-tablet was placed fronting the east, and on each side were ranged, three in a row, the tablets belonging to the six others, those of them which fronted the south being, in the genealogical line, the fathers of those who fronted the north. As fronting the south, the region of *brilliancy*, the former were called *chaou*, the latter, from the north, the *sombre* region, were called *muh*. As the dynasty was prolonged, and successive emperors died, the old tablets were removed, and transferred to what was called the "apartments of displaced

cestral vessels, displayed their various robes, and presented the offerings of the several seasons.

4. "By means of the ceremonies of the ancestral temple, they distinguished the imperial kindred according to their order of descent. By ordering the parties present according to their rank, they distinguished the more noble and the less. By the arrangement of the services, they made a distinction of talents and worth. In the ceremony of general pledging, the inferiors presented the cup to their superiors, and thus something was given the lowest to do. At the *concluding* feast, places were given according to the hair, and thus was made the distinction of years.

5. "They occupied the places of their forefathers, practised their ceremonies, and performed their music. They reverenced those whom they honoured, and loved those whom they regarded with affection. Thus they served the dead as they would have served them alive; they served the departed as they would have served them had they been continued among them.

shrines," yet so as that one in the *bright* line displaced the topmost of the row, and so with the *sombre* tablets. At the sacrifices, the imperial kindred arranged themselves as they were descended from a " bright" emperor, on the left, and from a "sombre" one, on the right, and thus a genealogical correctness of place was maintained among them. The ceremony of "general pledging" occurred towards the end of the sacrifice. To have anything to do at those services was accounted honourable, and after the emperor had commenced the ceremony by taking "a cup of blessing," all the juniors presented a similar cup to the seniors, and thus were called into employment. 5. "They occupied their places," according to K'ang-shing, is—"ascended their thrones;" according to Choo He it is "trod on—*i.e.*, occupied—their places in the ancestral temple." On either view, the statement must be taken with allowance. The ancestors of king Woo had not been emperors, and their place in the temples had only been those of princes. The same may be said of the four particulars which follow. By "those whom they "—*i.e.*, their progenitors —"honoured" are intended their ancestors, and by "those whom they loved," their descendants, and indeed all the people of their government. The two concluding sentences are important, as the Jesuits mainly based on them the defence of their practice in permitting their converts to continue the sacrifices to their ancestors. We read in " *Confucius Sinarum philosophus,*"—the work of Intorcetta and others, to which I have made frequent reference:—*Ex plurimis et clarissimis textibus Sinicis probari potest, legitimum predicti axiomatis sensum esse, quod eadem intentione et formali motivo Sinenses naturalem pietatem et politicum obsequium erga defunctos exerceant, sicuti erga eosdem adhuc superstites exercebant,*

6. "By the ceremonies of the sacrifices to Heaven and Earth they served God, and by the ceremonies of the ancestral temple they sacrificed to their ancestors. He who understands the ceremonies of the sacrifices to Heaven and Earth, and the meaning of the several sacrifices to ancestors, would find the government of a kingdom as easy as to look into his palm!"

XX. 1. The duke Gao asked about government.

2. The Master said, "The government of Wän and Woo is displayed in *the records*,—the tablets of wood and bamboo. Let there be the men, and the government will flourish; but without the men, the government decays and ceases.

ex quibus et ex infra dicendis prudens lector facile deducet, hos ritus circa defunctos fuisse mere civiles, institutos dumtaxat in honorem et obsequium parentum, etiam post mortem non intermittendum; nam si quid illic divinum agnovissent, cur diceret Confucius—Priscos servire solitos defunctis, uti iisdem servicbant viventibus." This is ingenious reasoning, but it does not meet the fact that sacrifice is an entirely new element introduced into the service of the dead. 6. I do not understand how it is that their sacrifices to God are adduced here as an illustration of the filial piety of king Wän and king Woo. What is said about them, however, is important, in reference to the views which we should form about the ancient religion of China. Both the old interpreters of the Han dynasty and the more eminent among those of the Sung, understand the two sacrifices first spoken of to be those to Heaven and Earth,—the former offered at the winter solstice, in the southern suburb of the imperial city, and the latter offered in the northern suburb, at the summer solstice. They think, however, that for the sake of brevity, the words for "and the sovereign earth," are omitted after "God," literally, "supreme ruler." Some modern interpreters understand that besides the sacrifices to Heaven and Earth, those to tutelary deities of the soil are spoken of. But these various opinions do not affect the judgment of the sage himself, that the service of one being—even of God—was designed by all those ceremonies. See my "Notions of the Chinese concerning God and Spirits," pp. 50—52.

20. ON GOVERNMENT: SHOWING PRINCIPALLY HOW IT DEPENDS ON THE CHARACTER OF THE OFFICERS ADMINISTERING IT, AND HOW THAT DEPENDS ON THE CHARACTER OF THE SOVEREIGN HIMSELF. We have here one of the fullest expositions of Confucius' views on this subject, though he unfolds them only as a description of the government of the kings Wän and Woo. In the chapter there is the remarkable intermingling, which we have seen in "The Great Learning," of what is peculiar to a ruler, and what is of universal application. From the concluding paragraphs, the transition is easy to the next and most difficult part of the Work. This chapter is found also in the "Family Sayings," but with considerable additions.

1. Duke Gao. The old commentators took what I have called an "easily-growing rush" as the name of an insect (so it is defined in the

3. "With the *right* men the growth of government is rapid, just as vegetation is rapid in the earth; and moreover *their* government *might be called* an easily-growing rush.

4. "Therefore the administration of government lies in *getting proper* men. Such men are to be got by means of *the ruler's* own character. That character is to be cultivated by his treading in the ways *of duty.* And the treading those ways of duty is to be cultivated by the cherishing of benevolence.

5. "Benevolence is *the characteristic element of* humanity, and the great exercise of it is in loving relatives. Righteousness is *the accordance of actions with what is* right, and the great exercise of it is in honouring the worthy. The decreasing measures of the love due to relatives, and the steps in the honour due to the worthy, are produced by *the principle of* propriety.

6. "When those in inferior situations do not possess the confidence of their superiors, they cannot retain the government of the people.

7. "Hence the sovereign may not neglect the cultivation of his own character. Wishing to cultivate his character, he may not neglect to serve his parents. In order to serve his parents, he may not neglect to acquire a knowledge of men. In order to know men, he may not dispense with a knowledge of Heaven.

Urh Ya), a kind of bee, said to take the young of the mulberry caterpillar, and keep them in its hole, where they are transformed into bees. So, they said, does government transform the people. This is in accordance with the paragraph, as we find it in the "Family Sayings." But we cannot hesitate in preferring Choo He's, as in the translation. The other is too absurd. 5. "Benevolence is man." We find the same language in Mencius, and in the Le-ke, XXXII. 15. This virtue is called MAN, "because loving, feeling, and the forbearing nature belong to man, as he is born. They are that whereby man is man." 6. This has crept into the text here by mistake. It belongs to paragraph 17, below. We do not find it here in the "Family Sayings." 7. I fail in trying to trace the connection between the different parts of this paragraph. "He may not be without knowing men."—Why? "Because," we are told, "it is by honouring and being courteous to the worthy, and securing them as friends, that a man perfects his virtue, and is able to serve his relatives." "He may not be without knowing Heaven."—Why? "Because," it is said, "the gradations in the love of relatives and the honouring the worthy, are all heavenly arrangements, and a heavenly order, natural, necessary principles." But in this explanation, "Knowing men" has a

8. "The duties of universal obligation are five, and the virtues wherewith they are practised are three. The duties are those between sovereign and minister, between father and son, between husband and wife, between elder brother and younger, and those belonging to the intercourse of friends. Those five are the duties of universal obligation. Knowledge, magnanimity, and energy, these three, are the virtues universally binding. And the means by which they carry *the duties* into practice is singleness.

9. "Some are born with the knowledge *of those duties*; some know them by study; and some acquire the knowledge after a painful feeling of their ignorance. But the knowledge being possessed, it comes to the same thing. Some practise them with a natural ease; some from a desire for their advantages; and some by strenuous effort. But the achievement being made, it comes to the same thing."

10. The Master said, "To be fond of learning is to be

---

very different meaning from what it has in the previous clause. 8. From this down to paragraph 11, there is brought before us the character of the "*men*," mentioned in paragraph 2, on whom depends the flourishing of "*government*," which government is exhibited in paragraphs 12—15. "The duties of universal obligation" is, literally, "the paths proper to be trodden by all under heaven"—the path of the Mean. Of the three virtues, the first is the *knowledge* necessary to choose the detailed course of duty; the second, is "benevolence," "the unselfishness of the heart" = *magnanimity* (so I style it for want of a better term), to pursue it; the third is the *valiant energy*, which maintains the permanence of the choice and the practice. The last clause is, literally, "Whereby they are practised is one," and this, according to Ying-tâ, means—"From the various kings downwards, in the practising these five duties, and three virtues, there has been but one method. There has been no change in modern times and ancient." This, however, is not satisfactory. We want a substantive meaning for "one." This Choo He gives us. He says:—"The *one* is simply sincerity;" the sincerity, that is, on which the rest of the work dwells with such strange predication. I translate, therefore, the term here by *singleness*. There seems a reference in the term to the being *alone* in ch. i. p. 3. The singleness is that of the soul in the apprehension and practice of the duties of the Mean, which is attained to by watchfulness over one's self, when *alone*. 9. Compare Analects, XVI. ix. But is there the threefold difference in the *knowledge* of the duties spoken of? And who are they who can practise them with entire ease? 10. Choo He observes that "The Master said " is here superfluous. In the "Family Sayings," however, we find the last paragraph followed by—"The duke said, Your words are beautiful and perfect, but I am stupid, and unable to accom-

near to knowledge. To practise with vigour is to be near to magnanimity. To possess the feeling of shame is to be near to energy.

11. "He who knows these three things knows how to cultivate his own character. Knowing how to cultivate his own character, he knows how to govern other men. Knowing how to govern other men, he knows how to govern the empire with all its States and families.

12. "All who have the government of the empire with its States and families have nine standard rules to follow; —viz. the cultivation of their own characters; the honouring of men of virtue and talents; affection towards their relatives; respect towards the great ministers; kind and considerate treatment of the whole body of officers; dealing with the mass of the people as children; encouraging the resort of all classes of artisans; indulgent treatment of men from a distance; and the kindly cherishing of the princes of the States.

13. "By the ruler's cultivation of his own character, the

plish this." Then comes this paragraph—"Confucius said," &c. The words in question, therefore, prove that Tsze-sze took this chapter from some existing document, that which we have in the "Family Sayings," or some other. Confucius' words were intended to encourage and stimulate the duke, telling him that the three grand virtues might be nearly, if not absolutely, attained to. 11. "These three things" are the three things in the last paragraph, which make an approximation at least to the three virtues which connect with the discharge of duty attainable by every one. What connects the various steps of the climax is the unlimited confidence in the power of the example of the ruler, which we have had occasion to point out so frequently in "The Great Learning." 12. These nine standard rules, it is to be borne in mind, constitute the government of Wăn and Woo, referred to in paragraph 2. Commentators arrange the fourth and fifth rules under the second; and the sixth, seventh, eighth, and ninth, under the third, so that after "the cultivation of the person," we have here an expansion of paragraph 5. By "the men of talents and virtue" are intended the "three Kung" and "three Koo," who composed the "Inner Council" of the Chow emperors; and by the "great ministers," the heads of the six departments of their government:—of all of whom there is an account in the Shoo-King, Pt V. Bk XX. 5—13. The emperors of China have always assumed to be the "fathers of the people," and to deal with them as their children. The eighth rule did not, probably, in Confucius' mind, embrace any but travelling merchants coming into the imperial domains from the other States of the empire; but in modern times it has been construed as the rule for the treatment of foreigners by the government of China,—which, moreover, would affirm that it has observed it. 13. This paragraph describes duties *of universal obligation* are set up. By honouring men of virtue and talents, he is preserved from errors of judgment. By showing affection to his relatives, there is no grumbling nor resentment among his uncles and brethren. By respecting the great ministers, he is kept from errors in the practice of government. By kind and considerate treatment of the whole body of officers, they are led to make the most grateful return for his courtesies. By dealing with the mass of the people as his children, they are led to exhort one another to what is good. By encouraging the resort of all classes of artisans, his resources for expenditure are rendered ample. By indulgent treatment of men from a distance, they are brought to resort to him from all quarters. And by kindly cherishing the princes of the States, the whole empire is brought to revere him.

14. "Self-adjustment and purification, with careful regulation of his dress, and the not making a movement contrary to the rules of propriety:—this is the way for the ruler to cultivate his person. Discarding slanderers, and keeping himself from *the seductions of* beauty; making light of riches, and giving honour to virtue:—this is the way for him to encourage men of worth and talents. Giving them places *of honour* and emolument, and sharing with them in their likes and dislikes: this is the way for him to encourage his relatives to love him. Giving them numerous officers to discharge their orders and commis-

---

the happy effects of observing the above nine rules. We read in the " Daily Lessons:" " About these nine rules, the only trouble is, that sovereigns are not able to practise them strenuously. Let the ruler be really able to cultivate his person, then will the universal duties and universal virtues be all-complete, so that he shall be an example to the whole empire, with its States and families. Those duties will be set up, and men will know what to imitate." On " the resources of expenditure being ample," Choo He says:—" The resort of all classes of artisans being encouraged, there is an intercommunication of the productions of labour, and au interchange of men's services, and the husbandman and the trafficker are aiding to one another. Hence the resources for expenditure are sufficient." I suppose that Choo He felt a want of some mention of agriculture in connection with these rules, and thought to find a place for it here. 14. After " The whole empire is brought to revere him," we have in the " Family Sayings," " The duke said, *How are these rules to be practised?* " and then follows this paragraph, preceded by " Confucius said." The blending together, in the first clause, as equally important, attention to inward

sions:—this is the way for him to encourage the great ministers. According to them a generous confidence, and making their emoluments large:—this is the way to encourage the body of officers. Employing them only at the proper times, and making the imposts light:—this is the way to encourage the people. By daily examinations and monthly trials, and by making their rations in accordance with their labours:—this is the way to encourage the classes of artisans. To escort them on their departure and meet them on their coming; to commend the good among them, and show compassion to the incompetent:—this is the way to treat indulgently men from a distance. To restore families whose line of succession has been broken, and to revive States that have been extinguished; to reduce to order States that are in confusion, and support those which are in peril; to have fixed times for their own reception at court, and the reception of their envoys; to send them away after liberal treatment, and welcome their coming with small contributions:—this is the way to cherish the princes of the States.

15. "All who have the government of the empire with its States and families have the above nine standard rules. And the means by which they are carried into practice is singleness.

16. "In all things success depends on previous preparation, and without such previous preparation there is sure to be failure. If what is to be spoken be previously determined, there will be no stumbling. If affairs be previously determined, there will be no difficulty with them. If one's actions have been previously determined, there will be no sorrow in connection with them. If principles

---

purity and to dress, seems strange enough to a western reader. The trials and examinations, with the rations spoken of in the seventh clause, show that the artisans are not to be understood of such dispersed among the people, but as collected under the superintendence of the government. Ambassadors from foreign countries have been received up to the present century, according to the rules in the eighth clause, and the two last regulations are quite in harmony with the moral and political superiority that China claims over the countries which they may represent. But in the case of travellers, and travelling merchants, passing from one State to another, there were anciently regulations, which may be adduced to illustrate all the expressions here. 16. The "all things" is to be understood

of conduct have been previously determined, the practice of them will be inexhaustible.

17. "When those in inferior situations do not obtain the confidence of the sovereign, they cannot succeed in governing the people. There is a way to obtain the confidence of the sovereign;—if one is not trusted by his friends, he will not get the confidence of his sovereign. There is a way to being trusted by one's friends;—if one is not obedient to his parents, he will not be true to friends. There is a way to being obedient to one's parents;—if one, on turning his thoughts in upon himself, finds a want of sincerity, he will not be obedient to his parents. There is a way to the attainment of sincerity in one's-self;—if a man do not understand what is good, he will not attain sincerity in himself.

18. "Sincerity is the way of Heaven. The attainment of sincerity is the way of men. He who possesses sincerity, is he who, without an effort, hits what is right, and apprehends, without the exercise of thought;—he is the sage who naturally and easily embodies the *right* way. He who attains to sincerity, is he who chooses what is good, and firmly holds it fast.

19. "To this attainment there are requisite the extensive study of what is good, accurate inquiry about it, careful reflection on it, the clear discrimination of it, and the earnest practice of it.

20. "The superior man, while there is anything he has not studied, or while in what he has studied there is anything he cannot understand, will not intermit his labour. While there is anything he has not inquired

with reference to the universal duties, the universal virtues, and the nine standard rules. 17. The object of this paragraph seems to be to show that the singleness, or sincerity, lies at the basis of that previous preparation, which is essential to success in any and every thing. The steps of the climax conduct us to it as the mental state necessary to all virtues, and this sincerity is again made dependent on the understanding of what is good, upon which point see the next chapter. 19. There are here described the different processes which lead to the attainment of sincerity. 20. Here we have the determination which is necessary in the prosecution of the above processes, and paragraph 21 states the result of it. Choo He makes a pause at the end of the first clause in each part of the paragraph, and interprets thus:—" If he do not study, well. But if he do, he will not give over till he understands what he studies," and so on. But it seems more natural to carry the supposition over the whole of every

about, or anything in what he has inquired about which he does not know, he will not intermit his labour. While there is anything which he has not reflected on, or anything in what he has reflected on which he does not apprehend, he will not intermit his labour. While there is anything which he has not discriminated, or while his discrimination is not clear, he will not intermit his labour. If there be anything which he has not practised, or if his practice fails in earnestness, he will not intermit his labour. If another man succeed by one effort, he will use a hundred efforts. If another man succeed by ten efforts, he will use a thousand.

21. "Let a man proceed in this way, and, though dull, he will surely become intelligent; though weak, he will surely become strong."

XXI. When we have intelligence resulting from sincerity, this condition is to be ascribed to nature; when we have sincerity resulting from intelligence, this condition is to be ascribed to instruction. But given the sincerity, and there shall be the intelligence, given the intelligence, and there shall be the sincerity.

The above is the twenty-first chapter. Tsze-sze takes up in it, and discourses from, the subjects of "the way of

part, as in the translation, which moreover substantially agrees with Ying-tă's interpretation. Here terminates the third part of the Work. It was to illustrate, as Choo He told us, how "the path of the Mean cannot be left." The author seems to have kept this point before him in chapters xiii.—xvi., but the next three are devoted to the one subject of filial piety, and the twentieth, to the general subject of government. Some things are said worthy of being remembered, and others which require a careful sifting; but, on the whole, we do not find ourselves advanced in an understanding of the argument of the Work.

21. THE RECIPROCAL CONNECTION OF SINCERITY AND INTELLIGENCE. With this chapter commences the fourth part of the Work, which, as Choo observes in his concluding note, is an expansion of the eighteenth paragraph of the preceding chapter. It is, in a great measure, a glorification of the sage, finally resting in the person of Confucius; but the high character of the sage, it is maintained, is not unattainable by others. He realizes the ideal of humanity, but by his example and lessons, the same ideal is brought within the reach of many, perhaps of all. The ideal of humanity,—the perfect character belonging to the sage, which ranks him on a level with Heaven,—is indicated by a single character, and we have no single term in English which can be considered as the complete equivalent of it. The Chinese themselves had great difficulty in arriving at that definition of it which is now generally acquiesced in. We are told that

Heaven" and "the way of men," mentioned in the preceding chapter. The twelve chapters that follow are all from Tsze-sze, repeating and illustrating the meaning of this one.

XXII. It is only he who is possessed of the most complete sincerity that can exist under heaven, who can give its full development to his nature. Able to give its full development to his own nature, he can do the same to the nature of other men. Able to give its full development to the nature of other men, he can give their full

"the Han scholars were all ignorant of its meaning. Under the Sung dynasty, first came Le Pang-Chih, who defined it by *freedom from all deception*. After him, Seu Chung-Keu said that it meant *ceaselessness*. Then one of the Ch'ing called it *freedom from all moral error*; and finally, Choo He added to this the positive element of *truth and reality*, on which the definition of the term was complete." Rémusat calls it — *la perfection*, and "*la perfection morale*." Intorcetta and his friends call it — *vera solidaque perfectio*. Simplicity or singleness of soul seems to be what is chiefly intended by the term; the disposition to and capacity of what is good, without any deteriorating element, with no defect of intelligence, or intromission of selfish thoughts. This belongs to Heaven, to Heaven and Earth, and to the sage. Men, not naturally sages, may, by cultivating the intelligence of what is good, raise themselves to this elevation.

Here, at the outset, I may observe that, in this portion of the Work, there are specially the three following dogmas, which are more than questionable:—1st, That there are some men—sages—naturally in a state of moral perfection; 2nd, That the same moral perfection is attainable by others, in whom its development is impeded by their material organization, and the influence of external things; and 3rd, That the understanding of what is good will certainly lead to such moral perfection.

22. THE RESULTS OF SINCERITY; AND HOW THE POSSESSOR OF IT FORMS A TERNION WITH HEAVEN AND EARTH. What I have called "giving full development to the nature," is, literally, "exhausting the nature;" but, by what processes and in what way, the character tells us nothing. The "giving full development to his nature," however, may be understood with Maou, as—" pursuing THE PATH in accordance with his nature, so that what Heaven has conferred on him is displayed without shortcoming or let." The "giving its development to the nature of other men" indicates the sage's helping them, by his examples and lessons, to perfect themselves. " His exhausting the nature of things," *i. e.*, of all other beings, animate and inanimate, is, according to Choo He, "knowing them completely, and dealing with them correctly," " so," add the paraphrasts, "that he secures their prosperous increase and development according to their nature." Here, however, a Buddhist idea appears in Choo He's commentary. He says:—" The nature of other men and things (= animals) is the same with my nature," which, it is observed in

development to the natures of animals and things. Able to give their full development to the natures of creatures and things, he can assist the transforming and nourishing powers of Heaven and Earth. Able to assist the transforming and nourishing powers of Heaven and Earth, he may with Heaven and Earth form a ternion.

XXIII. Next to the above is he who cultivates to the utmost the shoots *of goodness* in him. From those he can attain to the possession of sincerity. This sincerity becomes apparent. From being apparent, it becomes manifest. From being manifest, it becomes brilliant. Brilliant, it affects others. Affecting others, they are changed by it. Changed by it, they are transformed. It is only he who is possessed of the most complete sincerity that can exist under heaven, who can transform.

Maou's work, is the same with the Buddhist sentiment, that "a dog has the nature of Buddha," and with that of the philosopher Kaou, that " a dog's nature is the same as a man's." Maou himself illustrates the "exhausting the nature of things," by reference to the Shoo-king, IV. Bk IV. 2, where we are told that under the first sovereigns of the Hea dynasty, "the mountains and rivers all enjoyed tranquillity, and the birds and beasts, the fishes and tortoises, all realized the happiness of their nature. It is thus that the sage "assists Heaven and Earth." K'angshing, indeed, explains this by saying:—"The sage, receiving Heaven's appointment to the imperial throne, extends everywhere a happy tranquillity." Evidently there is a reference in the language to the mystical paragraph at the end of the first chapter. "Heaven and Earth" take the place here of the single term—"Heaven," in chapter xx., paragraph 18. On this Ying-tă observes:—"It is said above, *sincerity is the way of Heaven*, and here mention is made also of *Earth*. The reason is, that the reference above, was to the principle of sincerity in its spiritual and mysterious origin, and thence the expression simple,—*The way of Heaven;* but here we have the transformation and nourishing seen in the production of things, and hence *Earth* is associated with *Heaven*." This is not very intelligible, but it is to bring out the idea of a *ternion*, that the great, supreme, ruling Power is thus dualized. The original term means "a file of three," and I employ "ternion" to express the idea, just as we use "quaternion" for a file of four. What is it but blasphemy, thus to file man with the supreme Power?

23. THE WAY OF MAN;—THE DEVELOPMENT OF PERFECT SINCERITY IN THOSE NOT NATURALLY POSSESSED OF IT. There is some difficulty here about the term which I have translated *shoots*. It properly means "crooked," and, with a bad application, often signifies "deflection from what is straight and right." Yet it cannot have a bad meaning here, for if it have, the use of it will be, in the connection, unintelligible. One writer uses this comparison:—"Put a stone on a bamboo shoot, or where the shoot would show itself, and it will travel round the stone, and

XXIV. It is characteristic of the most entire sincerity to be able to foreknow. When a nation or family is about to flourish, there are sure to be happy omens; and when it is about to perish, there are sure to be unlucky omens. Such events are seen in the milfoil and tortoise, and affect the movements of the four limbs. When calamity or happiness is about to come, the good shall certainly be foreknown by him, and the evil also. Therefore the individual possessed of the most complete sincerity is like a spirit.

XXV. 1. Sincerity is that whereby self-completion is effected, and *its* way is that by which man must direct himself.

2. Sincerity is the end and beginning of things; without sincerity there would be nothing. On this account, the superior man regards the attainment of sincerity as the most excellent thing.

3. The possessor of sincerity does not merely accomplish the self-completion of himself. With this quality

---

come out *crookedly* at its side." So it is with the good nature, whose free development is repressed. It shows itself in shoots, but if they be cultivated and improved, a moral condition and influence may be attained, equal to that of the sage.

24. THAT ENTIRE SINCERITY CAN FOREKNOW. "Lucky omens;"—these are intimated by two terms, denoting respectively unusual appearances of things existing in a country, and appearances of things new. "Unlucky omens" are in the same way indicated by two terms, the former being spoken of "prodigies of plants, and of strangely dressed boys singing ballads," and the latter of prodigious animals. For the milfoil and tortoise, see the Yih-king, Appendix I. xi.; and the notes on the Shoo-king, V. Bk. IV. 20—30. The "four limbs" are by K'ang-shing interpreted of the feet of the tortoise, each foot being peculiarly appropriate to divination in a particular season. Choo He interprets them of the four limbs of the human body. "Like a spirit" must be left as indefinite in the translation as it is in the text.—The whole chapter is eminently absurd, and gives a character of ridiculousness to all the magniloquent teaching about "entire sincerity." The foreknowledge attributed to the sage,—the mate of Heaven,—is only a guessing by means of augury, sorcery, and other follies.

25. HOW FROM SINCERITY COMES SELF-COMPLETION, AND THE COMPLETION OF OTHERS AND OF THINGS. I have had difficulty in translating this chapter, because it is difficult to understand it. We wish that we had the writer before us to question him; but if we had, it is not likely that he would be able to afford us much satisfaction. Persuaded that what he denominates *sincerity* is a figment, we may not wonder at the extravagance of its predicates. 2. I translate the expansion of this in the "Daily

he completes *other men and things also.* The completing himself *shows his perfect* virtue. The completing *other men and things shows his* knowledge. Both these are virtues belonging to the nature, and *this is* the way by which a union is effected of the external and internal. Therefore, whenever he—*the entirely sincere man*—employs them,—*that is, these virtues,—their action will be right.*

XXVI. 1. Hence to entire sincerity there belongs ceaselessness.

2. Not ceasing, it continues long. Continuing long, it evidences itself.

3. Evidencing itself, it reaches far. Reaching far, it becomes large and substantial. Large and substantial, it becomes high and brilliant.

4. Large and substantial;—this is how it contains *all* things. High and brilliant;—this is how it overspreads *all* things. Reaching far and continuing long;—this is how it perfects *all* things.

5. So large and substantial, *the individual possessing it* is the co-equal of Earth. So high and brilliant, it makes

Lesson: "—" All that fill up the space between heaven and earth are things. They end and they begin again; they begin and proceed to an end; every change being accomplished by sincerity, and every phenomenon having sincerity unceasingly in it. So far as the mind of man is concerned, if there be not sincerity, then every movement of it is vain and false. How can an unreal mind accomplish real things? Although it may do something, that is simply equivalent to nothing. Therefore, the superior man searches out the source of sincerity, and examines the evil of insincerity, chooses what is good, and firmly holds it fast, so seeking to arrive at the place of truth and reality." Maou's explanation is:—" Now, since the reason why the sincerity of spiritual beings is so incapable of being repressed, and why they foreknow, is because they enter into things, and there is nothing without them;—shall there be anything which is without the entirely sincere man, who is as a spirit?" I have given these specimens of commentary, that the reader may, if he can, by means of them, gather some apprehensible meaning from the text.

26. A PARALLEL BETWEEN THE SAGE POSSESSED OF ENTIRE SINCERITY, AND HEAVEN AND EARTH, SHOWING THAT THE SAME QUALITIES BELONG TO THEM. The first six paragraphs show the way of the sage; the next three show the way of Heaven and Earth; and the last brings the two ways together, in their essential nature, in a passage from the She-king. The doctrine of the chapter is liable to the criticisms which have been made on the twenty-second chapter. And, moreover, there is in it a sad confusion of the visible heavens and earth with the immaterial power and reason which govern them; in a word, with God. 1, Choo He is condemned by recent writers for making a new chapter to commence here.

him the co-equal of Heaven. So far-reaching and long-continuing, it makes him infinite.

6. Such being its nature, without any display, it becomes manifested; without any movement, it produces changes; and without any effort, it accomplishes its ends.

7. The way of Heaven and Earth may be completely declared in one sentence.—They are without any doubleness, and so they produce things in a manner that is unfathomable.

8. The way of Heaven and Earth is large and substantial, high and brilliant, far-reaching and long-enduring.

9. The heaven now before us is only this bright shining spot; but when viewed in its inexhaustible extent, the sun, moon, stars, and constellations of the zodiac are suspended in it, and all things are overspread by it. The earth before us is but a handful of soil; but when regarded in its breadth and thickness, it sustains mountains like the Hwa and the Yoh, without feeling their weight, and contains the rivers and seas, without their leaking away. The mountain now before us appears only a stone; but when contemplated in all the vastness of its size, we see how the grass and trees are produced on it, and birds and beasts dwell on it, and precious things which men treasure up are found on it. The water now before us appears but a ladleful; yet extending our view to its unfathomable depths, the largest tortoises, iguanas, iguanadons, dragons, fishes, and turtles, are produced in them; articles of value and sources of wealth abound in them.

Yet the matter is sufficiently distinct from that of the preceding one. Where the "Hence" takes hold of the text above, however, it is not easy to discover. One interpreter says that it indicates a conclusion from all the preceding predicates about sincerity. "Entire sincerity" is to be understood, now in the abstract, now in the concrete. But the fifth paragraph seems to be the place to bring out the personal idea, as I have done. The last predicate is, literally, "without bounds,"— our *infinite*. Surely it is strange—passing strange—to apply that term in the description of any created being. 7. What I said was the prime idea in "sincerity," viz., "simplicity," "singleness of soul," is very conspicuous here. It surprises us, however, to find Heaven and Earth called "*things*," at the same time that they are represented as by their entire sincerity producing all things. 9. This paragraph is said to illustrate the unfathomableness of Heaven and Earth in producing things, showing how it springs from their sin-

10. It is said in the Book of Poetry, "The ordinances of Heaven, how profound are they and unceasing!" The meaning is, that it is thus that Heaven is Heaven. And again, "How illustrious was it, the singleness of the virtue of King Wăn!" indicating that it was thus that King Wăn was what he was. Singleness likewise is unceasing.

XXVII. 1. How great is the path proper to the sage!

2. Like overflowing water, it sends forth and nourishes all things, and rises up to the height of heaven.

3. All complete is its greatness! It embraces the three hundred rules of ceremony, and the three thousand rules of demeanour.

4. It waits for the proper man, and then it is trodden.

5. Hence it is said, "Only by perfect virtue can the perfect path, in all its courses, be made a fact."

6. Therefore, the superior man honours his virtuous nature, and maintains constant inquiry and study, seeking to carry it out to its breadth and greatness, so as to omit none of the more exquisite and minute points which it embraces, and to raise it to its greatest height and brilliancy, so as to pursue the course of the Mean. He cherishes his old knowledge, and is continually acquiring new. He exerts an honest, generous earnestness, in the esteem and practice of all propriety.

verity, or freedom from doubleness. I have already observed how it is only the material heavens and earth which are presented to us. And not only so:—we have mountains, seas, and rivers, set forth as acting with the same unfathomableness as those entire bodies and powers. The "Complete Digest" says on this:—"The hills and waters are what Heaven and Earth produce, and that they should yet be able themselves to produce other things, shows still more how Heaven and Earth, in the producing of things, are unfathomable." The confusion and error in such representations are very lamentable.

27. THE GLORIOUS PATH OF THE SAGE; AND HOW THE SUPERIOR MAN ENDEAVOURS TO ATTAIN TO IT. The chapter thus divides itself into two parts, one containing five paragraphs, descriptive of the PATH, and the other two, descriptive of the *superior man*, which two appellations are to be here distinguished. 1. "This paragraph," says Choo Hs̄, "embraces the two that follow." They are, indeed, to be taken as exegetical of it. 3. By the "rules of ceremony," we are to understand the greater and more general principles of propriety, "such as capping, marriage, mourning, and sacrifice;" and by those of "demeanour" are intended all the minuter observances of them. 300 and

7. Thus, when occupying a high situation, he is not proud, and in a low situation, he is not insubordinate. When the kingdom is well-governed, he is sure by his words to rise; and when it is ill-governed, he is sure by his silence to command forbearance to himself. Is not this what we find in the Book of Poetry,—"Intelligent is he and prudent, and so preserves his person?"

XXVIII. 1. The Master said, "Let a man who is ignorant be fond of using his own judgment; let a man without rank be fond of assuming a directing power to himself; let a man who is living in the present age go back to the ways of antiquity;—on the persons of all who act thus calamities will be sure to come."

2. To no one but the emperor does it belong to order ceremonies, to fix the measures, and to determine the characters.

3. Now, over the empire, carriages have all wheels of the same size; all writing is with the same characters; and for conduct there are the same rules.

2000 are round numbers. Reference is made to those rules and their minutiæ, to show how, in every one of them, as proceeding from the sage, there is a principle, to be referred to the Heaven-given nature. 4. Compare chapter xx. 2. In "Confucius Sinarum Philosophus," it is suggested that there may be here a prophecy of the Saviour, and that the writer may have been "under the influence of that spirit, by whose moving the Sibyls formerly prophesied of Christ." There is nothing in the text to justify such a thought.

28. AN ILLUSTRATION OF THE SENTENCE IN THE LAST CHAPTER— "IN A LOW SITUATION HE IS NOT INSUBORDINATE." There does seem to be a connection of the kind thus indicated between this chapter and the last, but the principal object of what is said here is to prepare the way for the eulogium of Confucius below,—the eulogium of him, a sage without the throne. 1. The different clauses here may be understood generally, but they have a special reference to the general scope of the chapter. Three things are required to give law to the empire: virtue (including intelligence); rank; and the right time. The " ignorant man " is he who wants the virtue; the next is he who wants the rank; and the last clause describes the absence of the right time.—In this last clause, there would seem to be a sentiment which should have given course in China to the doctrine of Progress. 2. This and the two next paragraphs are understood to be the words of Tsze-sze, illustrating the preceding declarations of Confucius. We have here the imperial prerogatives, which might not be usurped. " Ceremonies " are the rules regulating religion and society : " the measures " are the prescribed forms and dimensions of buildings, carriages, clothes, &c. The term translated " characters " is said by Choo He, after K'ung-shing, to be " the names of the written

4. One may occupy the throne, but if he have not the proper virtue, he may not dare to make ceremonies or music. One may have the virtue, but if he do not occupy the throne, he may not presume to make ceremonies or music.

5. The Master said, "I may describe the ceremonies of the Hea dynasty, but Ke cannot sufficiently attest my words. I have learned the ceremonies of the Yin dynasty, and in Sung they still continue. I have learned the ceremonies of Chow, which are now used, and I follow Chow."

XXIX. 1. He who attains to the sovereignty of the empire, having *those* three important things, shall be able to effect that there shall be few errors *under his government*.

2. However excellent may have been the regulations of those of former times, they cannot be attested. Not being attested, they cannot command credence, and not being credited, the people would not follow them. However excellent might be the regulations made by one in an inferior situation, he is not in a position to be honoured. Unhonoured, he cannot command credence, and not being credited, the people would not follow his rules.

characters." But it is properly the form of the character, representing, in the original characters of the language, the figure of the object denoted; and in the text must denote both the form and sound of the character. There is a long and eulogistic note here, in "*Confucius Sinarum Philosophus,*" on the admirable uniformity secured by these prerogatives throughout the Chinese empire. It was natural for Roman Catholic writers to regard Chinese uniformity with sympathy. But the value, or, rather, no value, of such a system in its formative influence on the characters and institutions of men may be judged, both in the empire of China and in the Church of Rome. 3. "Now" is said with reference to the time of Tsze-sze. The paragraph is intended to account for Confucius' not giving law to the empire. It was not the time. 4. "Ceremonies or music;"—but we must understand also "the measures" and "characters." In paragraph 2. The paragraph would seem to reduce most emperors to the condition of *role fainéants.* 5. See the Analects, III. ix., xiv., which chapters are quoted here; but in regard to what is said of Sung, with an important variation. This paragraph illustrates how Confucius himself "occupied a low station, without being insubordinate."

29. AN ILLUSTRATION OF THE SENTENCE IN THE XXVIITH CHAPTER— "WHEN HE OCCUPIES A HIGH SITUATION, HE IS NOT PROUD;" OR RATHER, THE SAGE AND HIS INSTITUTIONS SEEN IN THEIR EFFECT AND SWAY. 1. Different opinions have obtained as to what is intended by the

3. Therefore, the institutions of the Ruler are rooted in his own character and conduct, and sufficient attestation of them is given by the masses of the people. He examines them *by comparison* with those of the three kings, and finds them without mistake. He sets them up before heaven and earth, and finds nothing in them contrary to their mode of operation. He presents himself with them before spiritual beings, and no doubts about them arise. He is prepared to wait for the rise of a sage, a hundred ages after, and has no misgivings.

4. His presenting himself *with his institutions* before spiritual beings, without any doubts about them arising, shows that he knows Heaven. His being prepared, without any misgivings, to wait for the rise of a sage, a hundred ages after, shows that he knows men.

5. Such being the case, the movements of such a ruler, *illustrating his institutions*, constitute an example to the empire for ages. His acts are for ages a law to the empire. His words are for ages a lesson to the empire. Those who are far from him, look longingly for him; and those who are near him, are never wearied with him.

6. It is said in the Book of Poetry,—"Not disliked

" three important *things*." K'ang-shing says they are " the ceremonies of the three kings," *i.e.* the founders of the three dynasties, Hea, Yin, and Chow. This view we may safely reject. Choo He makes them to be the imperial prerogatives, mentioned in the last chapter, paragraph 2. This view may, possibly, be correct. But I incline to the view of the commentator Luh, of the T'ang dynasty, that they refer to the virtue, station, and time, which we have seen, in the notes on the last chapter, to be necessary to one who would give law to the empire. Maou mentions this view, indicating his own approval of it. 3. By "the Ruler" is intended the emperor sage of paragraph 1. " Attestation of his institutions is given by the masses of the people;" *i.e.* the people believe in such a ruler, and follow his regulations, thus attesting their adaptation to the general requirements of humanity. " The three kings," as mentioned above, are the founders of the three dynasties, viz. the great Yu, T'ang, the Successful, and Wăn and Woo, who are so often joined together, and spoken of as one. I hardly know what to make of " He sets them up before Heaven and Earth." Choo He says:—" Heaven and Earth here simply mean right reason. The meaning is—I set up *my institutions* here, and there is nothing in them contradictory to right reason." This, of course, is explaining the text away. But who can do anything better with it? I interpret " He presents himself with them before spiritual beings " with reference to sacrificial institutions, or the general trial of a sovereign's institutions by the efficacy of his sacrifice, in being responded to by the

there, not tired of here, from day to day and night to
night, will they perpetuate their praise." Never has
there been a ruler, who did not realize this description,
that obtained an early renown throughout the empire.

XXX. 1. Chung-ne handed down the doctrines of
Yaou and Shun, as if they had been his ancestors, and
elegantly displayed the regulations of Wăn and Woo,
taking them as his model. Above, he harmonized with
the times of heaven, and below, he was conformed to the
water and land.

2. He may be compared to heaven and earth, in their
supporting and containing, their overshadowing and curtaining, all things. He may be compared to the four seasons in their alternating progress, and to the sun and
moon in their successive shining.

3. All things are nourished together without their injuring one another. The courses *of the seasons, and of the
sun and moon*, are pursued without any collision among
them. The smaller energies are like river currents; the
greater energies are seen in mighty transformations. It
is this which makes heaven and earth so great.

XXXI. 1. It is only he, possessed of all sagely quali-

---

various spirits whom he worships. This is the view of Ho Ke-chen, and
is preferable to any other I have met with. 6. See the She-king, Pt IV.
Bk I. Sect. II. iii. 2. It is a great descent to quote that ode here, however, for it is only praising the feudal princes of Chow. "There" means
their own States; and "here" is the imperial court.

30. THE EULOGIUM OF CONFUCIUS, AS THE BEAU-IDEAL OF THE PER-
FECTLY SINCERE MAN, THE SAGE, MAKING A TERNION WITH HEAVEN
AND EARTH. 1. Chung-ne—See chapter II. The various predicates here
are explained by K'ang-shing, and Ying-tă, with reference to the "Spring
and Autumn," making them descriptive of it, but such a view will not
stand examination. Chinese writers observe that in what he handed
down, Confucius began with Yaou and Shun, because the times of Fuh-he
and Shin-nung were very remote. Was not the true reason this, that he
knew of nothing in China more remote than Yaou and Shun? By "the
times of heaven" are denoted the ceaseless regular movement, which
appears to belong to the heavens; and by the "water and the land," we
are to understand the earth, in contradistinction from heaven, supposed
to be fixed and immovable. The scope of the paragraph is, that the
qualities of former sages, of Heaven, and of Earth, were all concentrated
in Confucius. 2. "This describes," says Choo He, "the virtue of the
sage." 3. The wonderful and mysterious course of nature, or—as the
Chinese conceive—of the operations of Heaven and Earth, are described
to illustrate the previous comparison of Confucius.

31. THE EULOGIUM OF CONFUCIUS CONTINUED. Choo He says that

ties, that can exist under heaven, who shows himself quick in apprehension, clear in discernment, of far-reaching intelligence and all-embracing knowledge, fitted to exercise rule; magnanimous, generous, benign, and mild, fitted to exercise forbearance; impulsive, energetic, firm, and enduring, fitted to maintain a firm hold; self-adjusted, grave, never swerving from the Mean, and correct, fitted to command reverence; accomplished, distinctive, concentrative, and searching, fitted to exercise discrimination.

2. All-embracing is he and vast, deep and active as a fountain, sending forth in their due seasons his virtues.

3. All-embracing and vast, he is like heaven. Deep and active as a fountain, he is like the abyss. He is seen, and the people all reverence him; he speaks, and the people all believe him; he acts, and the people are all pleased with him.

4. Therefore, his fame overspreads the Middle kingdom, and extends to all barbarous tribes. Wherever ships and carriages reach; wherever the strength of man penetrates; wherever the heavens overshadow and the earth

---

this chapter is an expansion of the clause in the last paragraph of the preceding,—" The smaller energies are like river currents." Even if it be so, it will still have reference to Confucius, the subject of the preceding chapter. K'ang-shing's account of the first paragraph is:—" It describes how no one, who has not virtue such as this, can rule the empire, being a lamentation over the fact that while Confucius had the virtue, he did not have the appointment," that is, of Heaven, to occupy the throne. Maon's account of the whole chapter is:—" Had it been that Chung-ne possessed the empire, then Chung-ne was a perfect sage. Being a perfect sage, he would certainly have been able to put forth the greater energies, and the smaller energies of his virtue, so as to rule the world, and show himself the coequal of Heaven and Earth, in the manner here described." Considering the whole chapter to be thus descriptive of Confucius, I was inclined to translate in the past tense,—" It was only he, who could," &c. Still the author has expressed himself so indefinitely, that I have preferred translating the whole, that it may read as the description of the ideal man, who found, or might have found, his realization in Confucius. 1. The sage here takes the place of the man possessed of entire sincerity. Collie translates:—" It is only the most HOLY man." Rémusat:—" Il n'y a dans l'univers qu'un SAINT, qui.. So the Jesuits: " Hic commemorat et commendat summe SANCTI virtutes." But holiness and sanctity are terms which indicate the humble and pious conformity of human character and life to the mind and will of God. The Chinese idea of the "sage man" is far enough from this. 3. "He is seen;"—with reference, it is said, to "the robes and cap," the visibilities of the ruler. " He

sustains; wherever the sun and moon shine; wherever frosts and dews fall:—all who have blood and breath unfeignedly honour and love him. Hence it is said,—" He is the equal of Heaven."

XXXII. 1. It is only the individual possessed of the most entire sincerity that can exist under heaven, who can adjust the great invariable relations of mankind, establish the great fundamental virtues of humanity, and know the transforming and nurturing operations of Heaven and Earth;—shall this individual have any being or anything beyond himself on which he depends?

2. Call him man in his ideal, how earnest is he! Call him an abyss, how deep is he! Call him Heaven, how vast is he!

3. Who can know him, but he who is indeed quick in

---

speaks;"—with reference to his "instructions, declarations, orders." "He acts;"—with reference to his "ceremonies, music, punishments, and acts of government." 4. This paragraph is the glowing expression of grand conceptions.

32. THE EULOGIUM OF CONFUCIUS CONCLUDED. "The chapter," says Choo He, "expands the clause in the last paragraph of chapter xxix., that the greater energies are seen in mighty transformations." The sage is here not merely equal to Heaven:—he is another Heaven, an independent being, a God. 1. *King* and *Lun* are processes in the manipulation of silk, the former denoting the first separating of the threads, and the latter the subsequent bringing of them together, according to their kinds.—"The great invariabilities of the world." I translate the expansion of the last clause which is given in "*Confucius Sinarum Philosophus:*" "The perfectly holy man of this kind, therefore, since he is such and so great, how can it in any way be, that there is anything in the whole universe on which he leans, or in which he inheres, or on which he behoves to depend, or to be assisted by it in the first place, that he may afterwards operate?" 2. The three clauses refer severally to the three in the preceding paragraph. The first it speaks of is *virtuous humanity* in all its dimensions and capacities, existing perfectly in the sage. Of the sage being "a deep," I do not know what to say. The old commentators interpret the second and third clauses, as if there were an "as" before "deep" and "heaven," against which Choo He reclaims, and justly. In one work we read:—" Heaven and man are not originally two, and man is separate from Heaven only by his having this body. Of their seeing and hearing, their thinking and revolving, their moving and acting, men all say—*It is from* ME. Every one thus brings out his SELF, and his smallness becomes known. But let the body be taken away, and all would be Heaven. How can the body be taken away? Simply by subduing and removing that self-having of the *ego*. This is the taking it away. That being done, so wide and great as Heaven is, my mind is also so wide and great, and production and transformation cannot be

apprehension, clear in discernment, of far-reaching intelligence, and all-embracing knowledge, possessing all heavenly virtue?

XXXIII. 1. It is said in the Book of Poetry, "Over her embroidered robe she puts a plain, single garment," intimating a dislike to the display of the elegance of the former. Just so, it is the way of the superior man to prefer the concealment of *his virtue*, while it daily becomes more illustrious, and it is the way of the mean man to seek notoriety, while he daily goes more and more to ruin. It is characteristic of the superior man, appearing insipid, yet never to produce satiety; while showing a simple negligence, yet to have his accomplishments recognized; while seemingly plain, yet to be discriminating. He knows how what is distant lies in what is near. He knows where the wind proceeds from. He knows how what is minute becomes manifested. Such an one, we may be sure, will enter into virtue.

2. It is said in the Book of Poetry, "Although *the fish* sinks and lies at the bottom, it is still quite clearly seen."

separated from me. Hence it is said—*How vast is his Heaven*." Into such wandering mazes of mysterious speculation are Chinese thinkers conducted by the text:—only to be lost in them. As it is said, in paragraph 2, that only the sage can know the sage, we may be glad to leave him.

33. THE COMMENCEMENT AND THE COMPLETION OF A VIRTUOUS COURSE. The chapter is understood to contain a summary of the whole Work, and to have a special relation to the first chapter. There, a commencement is made with Heaven, as the origin of our nature, in which are grounded the laws of virtuous conduct. This ends with Heaven, and exhibits the progress of virtue, advancing step by step in man, till it is equal to that of High Heaven. There are eight citations from the Book of Poetry, but to make the passages suit his purpose, the author allegorises them, or alters their meaning, at his pleasure. Origen took no more license with the Scriptures of the Old and New Testament than Tsze-sze and even Confucius himself do with the Book of Poetry. 1. *The first requisite in the pursuit of virtue is, that the learner think of his own improvement, and do not act from a regard to others.* See the She-king, Pt I. Bk V. iii. 1. The ode is understood to express the condolence of the people with the wife of the duke of Wei, worthy of, but denied, the affection of her husband. 2. *The superior man going on to virtue, is watchful over himself when he is alone.* See the She-king, Pt II. Bk IV. viii. 11. The ode appears to have been written by some officer who was bewailing the disorder and misgovernment of his day. This is one of the comparisons which he uses;—the people are like fish in a shallow pond, unable to save themselves by diving to the bottom. The application of this to the superior

Therefore, the superior man examines his heart, that there may be nothing wrong there, and that he may have no cause for dissatisfaction with himself. That wherein the superior man cannot be equalled is simply this,—his *work which other men cannot see*.

3. It is said in the Book of Poetry, "Looked at in your apartment, be there free from shame, where you are exposed to the light of heaven." Therefore, the superior man, even when he is not moving, has *a feeling of reverence*, and while he speaks not, he has *the feeling of truthfulness*.

4. It is said in the Book of Poetry, "In silence is the offering presented, and *the spirit* approached to; there is not the slightest contention." Therefore, the superior man does not use rewards, and the people are stimulated to virtue. He does not show anger, and the people are awed more than by hatchets and battle-axes.

5. It is said in the Book of Poetry, "What needs no display is virtue. All the princes imitate it. Therefore, the superior man being sincere and reverential, the whole world is conducted to a state of happy tranquillity."

man, dealing with himself, in the bottom of his soul, so to speak, and thereby realizing what is good and right, is very far-fetched. 3. We have here substantially the same subject as in the last paragraph. The ode is the same which is quoted in chapter xvi. 4, and the citation is from the same stanza of it. We might translate it:

"When looked at in your chamber,
Are you there as free from shame in the house's leak?"

"The house's leak," according to Chou He, was the north-west corner of ancient apartments, the spot most secret and retired. But the single paces, in the roofs of Chinese houses, go now by the name, the light of heaven looking in through them. Looking at the whole stanza of the ode, we must conclude that there is reference to the light of heaven, and the inspection of spiritual beings, as specially connected with the spot intended. 4. *The result of the processes described in the two preceding paragraphs.* See the She-king, Pt IV. Bk. III. ii. 2. The ode describes the imperial worship of Tang, the founder of the Shang dynasty. The first clause belongs to the emperor's act and demeanour; the second to the effect of these on his assistants in the service. They were awed to reverence, and had no striving among themselves. The "hatchet and battle-axe" were anciently given by the emperor to a prince, as symbolic of his investiture with a plenipotent authority to punish the rebellious and refractory. The second instrument is described as a large-handled axe, eight catties in weight. I call it a battle-axe, because it was with one that king Woo despatched the tyrant Chow. 5. *The same subject continued.* See

6. It is said in the Book of Poetry, "I regard with pleasure your brilliant virtue, making no great display of itself in sounds and appearances." The Master said, "Among the appliances to transform the people, sounds and appearances are but trivial influences. It is said in another ode, 'Virtue is light as a hair.' Still, a hair will admit of comparison *as to its size*. 'The doings of the supreme Heaven have neither sound nor smell.'—That is perfect virtue."

The above is the thirty-third chapter. Tsze-sze having carried his descriptions to the extremest point in the preceding chapters, turns back in this, and examines the source of his subject; and then again from the work of the learner, free from all selfishness, and watchful over himself when he is alone, he carries out his description, till by easy steps he brings it to the consummation of the whole empire tranquillized by simple and sincere reverentialness. He further eulogizes its mysteriousness, till he speaks of it at last as without sound or smell. He here takes up the sum of his whole Work, and speaks of it in a compendious manner. Most deep and earnest was he in thus going again over his ground, admonishing and instructing men:—shall the learner not do his utmost in the study of the Work?

the She-king, Pt IV. Bk I. Sect. I. iv. 3. But in the She-king we must translate,—"There is nothing more illustrious than the virtue *of the sovereign*, all the princes will follow it." Tsze-sze puts another meaning on the words, and makes them introductory to the next paragraph. The "superior man" must here be "he who has attained to the sovereignty of the empire," the subject of chapter xxix. Thus it is that a constant shuffle of terms seems to be going on, and the subject before us is all at once raised to a higher and inaccessible platform. 6. *Virtue in its highest degree and influence.* See the She-king, Pt III. Bk I. viii. 7. The "*I*" is God, who announces to king Wăn the reasons why he had called him to execute his judgments. Wăn's virtue, not sounded nor emblazoned, might come near in the being without display of the last paragraph, but Confucius fixes on the word "great" to show its shortcoming. It had *some*, though not *large* exhibition. He therefore quotes again from Pt III. Bk III. vi. 6, though away from the original intention of the words. But it does not satisfy him that virtue should be likened even to a *hair*. He therefore finally quotes Pt III. Bk I. I. 7, where the imperceptible working of Heaven, in producing the overthrow of the Yin dynasty, is set forth as without sound or smell. That is his highest conception of the nature and power of virtue.

INDEXES.

INDEX I.

OF SUBJECTS IN THE CONFUCIAN ANALECTS.

Ability, various of Confucius, IX. vi.
Able officers, eight, of Chow, XVIII. xi.
Abroad, when a son may go, IV. xix.
Accomplishments come after duty, I. vi.; blended with solid excellence, VI. xvi.
Achievement of government, the great, XIII. ix.
Acknowledgment of Confucius in estimating himself, VII. xxxii.
Acting heedlessly, against, VII. xxvii.
Actions should always be right, XIV. iv.; of Confucius were lessons and laws, XVII. xix.
Adaptation for government of Yen Yung, &c., VI. i.; of Tsze-loo, &c., VI. vi.
Admiration, Yen Yuen's, of Confucius' doctrines, IX. x.
Admonition of Confucius to Tsze-loo, XI. xiv.
Advanced years, improvement difficult in, XVII. xxvi.
Adversity, men are known in times of, IX. xxvii.
Advice against useless expenditure, XI. xiii.
Age, the vice to be guarded against in, XVI. vii.
Aim, the chief, I. xvi.
Aims, of Tsze-loo, Tsăng-sih, &c., XI. xxv.
An all-pervading unity, the knowledge of, Confucius' aim, XV. ii.
Anarchy of Confucius' time, III. v.
Ancient rites, how Confucius cleaved to, III. xvii.
Ancients, their slowness to speak, IV. xxii.

Antiquity, Confucius' fondness for VII. xix.; decay of the monuments of, III. ix.
Anxiety of parents, II. vi.; of Confucius about the training of his disciples, V. ii.
Appearances, fair, are suspicious, I. iii., and XVII. xvii.
Appellations for the wife of a prince, XVI. xiv.
Appreciation, what conduct will insure, XV. v.
Approaches of the unlikely, readily met by Confucius, VII. xxviii
Approbation, Confucius', of Nan Yung, XI. v.
Aptitude of the *Keun-tsze*, II. xii.
Archery, contention in, III. vii.; a discipline of virtue, III. xvi.
Ardent and cautious disciples, Confucius obliged to be content with, XIII. xxi.
Ardour of Tsze-loo, V. vi.
Art of governing, XII. xiv.
Assent without reformation, a hopeless case, IX. xxiii.
Attachment to Confucius of Yen Yuen, XI. xxiii.
Attainment, different stages of, VI. xviii.
Attainments of Hwuy, like those of Confucius, VII. x.
Attributes of the true scholar, XIX. i.
Auspicious omens, Confucius gives up hope for want of, IX. viii.
Avenge murder, how Confucius wished to, XIV. xxii.

Bad name, the danger of a, XIX. xx.
Barbarians, how to civilise, IX. xiii.

21

Becloudings of the mind, XVII. viii.
Bed, manner of Confucius in, X. xvi.
Benefits derived from studying the Odes, XVII. ix.
Benevolence, to be exercised with prudence, VI. xxiv.; and wisdom, XII. xxii.
Blind, consideration of Confucius for the, XV. xli.
Boldness, excessive, of Tsze-loo, VII. x.
Burial, Confucius' dissatisfaction with Hwuy's, XI. x.
Business, every man should mind his own, VIII. xiv., and XIV. xxvii.

Calmness of Confucius in danger, VII. xxii.
Capacity of Mang Kung-ch'ö, XIV. xii.
Capacities of the superior and inferior man, XV. xxxiii.
Careful, about what things Confucius was, VII. xii.
Carriage, Confucius at and in his, X. xvii.; Confucius refuses to sell his, to assist a needless expenditure, XI. vii.
Caution, advantages of, IV. xxiii.; repentance avoided by, I. xiii.; in speaking, XII. iii., and XV. vii.
Ceremonies and music, XI. i.; end of, I. xii.; impropriety in, III. x.; influence of in government, IV. xiii.; regulated according to their object, III. iv.; secondary and ornamental, III. viii.; vain without virtue, III. iii.
Character (s), admirable, of Tsze-yu, &c., XV. vi.; differences in, owing to habit, XVII. ii.; different, of two dukes, XIV. xvi.; disliked by Confucius, and Tsze-kung, XVII. xxiv.; how Confucius dealt with different, XI. xxi.; how to determine, II. x.; lofty, of Shun and Yu, VIII. xviii.; of four disciples, XI. xvii.; of Kung-shuh Wǎn, XIV. xiv.; of Tan-t'ae Mëen-ming, VI. xii.; various elements of in Confucius, VII. xxxvii.; what may be learnt from, IV. xvii.
Characteristics, of perfect virtue, XIII. xix.; of ten disciples, XI. ii.
Claimed, what Confucius, VII. xxxiii.
Classes of men, in relation to knowledge, four, XVI. ix.; only two whom practice cannot change, XVII. iii.
Climbing the heavens, equalling Confucius like, XIX. xxv.

Common practices, some indifferent and others not, IX. iii.
Communications to be proportioned to susceptibility, VI. xix.
Comparison of Sze and Shang, XI. xv.
Comparisons, against making, XIV. xxxi.
Compass and vigour of mind necessary to a scholar, VIII. vii.
Compassion, how a criminal-judge should cherish, XVIII. xix.
Complete man, of the, XIV. xiii.; virtue, I. XIV., and VI. xvi.
Concealment, not practised by Confucius with his disciples, VII. xxiii.
Concubines, difficult to treat, XVII. xxv.
Condemnation of Tsang Woo-Chung. XIV. xv.; of Confucius for seeking employment, XIV. xli.
Condition, only virtue adapts a man to his, IV. ii.
Conduct that will be everywhere appreciated, XV. v.
Confidence, enjoying, necessary to serving and to ruling, XIX. x.
Connate, Confucius' knowledge not, VII. xix.
Consideration, of Confucius for the blind, XV. xli.; a generous, of others, recommended, XVIII. x.
Consolation to Tsze-new, when anxious about his brother, XII. v.
Constancy of mind, importance of, XIII. xxii.
Constant Mean, the, VI. xxvii.
Contemporaries of Confucius described, XVI. xi.
Contention, the superior man avoids, III. vii.
Contentment in poverty of Tsze-loo, IX. xxvi.; of Confucius with his condition, IX. xi.; of the officer King, XIII. viii.
Contrast of Hwuy and Tsze, XI. xviii.
Conversation, with Chung-kung, XII. ii.; with Tsze-chang, XII. vi., vii.; XX. ii.; with Tsze-kung, XIV. xviii.; with Tsze-loo, XIV. xiii., xvii.; with Tsze-new, XII. iii.; with Yen Yuen, XII. i.
Countenance, the, in filial piety, I. viii.
Courage, not doing right from want of, II. xxiv.
Criminal judge, should cherish compassion, XIX. xix.
Culpability of not reforming known faults, XV. xxix.

Danger, Confucius assured in time of IX. v.

Dead, offices to the, I. ix.
Death, Confucius evades a question about, XI. xi.; how Confucius felt Hwuy's, XI. viii., ix.; without regret, IV. viii.
Declined, what Confucius, to be reckoned, VII. xxxiii.
Defects of former times become modern vices, XVII. xvi.
Defence, of himself by Confucius, XIV. xxxvi.; of his own method of teaching, by Tsze-hea, XIX. xii.; of Tsze-loo, by Confucius, XI. xiv.
Degeneracy, of Confucius' age, VI. xiv.; instance of, XV. xxv.
Delusions, how to discover, XII. x., xxi.
Demeanour of Confucius, X. i. to v., xiii.
Departure of Confucius, from Loo, XVIII. iv.; from Ts'e, XVIII. iii.
Depreciation, Confucius above the reach of, XIX. xxiv.
Description of himself as a learner, by Confucius, VII. xviii.
Desire and ability, required in disciples, VII. viii.
Development of knowledge, II. xi.
Differences of character, owing to habit, XVII. ii.
Dignity, necessary in a ruler, XV. xxxii.
Disciples, anxiety about training, V. xxi.
Discrimination of Confucius in rewarding officers, VI. iii.; without suspiciousness, the merit of, XIV. xxxiii.
Dispersion of the musicians of Loo, XVIII. xi.
Distinction, notoriety not, XII. xx.
Distress, the superior man above, XV. i.
Divine mission, Confucius' assurance of a, VII. xxii., IX. v.
Doctrine of Confucius, admiration of, IX. x.
Dreams of Confucius affected by disappointments, VII. v.
Dress, rules of Confucius in regard to his, X. vi.
Dying counsels to a man in high station, VIII. iv.
Dynasties, Yin, Hea, and Chow, VIII. iv., III. xx.; Yin and Hea, III. ix.; Chow, &c., III. xiv.; certain rules exemplified in the ancient: eight able officers of the Chow, XVIII. xi.; three worthies of the Yin, XVIII. i.; the three, XV. xxiv.

Earnest student, Hwuy the, IX. xix.

Earnestness in teaching of Confucius, IX. vii.
Egotism, instance of freedom from, VIII. v.
Eight able officers of the Chow dynasty, XVIII. xi.
Emolument, learning for, II. xviii.; shameful to care only for, XIV. i.
End, the, crowns the work, IX. xxi.
Enjoyment, advantageous and injurious sources of, XVI. v.
Equalled, Confucius cannot be, XIX. xxv.
Error, how acknowledged by Confucius, VII. xxx.
Essential, what is, in different services, III. xxvi.
Estimate, Confucius' humble, of himself, VII. ii., iii., IX. xv., XIV. xxx.; of what he could do if employed, XIII. x.
Estimation of others, not a man's concern, XIV. xxxii.
Example, better than force, II. xx.; government efficient by, &c., XII. xvii., xviii., xix.; the secret of rulers' success, XIII. i.; value of, in those in high stations, VIII. ii.
Excess and defect equally wrong, XI. xv.
Expenditure, against useless, XI. xiii.
External, the, may be predicated from the internal, XIV. v.
Extravagant speech, hard to be made good, XIV. xxi.

Fair appearances are suspicious, I. iii., and XVII. xvii.
Fasting, rules observed by Confucius when, X. vii.
Father's vices, no discredit to a virtuous son, VI. iv.
Faults of men, characteristic of their class, IV. vii.
Feelings, need not always be spoken, XIV. iv.
Fidelity of his disciples, Confucius' memory of, XI. ii.
Filial piety, I. xi., IV. xix., xx., xxi.; argument for, II. vi; cheerfulness in, II. viii.; the foundation of virtuous practice, I. ii.; of Meen Tsze-keen, XI. iv.; of Mäng Chwang, XIX. xviii.; reverence in, II. vii.; seen in care of the person, VIII. iii.
Firmness of superior man, based on right, XV. xxxvi.
Five excellent things to be honoured, XX. ii.; things which constitute perfect virtue, XVII. vi.
Flattery of sacrificing to others' ancestors, II. xxiv.

Food, rules of Confucius about his, X. viii.
Foreknowledge, how far possible, II. xxiii.
Forethought, necessity of, XV. xi.
Formalism, against, III. iv.
Former times, Confucius' preference for, XI. i.
Forward youth, Confucius' employment of a, XIV. xlvii.
Foundation of virtue, I. ii.
Four bad things, to be put away, XX. ii.; classes of men in relation to knowledge, XVI. ix.
Frailties from which Confucius was free, IX. iv.
Fraternal submission, I. ii.
Friends, rules for choosing, I. viii., and IX. xxiv.; trait of Confucius in relation to, X. xv.
Friendship, how to maintain, V. xvi.; Tsze-chang's virtue too high for, XIX. xvi.
Friendships, what, advantageous and injurious, XVI. iv.
Frivolous talkers, against, XV. xvi.
Funeral rites, Confucius' dissatisfaction with Hwuy's, XI. x.; to parents, I. ix.
Furnace, the, and the S. W. Corner, of a house, III. xiii.

Gain, the mean man's concern, IV. xvi.
Generosity of Pih-e and Shuh-ts'e, V. xxii.
Glib-tongued, Confucius not, XIV. xxxiv.
Glibness of tongue and beauty, esteemed by the age, VI. xiv.
Glossing faults, a proof of the mean man, XIX. viii.
Gluttony and idleness, case of, hopeless, XVII. xxii.
God, address to, XX. i.
Golden rule, expressed with negatives, V. xi., XV. xxiii.
Good fellowship of Confucius, VII. xxxi.
Good, learning leads to, VIII. xii.
Good man, the, XI. xix.; we must not judge a man to be, from his discourse,' XI. xx.
Governing, the art of, XII. xiv.; without personal effort, XV. iv.
Government, good, seen from its effects, XIII. xvi.; good, how only obtained, XII. xi.; may be conducted efficiently, how, XX. ii.; moral in its end, XII. xvii.; principles of, I. v.; requisites of, XII. vii.
Gradual progress of Confucius, II. iv.;

communication of his doctrine, V. xii.
Grief, Confucius vindicates his, for Hwuy, XI. ix.
Guiding principle of Confucius, XVIII. viii.

Happiness of Confucius among his disciples, XI. xii.; of Hwuy in poverty, VI. ix.
Haste, not to be desired in government, XIII. xvii.
Heaven, Confucius rested in the ordering of, XIV. xxxviii.; knew him, Confucius thought that, XIV. xxxvii.; no remedy for sin against, III. xiii.
Hesitating faith, Tsze-chang on, XIX. ii.
High aim proper to a student, VI. x.; things, too much minding of, XIX. xv.
Home, Confucius at, X. xvi.; how Confucius could be not at, XVII. xx.
Hope, Confucius gives up, for want of auspicious omens, IX. viii.
Hopeless case, of gluttony and idleness, XVII. xxii.; of those who assent to advice without reforming, IX. xxiii.; of those who will not think, XV. xv.
House and wall, the comparison of a, XIX. xxiii.
Humble claim of Confucius for himself, V. xxvii.; estimate of himself, VII. ii., iii., IX. xv., XIV. xxx.
Humility of Confucius, VII. xxvi.
Hundred years, what good government could effect in a, XIII. xi.

Idleness of Tsae Yu, V. ix.; case of, hopeless, XVII. xxii.
Ignorant man's remark about Confucius, IX. ii.
Impatience, danger of, XV. xxvi.
Imperial rites, usurpation of, III. i., ii., vi.
Improvement, self, II. xviii.; difficult in advanced years, XVII. xxvi.
Incompetency, our own, a fit cause of concern, XV. xviii.
Indifference of the officer King to riches, XIII. viii.
Indignation of Confucius at the usurpation of imperial rites, III. i., ii.; at the support of usurpation and extortion by a disciple, XI. xvi.; at the wrong overcoming the right, XVII. xviii.
Inferior pursuits, inapplicable to great objects, XIX. iv.

Instruction, how a man may find, VII. xxi.
Instructions to a son about government, XVIII. x.
Insubordination, worse than meanness, VII. xxxv.; different causes of, VIII. x.
Intelligence, what constitutes, XII. vi.
Intercourse, character formed by, V. ii.; of Confucius with others, traits of, X. xi.; with others, different opinions on, XIX. iii.
Internal, the, not predicable from the external, XIV. v.
Ironical admonition, XIII. xiv.

Jealousy of others' talents, against, XV. x., iii.
Joy of Confucius independent of outward circumstances, VII. xv.
Judgment of Confucius concerning Tsze-ch'an, &c., XIV. x.; of retired worthy, on Confucius, XIV. xlii.

Keun-tsze. See Superior man.
Killing, not to be talked of by rulers, XII. xix.
Knowing and not knowing, II. xvii.
Knowledge, disclaimed by Confucius, IX. vii.; four classes of men in relation to, XVI. ix., not lasting without virtue, XV. xxxii.; of Confucius not connate, VIII. xix.; sources of Confucius', XIX. xxii.; subserves benevolence, II. xxii.

Lament over moral error added to natural defect, VIII. xvi.; sickness of Pih-new, VI. viii.; persistence in error, V. xxvi.; rarity of the love of virtue, IV. vi.; the rash reply of Tsao Go, III. xxi.; the waywardness of men, VI. xiv.; of Confucius, that men did not know him, XIV. xxxvii.
Language, the chief virtue of, XV. xl.
Learner, the, I. i., xiv.; Confucius describes himself as a, VII. xviii.
Learning and propriety combined, VI. xxv. and XII. xv.; Confucius' fondness for, V. xxvii.; different motives for, XIV. xxv.; end of, II. xviii.; how to be pursued, VI. xi. and VIII. xvii.; in order to virtue, XIX. vi.; necessity of, to complete virtue, XVII. viii.; quickly leads to good, VIII. xii.; should not cease or be intermitted, IX. xviii.; substance of, I. vii.; the indications of a real love of, XIX. v.; the student's workshop, XIX. vii.
Lesson, of prudence, XIV. ix.; to parents and ministers, XIV. viii.; to rulers, VIII. x.; to Tsze-loo, XIII. i.
Lessons and laws, Confucius' actions were, XVII. xix.
Libation, pouring out of, in sacrifice, III. x.
Life, human, valued by Confucius, X. xii.; without uprightness, not true, VI. xvii.
Likings and dislikings of others, in determining a man's character, XIII. xxiv. and XV. xxvii.
Literary acquirements, useless without practical ability, XIII. v.
Litigation, how Tsze-loo could settle, XII. xii.; it is better to prevent, XII. xiii.
Love of virtue rare, IV. vi. and IX. xvii.
Love to learn, of Confucius, V. xxvii.; of Hwuy, XI. vi.; rarity of, VI. ii.
Loving and hating aright, IV. iii.

Madman, the, of Ts'oo, XVIII. v.
Man, in relation to principles of duty, XV. xxviii.
Manhood, the vice to be guarded against in, XVI. vii.
Manner of Confucius when unoccupied, VII. iv.
Marriage-making, Confucius in, V. i.
Mat, rule of Confucius about his, X. ix.
Maturing of character, rules for, VII. vi.
Mean man, glosses his faults, XIX. viii. See Superior man.
Meanness of Wei-shang, V. xxiii.; not so bad as insubordination, VII. xxxv.
Mercenary officers, impossible to serve along with, XVII. xv.
Merit of Kung-shuh Wăn, XIV. xix.; of Kwan Chung, XIV. xvii., xviii.; virtue of concealing, VI. xiii.
Messenger, an admirable, XIV. xxvi.
Military affairs, Confucius refuses to talk of, XV. i.
Minding too much high things, XIX. xv.
Minister, the faithful, XV. xxxvii.
Ministers, great and ordinary, XI. xxiii.; importance of good and able, XIV. xix.; must be sincere and upright, XIV. xxiii.; should be strict and decided, XIV. viii.
Mission of Confucius, Yen Ywen's confidence in, XI. xxii.
Model student, fond recollections of a, IX. xx.

Moral appliances to be preferred in government, II. iii.
Mourners, Confucius' sympathy with, VII. ix., and X. xvi.
Mourning, three years for parents, XVII. xxi.; government, how carried on in time of, XIV. xliii.; the trappings of, may be dispensed with, XIX. xiv.
Murder of the duke of Ts'e, XIV. xxii.
Music, and ceremonies, vain without virtue, III. iii.; effect of, VIII. viii.; effect of, on Confucius, VII. xiii.; influence of, in government, XVII. iv.; of Shun and Woo compared, III. xxv.; on the playing of, III. xxiii.; service rendered to, by Confucius, IX. xiv.; the sound of instruments does not constitute, XVII. xi.
Musicians of Loo, the, dispersion of, XVIII. ix.
Music-master, praise of a, VIII. xv.

Name, danger of a bad, XIX. xx.; without reality, VI. xxiii.
Names, importance of being correct, XIII. iii.
Narrow-mindedness, Tsze-chang on, XIX. ii.
Natural duty and uprightness in collision, XIII. xviii.; case in ceremonies to be prized, I. xii.; qualities which are favourable to virtue, XIII. xxvii.
Nature of a man, grief brings out the real, XIX. xvii.
Neighbourhood, what constitutes the excellence of a, IV. i.
Nine subjects of thought to the superior man, XVI. x.
Notoriety, not true distinction, XII. xx.

Odes (s), the Chow-nan and Shaou-nan, XVII. x.; the Kwan-ts'eu, III. xx.; the Yung, III. ii.; Pih-kwō, X. v.; of Ch'ing, XV. x.; the Nga, IX. xiv.; XVII. xviii.
Odes, the study of the Book of, XVI. xiii. and XVII. ix., x.; quotations from the, I. xv., III. xviii., IX. xxvi., XII. x.; the pure design of the, II. ii.
Office, declined by Tsze-k'een, VI. vii.; desire for, qualified by self-respect, IX. xii.; Confucius, why not in, II. xxi.; when to be accepted, and when to be declined, VIII. xiii.
Officers, classes of men who may be styled, XIII. xx.; mercenary, im-

possible to serve with, XVII. xv.; personal correctness essential to, XIII. xiii.; should first attend to their proper work, XIX. xiii.
Official notifications of Ch'ing, why excellent, XIV. ix.
Old knowledge, to be combined with new acquisitions, II. xi.
Old man, encounter with an, XVIII. vii.
Opposing a father, disapproved of, VII. xiv.
Ordinances of Heaven necessary to be known, XX. iii.
Ordinary people could not understand Confucius, XIX. xxiii.; ordinary rules, Confucius not to be judged by, XVII. vii.
Originator, Confucius not an, VII. i.

Parents, grief for, brings out the real nature of a man, XIX. xvii.; how a son may remonstrate with, IV. xviii.; should be strict and decided, XIV. viii.; three years' mourning for, XVII. xxi.; their years to be remembered, IV. xxi.
People, what may and what may not be attained to with the, VIII. ix.
Perfect virtue, caution in speaking, characteristics of, XII. iii.; characteristics of, XIII. xix.; estimation of, V. xviii. and VI. xx.; five things which constitute, XVII. vi.; how to attain to, XII. i.; not easily attained, XIV. vii.; wherein realised, XII. ii.
Persuasion in error, lament over, V. xxvi.
Perseverance proper to a student, VI. x.
Personal attainment, a man's chief concern, I. xvi. and XIV. xxxii.; conduct, all in all in a ruler, XIII. xvi.; correctness, essential to an officer, XIII. xiii.
Perspicuity the chief virtue of language, XV. xl.
Pervading unity, Confucius' doctrine a, IV. xv.; how Confucius aimed at, XV. viii.
Phœnix, the, IX. viii. and XVIII. v.
Piety, see Filial.
Pity of Confucius for misfortune, IX. ix.
Plans, what is necessary to concord in, XV. xxxix.
Poetry, benefits of the study of the Book of, VIII. viii., and XVII. ix., x., and music, service rendered to by Confucius, IX. xiv.
Posthumous titles, on what principle conferred, V. xiv.

INDEX I. SUBJECTS IN THE ANALECTS. 327

Poverty, happiness in, VI. ix.; harder to bear aright than riches, XIV. xi; no disgrace to a scholar, IV. ix.
Practical ability, importance of, XIII. v.
Practice, Confucius' zeal to carry his principles into, XVII. v.
Praise of the house of Chow, VIII. xx.; of the music-master Ch'e, VIII. xv.; of Yaou, VIII. xix.; of Yu, VIII. xxi.
Praising and blaming, Confucius' correctness in, XV. xxiv.
Prayer, sin against Heaven precludes, III. xiii.; Confucius declines, for himself, VII. xxxiv.
Precaution, necessity of, XV. xi.
Preliminary study, necessity of, to governing, XI. xxiv.
Presumption, &c., of the chief of the Ke family, XVI. i.; and pusillanimity conjoined, XVII. xii.
Pretence, against, II. xvii.; Confucius' dislike of, IX. xi.
Pretentiousness of Confucius' time, VII. xxv.
Prince, and minister, relation of, III. xix.; Confucius' demeanour before a, X. ii.; Confucius' demeanour in relation to, X. xiii.
Princes, Confucius' influence on, I. x.; how to be served, III. xviii.
Principles, agreement in, necessary to concord in plans, XV. xxxix.; and ways of Yaou, Shun, &c., XX. i.; of duty, an instrument in the hand of man, XV. xxviii.
Prompt decision good, V. xix.
Propriety, and music, influence of, XVII. iv.; combined with learning, VI. xxv. and XII. xv.; effect of, VIII. viii.; love of, facilitates government, XIV. xliv.; necessary to a ruler, XV. xxxii.; not in external appurtenances, XVII. xi.; rules of, I. xii., III. xv.; rules of, necessary to be known, XX. iii.; value of the rules of, VIII. ii.
Prosperity and ruin of a country, on what dependent, XIII. xv. and XVI. ii.
Prowess conducting to ruin, XIV. vi.
Prudence, a lesson of, XIV. iv.
Pursuit of riches, against, VII. xi.
Pusillanimity and presumption, XVII. xii.

Qualifications of an officer, VIII. xiii.
Qualities that are favourable to virtue, XIII. xxvii.; that mark the scholar, XIII. xxviii.

Rash words cannot be recalled, III. xxi.
Readiness of Confucius to impart instruction, VII. vii.; of speech, V. iv. and XVII. xiv.
Reading and thought, should be combined, II. xv. and XV. xxx.
Rebuke to Yen Yew, &c., XVI, i.
Receptivity of Hwuy, II. ix. and XI. iii.
Reciprocity the rule of life, XV. xxiii.
Recluse, Tsze-loo's encounter with a, XVIII. vii.
Recluses, Confucius and the two, XVIII. vi.
Recollection of Hwuy, Confucius' fond, XI. xx.
Reflection, the necessity of, IX. xxx.
Regretful memory of disciples' fidelity, XI. ii.
Relative duties, necessity of maintaining, XII. xi.
Remark of an ignorant man about Confucius, IX. ii.
Remonstrance with parents, IV. xviii.
Repentance escaped by timely care, I. xiii.
Reproof to Tsze-loo, XI. xxiv.
Reproofs, frequent, warning against the use of, IV. xxvi.
Reputation not a man's concern, XV. xviii.
Resentments, how to ward off, XV. xiv.
Residence, rule for selecting a, IV. i.
Respect, a youth should be regarded with, IX. xxii.; of Confucius for men, XV. xxiv.; of Confucius for rank, IX. ix.
Retired worthy's judgment on Confucius, XIV. xlii.
Reverence for parents, II. vii.
Riches, pursuit of, uncertain of success, VII. xi.
Right way, importance of knowing the, IV. viii.
Righteous and public spirit of Confucius, XIV. xxii.
Righteousness the Keun-tsze's concern, IV. xvi.; is his rule of practice, IV. x.
Root of benevolence, filial and fraternal duty is the, I. ii.
Royal ruler, a, could, in what time, transform the empire, XIII. xii.
Ruin and prosperity dependent on what, XIII. xv. and XVI. ii.
Rule of life, reciprocity the, XV. xxiii.
Ruler, virtue in a, II. i.
Rulers, a lesson to, VIII. x.; personal conduct all in all to, XIII. xvi; should not be occupied with what is

the proper business of the people, XIII. iv.
Ruling, best means of, II. iii.
Running stream, a, Confucius how affected by, IX. xvi.
Sacrifice, Confucius' sincerity in, III. xii.; the great, III. x., xi.; wrong subjects of, II. xxiv.
Sagehood, not in various ability, IX. vi.
Scholar, attributes of the true, XIX. i.; his aim must be higher than comfort, XIV. iii.
Self-cultivation, I. viii. and IX. xxiv.; a man's concern, IV. xiv.; a characteristic of the Keun-tsze, XIV. xlv.; Confucius' anxiety about, VII. iii.; steps in, I. xv.
Self-examination, I. iv.
Selfish conduct means murmuring, IV. xii.
Self-respect should qualify desire for office, IX. xii.
Self-willed, Confucius not, XIV. xxxiv.
Sequences of wisdom, virtue, and bravery, IX. xxviii.
Servants, difficult to treat, XVII. xxv.
Shame of caring only for salary, XIV. i.
Shaou, a name of certain music, III. xxv.
Sheep, the monthly offering of a, III. xvii.
Shoo-king, quotation from, II. xxi.; XIV. xliii; compilation from, XX. i.
Silent mourning, three years of, XIV. xliii.
Simplicity, instance of, VIII. v.
Sincerity, cultivation of, I. iv.; necessity of, II. xxii.; praise of, V. xxiv.
Slandering of Tsze-loo, XIV. xxxviii.
Slowness to speak, of the ancients, IV. xxii.; of the Keun-tsze, IV. xxiv.
Small advantages not to be desired in government, XIII. xvii.
Social intercourse, qualities of the scholar in, XIII. xxiii.
Solid excellence blended with ornament, VI. xvi.
Son, a, opposing his father, against, VII. xiv.; Confucius' instruction of his own, XVI. xiii.
Sources of Confucius' knowledge, XIX. xxii.
Specious words, danger of, XV. xxvi.
Speech, discretion in, XV. vii.
Spirit of the times, against, III. xviii.
Spirits, Confucius evades a question about serving, XI. xi.: of the land, altars of, III. xxi.
Stages of attainment, VI. xviii.; of

progress, different persons stop at different, IX. xxix.
States of Ts'e and Loo, VI. xxii.
Strange doctrines, II. xvi.
Strength, not a fit subject of praise, XIV. xxxv.
Student's proper work, XIX. xiii.
Stupidity of King Woo, V. xx.
Subjects, avoided by Confucius, VII. xx.; of Confucius' teaching, VII. xxiv. See Topics.
Submission of subjects, how secured, II. xix.
Substantial qualities, and accomplishments, in the Keun-tsze, XII. viii.
Sun and moon, Confucius like the, XIX. xxiv.
Superficial speculations, against, XV. xvi.
Superior and mean man, II. xii., xiii., xiv., IV. xi., xvi., VI. xi., VII. xxxvi., XVI. viii.; different air and bearing of, XIII. xxvi.; different in their relation to those employed by them, XIII. xxv.; different manners of, XIII. xxiii.; different tendencies of, XIV. xxiv.; how to know, XV. xxiii.; opposite influence of, XII. xvi.
Superior man, above distress, XV. i.; changing appearances of, to others, XIX. ix.; cleaves to virtue, IV. v.; does not conceal, but changes, his errors, XIX. xxi.; firmness of, heard on right, XV. xxxvi.; four characteristics of, V. xv.; is righteous, courteous, humble, and sincere, XV. xvii.; more in deeds than in words, XIV. xxix.; nine subjects of thought to, XVI. x.; rule about his words and actions, IV. xxiv.; self-cultivation, characteristic of, XIV. xlv.; talents and virtues of, VIII. vi.; thoughts of in harmony with his position, XIV. xxviii.: truth the object of, XV. xxxi.; various characteristics of, XV. xx., xxii., xxiii.; wishes to be had in remembrance, XV. xix.
Superiority of Hwuy, VI. ii., v.
Superstitions of Tsang Wăn, V. xvii.
Supreme authority ought to maintain its power, XVI. ii.
Susceptivity of learners, teachers to be guided by, VI. xix.
Swiftness to speak, incompatible with virtue, XVII. xiv.
Sympathy of Confucius with mourners, VII. ix.; with sorrow, IX. ix.

Talents, men of, scarce, VIII. xx.; worthless without virtue, VIII. xi.

Taxation, light, advantages of, XII. ii.
Teacher, qualifications of a, II. xi.
Teaching, effect of, XV. xxxviii.; Confucius' earnestness in, IX. vii.; Confucius' subjects of, VII. xxiv.; graduated method of, XIX. vii.; necessary to prepare the people for war, XIII. xxix., xxx.
Temple, Confucius in the grand, XIII. xv. and X. xiv.
Thieves made by the example of rulers, XII. xviii.
Think, those who will not, the case of, hopeless, XV. xv.
Thinking without reading, fruitless, XV. xxx.
Thought and learning, to be combined, II. xv.
Three, errors of speech, in the presence of the great, XVI. vi.; families of Lu, III. ii.; friendships advantageous, and three injurious, XVI. iv.; sources of enjoyment, id. id., XVI. v.; things of which the superior man stands in awe, XVI. viii.; years' mourning, XIV. xliii., XVII. xxi.; worthies of the Yin dynasty, XVIII.i.
Thunder, Confucius how affected by, X. xvi.
Topics, avoided by Confucius, VII. xx.; most common of Confucius, VII. xvii.; seldom spoken on by Confucius, IX. i.
Traditions of the principles of Wan and Wu, XIX. xxii.
Training of the young, I. vi.
Transmitter, Confucius a, VII. i.
Trappings of mourning may be dispensed with, XIX. xiv.
Treatment of a powerful but unworthy officer by Confucius, XVII. i.
True turn, priority of, in Confucius' time, VII. xxv.
Truthfulness, necessity of, I. xxii.
Two classes only whom practice cannot change, XVII. iii.; recluses, Confucius and the, XVIII. vi.

Unbending virtue, V. x.
Unchangeableness of great principles, II. xxiii.
Unity of Confucius' doctrine, IV. xv. and XV. ii.
Unmannerly old man, Confucius' conduct to an, XIV. xlvi.
Unoccupied, Confucius' manner when, VII. iv.
Unworthy men, Confucius responds to the advances of an, XVII. vii.
Uprightness, and natural duty in collision, XIII. xviii.; measures inconsistent with, V. xxii.; necessary to true virtue, VI. xvii.
Usurped rites, against, III. i., ii., vi.
Usurping tendencies of the Ke family, XIII. xiv.
Utensil, Tsze-kung an, V. iii.; the accomplished scholar not an, II. xii.

Valour subordinate to righteousness, XVII. xxiii.
Various ability of Confucius, IX. vi.
View, how to correct, XII. xxi.
Vices, of a father, no discredit to a good son, VI. iv.; which youth, manhood, and age have to guard against, XVI. vii.
Village, Confucius' demeanour in his, X. i., x.
Vindication, Confucius', of himself, VI. xxvi.; of Confucius by Tsze-loo, XVIII. vii.
Virtue, alone adapts a man for his condition, IV. ii.; and not strength, a fit subject of praise, XIV. xxxv.; ceremonies and music vain without, III. iii.; complete, I. i.; contentment with what is vulgar injures, XVII. xiii.; devotion of the Kwun-tsze to, IV. v.; exceeding, of Tae-pih, VIII. i.; few really know, XV. iii.; how to exalt, XII. x., xxi; in concealing one's merit, VI. xiii.; influence of, II. i.; knowledge not lasting without, XV. xxxii.; leading to empire, XIV. vi.; learning necessary to the completion of, XVII. viii.; learning leading to, XIX. vi.; how of, rare, IV. vi., IX. xvii., XV. xii.; natural qualities which favour, XIII. xxvii.; not far to seek, VII. xxix.; the highest, not easily attained, and incompatible with meanness, XIV. vii.; the practice of, aided by intercourse with the good, XV. ix.; to be valued more than life, XV. viii.; true nature and art of, VI. xxviii.; without wealth, &c., XVI. xii.
Virtues, the great, demand the chief attention, XIX. xi.
Virtuous men, not left alone, IV. xxv.; only can love or hate others, IV. iii.
Vocation of Confucius, a stranger's view of, III. xxiv.
Vulgar ways and views, against contentment with, XVII. xiii.

War, how a good ruler prepares the people for, XIII. xxix., xxx.
Warning to Tsze-loo, XI. xii.
Waywardness, lament over, VI. xv.
Wealth without virtue, &c., XVI. xii.

Wickedness, the virtuous will preserve from, IV. iv.
Wife of a prince, appellations for, XVI. xiv.
Will, the virtuous, preserves from wickedness, IV. iv.; is unsubduable, IX. xxv.
Wisdom and virtue, chief elements of, VI. xx.; contrasts of, VI. xxi., IX. xxviii.
Wishes, different, of Yen Yuen, &c., V. xxv.; of Tsze-loo, &c., XI. xxv.
Withdrawing from public life, different causes of, XIV. xxxix.; of Confucius, XVIII. v., vi.; of seven men,

XIV. xl.
Withdrawing from the world, Confucius proposes, V. vi.; Confucius' judgment on, XVIII. viii.
Words, the force of, necessary to be known, XX. iii.
Work, a man's, is with himself, XIV. xxx.
Workshop, the student's, XIX. vii.

Young, duty of the, I. vi.; should be regarded with respect, IX. xxii.
Youth, the vice to be guarded against in, XVI. vii.

INDEX II.

OF PROPER NAMES IN THE CONFUCIAN ANALECTS.

Names in Italics will be found in their own places in this Index, with additional references.

Ch'ae, surnamed Kaou, and styled *Tsze-kaou*, a disciple of Confucius, XI. xvii.
Chang, *Tsze-chang*, XIX. xv., xvi.
Ch'ang-tseu, a worthy of Ts'oo, XVIII. vi.
Chaou, a prince celebrated for his beauty of person, VI. xiv.
Chaou, one of the three families which governed the state of Tsin, XIV. xii.
Ch'aou, the honourable epithet of Chow, duke of Loo, B. C. 540—509, VII. xxx.
Che, the Music-master of Loo, VIII. xv., XVIII. ix.
Ch'ih, surnamed *Kung-se*, and styled *Tsze-hwa*, a disciple of Confucius, V. vii., VI. iii., XI. xxv.
Ch'in, the state of, V. xxi., VII. xxx., XI. ii., XV. i.
Ch'in K'ang, *Tsze-k'in*, a disciple of Confucius, XVI. xiii.
Ch'in Shing, or Ch'in Hang, an officer of Keen, duke of Tsze, XIV. xxii.
Chin Wăn, an officer of Ts'e, V. xxii.
Ch'ing, the State of, XV. x.
Choo-chang, a person who retired from the world, XVIII. viii.

Chow dynasty, II. xxiii. III. xiv., xxi., VIII. xx., XV. x., XVI. v., XVIII. xi., XX. i.
Chow, the last emperor of the Yin dynasty, XVIII. i., XIX. xx.
Chow Jin, an ancient historiographer, XVI. i.
Chow-kung, or the duke of Chow, VII. v., VIII. xi., XI. xvi., XVIII. x.
Chuen-yu, a small territory in Loo, XVI. i.
Chung-hwŭh, an officer of Chow, XVIII. xi.
Chung-kung, the designation of Yen Yung, a disciple of Confucius, VI. i., iv., XI. ii., XII. ii., XIII. ii.
Chung-mow, a place in the state of Tsin, XVII. vii.
Chung-ne, Confucius, XIX. xxii.—xxv.
Chung-shuh Yu, the name as K'ung Wăn, XIV. xx.
Chung *Yew*, styled Tsze-loo, a disciple of Confucius, VI. vi., XI. xxiii., XVIII. vi.
Chwang of Peen, XIV. xiii.

E, a small town on the borders of the State of Wei, III. xxiv.

E., a famous archer, B.C. about 2150, XIV. vi.
E-yih, a person who retired from the world, XVIII. viii.
E Yin, the minister of T'ang, XII. xxii.

Fan Ch'e, by name Seu, and designated Tsze-ch'e, a disciple of Confucius, II. v., VI. xx., XII. xxi., xxii., XIII. iv., xix.
Fan Seu, the same as Fan Ch'e, XIII. iv.
Fang, a city in Loo, XIV. xv.
Fang-shuh, a musician of Loo, XVIII. ix.

Gae, the honourable title of Tseang, duke of Loo, B.C. 493—467, II. xix., III. xxi., VI. ii., XII. ix.
Gan P'ing, posthumous title of Gan Ying, principal minister of Ts'e, V. xvi.

Han, the river, XVIII. ix.
Hea dynasty, II. xxiii., III. ix., xxi., XV. x.
Heen, the name of Yuen Sze, a disciple of Confucius, XVI. i.
Hwan, the three great families of Loo, being descended from the Duke Hwan, are called the descendants of the three Hwan, II. v. note, XVI. iii.
Hwan, the duke of T'se, B.C. 683—642, XIV. xvi., xviii.
Hwan T'uy, a high officer of Sung, VII. xxii.
Hwuy, Yen Hwuy, styled Tsze-yuen, a disciple of Confucius, II. ix., V. viii., VI. v., ix., IX. xix., XI. iii., x., xviii., xxii.
Hwuy of Lew-Hea, posthumous title of Chen Hwŏ, an officer of Loo, XV. xiii., XVIII. ii., viii.

Joo Pei, a man of Loo, XVII. xx.

Kan, the Master of the band at Loo, XVIII. ix.
Kaou-tsung, the honourable epithet of the Emperor Woo-ting, B.C. 1323—1263, XIV. xliii.
Kaou-yaou, a minister of Shun, XII. xxii.
Ke, a small state in which sacrifices to the emperors of the Hea dynasty were maintained by their descendants, III. ix.
Ke, a small state in Shan-se, XVIII. i.
Ke family, the family of Ke K'ang of Loo, III. i., vi., VI. vii., XI. xvi., XVI. i., XVIII. iii.

Ke-Hwan, or Ke Sze, the head of the Ke family in the latter days of Confucius, XVIII. iv.
Ke K'ang, the honourable epithet of Ke-sun Fei, the head of one of the three great families of Loo, II. xx., VI. vi., XI. vi., XIII. xvii., xviii., xix., XIV. xx.
Ke-kwa, an officer of Chow, XVIII. xi.
Ke Loo, the same as Tsze-loo, V. xxv., XI. ii., xi., XIII. xiv., XVI. i.
Ke-sun, the same as Ke K'ang, XIV. xxxviii., XVI. i.
Ke-suy, an officer of Chow, XVIII. xi.
Ke Tsze-jen, a younger brother of the Ke family, XI. xxiii.
Ke Wăn, posthumous title of Ke Hangfoo, an officer of Loo, V. xix.
Kĕĕ-neih, a worthy of Ts'oo, XVIII. vi.
Kĕen, a duke of Ts'e, XIV. xxii.
Keu-foo, a small city on the western borders of Loo, XIII. xvii.
Keu Pih-yuh, the designation of Keu Yuen, an officer of the State of Wei, XIV. xxvi., XV. vi.
K'euth, a name of a village, XIV. xlvii.
Keuih, a musician of Loo, XVIII. iv.
Kew, brother of the Duke Hwan of T'se, XIV. xvii., xviii.
K'ew, Confucius' name, XIV. xxxiv., XVIII. vi.
K'ew, the name of Yen Yew, a disciple of Confucius, V. vii., VI. vi., XI. xvi., xxi., xxiii., xxv., XVI. i.
Kih Tsze-shing, an officer of the State of Wei, XII. viii.
King, a duke of Ts'e, XII. xi., XVI. xii., XVIII. iii.
King, a scion of the ducal family of Wei, XIII. viii.
K'ung, Confucius, IX. ii., XIV. xii., XVIII. vi.
Kung-Ch'ŏ, Mŏng Kung-chŏ, XIV. xiii.
Kung-ming Kea, XIV. xiv.
Kung-pih Leaou, a relative of the duke of Loo, XIV. xxxviii.
Kung-se Hwa, Tsze-hwa, a disciple of Confucius, VII. xxxiii., XI. xxi., xxv.
Kung-shan Fŭh-jaou, a confederate of Yang Ho, XVII. v.
Kung-shŭh Wăn, an officer of the State of Wei, XIV. xiv., xix.
Kung-sun Ch'aou, of Wei, XIX. xxii.
K'ung Wăn, posthumous title of Tszeyu, an officer of Wei, V. xiv.
Kung-yay Ch'ang, the son-in-law of Confucius, V. i.

Kwan Chung, by name E Woo, chief minister to the Duke Hwan of Ts'e, B.C. 683–640, III. xxii., XIV. x., xvii., xviii.
K'wang, the name of a town, IX. v., XI. xxii.

Laou, surnamed K'in, and styled Tse-h'ae or Tsze-chang, a disciple of Confucius, IX. vi.
Le, the name of T'ang, founder of the Shang dynasty, XX. i.
Le, a son of Confucius, who died early, XI. vii.
Leaou, a musician of Loo, XVIII. ix.
Lin Fang, styled Tsze-k'ew, a man of Loo, supposed to have been a disciple of Confucius, III. iv., vi.
Ling, a duke of Wei, XIV. xx., XV. i.
Loo, the native State of Confucius, II. v note, III. xxiii., V. ii., VI. xxii. IX. xiv., XI. xiii., XIII. vii., XIV. xv., XVIII. iv., vi., x.

Măng Che-fan, named Tsih, an officer of Loo, VI. xiii.
Măng Chwang, the head of the Măng family, anterior to Confucius' time, XIX. xviii.
Măng E, the posthumous title of Măng-sun, the head of the Măng family, II. v.
Măng family, one of the three great families of Loo, XVIII. iii., XIX. xix.
Măng King, honorary title of Chung-sun Tseë, son of Măng Woo, VIII. iv.
Măng Kung-ch'o, the head of the Măng or Chung-sun family, in the time of Confucius, XIV. xiii.
Măng-sun, named He-ke, the same as Măng E, II. v.
Măng Woo, honorary title of Che, the son of Măng E, II. vi., V. vii.
Min, the music-master of Loo, XV. xli.
Min, Min Tsze-k'een, XI. xii.
Min, Tsze-k'een, named Sun, a disciple of Confucius, VI. vii., XI. ii., iv., xiii.
Mung, the eastern, the name of a mountain, XVI. i.

Nan-kung K'woh, supposed to be the same as Nan Yung, XIV. vi.
Nan-tsze, the wife of the duke of Wei, and sister of Prince Chaou, VI. xxvi.
Nan-yung, a disciple of Confucius, V. i., XI. v.
Ngaou, the son of Han Tsuh (B.C. 2100), XIV. vi.

Ning Woo, honorary epithet of Ning Yu, an officer of Wei, V. xx.

P'ăng, an ancient worthy, VII. i.
Pe, a place in the state of Loo, VI. vii., XI. xxiv., XVI. i., XVII. v.
Pe-kan, an uncle of the tyrant Chow, XVIII. i.
Pe Shin, a minister of the State of Ch'ing, XIV. ix.
Pesin, the name of a city, XIV. x.
Peen, a city in Loo, XIV. xiii.
Peih Heih, commandant of Chung Mow, in the State of Tsin, XVII. vii.
Pih family, XIV. x.
Pih-e, honorary epithet of a worthy of the Shang dynasty, V. xxii., VII. xiv., XVI. xii., XVIII. viii.
Pih-kwăh, an officer of Chow, XVIII. xi.
Pih-new, the denomination of Tsze Kang, surnamed Yen, a disciple of Confucius, VI. viii., XI. ii.
Pih-tï, an officer of Chow, XVIII. xi.
Pih-yu, the eldest son of Confucius, XVI. xiii., XVII. x.

Seang, a musician of Loo, XVIII. ix.
Seu, the State of, XIV. xii.
Seen, an officer under Kung-shuh Wăn, XIV. xix.
Shang, name of Tsze-hea, a disciple of Confucius, III. viii., XI. xv.
Shaou, the music of Shun, III. xxv., VII. xiii.
Shaou Hwăh, minister of Duke Hwan's brother, Kew, XIV. xvii.
Shaou-leen, a person belonging to one of the barbarous tribes of the East, who retired from the world, XVIII. viii.
Shé, a district in the State of Ts'oo, VII. xviii., XIII. xvi.
She-shuh, named Yew-kaih, an officer of Ch'ing, XIV. ix.
Shih-mun, one of the frontier passes between Ts'e and Loo, XIV. xli.
Shin Ch'ăng, styled Tsze-chow, a disciple of Confucius, V. x.
Show-yang mountain, in Shen-se, XVI. xii.
Shuh-hea, an officer of Chow, XVIII. xi.
Shuh-sun, one of the three great families of Loo, II. v., note.
Shuh-sun, Woo-shuh, a chief of the Shuh-sun family, XIX. xxiii., xxiv.
Shuh-ts'e, honorary epithet of a worthy of the Shang dynasty, V. xxii., VII. xiv., XVI. xii., XVIII. viii.

Shih-yey, an officer of Chow, XVIII. xi.

Shun, the emperor, VI. xxviii., VIII. xviii., xx., XII, xxiii., XIV. xiv., XV. iv., XX. i.

Sin, Tsang-sin, a disciple of Confucius, IV. xv., XI. xvii.

Sung, a State in which sacrifices to the emperors of the Hea dynasty were maintained by their descendants, III. ix., VI. xiv.

Sze, the name of Tsze-chang, a disciple of Confucius, XI. xv., xvii.

Sze-ma New, named Kang, a brother of Hwan T'uy, and a disciple of Confucius, XII. iii., iv., v.

Tă-hwang, the name of a village, IX. ii.
T'ae mountain, on the border between Loo and Ts'e, III. vi.
T'ae pih, the eldest son of King T'ae, and grandfather of Wăn the founder of the Chow dynasty, VIII. i.
Tan-t'ae Mei-ming, styled Tsze-yu, a disciple of Confucius, VI. xii.
T'ang, the dynastic name of the emperor Yaou, VIII. xx.
T'ang, the founder of the Shang dynasty, XII. xxii., XX. i.
T'ăng, the State of, XIV. xii.
Tëen, the name of Tsang Sih, father of Tsăng Sin, and a disciple of Confucius, XI. xxv.
Ting, the posthumous epithet of Sung, prince of Loo, III. xix., XIII. xv.
Ts'ă, an officer of the State of Wei, styled Tsze-yu, VI. xiv., XIV. xx.
Tsze Go, by name Yu, and styled Tsze-go, a disciple of Confucius, III. xxi., VI. xxiv., XI. ii., XVII. xxi.
Tsae Yu, a disciple of Confucius, who slept in the day time, the same as the preceding, V. ix.
Ts'ae, the State of, XI. ii., XVIII. ix.
Tsăng Sih, named Tëen, the father of Tsăng Sin, and a disciple of Confucius, XI. xxv.
Tsăng Sin, styled Tsze-yu, a disciple of Confucius, I. iv., ix., IV. xv., VIII. iii.—vii., XII. xxiv., XIV. xxviii., XIX. xvi.—xix.
Tsang Wăn, the honorary title of Tsang-sun Chin, a great officer of Loo, V. xvii., XV. xiii.
Tsang Wu-chung, an officer of Loo, XIV. xiii., xv.
Ts'e, the State of, V. xviii., VI. iii., xxii., VII. xiii., XIV. xxii., XVI. iii., XVIII. iii., iv., ix.
Tsoë-yu, the designation of one Luh Tung, of Ts'oo, who feigned himself mad to escape public service, XVIII. v.

Tseih, How-tseih, the minister of agriculture to Yaou and Shun, XIV. vi.
Tsëih-tseaou K'ae, styled Tsze-jŏ, a disciple of Confucius, V. v.
Ts'in, the State of, XIV. xvi., XVIII. ix.
Tso-k'ew Ming, an ancient man of reputation, V. xxiv.
Ts'oo, the State of, XVIII. v., ix.
Ts'uy, a great officer of Ts'e, V. xviii.
Ts'ze, the name of Tsze-kung, a disciple of Confucius, i. xv., III. xvii., V. viii., ix., VI. vi., XIV. xxxi., XV. ii., XVII. xxiv.
Tsze-ch'an, named Kung-sun K'eaou, the chief minister of the State of Ch'ing, V. xv., XIV. ix., x.
Tsze-chang, the designation of Chuen-sun Sze, a disciple of Confucius, II. xviii., xxiii., V. xviii., XI. xix., XII. vi., xiv., xx., XIV. xliii., XV. v., xli., XVII. vi., XIX. i., ii., iii., XX. ii.
Tsze-fuh King-pih, an officer of Loo, XIV. xxxviii., XIX. xxiii.
Tsze-hea, the designation of Puh Shang, a disciple of Confucius, i. vii., II. vii., III. viii., VI. xi., XI. ii., XII. v., xxii., XIII. xvii., xxviii., XIX. iii.—xv.
Tsze-hwa, the designation of Kung-se, named Ch'ih, a disciple of Confucius, VI. iii.
Tsze-kaou, the designation of Ch'ae, a disciple of Confucius, XI. xxiv.
Tsze-kung, the designation of Twan-muh Ts'ze, a disciple of Confucius, I. x., xv., II. xiii., III. xvii., V. iii., viii., xi., xii., xiv., VI. xxviii., VII. xiv., IX. vi., xii., XI. ii., xii., xv., XII. vii., viii., xxiii., XIII. xx., xxiv., XIV. xviii., xxx., xxxi., xxxvii., XV. ii., v., xxiii., XVII. xix., xxiv., XIX. xx.—xxv.
Tsze-loo, the designation of Chungyew, often named simply Yew, a disciple of Confucius, II. xvii., V. vi., vii., xiii., xxv., VII. xxvi., VII. x., xxxiv., IX. xi., xxvi., X. xviii., XI. vii., xiv., xxi., xxiv., xxv., XII. xii., XIII. i., iii., xxviii., XIV. xiii., xvii., xxiii., xxviii., xli., xlv., XV. f., XVII. v., vii., xxiii., XVIII. vi., vii.
Tsze-sang Pih-tsze, VI. i., VII. xviii.
Tsze-se, the chief minister of Ts'oo, XIV. x.
Tsze-mëen, the designation of Pelh Puh-ts'e, a disciple of Confucius, V. ii.
Tsze-wăn, surnamed Tow, and named Kuh-yu-t'oo, chief minister of Ts'oo, V. xviii.

Tsze-yew, or Yen Yew, the designation of Yen Yen, a disciple of Confucius, II. vii., VI. xii., XI. ii., XVII. iv., XIX. vii.

Tsze-yu, a minister of the State of Ch'ing. XIV. ix.

Tung-le, XIV. ix.

Wǎn, the king, VIII. xx., IX. v., XIX. xxii.

Wǎn, a duke of Tsin. XIV. xvi.

Wǎn, a river dividing the States of Ts'e and Loo, VI. vii.

Wang-sun Kea, a great officer of Wei, III. xiii., XIV. xx.

We-shang Mow, XIV. xxxiv.

Wei, the State of, VII. xiv., IX. xiv., XIII. iii., vii., viii., ix., XIV. xx., xlii., XV. i., XIX. xxii.

Wei, one of the three families which governed the State of Tsin, XIV. xii.

Wei-shang Kaou, V. xviii.

Wei, a small State in Shan-se, XVIII. i.

Woo, the State of, VII. xxx.

Wǎn, the founder of the Chow dynasty, VIII. xx., XIX. xxii.

Woo, the music of King Woo, III. xxv.

Woo, a musician of Loo, XVIII. ix.

Wan-ma K'ǎ, VII. xxx.

Woo-shing, the name of a city in Po, VI. xii., XVII. iv.

Yang, a musician of Loo, XVIII. ix.

Yang Fou, a disciple of Tsǎng-sin, XIX. xix.

Yang Ho, or Yang Hoo, the principal minister of the Ke family, XVII. i.

Yaou, the emperor, VI. xxviii., VIII. xix., XIV. xlv., XX. i.

Yellow river, XVIII. ix.

Yen, Yen Yew, VI. iii., XVII. iv.

Yen Hwuy, styled Tsze-yuen, a disciple of Confucius, VI. ii., XI. vi.

Yen K'ew, Yen Yew, VI. x., XI. xxiii., XIV. xiii.

Yen-loo, the father of Hwuy, XI. vii.

Yen Pih-new, named Tsze Kăng, a disciple of Confucius, XI. ii.

Yen Yew, named K'ew, and designated Tsze-yew, a disciple of Confucius, III. vi., V. vii., VI. iii., VII. xiv., XI. ii., xii., xxi., xxv., XIII. ix., xiv., XVI. i., XIX. xii.

Yen Yuen, named Hwuy, and styled Tsze-yuen, a disciple of Confucius, V. xxv., VII. x., IX. x., xx., XI. ii., vii., viii., xix., xxii., XII. i., XV. x.

Yew, Chung Yew, styled Tsze-loo, a disciple of Confucius, II. xvii., V. vi., vii., VI. vi., IX. xi., xxvi., XI. xii., xiv., xvii., xx., xvi., xxiii., XII. xii., XIII. iii., XV. iii., XVI. i., XVI. viii.

Yew Jŏ, styled Tsze-jŏ, and Tsze-yew, a disciple of Confucius, I. ii., xii., xiii., XII. ix.

Yin dynasty, II. xxiii., III. ix., xxi., VIII. xx., XV. x., XVIII. i.

Yu, the emperor, VIII. xviii., xxi., XIV. vi., XX. i.

Yu, the dynastic name of the Emperor Shun, VIII. xx.

Yu, the historiographer of Wei, XV. vi.

Yu, Tsze Go, XVII. xxi.

Yu-chung, or Woo-chung, VIII. i. note, XVIII. viii.

Yuen Jang, a follower of Laou-tsze, XIV. xlvi.

Yuen Sze, named Hien, a disciple of Confucius, VI. iii.

Yen-yen Yung, styled Chung-kung, a disciple of Confucius, V. iv., VI. i.

INDEX III.

OF SUBJECTS IN THE GREAT LEARNING.

Ability and worth, importance of appreciating and using, comm., x. 14, 15.

Analects, quotations from the, comm., iv., x. 15.

Ancients, the, illustrated illustrious virtue how, text, 4.;

Empire, the, rendered peaceful and happy, text, 6, comm., x.

Family, regulating the, *text*, 4, 5, *comm.*, viii., ix.

Heart, the rectification of the, *text*, 4, 5, *comm.*, vii.

Illustration of illustrious virtue, *text*, 1, 4, *comm.*, i.

Kings, why the former are remembered, *comm.*, iii. 4, 5.

Knowledge, perfecting of, *text*, 4, 5, *comm.*, v.

Litigations, it is best to prevent, *comm.*, iv.

Master, the words of the, quoted, *comm.*, iii. 2, iv.

Measuring square, principle of the, *comm.*, x.

Middle kingdom, the, *comm.*, x. 15.

Mind, rectifying the, *text*, 4, 5, *comm.*, vii.

Odes, quotations from the, *comm.*, ii. 3, iii, ix. 6, 7, 8, x. 3, 4, 5.

Order of steps in illustrating virtue, *text*, 3, 4, 5.

Partiality of the affections, *comm.*, viii.

Passion, influence of, *comm.*, vii.

People, renovation of the, *text*, 1, *comm.*, ii.

Perfecting of knowledge, the, *text*, 4, 5, *comm.*, v.

Person, the cultivation of the, *text*, 4, 5, 6, *comm.*, vii., viii.

Renovation of the people, the, *text*, 1, *comm.*, ii.

Resting in the highest excellence, *text*, 1, 2, *comm.*, iii.

Root, the, and branches, *text*, 3, *comm.*, iv.; cultivation of the person the, *text*, 6; virtue the, *comm.*, x. 6, 7, 8.

Secret watchfulness over himself, characteristic of the superior man, *comm.*, vi. 1.

Shoo-king, the, quotations from, *comm.*, i. 1, 2, 3, ii. 2, ix. 2, x. 11, 14.

Sincerity of the thoughts, *text*, 4, 5, *comm.*, ii.

State, the government of the, *text*, 4, 5, *comm.*, ix., x.

Steps by which virtue may be illustrated, *text*, 4, 5.

Superior man, character of the, *comm.*, ii. 4.

Superior, and mean man, *comm.*, vi.

Virtue, illustrious, *text*, *comm.*, ii.; the root, *comm.*, x. 6, 7, 8.

Wealth a secondary object with a ruler, *comm.*, x. 7, &c.

INDEX IV.

OF PROPER NAMES IN THE GREAT LEARNING.

Ch'ing, the philosopher, *Introductory note*, *comm.*, v. *note*.

Chow, the State of, *comm.*, ii. 3.

Chow, the tyrant, *comm.*, ix. 4.

Confucius, *concluding note to text*.

Fan, the uncle of Duke Wăn, *comm.*, x. 13.

K'ang, honorary epithet of Fung, brother of King Woo, *comm.*, i. 1, ii. 2, ix. 2, x. 11.

K'e, the name of a river, *comm.*, iii. 4.

Këĕ, the tyrant, *comm.* ix. 4.

Măng Hëen, honorary epithet of Chung-sun Mĕĕ, a worthy minister of Loo, *comm.*, x. 22.

Mencius, *concluding note to text*.

Shun, the emperor, *comm.*, ix. 4.

T'ae Këă, the second emperor of the Shang dynasty, *comm.*, i. 2.

T'ang, the emperor, *comm.*, ii. 1.

Tsăng, the philosopher, *concluding note to text*, *comm.*, vi. 3.

Ts'in, the State of, *comm.*, x. 14.

Ts'oo, the State of, *comm.*, x. 12.

Wăn, the king, *comm.*, iii. 3.
Yaou, the emperor, *comm.*, i. 3, ix. 4.

Yin dynasty, *comm.*, x. 5.
Yin, an ancient officer mentioned in the She-king, *comm.*, x. 4.

INDEX V.

OF SUBJECTS IN THE DOCTRINE OF THE MEAN.

Analects, quotations from the, iii., xxviii. 5.
Ancestors, worship of, xviii. 2, 3, xix.
Antiquity, the regulations of, cannot be attested, xxviii. 5, xxix. 2.
Archery, illustrative of the way of the superior man, xiv. 5.

Benevolence, to be cherished in treading the path of duty, xx. 4, 5.
Burial and mourning, xviii. 3.

Ceremonies, music, &c., can be ordered only by the emperor, xxviii. 2, 3, 4.
Common men and women may carry into practice the Mean in its simple elements, xii. 2, 4.
Completion of everything effected by sincerity, xxv.

Emperor, certain exclusive prerogatives of the, xxviii. 2, 3, 4.
Emperor-sage, the, described, xxix.
Equilibrium, the mind in a state of, i. 4, 5.
Eulogium of Confucius, xxx., xxxi., xxxii.

Fame of Confucius universal, xxxi. 4.
Filial piety, of Shun, xvii.; of King Woo, and the duke of Chow, xix.
Five duties of universal obligation, xx. 8.
Forcefulness, in its relation to the practice of the Mean, x.
Four things to which Confucius had not attained, xiii. 4.

Government, easy to him who understands sacrificial ceremonies, xix. 6; dependent on the character of the officers, and ultimately on that of the sovereign, xx.

Harmony, the mind in a state of, i. 4,

5; combined with firmness, in the superior man, x. 5.
Heaven, rewarding filial piety in the case of Shun, and virtue in the case of Wăn, xvii.; Confucius the equal of, xxxi. 3.
Heaven and Earth, order of, dependent on the equilibrium and harmony of the human mind, i. 5; the perfectly sincere man forms a *ternion* with, xxii.; Confucius compared to, xxx. 2.

Instruction, definition of, i. 1.
Insubordination, the evil of, xxviii.
Intelligence, how connected with sincerity, xxi.

Knowledge of duties come by in three different ways, xx. 9.

Lamentation that the path of the Mean was untrodden, v.
Law to himself, man a, xiii.

Man has the law of the Mean in himself, xiii.
MEAN, only the superior man can follow the, ii. 1; the rarity of the practice of the, iii.; how it was that few were able to practise the, iv.; how Shun practised the, vi.; men's ignorance of the, shown in their conduct, vii.; how Hwuy held fast the course of the, viii.; the difficulty of attaining to the, ix.; on forcefulness in its relation to the, x.; only the sage can come up to the requirements of the, xi. 3; the course of the, reaches far and wide, but yet is secret, xii.; common men and women may practise the, xii. 2; orderly advance in the practice of the, xv.; Confucius never swerved from the, xxxi. 1.

INDEX V. SUBJECTS IN THE DOCTRINE OF THE MEAN.

Middle kingdom, Confucius' fame overspreads the, xxxi. 4.

Nature, definition of, i. 1.
Nine standard rules to be followed in the government of the empire, xx. 12, 13, 14, 15.

Odes, quotations from the, xii. 3, xiii. 2, xv. 2, xvi. 4, xvii. 4, xxvi., xxvii. 7, xxix. 6, xxxiii. 1, 2, 3, 4, 5, 6.

Passions, harmony of the, i. 4.
Path of duty, definition of, i. 1; may not be left for an instant, i. 2; is not far to seek, xiii.
Praise of Wăn and Woo, and the duke of Chow, xviii., xix.
Preparation necessary to success, xx. 16.
Principles of duty, have their root in the evidenced will of Heaven, i. 1; to be found in the nature of man, xii.
Progress in the practice of the Mean, xv.
Propriety, the principle of, in relation to the path of duty, xx. 5.

Reciprocity, the law of, xiii. 3, 4.
Righteousness, chiefly exercised in honouring the worthy, xx. 5.

Sacrifices, to spiritual beings, xvi. 3; instituted by Woo and the duke of Chow, xviii. 2, 3; to Heaven and Earth, xix. 6; to ancestors, xviii., xix.
Sage, a, only can come up to the requirements of the mean, xi. 3; naturally and easily embodies the right way, xx. 18; the glorious path of, xxvii.; Confucius a perfect, xxxi. 1.
Seasons, Confucius compared to the four, xxx. 2, 3.
Secret watchfulness over himself characteristic of the superior man, i. 3.
Self-examination practised by the superior man, xxxiii. 2.
Sincerity, the outgoing of, cannot be repressed, xvi. 5; the way of Heaven, xx. 17, 18; how to be attained, xx. 19; how connected with intelligence, xxi.; the most complete, necessa. to the full development of the natur xxii.; development of, in those not naturally possessed of it, xxiii.; when entire, can foreknow, xxiv.; the completion of everything effected by xxv.; the possessor of entire, is the co-equal of Heaven and Earth, and is an infinite and an independent being—a God, xxvi., xxxii. 1.
Singleness, necessary to the practice of the relative duties, xx. 8; necessary to the practice of government, xx. 15, 17; of King Wăn's virtue, xxvi. 10.
Sovereign, a, must not neglect personal and relative duties, xx. 7.
Spirit, the perfectly sincere man is like a, xxiv.
Spiritual beings, the operation and influence of, xvi.; the emperor-sage presents himself before, without any doubts, xxix. 3, 4.
Steps in the practice of the Mean, xv.
Superior man is cautious, and watchful over himself, i. 2, 5; only can follow the Mean, ii. 2; combines harmony with firmness, x. 5; the way of, is far-reaching and yet secret, xii.; distinguished by entire sincerity, xiii. 4; in every variety of situation pursues the Mean, and finds his rule in himself, xiv.; pursues his course with determination, xx. 20, 21; endeavours to attain to the glorious path of the sage, xxvii. 6, 7; prefers concealment of his virtue, while the mean man seeks notoriety, xxxiii. 1.

Three kings, the founders of the three dynasties, xxix. 3.
Three virtues, wherewith the relative duties are practised, xx. 8.
Three things important to a sovereign, xxix. i.
Three hundred rules of ceremony, and three thousand rules of demeanour, xxvii. 3.

Virtue in its highest degree and influence, xxxiii. 4, 5, 6.
Virtuous course, the commencement and completion of a, xxxiii.

INDEX VI.

OF PROPER NAMES IN THE DOCTRINE OF THE MEAN.

Ch'ing, the philosopher, *Introductory note*.
Chow dynasty, xxviii. 5.
Chow, the duke of, xviii. 3, xix.
Chung-ne, designation of Confucius, ii. 1, xxx. 1.
Confucian school, *Introductory note*.

Gae, the duke of Loo, xx. 1.

Hea dynasty, xxviii. 5.
Hwa, the name of a mountain, xxvi. 9.
Hwuy, a disciple of Confucius, viii.

Ke, a small State in which sacrifices were maintained to the emperors of the Hea dynasty, xxviii. 5.
Ke-leih, the duke, who received from Woo the title of king, xviii. 2, 3.

Mencius, *Introductory note*.

Shun, the emperor, vi., xvii. 1. xxx. 1.

Sung, a State in which sacrifices were maintained to the emperors of the Yin dynasty, xxviii. 5.

T'ae, the duke, T'an-foo, who received from Woo the title of king, xviii. 2, 3.
Tsze loo, a disciple of Confucius, x. 1.
Tsze-sze, *Introductory note*; *concluding notes to chapters* i., xii., xxi., xxxiii.

Wăn, the king, xvii. 4, xviii., xx. 2, xxvi. 10, xxx. 1.
Woo, the king, xviii., xix., xx. 2. xxx. 1.

Yaou, the emperor, xxx. 1.
Yin dynasty, xxviii. 5.
Yoh, the name of a mountain, xxvi. 9.
Yung, a distinguished scholar, A.D. 1064—1085, *concluding note to chapter* i.

END OF VOL. I.

JOHN CHILDS AND SON, PRINTERS.

www.ingramcontent.com/pod-product-compliance
Lightning Source LLC
Chambersburg PA
CBHW031849220426
43663CB00006B/557